WOMEN AS REVOLUTIONARY
AGENTS OF CHANGE

HQ 29 .H58 1994	Hite, Shere. Women as revolutionary agents of change.

$22.95

DATE			
10/94		-	

WOMEN AS REVOLUTIONARY AGENTS OF CHANGE

The Hite Reports and Beyond

Shere Hite

The University of Wisconsin Press

By the same author

Sexual Honesty, By Women, For Women (1974)
The Hite Report on Female Sexuality (1976)
The Hite Report on Men and Male Sexuality (1981)
Women and Love: A Cultural Revolution in Progress
(The Hite Report on Love, Passion and Emotional Violence) (1987)
Fliegen mit Jupiter (1993)

This compilation first published in Great Britain 1993
Copyright © 1993, 1994 by Shere Hite
Preface copyright © 1993 by Dale Spender

The University of Wisconsin Press
114 North Murray Street, Madison, Wisconsin 53715

Printed in the United States of America

For LC CIP information see p. 518

Contents

CONTENTS

CONTENTS

CONTENTS

CONTENTS

CONTENTS

Preface

Shere Hite has made history. She has helped to shape the beliefs and behaviors of Western society. When women were asking, "Who are we, and what do we want?" Shere Hite looked for answers. She began by getting women to speak for themselves, and then men to speak for themselves, and ultimately made some significant connections.

Shere Hite listened. In the early 1970s she listened to the questions and the responses of women, to the spoken and the unspoken, to the individual and the community meanings. In 1976 she carefully, conscientiously, and creatively put all the pieces together and returned to women their collective voices in *The Hite Report on Female Sexuality*.

Shere Hite's research on women's physical and emotional relations epitomizes the interactive process. For while it is obvious that her work is a product of the time (it would not have been so fitting in the Victorian era, for example), her contribution has also helped to shape the insights and interactions of many contemporary women (and men).

But her contribution did not stop with the documentation of women's attitudes and actions. Shere Hite understood that women's expressions about their physical and emotional reality raised a range of crucial issues about men, male values, and manhood. The publication of *The Hite Report on Male Sexuality* in 1981 confirmed the suspicion that sex, sexuality, and society meant very different things (and often incompatible things) to women and men.

"A Cultural Revolution in Progress" was the apt subtitle of *Women and Love,* the third Hite Report, published in 1987. Having taken soundings of women's experience for more than fifteen years, Shere Hite was able to show in this remarkable and reverberating study not just what women were thinking but how their thinking was changing. She has played a crucial part in bringing about a revolution that continues. Throughout this period of rapid change, she has both monitored and molded women's ideas and aspirations. In her three significant volumes, she has not only identified the issues and chronicled the critical changes, she has constructed a framework for their interpretation.

The substance of these different volumes—and many years of work— has now been integrated into a coherent overview. No matter what you call the subject matter—sex, love, passion, physicality, or emotionality—Shere Hite has gone to the core of the relationship between the sexes in her explorations and analyses. She has documented the shifts in power, prestige, and perception that are taking place at the most intimate of levels. At a time when the very nature of women and men—and their relationship or non-relationship—is in the throes of transformation, Shere Hite has been putting on public record the personal changes that are underway. *Women as Revolutionary Agents of Change* is a synthesis of these records and the radical research that supports them; as such it provides an historical account as well as a contemporary justification for women's stand.

Today it is often difficult to remember (let alone explain) what the world was like before the modern women's movement and in the pre-Hite era. Many of the women who lived through that period and look back upon it now consider the 1950s to be one of the worst decades for women in centuries. (This was the firm belief of Dora Russell, Rebecca West, and Betty Friedan, for example.)

Throughout the postwar period, when women were being banished from the workplace and "imaged" into homemaking, their autonomy and agency as human beings were steadily diminished. Freud was supposedly the only one who knew what women really wanted—and what they wanted, according to him, was an authoritative man to make up their minds for them. This was the time when the test of a true woman was the mature, vaginal orgasm, and when the term *penis envy* was used to devalue and deny the experiences of any woman which were not passive, pliant, and appropriately deferential to patriarchy. Such constraints now seem incredible, and are a measure of the distance women have traveled on the way to liberation.

Before the modern women's movement, it was existentially painful to be a woman. To find that fecund femininity and social servility were no recipe for self-fulfillment was to confront an absence of meaning, a "problem with no name." Yet any protests about such a state of "anomie" were disallowed, even before they were begun. Any woman who did not accept her lot in life, who did not cultivate the consciousness that would have her find her satisfaction in her husband, was simply advertising her own neurosis. She was displaying the symptoms of penis envy and revealing her dissatisfaction with being a woman and her desire to be a man. All such thinking was very reinforcing for men.

There was no room for women who did not relate to men, and so passive was the image of "womanliness" that it was not possible to officially acknowledge women's *labor*—neither in their own homes nor in anyone else's. Even the women who were in the paid workforce had to deny the reality of the hard work and the low pay and subscribe to the definition of docile, delicate, and devoted dependence.

No wonder the young cannot fully comprehend the conditions of the period. The way that women were socially, psychologically, and sexually enmeshed now seems beyond belief, even to those of us who experienced it. It is a mark of the hold that ideology can have over our minds and our mores that we should have been so deceived; that we have thrown off some of the old mind-sets is a testimony to the courageous individuals who defied the value system and the supposed evidence, and who insisted that there must be other ways of organizing and explaining the arrangements of society and the needs of individuals.

Shere Hite was one such person. It is perhaps no coincidence that her first interest and her training were in ideological history. She went beyond the boundaries of ideological scholarship, however, when she turned her attention to the physical and emotional elements of women's existence. It was one thing to critique scientific method as ideology; it was quite another to critique "sex" as the ideology of male dominance. She did so, however, and she did it by consulting thousands of women (and at one stage, thousands of men) about their lives, their thoughts, their feelings, and their sexual activities.

To call Shere Hite's monumental work *surveys* is to use an inadequate label. The ground-breaking questionnaires she designed (and to which so many thousands of women responded) became the underpinnings of a new and most illuminating frame of reference for analyzing power and the relationship between the sexes. She questioned beliefs; she amassed opinions and understandings; she sifted, sorted, and synthesized. In placing the experiences of women within her well-designed framework, she created unique data.

One of the most difficult problems that arose concerned language: how to express this new perspective and its new possibilities in words that would reflect the shift from men's definition of woman as other and object to women's definition of woman as self and subject? In her work Shere Hite has consistently drawn attention to the resistance of the language (and the semantic system) to women's meanings. She has shown that the experience of women is different from that of men, but no name represents their specific sense of it. One reason for this difference is that men encode women's experience from the "outside" and therefore reinforce the definition of women as other, as existing only in relation to men. Women, on the other hand, wish to encode their experience from the "inside," as the agent, the autonomous self. As Shere Hite points out, often no single word represents this value.

The language lag becomes apparent as women seek to encode their reality and find that no accurate term for it exists. (It is difficult to appreciate the "unreality" of the days before terms like *sexism* and *sexual harassment* became familiar.) Throughout her work Shere Hite alerts us to the role that language plays. At the macro level women are in the process of unlearning, of undefining what has been meant by sex, love, relationships, men, and self.

At the micro level they are finding that the names they have to work with do not accurately or authentically reflect their meaning as subject.

From the blatant political naming of the *mature vaginal orgasm*, to the equally loaded label of *foreplay*, Shere Hite asks, "Whose sexuality is being expressed and catered to here?"

Why is there no word for *pressing together*, she asks, "when it is one of the most important physical activities there is? Full-length body-to-body contact, so important to overall gratification," is reported by women frequently as a source of satisfaction and pleasure. But in the language in which men have had the privilege of being meaning-makers, such a term does not exist. One can only surmise that if pressing together held the same significance in the male scheme of values, the desire and the part they played in it would have an appropriate name.

Again and again, Shere Hite points to the links between language and reality; only in a context in which men are defined as active, and women as dependent—and object—would it be possible to describe the breakup of a relationship as one in which the woman was "being left," she states. "Deserted" and "abandoned" are used almost exclusively in relation to women [p284] even though, as Shere Hite's research suggests, it is the women who are moving on and the men who are being left—and being left behind.

The chorus of women whom Shere Hite has brought together is taking on a new role and insisting on new words. They are voicing ideas, possibilities, and criticisms that many men (and some women) do not want to hear. Their speaking out is one reason that Shere Hite and her reports have received a backlash press over the years. Disliking the message, some individuals have tried to shoot the messenger. So systematic and sustained has this negative reaction been that Susan Faludi uses it as a case study in her book *Backlash*. (Cheris Kramarae, a distinguished professor at the University of Illinois and an editor of *A Feminist Dictionary*, has studied the way Shere Hite's research has been distorted and devalued by those who did not want to see themselves portrayed so unflatteringly [see Appendix]. Given that I too have pointed out on numerous occasions that the English language offers no acceptable discourse for critiquing male power, no matter how justified such a critique might be, it is possible to see some of the sources of the antagonism to women's version of critical reality. And as Shere Hite has highlighted the responses of women that make it clear that anger toward men is an expression that is not to be tolerated—while men remain in charge of discourse and meanings—then it is hardly surprising that Shere Hite's work on the relationship between the sexes—and the shortcomings of men—should have been dismissed and discredited.)

Freud never let women speak for themselves; he was always there to say, "What she means is . . ." (According to my own research, variations on this theme constitute one of the most common statements that men make in conversation with women.) Until the modern women's movement it was accepted practice for men to speak for women in everything from marriage ceremonies to anthropological studies and research findings. No questions were asked about the validity of the "male only" opinions. But when Shere Hite presented the *women speaking for themselves,* she was denounced for her use of flawed methodology!

Like so many other feminist researchers, however, Shere Hite made no false claims for her research, no appeals to authority or universality, as Freud had done. Shere Hite gave us women's words and an interpretative framework. "This is what women said," she stated, "and this is what I think it means," she declared. That millions of women who have read her work on psychology and gender have been able to hear echoes of their own voices within her reports suggests that there can be no quarrel on these grounds either.

But if it was not possible to disqualify the reports on methodological grounds, attempts could be made to devalue the entire enterprise. This was another line of attack that was used against Shere Hite's account of a revolution in progress. Certain members of the media have branded Shere Hite as a "sex therapist" and discounted her intellectual commentary as some sort of sex manual. But such an appraisal of her work is seriously misleading. For while sex may have been the starting point—and there's no doubt that in the absence of a reliable data base Shere Hite consulted women about what they actually did in their sex lives—Shere Hite's definition and documentation did not stay within the narrow confines of sex as conventionally (or patriarchally) decreed.

One of the most valuable contributions of her research has been to re-map and rename the territory of sexuality from women's perspective. It is here that the report on male sexuality can offer useful comparisons. For while it seems that women seek to define sex as part of the fabric of their physical and emotional lives, most men who responded to the questionnaire defined sex surely and simply as sexual intercourse. That Shere Hite has been able to break with this distressingly and distortingly limited concept of sexuality, that she has been able to provide women with an alternative focus that makes sense of their different experience of the world, is testimony to her achievement. For that reason, *Women as Revolutionary Agents of Change: Essays in Psychology and Gender* is the appropriate title for this volume. It takes account of the transformations that have occurred in women's psyche. Yet these collected essays not only record the ways that women have changed over the decades but also emphasize that it is now *women who are doing the changing*.

Women have changed and in the process they have put men on notice. As is evident from *The Hite Report on Love, Passion and Emotional Violence,* women are now saying loudly, and clearly, that enough is enough. They have looked at everything that has been demanded of them in the name of love and they have decided that they want something different. They want love to include emotional nurturance for women and not, as in the past, simply emotional nurturance by women. Women have been shocked to realize that men fail to reciprocate; many have come to understand—and to state—that if relationships were left to men, there wouldn't be any. Women have been politicized by the recognition that they count for so little with so many men that they have determined that it just isn't good enough anymore. And despite all the difficulties and dangers, women are in a better position, psychologically and materially, to do something about it.

Shere Hite's essays have broken the silence so that women now know what's happening in relationships other than their own. They are beginning to appreciate that they are not alone with their "problems." With the personal testimony of so many women respondents about the violations and the disappointments in their relationships with men has come the realization that many men are doing things in the private sphere that have been made illegal in public.

Increasingly women gain strength from hearing each other and feel sufficiently empowered to insist that they will no longer put up with such abuse. Perhaps we are witnessing the emergence of a Lysistrata campaign ("Lysistrata, [who] organized the women of ancient Greece to withhold sex from their husbands as an anti-war protest": A Feminist Dictionary, 1985, p. 30). In women's own words they are negotiating the conditions of their lives so that men are no longer the priority; now it is women who are drawing up the rules and determining that *unless men start to change* there will be no relationships.

Many of them are as good as their word. I cannot be the only one who has registered that a significant number of women now live with women. "Why have you left husband, home, children?" I have asked more than a hundred professional women in their forties and fifties. They replied, "Because I wanted companionship . . . because I only wanted to do half the housework . . . because I got tired of trying to establish my right to life." They make no attempt to disguise their reasons, and there is no way of denying their choices. It could be the first time in human history that women have begun to enjoy and exercise options about their living and loving relationships. And it could be that this growing—albeit uneven—freedom of women fuels male feelings of irrelevance and resentment.

Throughout the Western world, Susan Faludi reminds us, women's lives have been radically transformed. Few women now live as their mothers did; few women today could have envisaged their present lives in their youth. And it has to be recognized that while women have been engaged in a process of rapid change and constant re-evaluation, many men have stayed locked into the old realities, trying to live the way their fathers did. So stark is this contrast between the development of women and the stagnation of men that the question which must arise is, Are only women evolving now?

Thirty years ago—and for many of the preceding centuries—women were thought to have had a problem with sex. That a revolution has indeed taken place can be seen by the way the situation is defined today; it is society—and specifically a male-dominated society—that is seen to have a problem dealing with women and their autonomous sexuality. Shere Hite has played a vital part in this revolution. She has been both the chronicler and the predicter of cultural change. She has been a pioneer in women's liberation, in women-centered research, and in redefining the language and reality of women's lives. She has shown how women have changed and how women are now bringing about change; she has empowered women in their relationships with the dominant sex. For the last three decades she has been rewriting the scripts of love, passion, emotional violence, and women's autonomy. She is a woman who is a revolutionary agent of change.

Dale Spender
September 1992

An Introduction to The Hite Reports: Theory and Importance

Naomi Weisstein, Professor of Psychology, State University of New York, 1987

These essays represent the theoretical structure of a series of three books (*The Hite Report on Female Sexuality*, 1976, *The Hite Report on Male Sexuality*, 1981, and *The Hite Report on Love, Passion, and Emotional Violence*—originally published as *Women and Love*, 1987) dealing with private life and gender definition in the United States. Through these essays, one sees a combination of discussion and impressive empirical research. Published internationally with widespread influence, these books comprise complex and fascinating portraits of a crucial fifteen-year period in American culture—a period in which society came into an extraordinary confrontation with the traditional ideas of home and family.

This confrontation is examined in the Hite Reports by looking at what really is there—i.e., documentation consisting of the responses of thousands of people to anonymous open-ended questionnaires—rather than at what reigning theory tells us should be there, and by a debate carried on sometimes among the participants, sometimes between Hite and the participants, a debate based on a coherent theoretical perspective. Perhaps we will look back and say that what is documented here is the ideological revolution in personal life of the end of the twentieth century.

The Hite Report on Female Sexuality: The redefinition of sexuality: sex is cultural

Hite began this project in 1971 when, on leave of absence from graduate school, she became involved with the feminist movement, and taking seriously the idea that the personal is the political, undertook a major effort to find out what really happens in women's sexual lives.

1

From 1972 to 1976 she distributed a lengthy essay questionnaire to women all over the country; in 1976, on publication of the findings from the responses of 3,500 women, she explained her goals: "The purpose of this project is to let *women* define their own sexuality—instead of doctors or other (usually male) authorities. Women are the real experts on their own sexuality; they know how they feel and what they experience, without needing anyone to tell them. This is not to say that Masters and Johnson's and Kinsey's work is not invaluable—it is. However, their work continued to view sex through certain cultural blinders which kept them from understanding the whole truth about female sexuality. In this study, for the first time, women themselves speak out about how they feel about sex, how they define their own sexuality, and what sexuality means to them." Hite's background in social and cultural history helped her to provide a cultural framework for this discussion, to see female sexuality for what it is, rather than how it fit into the prevalent patriarchal ideology.

Hite's basic finding was that 70 percent of women do not have orgasms from intercourse, but *do* have them from more direct clitoral stimulation. This testimony from thousands of women blew the lid off the question of female orgasm. Masters and Johnson had brought up the importance of the clitoris, but had emphasized that women should get enough clitoral stimulation from simple thrusting during intercourse to lead to orgasm; if they did not, they had a "sexual dysfunction." Kinsey had hinted at this issue by noting briefly that women like cuddling and that they have their highest rate of orgasm during masturbation, but he did not define masturbation beyond a few sentences, nor did he come to the logical conclusion implied, or reach the new understanding of women's sexuality that Hite formulated.

Ann Koedt had first questioned whether women have orgasms during intercourse and suggested that the issue involved a patriarchal definition of female sexuality in her ground-breaking 1968 essay "The Myth of the Vaginal Orgasm."

Following publication of Hite's work, one commentator placed the discussion in historical perspective: "Ann Koedt's . . . 'The Myth of the Vaginal Orgasm' and Shere Hite's *The Hite Report on Female Sexuality* . . . are unique discussions of female sexuality because they treat sexuality as the unity of both human biology and psychology imbedded in a political formation. Advancing from the personal 'sharing of experiences,' Koedt and Hite both revealed how men have constructed sexuality to their advantage. In particular, Hite illustrated that within the dominant pattern of heterosexual interaction male pleasure is primary. The importance of her work lies in the fact that Hite clearly views sexual patterns as social constructions. Her book not only sheds light on contemporary sexual practice, but works to direct the creation of noninstitutionalized sexuality."*

Hite's documentation with such a large sample of exactly how women do have orgasms easily—during self-stimulation—and that they do not usually have orgasms during simple intercourse without additional stimulation, as well as her declaration that there was nothing "wrong" with this, that if the majority of women said this, it must be "normal" for women—no matter what "professional sexologists" said—was, after an initial period of shock among some in the sex research community, accepted widely, and eventually Hite received the distinguished service award from the American Association of Sex Educators, Counselors and Therapists.

Hite's finding that women could easily reach orgasm with clitoral stimulation (although society had said women had a "problem" having orgasms) also raised a further question—i.e., is sex as we know it (the basic set of physical activities with its focus on coitus) a social or a biological phenomenon? Hite had raised this question in the sense that she showed that for the majority of women, intercourse itself doesn't necessary lead to orgasm, although clitoral stimulation does. Therefore we are forced to ask ourselves whether sex was "created" for pleasure and intimacy, or simply for reproduction. If the former, then the fact that the kind of stimulation the majority of women need for orgasm should be included in the definition of sex forces us to consider redesigning sex.

If women had been compelled to hide how they could easily reach orgasm during masturbation, then the definition of sex, it follows, is sexist and culturally linked. Hite, again, writing in 1976: "Our whole society's definition of sex is sexist—sex for the overwhelming majority of people consists of foreplay, eventually followed by vaginal penetration and then by intercourse, ending eventually in male orgasm. This is a sexist definition of sex, oriented around male orgasm and the needs of reproduction. This definition is *cultural*, not biological."

In other words, Hite's study showed that sex is part of the whole cultural picture; a woman's place in sex mirrors her place in the rest of society. Although, until that time, female sexuality had been seen essentially as a response to male sexuality, this was not a scientific or objective summation of the facts. It was a view of female sexuality through a certain ideological perspective.

Thus, *The Hite Report on Female Sexuality* linked the definition of

---

* Rhonda Gottlieb, "The Political Economy of Sexuality" in *Review of Radical Political Economics* 16 (1): 143–65.

sex as we know it to a particular society and historical cultural tradition, saying sex as we know it is *created* by our social system; it is a social institution.

While it is currently fashionable in academic circles to credit French philosopher Michel Foucault with the discovery that sex is cultural, that the way sexuality is defined is tied to a certain historical time and place, certain social structures, in fact, the idea grew out of early feminist discussions which were widely circulated both in the U.S. and France. *The Hite Report* contains the earliest full-scale statement of the clear connection between sexuality, its formation, shaping and definition, and the society that channels it in certain directions.

Carrying these thoughts further, into an "un-definition" of sexuality, the first Hite Report continued, "Touching friends and sitting together intimately should be possible. . . . Intense physical contact should be possible in many varied ways. In short, our whole idea of sex must be reevaluated."

Not the least of the contributions of the first Hite Report was the presenting of women's own voices on this topic for the first time—as Hite said, "The statements women sent were full of beautifully written, moving descriptions of their feelings—an anonymous and powerful, deep communication, almost a soul to soul communication, from the women who answered to all the women of the world. Receiving these replies was one of the most emotionally fulfilling experiences of my life—and it is this I want to share with other women who read the book."

The Hite Report on Male Sexuality: toward a new definition of masculinity

The second Hite Report, *The Hite Report on Male Sexuality*, was the first study of how men feel about themselves, their relationships and their sexuality: no such book had ever been done, certainly none using a data base approaching Hite's in size and representativeness. Although comparisons are often made with Kinsey, in fact Kinsey measured the frequency of sexual behaviors, not attitudes or feelings about sex, and he was dealing only with sexuality, not love or relationships.

Here also, Hite followed the format of anonymous essay questionnaires, asking men questions not only about sexuality, but also about love—about how it feels to fall in love for the first time, about their feelings concerning growing up with their fathers, their current relationships with women, their marriages, and what they would like to change about their sexuality and their lives if they could.

All told, *The Hite Report on Male Sexuality* presents a staggering picture of men, told in men's own words. The heart of this book is about ideology, that is, about why people behave as they do—and specifically, about the patriarchal ideology and how it permeates men's behaviors in every area, including sexuality, which is supposedly biologically determined. In other words, what we call "sex"—as stated in the first Hite Report—comes down to a reflection of attitudes and values (i.e., an ideology) that extend through large segments of the overall society. These sexual behaviors are socially created, not just biological; further, this socially directed institution of sex does not equally value the needs and possibilities of women and men.

In effect, with this volume, Hite was beginning a re-evaluation of "male psychology" and "male sexuality," which are so intimately linked —something rarely done,* since the assumption has been that the psychology of men is human psychology itself, that the way men are is "natural": not a socially constructed set of behaviors and perceptions, but "biological human nature in action."

To understand "male sexuality" it is necessary to understand the culture and what it informs men "male sexuality" and "masculinity" are—the whole context in which men are taught to see/express their "sexuality," and, especially, to see their emotional world. Men are offered a very limited repertoire of admissible (or at least publicly admissible) emotions; if a man feels other emotions, he must hide them. Therefore, most men, if asked on the street for their opinion, are quick to say, "Well, I don't think I'm a typical male." And they are probably right; there *are* almost no "typical males," since few humans could live with the limited set of feelings they are "permitted." Furthermore, not being allowed to express their emotions, not even (in a way) being allowed to *feel* all the things humans feel, makes men confused and uncomfortable when asked to talk about their "feelings," and this, in turn, causes deep problems for them in their relationships with women.

While in this book Hite has sympathetically pointed out the difficulties for many men—the awkwardness of some male rituals, how many men are stuck in these ritual patterns, this system, and suffering from it—possibly all this was a shock to men, since they are not used to seeing themselves as the object of studies, not to mention

---

* Psychologists earlier in the century such as Karen Horney and Beatrice Hinkle commented and wrote on these issues.

a study done by a woman. Perhaps because it is so shocking for men to be treated as a specific group, rather than as a universal standard, the second Hite Report received dismayed and sometimes even lunatic reaction from some male critics.

Hite, in effect, was receiving criticism for her bold dissection of the current socio-sexual system: by daring to claim that socialization pressures the male to adapt and perform in a particular sexual manner, she challenged the usual and highly touted idea that male physiology and evolutionary processes create and control male sexuality. As a result, she was subject to a deeply entrenched prejudice based upon her sex and the topic of her study. In effect, male critics attacked her expertise and her commentary on a matter which men consider to be extremely personal and important to their sense of being male. In other words, she was viewed as treading on sacred ground, daring to investigate an area which so greatly forms the male ego.

Again, in this volume, Hite stressed the cultural relativism of sexuality. In a section on the politics of intercourse, she argued that a man's "sexual drive" is not a biological imperative, but that our society's definition of sex is culturally created: if you can show that there are cultural pressures on people to behave in a certain way, then you cannot make the assumption that the behavior is a biological given.

But what we know as "male sexuality," Hite explains, is not only a socially constructed but also a very limited version of what male sexuality might be. Just as men are offered a very narrow range of emotions by the culture, also their sexuality is narrowly defined and subtly inhibited. As she states in the preface to that work, society tells men to "define love as sex, and sex as penetration and ejaculation within a woman . . . [therefore] it is not simply by looking at the small details of men's sexual lives and understanding how they may hurt or give pleasure that will change our idea of what male sexuality is—discussing them rationally as if more 'pleasure' were the aim—because that is not the definition of male sexuality—male sexuality is not based on simple pleasure. Male sexuality, and masculinity, is based on a larger ideology; [in fact, 'sex' in general] is not so much about pleasure as it is about a certain emotional symbolism that is a part of that ideology, a ritual drama re-enacted over and over."*

Hite, in essence, is appealing for a redefinition of masculinity, for men to stop and look at what it is they are doing with their lives. This is a book full of possibilities for the future.

* The Hite Report on Male Sexuality (New York: Alfred A. Knopf, 1981), p. xvii.

The Hite Report on Love, Passion, and Emotional Violence: redefining the nature of emotional life

I have always felt that "love," perhaps because it is considered to be the center, if not the totality of a woman's life, is a risky business, and one to which feminists should address much energy and ingenuity. When I was in graduate school in the early 60s, I was appalled by the abuse that my female colleagues sustained in the pursuit and achievement of love. Indeed, I organized a "syndicate" (modeled after Milo Minderbinder's in Joseph Heller's *Catch-22*) to resist such abuse, collectively taking the initiative in dating and blacklisting men who mistreated members of the syndicate. The outrage which resulted from these efforts convinced me that I was tampering with what men considered their sacred rights. I continued this work later, when, as a member of the Chicago West Side Group, I led a drive to organize women in singles bars to rationalize and dignify the pursuit of love. But although the members of the group had previously demonstrated extraordinary courage, facing police, tear gas, going to jail in draft resistance demonstrations, when it came to the singles bars, their courage faltered. The project was abandoned because only two of us would regularly show up for planned actions at the bars, no matter how many had promised to come. At an early meeting of feminists from across the country in 1968, I spoke of the need for a task force of feminists to fight the oppression and dehumanization of women that went along with our pursuit and achievement of love.

But the politics of heterosexual love and romance have never been fully explored nor documented on a large scale. In the first Hite Report, in 1976, Hite had announced her intention of studying women's feelings about love, asking women to define the nature of love*—because "it is in the emotional dynamics of love relationships, and in the psychological assumptions, that stereotypes about women remain most deeply embedded."† And also, women have been defined by the society for a very long time in terms of "love"—i.e., told that they must raise a family, be loved by a man, married, or face being an "outcast."

---

* See *The Hite Report on Female Sexuality* (New York: Macmillan, 1976), Chapter 6.
† This explains the explosion of popular psychology books in which the subject of relationships between women and men is now being talked about: as women become more and more unafraid of the social system and of men, more independent financially and ideologically, yet find themselves in love with or living with men who still express (perhaps unconsciously) old stereotypes about women's "nature"--expecting women will be loving, take second place emotionally in relationships, not being angry when the man does not reciprocate with this emotional support—women wonder what to do about the situation, whether to leave or stay, what to think.

Much of this feeling, that women's basic function in life is to be loving and nurturing, still remains; it has not been fully accepted that women are complete above and beyond their biological capabilities, or ability to take care of, "service" others. This does not mean, of course, that it is "wrong" to be nurturing; the question here is whether all of the nurturing of society is supposed to be done by women.

In particular, there is a bias against women that often comes out in personal relationships—i.e., that men express by their behavior, actions and statements to women in private. Love between women and men is an area that needs to be analyzed more deeply than it has been. As Carol Gilligan has pointed out, "Among the most pressing items on the agenda for research on adult development is the need to delineate *in women's own terms* the experience of their adult life."*

Several earlier works broached these issues. Simone de Beauvoir's *The Second Sex* opened up some of the deeper areas of women's concerns about love, bringing out poignantly the mixed sense that love is great and yet somehow involves pain and humiliation for women—so that, according to de Beauvoir at the time, we finally may come to learn to love humiliation in love. In the 1970s Kate Millett's *Sexual Politics* shook the world with its statements about love between women and men, exposing the violence in much of men's writing about women they love, or supposedly love. Ti-Grace Atkinson, in *Amazon Odyssey*, coined the phrase, "Scratch his love, and you'll find your fear." Shulamith Firestone and Laura X also presented interesting theoretical statements, and additional work was done by Elaine Walster-Hatfield and Dorothy Tennov.

However, after the early 70s, issues of love between women and men did not receive as much attention as issues of sexuality (notable exceptions were Jessie Bernard, Letty Cottin Pogrebin, Barbara Ehrenreich and Andrea Dworkin). Indeed, in a strange sort of reverse Victorianism, theorizing and writing about sex became more acceptable than writing about love, and some interesting theoretical works were produced by Alison Jagger, Catherine Stimpson, and a group of women editing *Powers of Desire*. But feminists rarely confronted the politics of heterosexual love head-on. Rather, two trends, both of which skirted the issue, arose. One went off men entirely, embarking on a stunningly revolutionary exploration of how women can love women without reservation. However, a sectarian part of this trend claimed that women still attached to males were "consorting with the enemy,"

---

* Carol Gilligan, *In a Different Voice* (Cambridge: Harvard University Press, 1982), pp. 172–73.

thereby dismissing millions of women who had associations with men either by choice or circumstance. The other trend was of the position that "Men are changing, so why talk about it? There *is* no problem—a smart woman should be able to find herself one of the 'new men' out there."

Thus heterosexual love relationships became almost a taboo subject in feminist circles, not politically "correct" or "relevant." And yet this is one of the most important political topics there is, if one takes seriously the original slogan of the women's movement, that is, "the personal is political."

Academic psychological studies in recent years have come to focus on gender issues, but have also shied away from the study of love and emotion, perhaps since they are not easily quantified, and therefore the work might not be considered "scientific" by colleagues. Studying love, in other words, is difficult, and could easily leave one open to attack—as Elaine Walster-Hatfield found in 1972 when, after obtaining a government grant to study love, she was berated publicly by Senator William Proxmire, who thought the taxpayers' money was being wasted on such a frivolous topic, and as a result lost her grant. Nevertheless, in recent years, Pepper Schwartz and Philip Blumstein of the University of Washington have published in this area, as have philosophers such as Joseph Fell, Irving Singer and Emilie Rorty.

In *Women and Love* (*The Hite Report on Love, Passion, and Emotional Violence*) Hite and the 4,500 women participating begin the process of re-naming what is going on in personal life, re-seeing the emotions involved and the patterns of behavior, debating with each other the definition of love and various emotions felt for another—not only for men but also for women.

What do women say here about love, and what is going on in their lives? Basically, whether married or single, most say they do not feel emotionally satisfied in their relationships with men, often finding themselves frustrated, alienated, distanced and unable to break through to a man who doesn't see what is missing. Many women leave these relationships, while others stay, but often stay physically only, looking elsewhere for their primary emotional connection—often with women friends. The frustration women feel in these situations, in fact, the tragic aspect of many relationships—is staggering and profoundly moving.

We know that the home has been women's ghetto, and were surprised when we first began to hear of the incidence of physical violence in these private settings. Now we see here something harder to pinpoint, that is the terrible emotional draining of women that has been and is going on in relationships, the subtle ways women are badgered

9

emotionally in private (even just by "standard" and "acceptable" usage of language which inherently puts women down)—and still expected to provide loving and nurturing.

Love relationships take place in private, there is no one to witness what goes on there, to name what is happening; each individual has to name it for herself, by herself—amidst the confusion of also loving and perhaps being loved—and doubt that she is ever right in her naming. (If a relationship is painful, a woman may feel she cannot or "should" not complain, lest she be seen as having "problems.") So, many of these things are not said in daily life—in fact some of the voices we hear here seem almost to be voices from hidden bedrooms, sobs never before heard by anyone—or voices surfacing finally after months and years of numbness, of having almost forgotten how to speak because of the futility of it, since one's own "voice" was never heard. And yet there is also in these voices a great strength and determination to be heard, to speak, to no longer remain silent or be told what "reality" is.

The documentation women give here of their inner emotional lives should finally provide much of the material necessary to replace the Freudian-descended systems of "women's psychology."

Was Freud wrong about women? Yes, indeed, as I first argued in 1968.* Personality theory in general, whether Freudian or not, has missed the central importance of social expectation and culture in determining what we do and how we feel, and thus is largely irrelevant to an understanding of our lives and our behavior. As I showed, Freudians and others can neither predict what we do, nor seriously explain what we have done. Nonetheless, the idea of women's inherent "passivity" or "masochism" has remained a bedrock of the cultural myth about women, a myth strengthened by the cultural recidivism of the current era. Here this myth is annihilated by a large body of proof and documentation.

What women say in *Women and Love* (*The Hite Report on Love, Passion, and Emotional Violence*) supersedes Freud and many other current schools of therapy, none of which are based on large data bases, and especially not on what *women* say. This book shows the fallacy of many of the stereotypes placed on women ("defining" women) by, as Hite describes it, "Freudian Mysticism—i.e., that particular brand

* An early version of this argument appeared in "Psychology Constructs the Female," published as a pamphlet in 1968 (Boston: New England Free Press); it was then reprinted as " 'Kinder, Kuche, Kirche' as Scientific Law: Psychology Constructs the Female" in Robin Morgan's *Sisterhood is Powerful: An Anthology of Writings From the Women's Liberation Movement* (New York: Random House, 1970, pp. 205–20); and was later revised and updated as "Psychology Constructs the Female; or the Fantasy Life of the Male Psychologist—With Some Attention to the Fantasies of His Friends, the Male Biologist and the Male Anthropologist" (*Social Education*, April 1971, pp. 363–73).

of mystifing women Freud had which was a retort to the feminism of the 1900s; women are not 'dissatisfied,' he said, because of their secondary social status, or because they are in fact overworked; women are 'dissatisfied' for neurotic personal reasons.'' Hite goes on: ''This line of 'thinking' continues today in abstruse academic theory and in popular advice books which tell women they 'love too much' and should change their 'crippled,' 'neurotic' patterns of behavior. But women are confronted by very real, negative situations in their lives. The question for any group in this situation is, what to do about it. Women are trying to get men to see personal relationships differently, to change their values, but when they don't, women now feel forced either to leave, or if they stay, to become less committed emotionally—they feel psychologically divided and frequently confused and depressed. Freud may have, with his sample of three women, documented this stage of the process, but it was not correct to build an entire 'theory of women' or 'psychology of women' around it. What we are documenting here, by listening to women, is the *whole* panorama, and not forgetting the cultural milieu in which we are living.''

Some readers may be surprised by the small focus on class analysis here, since it has become so prominent in some feminist scholarship. Hite's data (as seen in particular in the statistical appendixes) simply do not warrant such a breakdown. How women are ''seen'' by the culture transcends class: almost all women are expected to be ''loving'' and not ''bitchy,'' no matter what their class, education or socioeconomic group. Indeed, class analysis has never struck me as appropriate in an understanding of women's oppression. Rather I have always suspected that it is a scam whose aim is to keep women in the place assigned to them by Marxists.★ Interestingly, however, an important part of what Hite has done in her work is to involve a great number of people in significant discussions and in the political process of defining their own lives and the culture.

Hite's theoretical framework for understanding what is happening today in personal relationships and in the culture is neither Freudian nor Marxist, but builds on feminist analyses of patriarchy. As she says Freud eventually came to believe that aggression was inherent in biology, and could not be eradicated from society in order to make a better society; Marx, however, declared that aggression was caused by the economic system, a system which should be changed; Hite, like many feminists, believes that the society we have, with so much emphasis on aggression

★ Naomi Weisstein, Virginia Blaisdell and Jesse Lemisch, *The Godfathers: Freudians, Marxists and the Scientific and Political Protection Societies* (New Haven: Belladonna Publishing, 1981).

and competition, is not necessary—we simply don't have to live this way—and what is needed to change it is a complete understanding and revision of the ideological system at hand. It is to this that her books are dedicated.

We seem to be living in a time of a radical shift: we are in the midst of a very real revolution. Despite the cultural backlash, despite the media blitz and the mocking of feminism, what the modern women's movement started continues its explosive growth. Women all over the United States have come to some very important conclusions; indeed, their whole perspective on the world seems to be changing. What we see in *Women and Love* (*The Hite Report on Love, Passion, and Emotional Violence*) is women defining themselves emotionally, defining themselves on their own terms, leaving behind a "male" view of the world, saying goodbye to an allegiance to "male" cultural values which define women as second-class emotionally or any other way, and which insist that competition and aggression are the basic realities of "human nature."

Women are finding new strength in their women friends, and women as lovers—although women's friendship may have been even stronger in Victorian society, when friends walking arm in arm or holding hands was commonplace, as was writing passionately affectionate letters to one's friends, and although in general women have throughout history taken strength from each other.★ In fact here, a significant number of previously married women over forty are finding love with another woman to be a new and satisfying way of life.

This debate is in part about what "women's revolution" will mean to the society: if we change our status, will the whole society be changed, thereby transformed? Will women's consciousness change the culture, or will women be totally assimilated into "male" ways of thinking and perceiving the world? Women here, while taking on some "male" ways of dealing with the world, seem quite clearly to be rejecting the "male" value system, and taking a new path—although where that new path will lead is as yet unclear.

In other words, women are leaving "home" and creating a new culture—radically altering the psychological structure of their lives,

★ While it is likely that for most times and places, women have had close friendships with each other, in the twentieth century before the second wave of feminism, intense friendships between women became socially unacceptable, deemed sick and abnormal by the early sexologists and other patriarchal enthusiasts. In her brilliant book, *Surpassing the Love of Men: Romantic Friendships and Love Between Women from the Renaissance to the Present* (New York: William Morrow, 1981), Lillian Faderman documents the passionate attachments between women that were the social norm throughout the seventeenth, eighteenth, and nineteenth centuries, and which we see women re-claiming here.

leaving behind an authoritarian allegiance to "male" dominance and to the acceptance of male definitions of who women are. Hite calls this, "Seeing the world through new eyes: if women have been the 'Other,' in the famous phrase of Simone de Beauvoir, now the 'Other' have turned that role to advantage, 'Seeing' in a new way. From our role as 'outsider,' we have found we are able to see and analyze what is going on much more clearly than those at its center. Women are changing the role of 'Other' from outsider to that of Seer, inventing a new analysis of culture."

Here then, is a massive wealth of deeply perceptive theoretical treatises, juxtaposed with rich, personal and subjective material from thousands of women and men about their personal private thoughts, current struggle in personal life against ideology. This volume is a scholarly landmark, ahead of its time, and an invaluable contribution to the transformation of our culture currently going on.

PART ONE

Beginnings

1972–1976

1972: Original Letter to Women

Many years ago, I started asking women questions about their sexuality. To explain, I wrote this:

Questionnaire

Shere Hite

★NATIONAL ORGANIZATION FOR WOMEN, N.Y.C. CHAPTER

The purpose of the questionnaire is to try to understand ourselves better, both collectively and individually. On the one hand, asking yourself these questions is a good way to get further acquainted with your sexual feelings, and on the other hand, it is wonderful to hear what other women are thinking and feeling about the same things—especially since we never talk about them. The results will be published as a general discussion of what was said, with a few statistics, and a lot of quotes, like a giant "rap session" on paper.

The questionnaire is anonymous, so don't sign it. If any questions do not apply to you, just write "nonapplicable." Please use a separate sheet of paper and number your answers accordingly. **Don't feel that you have to answer every single question** (although we would really like it if you did). You can just skip around and answer the ones that interest you—Just let us hear from you!!!

---

* See reference to NOW in 1974: Introduction to *Sexual Honesty, By Women, For Women*, page 30.

Hite Research Questionnaire on Female Sexuality

1. Is having sex important to you? What part does it play in your life?

2. Do you think your age and background make any difference as far as your sex life is concerned? What is your age and background—education, upbringing, occupation, race, economic status, etc.?

3. Do you usually prefer sex with men, women, either, yourself, or not at all? Which have you had experience with and how much?

4. Do you have orgasms? When do you usually have them? During masturbation? Intercourse? Clitoral stimulation? Other sexual activity? How often?

5. Is having orgasms important to you? Do you like them? Do they ever bore you? Would you enjoy sex just as much without ever having them? Does having good sex have anything to do with having orgasms?

6. If you almost never or never have orgasms, are you interested in having them? Why or why not? If you are interested, what do you think would contribute to having them? Did you ever have them?

7. Could you describe what an orgasm feels like to you? Where do you feel it, and how does your body feel during orgasm?

8. Is having orgasms somewhat of a concentrated effort? Do you feel one has to learn to have orgasms?

9. Is one orgasm sexually satisfying to you? If not how many? How many orgasms are you capable of? How many do you usually want? During masturbation? During clitoral stimulation with a partner? During intercourse?

10. Please give a graphic description or drawing of how your body could best be stimulated to orgasm.

11. Do you enjoy arousal? For its own sake, i.e. as an extended state of heightened sensitivity not necessarily leading to orgasm? What does it feel like?

12. Do you like to remain in a state of arousal for indefinite or long periods of time? Or do you prefer to have arousal and orgasm in a relatively short period of time?

13. Do you ever go for long periods without sex? (Does this include masturbation or do you have no sex at all?) Does it bother you or do you like it?

14. How often do you desire sex? Do you actively seek it? Is the time of the month important? Do you experience an increase in sexual desire at certain times of the month?

15. Do you enjoy masturbation? Physically? Psychologically? How often? Does it lead to orgasm usually, sometimes, rarely, or never? Is it more intense with someone or alone? How many orgasms do you usually have?

16. What do you think is the importance of masturbation? Did you ever see anyone else masturbating? Can you imagine women you admire masturbating?

17. How do you masturbate? What is the sequence of events which occur? Please give a detailed description.

18. What positions and movement are best for stimulating yourself clitorally with a partner? Do you have orgasms this way usually, sometimes, rarely, or never? Please explain ways you and your partner(s) practice clitoral stimulation. Can you think of other ways?

19. What other sexual play do you enjoy? Is it important for reaching orgasm? How important is kissing (mouth stimulation), breast stimulation, caressing of hips and thighs, general body touching, etc?

20. Do you like vaginal penetration/intercourse? Physically? Psychologically? Why? Does it lead to orgasm usually, sometimes, rarely, or never? How long does it take? Do you ever have any physical discomfort? Do you usually have adequate lubrication? Do you ever have a decrease in vaginal–genital feeling the longer intercourse lasts?

21. What kinds of movement do you find most stimulating during penetration—soft, hard, pressure to the back or front or neither,

with complete or partial penetration, etc? Which positions do you find most stimulating? Does size or shape of penis or penetrating "object" concern you?

22. Do you have intercourse during your period? Oral sex?

23. Is it easier for you to have an orgasm when intercourse is not in progress? In other words, do you have orgasms more easily by clitoral stimulation than intercourse? Are the orgasms different? How?

24. Do you enjoy cunnilingus? Do you have orgasms during cunnilingus usually, sometimes, rarely, or never? Do you have them during oral/clitoral and anal/vaginal contact or both? Explain what you like or dislike about it.

25. Do you use a vibrator to have orgasms?

26. Do you enjoy rectal contact? What kind? Rectal penetration?

27. What do you think about during sex? Do you fantasize? What about?

28. Does pornography stimulate you? What kinds? What actions?

29. What do you think of sado-masochism? Of domination-submission? What do you think is their significance?

30. Do you prefer to do things to others or to have things done to you, or neither?

31. Which would cause you to become more excited—physical teasing, direct genital stimulation, or psychological "foreplay"?

32. Who sets the pace and style of sex—you or your partner? Who decides when it's over? What happens if your partner usually wants to have sex more often than you do? What happens if you want to have sex more often than your partner?

33. Do you usually have sex with the people you want to have sex with? Who usually initiates sex or a sexual advance—you or the other person?

34. Describe how most men and women have had sex with you (if there are any partners, etc).

35. Do most of your partners seem to be well informed about your sexual desires and your body? Are they sensitive to the stimulation you want? If not, do you ask for it or act yourself to get it? Is this embarrassing?

36. Do you feel guilty for taking time for yourself in sexual play which may not be specifically stimulating to your partner? Which activities are you including in your answer?

37. Are you shy about having orgasms with a partner? With only new partners or with everyone? Why?

38. Do you think your vagina and genital area are ugly or beautiful? Do you feel that they smell good?

39. Do you ever find it necessary to masturbate to achieve orgasm after "making love"?

40. How long does sex usually last?

41. Do you ever fake orgasms? During which sexual activities? How often? Under what conditions?

42. What would you like to try that you never have? What would you like to do more often? What changes would you like to make in the usual "bedroom" scene?

43. What are your best sex experiences?

44. How old were you when you had your first sexual experience? With yourself? With another person? What were they? How old were you when you had your first orgasm? During what activity? At what age did you look carefully at your vagina and genitals?

45. What is it about sex that gives you the greatest pleasure? Displeasure?

46. What can you imagine you would like to do with another person's body? How would you like to relate physically to other bodies?

47. Do you enjoy touching? Whom do you touch—men, women, friends, relatives, children, yourself, animals, pets, etc? Does this have anything to do with sex?

48. How important are physical affection and touching for their own sakes (not leading to sex)? Do you do as much of them as you would like? Do you ever have sex with someone mainly to touch and be touched and be close to them? How often?

49. Do you ever touch someone for purposes of sensual arousal but not "real" sex? Explain.

50. Is there a difference between sex and touching? If so, what is that difference?

51. In the best of all possible worlds, what would sexuality be like?

52. What do you think of the "sexual revolution"?

53. How does or did contraception affect your sexual life? What methods have you used? Did you ever take birth control pills? Aids?

54. Do you feel that having sex is in any way political?

55. Have you read Masters and Johnson's recent scientific studies of sexuality? Kinsey's? Others? What do you think of them?

56. Please add anything you would like to say that was not mentioned in this questionnaire.

57. How did you like the questionnaire?

1974: Introduction to *Sexual Honesty, By Women, For Women**

This book is a forum for our public discussion with each other of the nature of our sexuality, the first in a series intended for the re-examination and redefinition of our sexuality. We have never before attempted as a group to define or discover what the physical nature of our sexuality might be, and have sometimes just accepted the role which society handed to us. The purpose here is to begin to determine what feelings might lie buried beneath the layers and layers of myth we live by, or buried beneath the weight of the many "authoritative" books written by male "experts" who presume to tell us how we feel. It is time we made up our own minds, ended the ban on talking about sex, and came to terms with our own personal lives and how we intend to live them.

Most of the extant works on female sexuality contain distortions related to not knowing what female sexuality is about. The most damaging of this literature, often written by male doctors,† is nothing more than the reiteration of "marriage manual" techniques for improving our "responsiveness," with some worn-out platitudes thrown in to "liberate" us from our "hang-ups." The most helpful of this literature has been the more scientific clinical studies, which, while in themselves valid and necessary, have also unfortunately been interpreted through the perspectives of unexamined preconceptions about our sexuality. There has rarely been any acknowledgment that female sexuality might have a nature of its own, which would involve more than merely being the logical counterpart of male sexuality. Actually, no one really knows much about the subject yet because women are just beginning to think about it. Therefore, even though some of these clinical efforts have been helpful, it is

---

* Published by Warner Paperback Library, a division of Warner Books, Inc.
† Almost nothing has been written by women themselves, but there are some outstanding exceptions: *The Nature and Evolution of Female Sexuality* by Mary Jane Sherfey; *Free and Female* by Barbara Seaman; articles by Ann Koedt and Ti-Grace Atkinson; and the material on sex in *Our Bodies, Our Selves* by the Boston Women's Health Collective.

time we as women speak out ourselves, and begin to define our own sexuality.

What exactly is meant by "defining our own sexuality"? Perhaps we have become so submerged in our culture's idea of what we are supposed to be, that we have lost touch with what we really feel, and how to express it. So our first step, for which the questionnaires were designed, should be to get back in touch with our more instinctive feelings, and even perhaps to discover feelings never before articulated or consciously felt. Not only are we out of touch with ourselves, but we are also out of touch with each other, and with each other's feelings about sex, since no channels exist for communication on this subject. If we were lucky, our mothers or friends shared their experiences with us, but all too often this was not the case. Perhaps this lack of real information made us wonder if we were somehow "different" from other women.

Although the kind of material presented here is always part of the scientific investigation of sexuality, access to primary data is something the public is not ordinarily trusted with, and so even this possible channel of communication has been closed off. With this book we have, perhaps for the first time, a means of sharing our feelings about sex and getting acquainted on a broad scale, a forum for discovering common experiences and needs, and for beginning this redefinition of who we are. Of course this book does not pretend to represent any kind of final definition of our sexuality, nor is it a statistical sample of all the replies received. It merely represents forty-five out of the over two thousand replies received to the questionnaires to date. Neither will this book be the end of our newly opened dialogue, but rather a beginning, as it will be followed by the publication of more of these answers, and eventually by the complete analysis of all the answers received. Therefore it is vitally important that you participate in this discussion by sending in your own answers to the questions, and thus adding your own feelings to this redefinition.

The ultimate intention of this research is to formulate a critique of our current cultural definitions of sex, based on what we have all said. This book,* to be published in 1975, perhaps together with some concluding original replies, will not be statistically oriented in that it will not attempt to correlate such things as age and background with attitude and "performance." Rather, it will attempt to answer the questions which formed the basis for this study, namely:

1) Insofar as we can possibly know them, what are the "instinctive"

---

* This book was to be *The Hite Report on Female Sexuality*, 1976.

24

(natural, not socially conditioned) physical expressions of our sexuality?

2) How do these compare with the basic physical activities we usually engage in?

3) What changes, based on the findings of 1) and 2), might we want to make in our sexual definitions and in our actual physical relations? What would be the implications of these changes for our present cultural definitions of sexuality, for the institutions related to them, and for men's perceptions of their own sexuality?*

It does, even now, seem fairly clear that this reawakening of our sensitivity to what is instinctive and natural to us will be part of larger changes which involve not only such things as bedroom habits, but which will also have profound and far-reaching effects on all of our social relations.

My academic training was as an historian. My M.A. thesis, and major area of interest before this study, concerned the origins of the belief in scientific method as the ultimate road to truth and reality. My Ph.D. coursework centered on the history of Western thought since the Enlightenment, with specific emphasis on contemporary ideas, institutions and their origins.

I began to see sexuality as one of those institutions, and thus this project was begun. It was neither originated nor funded by the New York chapter of the National Organization for Women, nor was it conducted jointly with them. The connection was simply that, as a member, I was granted permission to use the name and address as a heading for the questions, with the purpose of providing the reader with a quick orientation as to their viewpoint.

The questionnaires were printed in New York at the Come! Unity Press, 13 East 17 Street. This is an offset press available completely free to anyone for printing their own non-commercial material. Its only support is donations of printing supplies, food, money for rent, mechanical skills and so on. Unfortunately, these donations are not always regular, and so this press, without which my project and others like it could not exist, may not continue for lack of adequate support. However, the contribution of this press and the many

---

* For purposes of checking our assumptions about male sexuality, I have prepared a questionnaire for men.

people I have met there to this project has been enormous, and I thank them.

I would also like to extend my personal thanks to Veronica Di Napoli, Dorothy Crouch, Sydelle Beiner and Joyce Snyder; also to *Majority Report*, KNOW Inc., the *New York Woman*, and the Manhattan Women's Political Caucus. Many others helped with this project and continue to help it in many ways, among them Joyce Gold, Dorothy Petrak, Jackie Starkey, Ann Diamond, Penny Otton, Polly Kellog, Anne Pride, Susan Robinson, C. K. Yearley, Helen Ferraioli, Catherine Wagner, Tracy Young and Howard Smith, and Cecile Rice, and I thank them. A special note of appreciation goes to Michael Wilson. I would also like to send my personal thanks to all the women all over the country who distributed questionnaires in their areas, and to those who sent postage.

Of course the most important vote of thanks for this book go to all the 2,000 women who have answered the questionnaires. Without all of you, this project would not have been possible. Please accept my deepest thanks and my warmest personal greetings.

Shere Hite
January 17, 1974

1976: Speech Delivered to Harvard Forum and also to the University of Pennsylvania, 1977

Starting in 1972, with the cooperation of the National Organization for Women (NOW, New York Chapter), I distributed a long, essay-type questionnaire to women all over the United States, asking such questions as, "How do you masturbate?", "Do you ever fake orgasms?", and "How do you feel about the sexual revolution?". At first, I didn't plan to do such a large-scale study, but the more I saw women's answers, the more I became determined to let every woman know what I was finding out. Eventually, 3,019 women—including every type of woman imaginable, ages 14 to 78, from radical to conservative—sent back their replies.

These answers were more than I ever hoped for—long, personal letters from women of all backgrounds and points of view, full of beautifully written, moving descriptions of their feelings, and things they had experienced—a joy to receive. Of course, the replies were all anonymous, so I have never met any of the women; as much as I wanted to write to some of them, it was never possible, and the whole exchange has remained an anonymous and powerful communication, almost a soul-to-soul communication, from the women who answered to all the women of the world. Receiving these replies was one of the most emotionally fulfilling experiences of my entire life, something enriching and indescribably beautiful which expanded my horizon tremendously: and it is this experience I want to share with those who read the book. Almost nine-tenths of the book is made up of direct quotes from the women who answered.

Usually a project of this size would have been funded by some national foundation; however, there was no funding involved in this project, from NOW or any other source. (NOW simply could not afford it.) Instead, friends (both women and men) and I went into debt to finance it because we felt very strongly that it should remain totally woman-run. It took four years of 7-day-a-week, 15-hour-a-day work—approximately 23,000 woman-hours. It was quite a long process to record, code, and analyze 3,000 replies to 50 long, essay questions. Many people worked with me over the years, for a very small, minimal wage, but mostly for love. We sat packed close together in a small room, deciphering all types of handwriting, slowly and laboriously, onto long charts which never seemed to end. But every minute was worth it, both for the long-term result and for our own personal growth.

My background is in social and intellectual history, which was perfect for this study. It was my training, plus the inspiration of the women's movement, which enabled me to see that sex as we know it is a cultural institution, rather than the biological given we assume. My master's thesis had been written on social science methodology, which provided me with a good background in research techniques and values. However, a dissertation on female sexuality was difficult for a conservative school like Columbia University to understand, so I didn't finish my doctorate. And I was still paying off college tuition debts during this entire period, and so held innumerable jobs, from secretary to waitress to model—which was also a part of my education.

The Hite Report on Female Sexuality is so long that very often it is understood on one level only. However, in reality there are three important levels on which to understand it. First, to hear women's voices on this subject is an historic breakthrough. Can you believe that, before this, we had almost no recorded descriptions of how orgasm feels to women, only how it feels to men? The second contribution of *The Hite Report on Female Sexuality* is that it provides a new cultural and historical framework for the definition of physical relations as we know it, i.e., "sex." And finally, *The Hite Report on Female Sexuality* provides many new findings for sex research, especially relating to how women achieve orgasm.

Perhaps one of the most widely publicized of those findings, and deservedly so, is that intercourse/coitus itself does not automatically lead to orgasm for most women. For centuries, women have been described as having "problems" with sex. However, it is now becoming clear that it is not women who have a problem with sex, but the society that has a problem with its definition of sex, a definition that hurts both women and men, but a definition we can change.

Below is a brief list of some of the findings of *The Hite Report on Female Sexuality*:

★ Most women do not orgasm as a result of intercourse per se. The overwhelming majority of women require specific clitoral contact for orgasm. Women know how to orgasm whenever they want, easily and pleasurably. Women who masturbate can orgasm easily and regularly. Women are free to use this knowledge during sex with others. The stereotype of female sexuality which says it is more difficult for a woman to orgasm than a man is untrue. Women are not "dysfunctional" or slow to arouse; it is our definition of sex which makes women "dysfunctional."

★ Why do we define sex as "foreplay"—followed by intercourse to male orgasm? This is a sexist definition of sex, with a cultural, rather than a biological, base. We can change it. Historically, this definition is only 3,000 years old.

★ Men make their own orgasms during sex; women should be able to, too. Men should not be in charge of both their own and women's orgasms.

★ The Sexual Revolution did not "free" women, but in many ways was a step backward for women.

★ Age is not a factor in female sexuality. Older women are NOT less sexual than younger women—and they are often *more* sexual. Young women and girls are not less sexual than adults, but are often misinformed about the nature of their sexuality.

It's not specifically just *orgasms* we are talking about here; we are talking about a complete re-definition, or *un*-definition, of what sex is. What is the meaning of physical relations anyway? Our whole definition of sex is oriented around male orgasm during intercourse, because of our definition of sex as reproductive activity. This definition must be seen as part of a total culture and way of life, and not as biological imperative. Sexuality or physical pleasure has not always been defined as we define it; the earliest Hebrew codes did not condemn homosexuality, and reproductive activity has not always been the only form of intense intimacy which was glorified. Touching friends and sitting together intimately should be possible, without it having overtones of anything else. Intense physical contact should be possible in many varied ways. In short, our whole idea of "sex" must be re-evaluated. We need to make a new kind of physical relations to go with a new, more humane and pro-life society.

PART TWO

The Hite Report on Female Sexuality

1976

Sexuality As a Social Construction: Toward a New Theory of Female Sexuality

Undefining* Sex

Our definition of sex belongs to a world view that is past—or passing. Sexuality, and sexual relations, no longer define the important property right they once did; children are no longer central to the power either of the state or the individual. Although all of our social institutions are still totally based on hierarchical and patriarchal forms, patriarchy as a form is really dead, as is the sexuality that defined it. We are currently in a period of transition, although it is unclear as yet to what. The challenge for us now is to devise a more humane society, one that will implement the best of the old values, like kindness and understanding, cooperation, equality, and justice throughout *every* layer of public and private life—a metamorphosis to a more personal and humanized society.

Specifically in sexual relations—which we should perhaps begin calling simply physical relations—we can again reopen many options. All the kinds of physical intimacy that were channeled into our one mechanical definition of sex can now be reallowed and rediffused throughout our lives, including simple forms of touching and warm body contact. There need not be a sharp distinction between sexual touching and friendship. Just as women described "arousal" as one of the best parts of sex, and just as they described closeness as the most pleasurable aspect of intercourse, so intense physical intimacy can be one of the most satisfying activities possible—in and of itself.

Although we tend to think of "sex" as one set pattern, one group of activities (in essence, reproductive activity), there is no need to limit ourselves in this way. There is no reason why physical intimacy with

---

* This was "undefining" in the original text, but changed to "redefining" by a copyeditor since the word "undefining" did not exist. However, the concept I meant to indicate was not to create one new definition (i.e. redefinition) of sexuality, but allow for many – hence, "undefining."

men, for example, should always consist of "foreplay" followed by intercourse and male orgasm;* and there is no reason why intercourse must always be a part of heterosexual sex. Sex is intimate physical contact for pleasure, to share pleasure with another person (or just alone). You can have sex to orgasm, or not to orgasm, genital sex, or just physical intimacy—whatever seems right to you. There is never any reason to think the "goal" must be intercourse, and to try to make what you feel fit into that context. There is no standard of sexual performance "out there," against which you must measure yourself; you aren't ruled by "hormones" or "biology." You are free to explore and discover your own sexuality, to learn or unlearn anything you want, and to make physical relations with other people, of either sex, anything you like.

Turning Theory on Its Head: A New Theory of Female Sexuality and Orgasm
Do most women orgasm from intercourse?

"This is one of the last questions I've answered—I'm afraid to admit it—but I'm not really sure yes or no—although I've had many orgasms through masturbation, I'm not sure what orgasm from vaginal intercourse is like—I've had very high feelings, but I guess since it wasn't like a masturbatory orgasm I didn't think it was an orgasm. At first, this questionnaire made me feel totally inexperienced—but it's just that I guess I don't always *think* about these things during sex. Like I remember when I had my first coitus I just kept thinking, 'My god, I've got to remember all the details about this—the big important time of my life, when I chose to give up my virginity' and you know something—I don't really remember that much about that specific time."

"I really don't know if I've had an orgasm with a man, unless it's just that I don't really know what to be aware of because if it's supposed to be like when I'm masturbating then I think not. I would like to know if that makes me abnormal."

"I don't think I've ever really experienced an orgasm. In any event, not the way I've read about them. My husband's clitoral stimulation usually leads to a climax for me but never during vaginal stimulation. I keep hoping and working at it. Sometimes I tend to think maybe I'm not supposed to experience a vaginal climax. Sometimes it bothers

---

* This is discussed from men's point of view in the analysis of replies received from men, published as *The Hite Report on Male Sexuality*, 1981.

my husband more than it does me. He really feels badly that I don't experience the same type of pleasure he does. Sometimes I think we work at it too hard and sometimes we think we're getting closer to it, but I never experience anything physically ecstatic."

"I am rather hung up when it comes to orgasms. Because I never have them during intercourse, I feel deeply ashamed and inferior. I grew up with that wretched word 'frigid'—and I think that a lot of my desire to have orgasms during intercourse comes from this shame and feelings of inadequacy. I think the only thing that will contribute to my having them is when I change the feelings I have mentioned before—when I stop pressuring myself and hating myself because I don't have orgasm—hell, I don't know—I've been in therapy for two years and it has helped me personally a lot, but I'm still no closer to having them during intercourse. I think it will take some radical change in my perception and attitude toward myself."

Findings of this study

Did most of the women in this study orgasm regularly during intercourse (the penis thrusting in the vagina), without additional clitoral stimulation? No. *It was found that only approximately 30 percent of the women in this study could orgasm regularly from intercourse*—that is, could have an orgasm during intercourse without more direct manual clitoral stimulation being provided at the time of orgasm.

In other words, the majority of women do not experience orgasm regularly as a result of intercourse.

For most women, orgasming during intercourse as a result of intercourse alone is the exceptional experience, not the usual one. Although a small minority of women *could* orgasm more or less regularly from intercourse itself, since almost *all* women orgasm from clitoral stimulation (during manual stimulation with a partner or masturbation), henceforth we will refer to the stimulation necessary for female orgasm as *clitoral*.

It is clear that intercourse by itself did not regularly lead to orgasm for most women. In fact, for over 70 percent of the women, intercourse—the penis thrusting in the vagina—did not regularly lead to orgasm. What we thought was an individual problem is neither unusual nor a problem. In other words, *not* to have orgasm from intercourse is the experience of the majority of women.

We shall see later on that, often, the ways in which women do orgasm during intercourse have nothing much to do with intercourse itself. In fact, these methods could probably be adopted by other women who wished to orgasm during intercourse—if this was felt to be a desirable goal.

The Glorification of Intercourse: A Reproductive Model of Sexuality

Why have we thought women should orgasm from intercourse?

There are three basic reasons for this insistence, which will be developed in the following pages:

A. The explanation of sexual pleasure as the means of insuring reproduction.

B. The crucial role of monogamous intercourse in patrilineal inheritance.

C. The widespread influence of the Freudian model of female psychology.

A. Sexual pleasure and the reproductive model

First the idea that since nature gave us a "sex drive" and the capacity for sexual pleasure in order to insure reproduction, therefore coitus is "the real thing," and all other forms of sexual gratification are substitutions for, or perversions of, this "natural" activity.

It is important to scrutinize this assumption. Intercourse *is* necessary for reproduction, and sexual pleasure and orgasm *are* involved with reproduction. But exactly how? Looking closer, one sees that only *male* orgasm during intercourse is necessary for reproduction. It would make sense, from the point of view of the necessity to deposit semen inside the vagina, that intercourse provide almost automatic, perfect stimulation for male orgasm, and, of course, it does: men orgasm as regularly during intercourse as women (and men) do during masturbation.

However, since female orgasm is not necessary during intercourse for reproduction to occur, why should nature provide stimulation for female orgasm during intercourse? (As a matter of fact, what is the reason for the existence of female orgasm at all?) There are several possibilities:

1. Some researchers claim that female orgasm helps "suck" the sperm up into the uterus. However, Masters and Johnson believe that this is doubtful, since the contractions of the uterus progress downward, and so are "more likely to have an expulsive action than a sucking action." To check this, they placed a fluid resembling semen but opaque to X rays in a cap covering the cervix, so that if there were any sucking, the fluid would be taken into the cervix. However, X ray films showed no significant gaping of the cervical opening at all. Several respondents in this study mentioned that their contractions move downward, or outward. One woman described her orgasm this way: "A clitoral orgasm is a sharp, shuddering, breath-taking pleasure/pain gripping of the muscles in my rectum and vagina. Whatever is in me—a finger, or penis, or dildo—is gripped and pushed outward."

2. Dr. Mary Jane Sherfey says: "In general, the orgasm in the male is admirably designed to deposit semen where it will do the most good, and in the female, to remove the largest amount of venous congestion in the most effective manner." But orgasm does this for men, too, and Sherfey herself has made a point of emphasizing that after one orgasm women do not completely decongest but remain in a state of partial arousal, and sometimes after one orgasm arousal can become *stronger*. Can this be, then, the only function of female orgasm?

Dr. Sherfey has also given a reason why, from the point of view of reproduction, women should *not* have orgasms during intercourse: "In a woman with a lax perineal body who has borne children, semen easily escapes with premature withdrawal, whereas if the woman does *not* have an orgasm, the still-swollen lower third acts as a stopper to semen outflow. . . ." Masters and Johnson have also mentioned that there is a greater chance for impregnation for some women if they do not orgasm, for the same reason.

3. Another possibility is that perhaps our orgasmic contractions are for the purpose of further insuring male orgasm, gripping the penis and pulling slightly downward rhythmically. In this model of intercourse, thrusting would not be considered as necessary as it now is, and perhaps intercourse in another culture would be less gymnastic and male-dominated—more a mutual lying together in pleasure, penis-in-vagina, or vagina-covering-penis, with female orgasm providing much of the stimulation necessary for male orgasm.

4. On the other hand, perhaps the function of female orgasm is to provide arousal and "receptivity," or interest in the woman in initiating

intercourse. Most female primates have a period of estrus, a specific period of time during which arousal is more or less constant, which guarantees that fertility and intercourse will coincide. Women do not have estrus; they are theoretically capable of becoming aroused at any time. We become aroused in many ways—by kissing, hugging, and even talking. During all these activities, if we find them arousing, a warm, tickling sensation—the desire for clitoral stimulation, perhaps—becomes stronger and stronger. If clitoral stimulation follows, it often leads to a kind of vaginal tickle ("vaginal ache") that feels to many women like a desire to "be penetrated." While continued stimulation brings orgasm, and, for many women, a return to arousal, intercourse seems to quiet this feeling. Perhaps one of the functions of our orgasm is continuing arousal—and "receptivity."

It is unclear whether the "vaginal ache" part of the outline just presented holds true for most women, or even for very many women, since most women generally don't use any kind of vaginal entry during masturbation. However, the general idea of our orgasms perhaps serving the function of continuing our arousal and keeping it at just manageable levels for the body is an interesting possibility.

In the same way, it could be argued that since women do not have estrus, it is necessary for our clitoris to be located on the outside of our bodies rather than closer to the vagina, so that stimulation might happen in the normal course of things. In other words, since we are not periodically receptive like other mammals, there must be some mechanism provided for arousal that can be activated at will and that will not leave us constantly in a state of arousal.

However, none of these theories may be right. For example, if the purpose of arousal and sexuality in general is really connected only with reproduction, why can we have just as much if not stronger arousal and orgasm(s) at times when we are not capable of conception—i.e., during pregnancy, after menopause, during menstruation, and at other times of the month when conception is not possible, and during childhood?

Perhaps orgasm is basically a release mechanism for the body, as are other body reactions, such as laughing, crying, or bodily convulsions. Maybe one function of orgasm is the discharge of *all* kinds of tensions through this release. Or could it be possible that there is no "reason" for the existence of female orgasm other than pleasure? In any case, whether or not continuing arousal is the function of female orgasm, or the release of all kinds of bodily tensions, it is definitely clear that there is no logical reason for insisting that we have our orgasms during intercourse.

B. Patriarchy and monogamous intercourse

A second reason for insisting women (and men) should find their greatest sexual pleasure in intercourse, and for seeing intercourse as *the* basic sexual act, *the* basic form of sex—is that our form of society demands it. With a very few isolated exceptions, for the last three or four thousand years all societies have been patrilineal or patriarchal. Family name and inheritance have passed through men, and religious and civil laws have given men authority to determine the course of society. In a non-patriarchal society, where there is either no question of property right or where lineage goes through the mother, there is no need for institutionalizing intercourse as the basic form of sexual pleasure. In the earliest societies we know about, families were mostly extended groups of clans, with aunts and brothers sharing equally in the upbringing of the child; the mother did not particularly "own" the child, and there was no concept of "father" at all. In fact, the male role in reproduction was not understood for quite a long time, and intercourse and male orgasm were not connected with pregnancy which of course only became apparent many months later.

But with changeover to a patrilineal or patriarchal society,* it becomes necessary for the man to control the sexuality of the woman. Nancy Marval, in a paper printed by The Feminists, explains this further:

In a patriarchal culture like the one we were all brought up in, sexuality is a crucial issue. Beyond all the symbolic aspects of the sexual act (symbolizing the male's dominance, manipulation, and control over the female), it assumes an overwhelming practical importance. This is that men have no direct access to reproduction and the survival of the species. As individuals, their claim to any particular child can never be as clear as that of the mother who demonstrably gave birth to that child. Under normal circumstances it is agreed that a man is needed to provide sperm to the conception of the baby, but it is practically impossible to determine *which* man. The only way a man can be absolutely sure that he is the one to have contributed that sperm is to control the sexuality of the woman.

To do this, he had to insist she be a virgin at marriage, and monogamous thereafter. As Kinsey put it:

* Books related to this subject include *The First Sex*, by Elizabeth Gould Davis; *The Mothers*, by Robert Briffault; *The White Goddess*, by Robert Graves; *The Cult of the Mother Goddess*, by E. O. James; *Woman's Evolution*, by Evelyn Reed; and *Prehistory and the Beginning of Civilization*, by Jacquetta Hawkes and Sir Leonard Woolley.

Sexual activities for the female before marriage were proscribed in ancient codes primarily because they threatened the male's property rights in the female whom he was taking as a wife. The demand that the female be virgin at the time of her marriage was comparable to the demand that cattle or other goods that he bought should be perfect, according to the standards of the culture in which he lived.

In addition to these practical reasons for controlling sexuality (to maintain the form of social organization we know), in the early period of the changeover to patriarchy there were political reasons as well, in that other forms of sexuality represented rival forms of social organization. For example, it is generally accepted by Bible scholars that the earliest Jewish tribes mentioned in the Old Testament accepted cunnilingus and homosexuality as a valid part of life and physical relations, as did the societies around them—which were not, for the most part, totally patriarchal. In fact, prior to the seventh century B.C.,* homosexual and other sexual activities were associated with Jewish religious rites, just as in the surrounding cultures. But as the small and struggling Jewish tribes sought to build and consolidate their strength, and their patriarchal social order, and to bind all loyalty to the one male god, Yahweh, all forms of sexuality except the one necessary for reproduction were banned by religious code. The Holiness Code, established at the time of their return from the Babylonian exile, sought to fence out the surrounding cultures and set up rules for separating off the Chosen People of God. It was then that non-heterosexual, non-reproductive sexual acts were condemned as the way of the Canaanite, the way of the pagan. But these activities were proscribed as an indication of allegiance to another culture, an adjunct to idolatry—and *not* as "immoral" or as sexual crimes, as we consider them. They were political crimes.

These codes have continued in our religious and civil law up to this day. Judeo-Christian codes still specifically condemn all sexual activity that does not have reproduction as its ultimate aim. Our civil law is largely derived from these codes, and the laws of most states condemn non-coital forms of sexuality (in and out of marriage) as punishable misdemeanors or crimes. Thus, intercourse has been *institutionalized* in our culture as the only permissible form of sexual activity.

Forms of sexuality other than intercourse are now also considered *psychologically* abnormal and unhealthy, as we shall see in a few pages. However, the full spectrum of physical contact is enjoyed by the other

---

* Although according to *The Jews: Biography of a People*, by Judd Teller, it was the sixth century B.C.

mammals, and their mental health has not been questioned. Furthermore, intercourse is not the main focus of their sexual relations either, but only one activity out of many. They spend more time on mutual grooming than they do on specifically sexual contact, as Jane Goodall and many other primate researchers have described in great detail. They also masturbate and have homosexual relations quite commonly. Among the animals for whom these activities have been recorded are the rat, chinchilla, rabbit, porcupine, squirrel, ferret, horse, cow, elephant, dog, baboon, monkey, chimpanzee, and many others. Although our culture seems to assume that since sexual feelings are provided by nature to insure reproduction, and therefore intercourse is or should be the basic form of our sexuality—even though women's sexual feelings are often strongest when women are *not* fertile—it is patently obvious that other forms of sexuality are just as natural and basic as intercourse, and perhaps masturbation is more basic since chimpanzees brought up in isolation have no idea of how to have intercourse, but do masturbate almost from birth.

Redefining sexuality
To try to limit physical relations between humans to intercourse is artificial. But perhaps it was also necessary to channel all forms of physical contact into heterosexual intercourse to increase the rate of population growth. A high rate of reproduction is the key to power and wealth for a small group, and in the early Jewish tribes, barrenness was a curse. In fact, children have been the basic form of wealth in almost every society up to the present. From the point of view of the larger society, increase in numbers provides the ability to consolidate more territory and to defeat other tribes. On a personal level, children could inherit one's property and also consolidate the family's holdings, and they could till the fields, hunt, gather food, or tend flocks (and later, work in factories) for their parents.

The desire for maximum population growth was institutionalized in our culture, and out of this grew the definition of women as basically serving this ideal. The glorification of marriage, motherhood, and intercourse is part of a very strong pro-natalist bias in our culture, which is discussed in detail in the book *Pronatalism: The Myth of Mom and Apple Pie*, edited by Ellen Peck and Judy Senderowitz.

In summary, since intercourse has been defined as the basic form of sexuality, and the only natural, healthy, and moral form of physical contact, it has automatically been assumed that this is when women should orgasm. Heterosexual intercourse has been *the* definition of sexual expression ever since the beginning of patriarchy, and is the only form of sexual pleasure really condoned in our society. The corollary of this institutionalization of heterosexual intercourse is the villainization and suppression of all other forms of sexuality and pleasurable intimate contact—which explains the historic horror of our culture for masturbation and lesbianism/homosexuality, or even kissing and intimate physical contact or caressing between friends.

C. The Freudian model of female sexuality

The third and final basic reason why women have been expected to orgasm during intercourse is the general acceptance of the Freudian model of female sexuality, the model of female psychology based on it, and in general the acceptance of the concept of "mental health."

Freud was the founding father of vaginal orgasm. He theorized that the clitoral orgasm (orgasm caused by clitoral stimulation) was adolescent and that, upon puberty, when women began having inter-course with men, women should transfer the center of orgasm to the vagina. The vagina, it was assumed, was able to produce a parallel, but more mature, orgasm than the clitoris. Presumably, this vaginally produced orgasm would occur, however, only when the woman had mastered important major conflicts and achieved a "well-integrated" "feminine" identity. The woman who could reach orgasm only through clitoral stimulation was said to be "immature" and not to have resolved fundamental "conflicts" about sexual impulses. Of course once he had laid down this definition of our sexuality, Freud not so strangely discovered a tremendous "problem" of "frigidity" in women.

These theories of Freud's were based on faulty biology. Freud himself did mention that perhaps his biological knowledge was faulty and would turn out, on further study, to be incorrect—and indeed it has been demolished for some thirty years now. Undoubtedly, Freud would have accepted this research by now, but the profession he originated has been unwilling or slow to do so. All too many psychoanalysts and various "authorities" writing in popular women's magazines continue to insist that we should orgasm through intercourse, via thrusting, with no hands, and still see "vaginal primacy" as a crucial criterion of "normal" functioning in women. They continue to regard orgasm produced by intercourse as the only "authentic" female sexual response, and climax caused by any other form of stimulation (like "clitorism," as they call it) as a symptom of neurotic conflict.

Freud's theory of female sexuality has also been refuted on psychological grounds. Not only, in Freudian psychology, must a woman orgasm by the movement of the penis in the vagina, but if she doesn't, she is "immature" and psychologically flawed. Her difficulty is supposedly a reflection of her over-all maladaptive character structure. She is seen as being significantly disturbed and lacking in "ego integration." It is said that she is struggling with unconscious conflicts that make her anxious and unstable; and her lack of orgasm is only one facet of this general unhappiness.

No major studies in the field of psychology have detected these correlations between personality structure and ability to orgasm during intercourse. If anything, as the most recent large-scale study has shown (Seymour Fisher, *The Female Orgasm*, 1975), there is almost an opposite correlation:

There seems to be good reason for concluding that the more a woman prefers vaginal stimulation, the greater is her level of anxiety. The strongly vaginally oriented woman is tense and has a low threshold for feeling disturbed. This was demonstrated not only in her overt behavior but also her fantasies. As reported, the relatively high anxiety of the vaginally oriented woman was detected by multiple observers who got to know her while she was in the psychology laboratory. It was also revealed in her self-ratings. . . . Obviously, the facts, as they have emerged in the present studies, blatantly contradict existing theories. If these facts receive support from other investigators, a gross revision of such theories will be required.

Despite these demonstrations of the fallacies of Freudian theory about women, "treatment" of women along Freudian lines is still being widely performed, with the large majority of psychiatrists having complete faith in this version of female sexuality and female psychology! Even with all the advances in biological knowledge that make Freud's biology obsolete, and even with the findings of Masters and Johnson, and Fisher, and many others, psychoanalytic theory has not changed! As Sherfey, herself a psychiatrist, asks, "The question must be put and answered within the profession . . . Could many of the sexual neuroses which seem to be almost endemic to women today be, in part, induced by doctors attempting to treat them?"

Probably millions of women could agree with one woman who wrote, "It would give me a great deal of personal pleasure to give Freud a black eye."

"If you don't have orgasms during intercourse, you're hung up"

The influence of these psychiatric theories on women has been strong and pervasive. Whether or not a woman has been in analysis, she has heard these unfounded and anti-woman theories endlessly repeated—from women's magazines, popular psychologists, and men during sex. *Everyone*—of all classes, backgrounds, and ages—*knows* a woman should orgasm during intercourse. If she doesn't, she knows she has only herself and her own hangups to blame.

"I see my failure to have orgasms during intercourse as *my* failure largely, i.e., I've had plenty of men who were 1) adept, 2) lasted a long time, 3) were eager for my orgasm to occur, and 4) etc. but none of them were successful. I guess I have a fear of childbearing, a fear of responsibility—I don't know."

There was a lot of psychiatric jargon in the women's answers. The women may have been in therapy, but it's just as easy to pick up these terms from numerous articles by therapists and others in the women's magazines, and also from male "experts" with whom you may have "sex."

The idea that if we would "just relax and let go" during intercourse we would automatically have an orgasm is, of course, based on the fallacious idea that orgasm comes to us automatically by the thrusting penis, and all we have to do is to give ourselves over to what our bodies will naturally and automatically do—that is, orgasm. As one woman put it, "It's our fault that we can't be as natural as they are."

I wish we could have back all the time and energy we have spent blaming ourselves and searching our souls about why we didn't have orgasms during intercourse. And all the money we spent "flocking to the psychiatrists" looking for the hidden and terrible repression that kept us from our "vaginal destiny." I would like to have what we would have built with that energy.

Conclusion

Insisting that women should have orgasms during intercourse, from intercourse, is to force women to adapt their bodies to inadequate stimulation, and the difficulty of doing this and the frequent failure that is built into the attempt breeds recurring feelings of insecurity and anger. As Ann Koedt★ put it, in *The Myth of the Vaginal Orgasm*:

★ Ti-Grace Atkinson has also written about this in *Amazon Odyssey* (Links Books), 1974.

Perhaps one of the most infuriating and damaging results of this whole charade has been that women who were perfectly healthy sexually were taught that they were not. So in addition to being sexually deprived, these women were told to blame themselves when they deserved no blame. Looking for a cure to a problem that has none can lead a woman on an endless path of self-hatred and insecurity. For she is told by her analyst that not even in her one role allowed in a male society—the role of a woman—is she successful. She is put on the defensive, with phony data as evidence that she better try to be even more feminine, think more feminine, and reject her envy of men. That is: Shuffle even harder, baby.

Finally, there are two myths about female sexuality that should be specifically cleared up here.

First, supposedly women are less interested in sex and orgasms than men, and more interested in "feelings," less apt to initiate sex, and generally have to be "talked into it." But the reason for this, when it is true, is obvious: women often don't expect to, can't be sure to, have orgasms:

"I suspect that my tendency to lose interest in sex is related to my having suppressed the desire for orgasms, when it became clear it wasn't that easy and would 'ruin' the whole thing for him."

The other myth involves the mystique of female orgasm, and specifically the idea that women take longer to orgasm than men, mainly because we are more "psychologically delicate" than men, and our orgasm is more dependent on feelings. In fact, *women do not take longer to orgasm than men*. The majority of the women in Kinsey's study masturbated to orgasm within four minutes, similar to the women in this study. It is, obviously, only during inadequate or secondary, insufficient stimulation like intercourse that we take "longer" and need prolonged "foreplay."

Another Myth: Abnormal Genitals

Fears that we are abnormal

"I really believe my clitoris may not be physically positioned quite right because I almost never can find a position for stimulating it while his penis is in my vagina."

The truth is that clitoral and labial anatomy are highly variable in size, shape, placement, texture, and other factors. However, that does not mean that our anatomy is *wrong*, deformed. It is the cultural pressure on women to orgasm during intercourse that is wrong, and the stereotyped way in which we define sex.

It is doubtful whether anatomy is an important factor in whether or not we orgasm during intercourse. Masters and Johnson found no evidence to support the belief that differences in clitoral anatomy can influence sexual response. However, Barbara Seaman, who wrote *Free and Female*, cautions that "this must be viewed as a highly tentative finding since they were unable to observe any clitorises during orgasm." Sherfey also feels that more research should be done in this area. Masters and Johnson have said that they think certain *vaginal* conditions can operate to prevent the thrusting penis from exercising traction on the labia and clitoral hood. But it's all animal crackers in the end. The real thing to keep in mind is that it is more unusual than not to orgasm from intercourse, especially without making some kind of special effort to do so by getting additional clitoral stimulation at the same time.

A Critique of Masters and Johnson: How Do Women Orgasm During Intercourse?

Masters and Johnson: A Rube Goldberg Model?

Before describing the methods women in this study used to orgasm during intercourse, it remains to mention how Masters and Johnson have explained the way in which orgasm during intercourse occurs.

Stressing that all women's orgasms are caused by stimulation of the clitoris, whether direct or indirect, they have explained that orgasm during intercourse comes from the indirect clitoral stimulation caused by thrusting: as the penis moves back and forth, it pulls the labia minora, which are attached to the skin covering the clitoris (the hood), back and forth with it, so indirectly moving the skin around over the clitoral glands. In Masters and Johnson's own words:

A mechanical traction develops on both sides of the clitoral hood of the minor labia subsequent to penile distension of the vaginal outlet. With active penile thrusting, the clitoral body is pulled downward toward the pudendum by traction exerted on the wings of the clitoral hood. . . .

When the penile shaft is in the withdrawal phase of active coital stroking, traction on the clitoral hood is somewhat relieved and the body and glans return to the normal pudendal-overhang positioning . . . the rhythmic movement of the clitoral body in conjunction with active penile stroking produces significant indirect or secondary clitoral stimulation.

It should be emphasized that this same type of secondary clitoral stimulation occurs in every coital position when there is a full penetration of the vaginal barrel by the erect penis.

In other words, the clitoris is surrounded by skin known as the "clitoral hood" that is connected, in turn, to the labia minora. Supposedly, during intercourse the thrusting penis (notice the assumption of female passivity) exerts rhythmic mechanical traction on the swollen labia minora, and so provides stimulation for the clitoris via movements of the clitoral hood. Sherfey has termed this the "preputial–glandar mechanism" wherein "the thrusting movement of the penis in the vagina pulls on the labia minora which, via their extension around the clitoris (the clitoral hood or prepuce) is then pulled back and forth over the erect clitoris." That is, the final stimulation is provided to the clitoris by friction against its own hood.

The development of this theory was a great advance in that it no longer said friction against the walls of the vagina had anything to do with stimulating female orgasm. However, the existence of this model, and its publicity, has left women with the impression that orgasm during intercourse is still to be expected as part of the automatic "normal" course of things.

Masters and Johnson developed this model of how women's sexuality works by observing the women they had selected for study, all of whom were chosen only if they were able to have orgasms during intercourse. It would seem that to analyze what is probably an unusual group of women, and then to generalize from these women, is a mistake. Indeed, it is only possible if you assume that to orgasm during intercourse is somehow "normal," and not "dysfunctional." (Masters and Johnson have labeled the "inability" to orgasm during intercourse "coital orgasmic inadequacy"; "primary sexual dysfunction" is never having an orgasm in any way.)

Besides the fallacy of generalizing from a special population about just that very thing which makes them special, there is a second problem with this model. That is, there can only be traction between the penis and vagina when the woman is already at a certain stage of arousal, because only then do the labia swell up enough to cause traction (the stage Masters and Johnson call late plateau arousal). In other words, the penis can only pull the labia back and forth with it if the woman is at the last stage of arousal before orgasm so that there is sufficient engorgement of the area to cause a tight fit between penis and vaginal opening. (You can check how well this mechanism works for you, by the way, by placing a dildo or similarly sized inanimate object in your vagina when you reach this state of arousal, and then moving it in and out and seeing what you feel.)

Masters and Johnson have not explained how they arrived at the conclusion that this mechanism is the means of orgasm during intercourse of the women they studied. It does seem clear that this mechanism is indeed the means by which most women orgasm during clitoral stimulation or masturbation, in that during masturbation the skin of the clitoral area, or the upper lips, are pulled around or moved around slightly, thus causing the skin to move back and forth over the clitoral glans. As Sherfey puts it: "Mons area friction will have exactly the same effect on the prepuce-glans action as the penile thrusting motion: *the prepuce is rhythmically pulled back and forth over the glans.*"

It seems that the thrusting activates this mechanism for very few women, however. Most researchers and sex therapists agree that thrusting is less efficient in causing female orgasm than clitoral area stimulation. Pulling your ear slightly back and forth can also pull the skin on your cheek. Just so, it is possible for thrusting to pull the skin near your clitoris in just the right way to stimulate you to orgasm, and it may happen regularly for a small percentage of women—but not for most women most of the time.

This brings to mind the fact that Masters and Johnson have insisted on treating women, but not men, with their *usual* sexual partners, whom they must bring with them. (Men were allowed surrogates.) This is usually understood to imply adherence to a moral double standard, but the reason for this rule may in fact have been that, for a woman to orgasm during intercourse, she must adapt her body to inadequate stimulation, and so it is essential that she work out this procedure with a regular partner.

Later, in lectures and private therapy, Masters and Johnson emphasized the specific techniques women can use to orgasm during intercourse, such as being on top of the man, doing most of the moving, etc. Perhaps they have too found that the "preputial-glandar mechanism" does not work for most women. However, if this is indeed the case, the message has not reached the general public. The woman-in-the-street (most of us) still has the impression that it is "normal" to orgasm from male thrusting.

There is nothing wrong with saying that the movement of the clitoral hood over the clitoris is what is responsible for orgasm; this is true. What *is* wrong is to say that thrusting in itself will activate this mechanism in most women. As Alex Shulman has pointedly remarked:

49

Masters and Johnson observe that the clitoris is automatically "stimulated" in intercourse since the hood covering the clitoris is pulled over the clitoris with each thrust of the penis in the vagina—much, I suppose, as a penis is automatically "stimulated" by a man's underwear whenever he takes a step.

But let's apply this same logic to men with more scientific precision. As Dr. Sanford Copley put it, when interviewed on the television show "Woman," this indirect stimulation of women could be compared to the stimulation that would be produced in a man by the rubbing of the scrotal skin (balls), perhaps pulling it back and forth, and so causing the skin of the upper tip of the penis to move, or quiver, and in this way achieving "stimulation." Would it work? Admittedly, this form of stimulation would probably require a good deal more foreplay for the man to have an orgasm! You would have to be patient and "understand" if it did not lead to orgasm "every time."

Masters and Johnson's theory that the thrusting penis pulls the woman's labia, which in turn pull the clitoral hood, which thereby causes friction of the clitoral glans and thereby causes orgasm sounds more like a Rube Goldberg scheme than a reliable way to orgasm.*

It is not that the mechanism doesn't work. It does: if you pull any skin around the area it can stimulate the clitoris. But the question is, does thrusting do this effectively? The answer would seem to be that, for most women, without some special effort or some special set of circumstances, it does not.

Perhaps, finally, it is important to point out that, if this mechanism works so well, why hasn't it been working all along, for centuries? Why is "coital frigidity" the well-known "problem" that it is? And why don't women masturbate this way sometimes? No, having an orgasm during intercourse is an adaptation of our bodies. Intercourse was never meant to stimulate women to orgasm.

A New Theory of Why and How Women Orgasm During Intercourse

Orgasms during intercourse in this study usually seemed to result from a conscious attempt by the woman to center some kind of clitoral area contact for herself during intercourse, usually involving contact with the

* This analogy may have first been made by Dr. Pauline Bart.

man's pubic area. The clitoral stimulation during intercourse could be thought of, then, as basically stimulating yourself while intercourse is in progress. Of course the other person must cooperate. This is essentially the way men get stimulation during intercourse: they rub their penises against our vaginal walls so that the same area they stimulate during masturbation is being stimulated during intercourse. In other words, *you* have to get the stimulation centered where it feels good.

To have an orgasm during intercourse, there are two ways a woman can increase her chances, always remembering that she is adapting her body to less than adequate stimulation. First and most important, she must consciously try to apply her masturbation techniques to intercourse, or experiment to find out what else may work for her to get clitoral stimulation; or, she can work out a sexual relationship with a particular man who can meet her individual needs.

Do it yourself

The women who had orgasm during intercourse were usually those who, in a sense, did it themselves. They did not expect to "receive" orgasm automatically from the thrusting of the partner. There is an old myth that masturbation causes "clitoral fixation" and "frigidity."

"Perhaps if you masturbate, you can get a fixation on your clitoris and are thus unable to come during intercourse."

"The fact that I've been masturbating since I was ten has made it more difficult for me to orgasm vaginally."

"Having been used to masturbating for years as a teenager and repressing my desire for actual intercourse with boys, I feel I developed a conditioned reflex that did not allow me to have a vaginal orgasm with my husband even though I enjoyed the act itself."

The truth, however, is just the opposite: masturbation increases your ability to orgasm in general, and also your ability to orgasm during intercourse. Why not? It's the same stimulation. Only 19 percent of the women in this study who did not masturbate orgasmed regularly from intercourse—quite a drop from the 30 percent in the over-all population. Of course, masturbating to orgasm does not automatically enable you to orgasm during intercourse. There is no mystical connection between the two—just the practical experience with orgasm—how it feels and how to get it.

Finally, was there a correlation between type of masturbation and "ability" to orgasm during intercourse? Were some orgasm types more likely to orgasm during intercourse than others? My impression was that these figures are imprecise because too many women were disqualified from being counted; they included those who did not specify how they had orgasmed during intercourse, those who masturbated in more than one way, and the "questionable-orgasm-definition" group. This left a very small number from which to make correlations.

However, despite all these problems, two definable trends did appear. Most likely to orgasm during intercourse were those who masturbated on their stomachs, especially those who did not use their hands. Least likely were those who held their legs together or crossed.

Other than this there were no really clear-cut correlations, and many women whose type of orgasm suggested they might be able to were still not able to orgasm during intercourse. A lot seemed to depend on how interested the individual was in applying her own knowledge of her body to intercourse and actively directing the stimulation unabashedly to herself.

Of course it remains an unanswered question whether these body types are made or born. That is, once you learn to orgasm a certain way, does that become a basically fixed pattern for you? For example, if you learned with your legs together, could you later learn with them apart? Or, are some types of bodies only able to orgasm in certain positions?

This question is, however, important only academically. Women who masturbate with their legs together, for example, can just as well adapt this position to intercourse as other masturbation types. No one type is "better" than another. While a woman who needs to have her legs together to orgasm may have slightly more trouble teaching new lovers ways to have intercourse in which she can orgasm, it is also true that women who hold their legs together are more likely to be able to have many sequential orgasms than other women, since they do not stimulate their clitorises so directly (the bunched-up skin forms a protective cushion). Whatever type a woman is, she can have fully as much pleasure as every other woman. All she has to do is be active and explore.

Why "orgasm" should be a verb

What is the difference between "to orgasm" and "to have an orgasm"?
This idea that we really make our own orgasms, even during intercourse, is in direct contradiction to what we have been taught. Most of us were taught that "you should relax and enjoy it"—or at most help him out with the thrusting—because *he* would "give" you the orgasm.

It should be mentioned that many of the women who answered in this way were also not having orgasms regularly in sex. As we saw in the preceding section, orgasm is most likely to come when the woman takes over responsibility for and control of her own stimulation. You always, in essence, create your own orgasm.

"I create my own orgasm. Sometimes no amount of stimulation will turn me on, because I don't want it. I really resent men who boast of 'giving' a woman a good come. I always feel I have created it myself, even if he was doing the stimulating."

"My orgasm is my own. I control it, produce it, and dig it."

"Although I think mutual pleasure is wonderful, the orgasm is in the end one's own. You have to put in the concentration and physical effort yourself."

We do give ourselves orgasm, even, in a sense, when someone else is providing us with stimulation, since we must make sure it is on target, by moving or offering suggestions, and by tensing our bodies and getting into whatever position(s) we need—and then there is a final step necessary in most cases: we need to focus on the sensation and concentrate, actively desire and work toward the orgasm.

In conclusion, it could perhaps be said that the two reasons women don't orgasm during intercourse are: they are given false information, specifically they are told that the penis thrusting in the vagina will cause orgasm; and they are intimidated from exploring and touching their bodies—they are told that masturbation is bad and that they should not behave "aggressively" during sex with men. They do not control their own stimulation.

This emphasis on getting your own stimulation does not in any way imply a lack of feeling for the man you are with during intercourse. However, orgasm has been very importantly the focus of this discussion, because it is symbolic for women: the ability to orgasm when we want, to be in charge of our stimulation, represents owning our own bodies, being strong, free, and autonomous beings.

Masturbation: Theory, Practice, and New Beginnings

Masturbation is, in a very real sense, one of the most important subjects discussed in *The Hite Report on Female Sexuality* and a cause for celebration, because it is such an easy source of orgasms for most women. Women in this study said they could masturbate and orgasm with ease in just a few minutes. Of the 82 percent of women who said they masturbated, 95 percent could orgasm easily and regularly, whenever they wanted. Many women used the term "masturbation" synonymously with orgasm: women assumed masturbation included orgasm.

The ease with which women orgasm during masturbation certainly contradicts the general stereotypes about female sexuality—that women are slow to become aroused, and are able to orgasm only irregularly. The truth seems to be that female sexuality is thriving—but unfortunately underground.

How many women masturbate is one of the most important keys to understanding female sexuality (from the point of view of orgasm): since it is almost always done alone and since in most cases no one is taught how to do it, masturbation provides a source of almost pure biological feedback—it is one of the few forms of instinctive behavior to which we have access. Although some women did not masturbate until after they had had sex with another person, most women discovered it on their own, very early: "I've never needed anyone to tell me where I have to be touched to have an orgasm; I've just been masturbating ever since I can remember."[*]

Surprisingly, most researchers have not shown[†] much interest in

---

[*] As Betty Dodson has written in "Liberating Masturbation," "Masturbation is our primary sex life. It is the *sexual base*. Everything we do beyond that is simply how we choose to socialize our sex life." In addition, primates also masturbate more or less instinctively from childhood on.

[†] And still, in 1992, *The Hite Report on Female Sexuality* is the only work (not to mention the only research work) in which the masturbation practices of thousands of women are detailed and catalogued. One unique aspect of *The Hite Report on Female Sexuality* is that the actual words of women participating in the study are used. The women themselves explain their experiences, enabling us to see all the detail of individual human uniqueness. No study has as yet followed up on the finding here that some women can only orgasm with their legs apart, others with their legs together.

masturbation. Generally, they approach the study of sexuality through intercourse, with masturbation as a sidelight—since, it is argued, the "sex drive" is fundamentally for purposes of reproduction. However, to take intercourse as the starting point is an assumption—one that has led to widespread misunderstanding of female sexuality. To assume that intercourse is the basic expression of female sexuality, during which women should orgasm, and then to analyze women's "responses" to intercourse—is to look at the issue backwards. What should be done is to look at what women are actually experiencing, what they enjoy, and when they orgasm—and then draw conclusions. In other words, researchers must stop telling women what they *should* feel sexually, and start asking them what they *do* feel sexually. This is what these questionnaires have attempted to do.

The fact that women can orgasm easily and pleasurably whenever they want (many women several times in a row) shows beyond a doubt that women *know* how to enjoy their bodies; no one needs to tell them how. It is not female sexuality that has a problem ("dysfunction") but society that has a problem in its definition of sex and the subordinate role that definition gives women. Sharing our hidden sexuality by telling how we masturbate is a first step toward bringing our sexuality out into the world and toward redefining sex and physical relations as we know them.

Masturbation seems to have so much to recommend it—easy and intense orgasms, an unending source of pleasure—but, unfortunately, we are all suffering in some degree from a culture that says people should not masturbate. This deeply ingrained prejudice is reflected in a quote from a woman who was in other ways very aware of the culture's influences on her: "A problem is definitions and usage of words. Probably one of the most offensive statements I've seen in this regard in a long, long time is your question, 'Do most men masturbate you?' To some extent, my difficulty with that is that I give a negative connotation to masturbation when compared with intercourse; that is, I would rather have intercourse than masturbation. I take masturbation to mean what I do to myself, alone. Intercourse is what I do with another person, regardless of what takes place. To call vaginal stimulation of the penis intercourse, and to call manual stimulation of the clitoris masturbation, insults me and makes me angry."

Actually the term "masturbate" had been used (really, misused) as a euphemism for someone giving someone else manual clitoral stimulation with the express purpose of gauging the reaction to this usage. The meaning was perfectly understood by the overwhelming majority of women, but the implication was *hated*: sex with a partner legitimizes the activity, whatever it is, and to call it masturbation demeans it.

We have arrived at a point in our thinking as a society where it has become acceptable for women to enjoy sex, as long as we are fulfilling our roles as women—that is, giving pleasure to men, participating in mutual activities. Perhaps in the future we will be able to feel we have the right to enjoy masturbation too—to touch, explore, and enjoy our own bodies in any way we desire, not only when we are alone but also when we are with another person. "The importance of masturbation," as one woman put it, "is really to love and care for yourself totally, as a natural way of relating to your own body. It is a normal activity that would logically be a part of any woman's life."

Leg position for orgasm: an unanswered question*

An interesting and important but as yet unanswered puzzle about female orgasm is why some women need to have their legs apart for orgasm while others must have them together; still others prefer to have them bent at the knees or up in the air. Just as different women need different kinds of stimulation for orgasm, they also *need* different leg positions to orgasm.

Unfortunately, many women did not answer this final part of the masturbation question, probably due to the length of the question, and because they assumed their leg position was the same as everyone else's. However, most of the women who did answer usually had their legs apart. Still, a significant number of women in all the masturbation types did hold their legs together.

Reasons women gave for keeping their legs together included the following.

"I like my legs together because then everything (the whole genital area) is tighter and the vibrations travel better."

"If I have my legs *apart*, I feel almost nothing, no matter what I do!"

"Legs *together* intensifies orgasm—to have everything as tight and tense as possible is best, like a drum."

* Still unanswered in 1992. No other research has followed up on this interesting question.

56

On the other hand, some women could feel nothing with their legs *together*.

Some women who liked their legs apart also liked their knees bent.

"My legs are apart, either with my knees bent while my feet are flat on the bed, or with my knees at right angles and my feet together. I can masturbate sitting also, and standing, but I prefer lying down in this position."

Some women moved their legs together for orgasm, as the feeling intensified, after having them apart during stimulation (and a very small number did the opposite).

Most women had only one basic leg position that worked best for them, but a few women found leg position interchangeable.

"I hold my legs together or apart depending on the type of fantasy I am using."

"My muscles usually tense up, and then right before orgasm my hips start moving back and forth. My legs are the tensest of all, usually bent at the knees, one up and one sideways when I'm by myself. With a partner, there are other considerations that determine what I do with my legs—sometimes they stiffen out straight."

The reason for the difference in leg positions for different women is still a mystery. Does it depend on how the woman first learned how to orgasm? Or does the anatomy of our genitals (both interior and exterior) vary just enough from woman to woman to make different positions necessary for different individuals? Answers to these questions are simply not known.

The New Meaning of Clitoral Stimulation: Orgasm and Identity

The Social Construction of Sexuality

"How have most men had sex with you?"

The following answers represent the overwhelming majority of answers received to this question: that sex—whether enjoyable or exploitative—generally follows the reproductive pattern previously described: "foreplay" followed by "penetration" and "intercourse" (thrusting) followed by orgasm (especially male orgasm), which is then defined as the "end" of sex. Answers not falling into this category, not including the lesbian replies, composed less than 5 percent of those in the study.

"In bed with the man above me, in the dark."

"I've only had sex with my husband. (We were just married for a few months.) He always initiates it. We kiss and he plays with my breasts. He puts one hand down and sticks his finger into my vagina and moves it back and forth like a penis would go. When he's doing this, I lie on my back, and he lies on his side so his body is pressed against my side. He moves his hips back and forth so that his penis rubs against the side of my leg. When he's ready, he has me get on my hands and knees, and he gets in back of me. He sticks his penis into me and moves it back and forth until he finishes."

"Most of the men I've slept with have had absolutely no idea of what I want or need and no interest in finding out. There have been several men who seemed to care whether I was happy, but they wanted to make me happy according to *their* conception of what ought to do it (fucking harder or longer or whatever) and acted as if it was damned impertinent of me to suggest that my responses weren't programmed exactly like those of mythical women in the classics of porn. All I can say is, after years of sexual experience that ranged from brutal to trivial to misguided, etc., it's a wonder I didn't just blow off the whole thing

58

a long time ago. I'm glad I stuck with it until I found a partner whose eroticism complements mine so beautifully."

Orgasm from clitoral stimulation by hand

Do most women orgasm regularly from clitoral stimulation by hand?
In the reproductive pattern of sex just described, which is far and away the most prevalent in our culture—if not the *only* definition for most people—were women having orgasms during "foreplay" with clitoral stimulation?

Those who orgasm regularly (those who answered "yes," always or usually) during clitoral stimulation by hand during sex with a partner comprise approximately 44 percent of the total.

In other words, although nowhere near the overwhelming majority of women who orgasmed regularly with masturbation, those who orgasmed with the manual clitoral stimulation of their partners comprised a much larger number than those who orgasmed during intercourse (30 percent). But why don't women orgasm as easily during clitoral stimulation with others as they do with themselves?

The first reason women don't orgasm as frequently from clitoral stimulation by another person as they do on their own, is that, more often than not, clitoral stimulation is not *intended* to lead to orgasm. The reproductive model of sex has traditionally included just enough clitoral stimulation in "foreplay" for purposes of arousal but not for orgasm—which is perhaps worse than no clitoral stimulation at all, a kind of "cock teasing" in reverse.

Feelings about clitoral stimulation

"Do you feel guilty about taking time for yourself in sexual play which may not be specifically stimulating to your partner? Which activities are you including in your answer?"
Many women interpreted this question to mean, did they feel guilty about needing "foreplay"—rather than interpreting "taking time for yourself" to mean to have an orgasm. This only underscores more strongly the picture already presented—that clitoral stimulation is commonly used for purposes of arousal but not orgasm. And nevertheless, many women felt guilty—even *without* orgasm—for "needing" this kind

59

of "extra" stimulation. As one woman put it, "Women are made to feel *sexy* women don't require it."

"Yes, I definitely feel guilty about taking time for myself in activities such as clitoral stimulation, erotic massage, and cunnilingus simply because these activities are not specifically stimulating to my partner. I feel selfish, I imagine that my partner is either impatient to 'get on with it' or is not enjoying himself very much, or feels uncomfortable because he doesn't quite know what he's doing (which he usually doesn't because he does it so seldom and doesn't ask for any feedback from me, and I'm so reluctant to volunteer it); in other words I can't relax very well when things are being done to me, only, and I don't come very easily as a result."

"Men think they are really being hip and up front in the vanguard if they do it without your asking. Out of all the information popularized about female sexuality since the 'sexual revolution,' the idea of clitoral stimulation has really made the heaviest impact. But I still feel my partner is doing something that for him is a mere technical obstacle to deal with before going on to the "main event.""

Remember how beautiful and enthusiastic the language was that was used to describe intercourse and general arousal? But notice how spare and tight, unenthusiastic and secretive the language has become here. Obviously women do not feel proud about clitoral stimulation in any form. Our culture had discouraged clitoral stimulation, even to the point of not giving it a name. "Cunnilingus" at least is a name, even if its meaning is not clear to everyone, but "manual clitoral stimulation" is just a phrase that is used to describe an activity that has no name. Our language for, as well as our respect for, clitoral stimulation, is almost nonexistent. Our culture is still a long way from understanding, not to mention celebrating, female sexuality.

"Do you ever find it necessary to masturbate to achieve orgasm after 'making love'?"

	Q. I	Q. II	Q. III
Yes	120	170	55
Sometimes	90	117	29
Rarely	35	41	11
No	275	349	73
Used to	19	23	11
Would like to	20	22	19

Yes, *with* partner (or, *he* does it)	12	25	1
Would be embarrassing	6	20	2
I don't bother	2	5	6
It wouldn't be right	1	3	
It doesn't work	6	6	
Do it *during* intercourse!	1	5	
For an *extra* orgasm	5	2	
Total	592	798	207

Why has clitoral stimulation been left out of the standard pattern of sex?
During "sex" as our society defines it both people know what to expect
and how to make it possible for the man to orgasm. The whole thing
is prearranged, preagreed. But there are not really any patterns or
prearranged times and places for a woman to orgasm—unless she
can manage to do so during intercourse. So women are put in the
position of asking for something "special," some "extra" stimulation,
or they must somehow try to subliminally send messages to a partner
who often is not even aware that he should be listening. If she does
get this "extra," "special" stimulation, she feels grateful that he was
so unusually "sensitive." So all too often women just do without—or
fake it.

Do it yourself
But we can change this pattern, and redefine our sexual relations with
others. On one level, we can take control over our own orgasms. We
know how to have orgasms in masturbation. How strange it is, when
you think about it, that we don't use this knowledge during so much of
the sex we have with men. Why, in our pattern of sexual relations, does
the man have charge of both his stimulation and ours? A man controls
his own orgasm in the sense that during intercourse he thrusts his penis
against the walls of the vagina in ways that provide the best stimulation
for him; this is not considered "selfish" or "infantile" because there is
an ideology to back it up.

However, women do not usually, are not supposed to, control their
own stimulation:

"I have never tried to stimulate myself clitorally with a partner—I
have always been afraid to."

"It seems too aggressive when I act to get the stimulation I
want."

"During sex, I must depend on a man's willingness to do an

61

aggressive action for me, while I am passive. (Passive about my *own* stimulation; moving for *his* pleasure doesn't count.) Whereas during intercourse a man climaxes through his own aggressiveness."

"I always dreamed of the ecstasy of physical love. I have never been able to reach this kind of feeling with another person. The sensations, the orgasms I can give myself, are more than just in the sex organs, they are feelings of relaxation and pleasure throughout the body, mind, and soul. A sort of sailing feeling, a flowing, rich in colors, rich in well-being, joy. They are 'multiple orgasms,' each richer than the previous one. A *whole, complete* feeling. I can have orgasms with a partner, but not these complete intense sensations."

But why can't we touch ourselves? Why can't we do whatever we need to make orgasm happen? Although sharing sex with a man can be wonderful, why does "sharing" for a woman mean that the man must "give" her the orgasm? Why can't a woman use her own hand to bring herself to orgasm? In sex as elsewhere, women are still in the position of waiting for men to "mete out the goodies."

We have the power to make our own orgasms, if we want. You can get control of your own stimulation by moving against the other person, or by stimulating yourself directly in the same way as you do during masturbation. Although this suggestion may sound strange at first, it is important to be able to masturbate with another person, because it will give you power over your own orgasms. There is no reason why making your own orgasms should not be as beautiful or as deeply shared as any other form of sex with another person—perhaps even more so. The taboo against touching yourself says essentially that you should not use your own body for your own pleasure, that your body is not your own to enjoy. But we have a right to our own bodies. Controlling your own stimulation symbolizes owning your own body, and is a very important step toward freedom.

Clitoral Anatomy

Even after the well-known work of Masters and Johnson has conclusively proved that all orgasms in women are caused by clitoral stimulation (whether direct or indirect), there is still enormous confusion over the terms "clitoral orgasm" and "vaginal orgasm." Why does this confusion continue? There are several reasons: the first is that we lack complete understanding of our anatomy, mainly because most of our sexual organs, unlike those of men, are located inside our bodies. The following description of our sexual anatomy will try to give a fundamental picture of the basic underlying structures.

Anatomy*

Sherfey's book *The Nature and Evolution of Female Sexuality* is, although technical, definitely the best and most complete explanation available of our anatomy, and worth the time a thorough reading requires. Here I quote from Edward Brecher's analysis of her main points, in *The Sex Researchers*:

> The truth is . . . that the glans and shaft of the human clitoris are merely the superficially visible or palpable manifestations of an underlying *clitoral system* which is at least as large, as impressive, and as functionally responsive as the penis—and which responds as a unit to sexual stimulation in much the same way that the penis does.
>
> The penis, for example, has two roots known as *crura* which play an essential role in its functioning. During sexual excitation these crura become engorged with blood and contribute to erection of the penis. The clitoris, too, has two broad roots, of approximately the same size as in the male. The clitoral crura, too, become engorged with blood early in the woman's sexual excitation.

* See anatomy update after new study, 1978, on pages 190–1.

Again, the penis contains within its shaft two caverns or spaces known as *corpora cavernosa*, which fill with blood during sexual excitation, and contribute to the expanded size of the erect penis. The female clitoral system has a precisely analogous pair of bulbous *corpora cavernosa*, which similarly fill with blood during sexual excitation. They are not inside the shaft of the clitoris, however. Rather, they are located surrounding the vestibule and outer third of the vagina. The vestibular bulbs and the circumvaginal plexus (a network of nerves, veins, and arteries) constitute the major erectile bodies in women. These underlying structures are homologous to, and about the same size as, the penis of a man. They become engorged (swollen) in the same way that a penis does. When fully engorged, the clitoral system as a whole is roughly thirty times as large as the external clitoral glans and shaft—what we commonly know as the "clitoris."

Our sex organs, though internal and not as easily visible as men's, expand during arousal to approximately the same volume as an erect penis. The next time you are aroused, notice how swollen your vulva and labia majora become; this reflects the swelling of the vestibular bulbs and other tissues which lie just below this area.

In short, the only real difference between men's and women's erections is that the men's are on the outside of their bodies, while women's are on the inside. Think of your clitoris as just the *tip* of your "penis," the rest of which lies underneath the surface of your vulva—or think of a penis as just the externalization of a woman's interior bulbs and clitoral network. (They are therefore known as the vestibular bulbs.) The spongelike body (*corpus spongiosum*) inside the penis is paralleled by a similar spongelike structure in the clitoral system which functions in the same way.

The penis, Dr. Sherfey continues, is associated with sets of muscles which help to erect it during sexual excitation. The clitoris is associated with precisely homologous sets of muscles which serve to retract it, too—though, as Masters and Johnson have shown, at a somewhat later stage in the sex act. Other male muscles contract during orgasm, forcing the ejaculation of semen. Precisely homologous muscles function during the female orgasm, causing a rhythmic contraction of the outer third of the vagina. Indeed, as Masters and Johnson have also shown, the male and female sets of muscles respond in the *same* rhythm—one contraction every four-fifths of a second.

There are also differences, Dr. Sherfey concedes, between the penis and the clitoral system—but the differences, astonishing as it may seem to readers brought up in a male-dominated society, are in favor of the clitoral system. That system, for example, includes at least three (and possibly four or five) networks of veins called *venous plexi*, which extend diffusely throughout the female pelvic area—but especially through the regions immediately to the left and right of the vagina. These networks are also, Dr. Sherfey reports, a part of the clitoral system; and in addition they merge with the venous networks of the vaginal system. Together the clitoral and vaginal networks become engorged with blood during female sexual excitation.* Thus the clitoris itself, far from being a vestigial or rudimentary organ, is merely the visible tip and harbinger of a vast anatomical array of sexually responsive female tissue. When fully engaged, the clitoral system as a whole overshadows the clitoral glans and shaft *in the ratio of almost thirty to one.* The total blood-vessel engorgement of the clitoral system during sexual excitation may actually exceed the more obvious engorgement of the male.

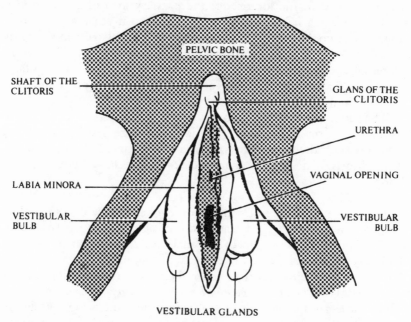

Redrawn by Charlotte Staub from Atlas der deskriptiven Anatomie des Menschen *by J. Sobotta, Berlin: Urban and Schwarzenberg, 1948.*

* Ruth Herschberger has made some pointed comments about terminology in her chapter of *Adam's Rib*, "Society Writes Biology": "The patriarchal biologist employs *erection* in regard to male organs and *congestion* for female. Erection of tissue is equivalent to the filling of the local blood vessels, or congestion; but erection is too aggressive-sounding for women. Congestion, being associated with the rushing of blood to areas that have been infected or injured, appears to scientists to be a more adequate characterization of female response."

As Barbara Seaman has explained in *Free and Female*, our sexual structures expand as much or more during arousal as men's; the only difference is that male erection (engorgement) takes place outside the body, and is therefore more visible, while ours takes place underneath the surface—under the vaginal lips. The total size of our engorgement is no smaller than the size of an erect penis.

Helen Kaplan, in *The New Sex Therapy*, explains a further anatomical cause of the continuing confusion between "clitoral" and "vaginal" orgasm:

Apparently, it is this dichotomy—on the one hand, the location of orgasmic spasms in and around the *vagina* and concomitant perception of orgasmic sensation in the general vaginal and deep pelvic region; on the other hand, the location of the primary area of stimulation in the *clitoris*—which has served to perpetuate the myth that the female is capable of two distinct types of orgasms, and has also given rise to the incredibly stupid controversy surrounding female orgasm. The orgasm is, after all, a reflex and as such has a sensory and a motor component. There is little argument over the fact that the motor expression of this reflex is "vaginal". . . .

The entire argument really only revolves around the location of the sensory arm of the reflex. Is orgasm normally triggered by stimulating the vagina with the penis? Or is it produced by tactile friction applied to the clitoris? The clinical evidence reviewed clearly points to the clitoris.

In other words, clitoral stimulation evokes female orgasm, which takes place deeper in the body, around the vagina and other structures, just as stimulation of the tip of the male penis evokes male orgasm, which takes place inside the lower body of the male.

Despite the seeming surface contradictions of those responding (on pages 185–90 of *The Hite Report on Female Sexuality*) it seems clear that both of these groups of women are saying the same thing. While one group terms clitoral orgasm "more intense and focused," the other group calls it more "localized" and therefore more "limited"—in much the same way as one person will see a glass as being half full of water, while another sees it as half empty. While some women found orgasm during intercourse "more diffused" and more "whole body," and therefore not as exciting as the locally intense clitoral orgasm, other women found the "whole body" feeling during intercourse more fulfilling than the "locally intense" and "limited" clitoral orgasm.

Which way you interpret these feelings is a question of your own individual feelings, what is going on in your life regarding feelings for another person (that is, especially in this case, for a man), and of course the cultural pressures to find intercourse more fulfilling. Whichever way you interpret the physical feelings, however, there is no argument that the sensations differ: a clitorally stimulated orgasm without intercourse feels more locally intense, while an orgasm with intercourse feels more diffused throughout the area and/or body.★

Thus, it can be concluded that the presence of a penis seems to diffuse and generalize the sensation of orgasm. This is not to say that orgasm without intercourse is "better" or to make any other value judgment, since only individuals can make those. The sole purpose here is to define the actual physical feelings as most women experience them.

The fact is that clitorally stimulated, non-intercourse orgasms—especially in masturbation—are physically stronger than orgasms during intercourse. Masters and Johnson have also reported that not only were contraction patterns stronger in masturbation orgasms than in intercourse orgasms, but also that their study subjects gave the same subjective opinions. As a matter of fact, the highest cardiac rates of all the orgasms they studied occurred during female masturbation.

Is the feeling of orgasm weaker during intercourse because of the presence of the penis, or because of other factors?
There may, for some women, be an increased intensity in orgasm during masturbation because of being totally unselfconscious when alone. But other women felt just the opposite: intercourse is more acceptable than masturbation, and therefore one can "let go" more then. Perhaps orgasm during masturbation is stronger because you can get the stimulation more perfectly centered and coordinated, including your leg position.

"For me, the intensity seems to depend on 1) not rushing the orgasm but trying to hold on as long as possible, when the peak excited stage has been reached. The longer I hold on (I can't wait longer than about one minute at that stage) the more intense the orgasm. The second factor is 2) letting go at just the right moment. This leads to very intense orgasms. If I let go too soon, or a little too late, I have a less intense orgasm."

★ These findings are quite similar to those of Seymour Fisher's study of three hundred women. Fisher wrote: "Scanning the comments the women offered, I was struck by how often clitoral stimulation is described with words like 'warm,' 'ticklish,' 'electrical,' and 'sharp,' whereas vaginal stimulation is more often referred to as 'throbbing,' 'deep,' 'soothing,' and 'comfortable.' "

The Pleasures of Intercourse: "Vaginal Ache" and Emotional Orgasm

Orgasms during intercourse may feel stronger psychologically because of very real feelings for the man, or because we are culturally conditioned to feel intercourse is the highest expression of our sexuality.

Orgasms during intercourse may feel more whole body partially because there is usually a longer build-up period than during masturbation. However, none of the factors just mentioned changes the basic conclusion that the physical intensity of orgasm per se is greater for most women when intercourse is not in progress, and especially during self-stimulation.

Despite this, a majority of women stated flatly that, no matter what the difference in feeling might be, they would always prefer orgasm during intercourse because of the psychological factors of sharing with and being loved by another person, the warmth of touching all over body to body.

"Love of another is what makes intercourse orgasm better, in its way, and self-manipulation is more intense in its way."

"Orgasm during intercourse is less intense, but more emotionally satisfying."

"With penetration I feel more whole and loved."

"I feel the contractions less during intercourse, but I enjoy the feeling of fullness, and psychologically, being seen as complete."

"But isn't intercourse great anyway?"—"vaginal ache"

There is a very specific but important question that has been saved until last, something that is referred to as the phenomenon of "vaginal ache," that is often perceived as the desire for vaginal penetration. It is part of the same question just discussed, i.e., the difference in feeling between orgasm with intercourse or without. This feeling of intense desire or "ache" (desire to be filled), comes during the buildup to orgasm, very near the moment of orgasm itself, and then spills over into the orgasmic contractions.

What happens is this: sometimes building up to and just at the moment of orgasm there is an intense pleasure/pain feeling deep inside the vagina, something like a desire to be entered or touched inside, or just an exquisite sensation of pleasure, or "vaginal ache." It is an almost hollow feeling, and is caused because the upper end, the deeper portion of the vagina, is ballooning out, expanding into what has theoretically been pictured as a little lake for the collection and holding of semen.

Some women perceive this feeling as hollow, empty, and unpleasant, while others find it intensely pleasurable. Whether you prefer to have a penis there or not at that moment depends on your own personal preference, of course. For most women, "vaginal ache" is not felt so intensely with a penis present; the penis seems to "soothe" and diffuse the feeling, so it depends on whether you prefer to feel the sensation or not.

Without intercourse the sensation of "vaginal ache" was described like this

"I feel an urgent yearning way deep inside to envelop and take him inside me."

"During arousal, there is a craving in my vagina—which is, by the way, disappointed if satisfied."

"Sometimes while masturbating, I'll feel the urge to push something up me—usually always I am disappointed with the result."

"After cunnilingus, just at the moment she reaches orgasm, she likes me to place my tongue in her vagina, as it seems to soothe the ache."

"Just at the moment when I orgasm, there is a beautiful, painful feeling in the vagina."

Conclusion

We have seen in this section that with the presence of a penis, the orgasm and contractions are felt less concretely, and that the "vaginal ache" (which is an exquisitely pleasurable feeling—not pain) is either soothed or not felt during intercourse. In general, then, vaginal penetration or the presence of a penis seems to have a soothing, diffusing, or blanketing effect.

There are two ways of interpreting this phenomenon. You could say either:

1. During intercourse the penis works as a pacifier—the touching and rubbing kills feeling, allows less intense contractions and sensations, and disperses and diffuses the focus of orgasm—making it less intense and less pleasurable.

2. During intercourse the penis, by soothing or quietening arousal, gives more of a feeling of peace and completeness, relaxation and satisfaction, than non-intercourse orgasm, which in many cases only leaves you a second later with continued arousal. Thus, intercourse (actually, with or without orgasm) is more "fulfilling" than orgasm without intercourse.

Whichever you prefer is a personal decision and a matter of temperament—whether you define pleasure as desire or its satisfaction. Is the greater pleasure desire (arousal), or its fulfillment?

Finally, you could prefer either sensation at different times:

"I cannot describe the difference, it is neither better nor worse, just different. Sometimes I want penetration, and other times I am happier engaging in other activities. It depends on my mood."

Emotional orgasm

Some women who mentioned that they have a different type of orgasm during clitoral stimulation or masturbation than during intercourse meant that they have "real" orgasm during clitoral stimulation and something else during intercourse—what has often been called "vaginal orgasm." By this they did not mean they felt vaginal contractions, or intense clitoral or vaginal sensations, but that they felt an intense emotional peak (sometimes felt as an extreme opening sensation both in the vagina and the throat)—accompanied by strong feelings of closeness, yearning, or exaltation. We will call this "emotional orgasm":

"Clitoral orgasm gives me a full-blown climax. During intercourse, none of the flash sensations occur, but there is a tremendous calm and loving feeling that makes me cry—kind of like having an emotional (rather than physical) orgasm."

"It's difficult not to use clichés I've heard or read, but some of them are so accurate. It is a full, warm sensation in the vagina, lips, and surrounding pubic area, that spreads out, plus a feeling of tremendous exhilaration in my chest. If the man is an important part of my life, I find myself wishing his penis could reach clear up to my neck, that he would just crawl inside of me. He can't seem to get deep enough or close enough."

"First all feeling seems centered in the genital area and it spreads

70

through my entire body in great waves of sensation and sensitivity. Sometimes I feel as though I want to sing, as though the sensation has traveled to my vocal cords and has set them vibrating in a key yet to be discovered."

"This kind of orgasm for me is metaphysical immersion in another world, religious, ascending a mountain. It happens mostly in my mind, which is flushed with sensation, and sends me very close emotionally to the person I am with."

"Orgasm: a compelling sensation of light. My vision dissolves into brilliance behind my eyes, blinding me; my body dissolves into pure light. I see nothing but light, hear nothing at all, feel nothing that can be named—but every blood cell is dancing and every pore outpouring radiance—and the spiders in the closets and the ants on the floor must be full of joy at receiving the overflow of love."

Emotional orgasm is a feeling of love and communion with another human being that reaches a peak, a great welling up of intensity of feeling, which may be felt physically in the chest, or as a lump in the throat, or as a general opening-up sensation, a feeling of wanting deeper and deeper penetration, wanting to merge and become one person. It could be described as a complete release of emotions, what one woman called "a piercing feeling of love," or an orgasm of the heart.

The Suppression of Female
Sexuality and Orgasm

We have seen that the basic value of sex and intercourse for women is closeness and affection. Women liked sex more for the feelings involved than for the purely physical sensations of intercourse per se.* As most women's answers reflected, it is the emotional warmth shared at this time, and the feeling of being wanted and needed (not the plain physical act), which are the chief pleasures of sex and intercourse.

Sex in our society is an extremely important way of being close—almost the only way we can be really physically or even spiritually intimate with another human being. And sex is one of the few times we tangibly feel we are being loved and demonstrate our love for another person. And yet, in another, as yet unborn (uncreated) society, it would not be necessary to define "sex" in such a closed and rigid way. It would not be necessary for women to accept an oppressive situation in order to get closeness and affection.

It is not the fact that women don't want or don't like intercourse that makes them sexual slaves (since they do like it), but rather the fact that they have few or no alternative choices for their own satisfaction.

"I have wanted to have orgasms with a man for years—about twelve. Seems like the impossible dream. I can be a loving eunuch with him, but only a full sexual person by myself."

Why does this woman say this? Why, if she can be "a full sexual person" by herself, can she be only "a loving eunuch" with a man? This woman's comment points up a dilemma that has become clearer and clearer throughout this book. We have seen that heterosexual sex usually involves the pattern of foreplay, penetration, and intercourse ending with male ejaculation—and that all too often the woman does not orgasm. But

---

* As far as the physical sensations in intercourse themselves are concerned, the moment of penetration was by far the favorite sensation mentioned by most women. What sex researchers call "proprioceptive feeling"—pleasurable physical sensations having nothing to do with orgasm—were very rarely mentioned.

women *know* very well how to orgasm during masturbation, whenever they want. If they know how to have orgasms whenever they want, why don't they feel free to use this knowledge during sex with men? *Why do women so habitually satisfy men's needs during sex and ignore their own?*

The fact is that the role of women in sex, as in every other aspect of life, has been to serve the needs of others—men and children. And just as women did not recognize their oppression in a general sense until recently, just so sexual slavery has been an almost unconscious way of life for most women—based on what was said to be an eternally unchanging biological impulse. We have seen, however, that our model of sex and physical relations is *culturally* (not biologically) defined, and can be redefined—or undefined. We need not continue to have only one model of physical relations—foreplay, penetration, intercourse, and ejaculation.

Women are sexual slaves insofar as they are (justifiably) afraid to "come out" with their own sexuality, and forced to satisfy others' needs and ignore their own. As one woman put it, "sex can be political in the sense that it can involve a power structure where the woman is unwilling or unable to get what she really needs for her fullest amount of pleasure, but the man is getting what he wants, and the woman, like an unquestioning and unsuspecting lackey, is gratefully supplying it." The truth is that almost everything in our society pushes women toward defining their sexuality only as intercourse with men, and toward not defining themselves as full persons in sex with men. Lack of sexual satisfaction is another sign of the oppression of women.

This, of course, is not to say that women don't like sex, or that they don't enjoy intercourse in many ways. When asked if they enjoyed sex, almost all women said yes, they did. Furthermore, there was no correlation with frequency of orgasm: women who did not orgasm with their partners were just as likely to say they enjoyed sex as women who did. And women who never orgasmed during intercourse were just as likely to say they enjoyed intercourse as women who did. However, the important question is: What is it that women enjoy about sex/intercourse, and what do women mean when they say they like them?

The Clitoral–Vaginal Controversy

"Do orgasms with the presence of a penis (intercourse) feel different from those without? In what way?"
Another reason the clitoral–vaginal controversy remains with us is that

the mystique of orgasm during intercourse is still very strong. The idea is that orgasm during intercourse ("vaginal orgasm") feels much better than orgasm without intercourse ("clitoral orgasm"). It is this idea which will be examined here. The fundamental question is: Does orgasm with a penis inside feel different from orgasm without a penis inside? Have women who orgasm during intercourse, by whatever means, defined their orgasms in any way that is different from the general definition of orgasm? And what comparisons have they made when asked if orgasm felt different with or without the presence of a penis during intercourse?

Sex is defined as a certain pattern—foreplay, penetration, intercourse, and ejaculation—and intercourse is always part of that pattern, indeed, intercourse *is* the pattern (at least insofar as it ends with male ejaculation, and this ends sex). This pattern is what oppresses women, and in fact it oppresses men too, as we shall see later on.

But the original question of this chapter is still not answered—If women know how to have orgasms, why don't they use this knowledge during sex with men? Why don't they break out of the pattern? There is no reason why using this knowledge and taking the initiative in new directions would diminish the warmth and closeness of sex. Or is there?

Habit

On one level, it could be said that we think of "sex" as we do—as "foreplay," "penetration," and intercourse followed by male ejaculation—because we are taught that this is what sex is, because we are taught that these are the proper physical relations between people, and that this is what you are "supposed" to do. Our idea of sexual relations is structured around reproductive activity, which is defined as "instinctual." Although sexual feelings of pleasure are instinctual, or at least innate, intercourse is not, strictly, their instinctive or innate goal. One of our society's myths is that it is "nature" or our "instincts" that make us have "sex" as we do. Actually, most of the time we do it the way we do because we have learned to do it that way. Even chimpanzees and other animals must learn to have intercourse (Yerkes; Harlow and Harlow; H. C. Bingham). Sex and all physical relations are something *we* create; they are *cultural* forms, not biological forms. Most often, however, we do not think of ourselves as free to explore and discover or invent whatever kinds of varied physical relations we might want, or which might seem natural to us at any given time, corresponding to our own individual feelings and needs. Instead, we tend to act as if there were one set formula for having intimate physical contact with other people (who "must" be of the opposite sex), which includes foreplay, intercourse, and male orgasm.

From this point of view, the answers women gave when asked if they like "sex" can be seen as reflecting their feelings about this standard definition: if intercourse is instinctive, and if the way we have sex is nature itself, how can anyone (who is not "neurotic") say they don't like it? Or how can anyone say they would like to change it? Sex is sex, and either you like it or you don't. However, as we have seen, the more specific questions did bring out all kinds of satisfactions and dissatisfactions with sex as we know it.

There is great pressure on women in our society now to say they like "sex." As one woman put it, "With the current spotlight on sex, the knowledge that I have a good sex life protects me from damaging doubts about myself every time I read an article about sex." Women *must* "do it right" and especially they must enjoy it. Any woman who says she does not like sex is labeled "neurotic," "hung up," "weird," or "sick," by the psychiatric profession and others. Women, for all kinds of reasons, *must* like "sex." This means, essentially, that women must like heterosexual intercourse.

In fact, to even hint at questioning the glory and importance of intercourse as a primary value is like questioning the American flag or apple pie. One is not even allowed to *discuss* feelings about intercourse, or whether one likes it, etc., without arousing a strong emotional reaction in many people, who feel you are attacking "*men.*" But this is not true. The fact that it is so perceived is merely another indication of how stereotyped our ideas about physical relations are and, further, how emotionally and politically sensitive a topic sex is.

To reinforce us in these ideas of what sex is, and especially that heterosexual intercourse is *the* high point in every case, we have all kinds of people—from physicians to clergymen to self-styled sex experts in books and women's magazines to our own male lovers—instructing us in what sex is, and in the proper ways of having it. But, how can there be a "proper" way of touching another human being? Sex manuals tell us with mechanical precision where to touch, how to touch, when to Orgasm, that it is Bad not to Orgasm, and so On. But especially we learn that, no matter what else, intercourse and male orgasm *must* take place. Although this subject will be pursued further in a later chapter, it is important to stress here that, although sex manuals can be helpful, it is *we* who know what we want at any given time, and we who can create sex in whatever image we want. There is no need to follow any one mechanical pattern to be close to another human being.

Love and Sexual Slavery

But somehow, the truth is more complicated than the simple idea that women are oppressed in bed as elsewhere out of "habit"—simply because "just as women are used to serving men their coffee, so they are used to serving them their orgasms." It is still remarkable how easily we bring ourselves to orgasm during masturbation, and how totally we can ignore this knowledge during sex with men. It seems clear that we are often afraid to use this knowledge during sex with men because to do so would be to challenge male authority. Somehow it is all right for a woman to demand equal pay, but to demand equality in sex is not considered valid.

Why are women afraid to challenge men in bed? First, they fear losing men's "love." The question of what love is, of course, is very complicated,* but it is clear that as seen throughout this chapter, the importance of sex for women is inextricably bound up with love:

"Sex for me is a very private and almost sacred thing. To me sex means the supreme proof of love."

"In my own case, I desire happiness, togetherness, love, etc., and I know that if for no apparent reason I kept refusing sex, I would lose some of the happiness in my life, and I might lose the love my man has for me. He would assume that something was wrong and make changes, perhaps excluding me from his life."

"It's a trade. Like my mother says, men give love for sex, women give sex for love."

It does seem to many sex researchers and therapists that fear of losing a man's love *is* holding many women back from having orgasms with men. For example, Seymour Fisher, of the State University of New York, the author of *The Female Orgasm*, has written:

The psychological factors—for example, fear of object loss—which my work suggests may interfere with orgasm attainment in many women may exemplify at another level the general cultural feeling transmitted to woman that *her place is uncertain and that she survives*

* See *Women and Love* (*The Hite Report on Love, Passion, and Emotional Violence*).

76

only because the male protects her. The apparent importance of fear of object loss in inhibiting orgasm can probably be traced to the fact that the little girl gets innumerable messages which tell her that the female cannot survive alone and is likely to get into serious trouble if she is not supported by a strong and capable male. *It does not seem too radical to predict that when women are able to grow up in a culture in which they are less pressured to obedience by threats of potential desertion, the so-called orgasm problem will fade away.* [Italics mine.—Au.]

Although Fisher, as a psychologist, tends to see these fears of loss of love as emanating from childhood experiences, it is obvious that they also can be reactions to very real current, adult conditions, such as fears that as you get older the man you love will stop loving you, that he needs you less than you need him, and so forth.

Economics

Not only may a woman be afraid of losing a man's love, if she asserts herself, or "challenges" him sexually, but all too often economic intimidation is also involved. This can take many forms, some subtle, some overt. The most obvious form of economic intimidation occurs when a woman is totally dependent on the man with whom she has sex for food and shelter, and has no economic alternatives such as being able to get a job herself if she wants—that is, marriage as it was traditionally defined. We have all seen the connection between affection and economics in a mild form on "I Love Lucy," where affectionate words and embraces were always a standard part of talking Ricky into a new sofa, a new hat, or a vacation. Some of the women in this study also mentioned the connection between sex and economics in their lives, in answer to *"Do you feel that having sex is in any way political?"*:

"I'm not sure if it's political, but it's economic. I really felt I was earning my room and board in bed for years, and if I wanted anything, my husband was more likely to give it to me after sex. Now that I am self-supporting, I don't need to play that game any more. What a relief!"

"I think it is used for 'horse trading.' I know I have used it that way, and I think most women have been forced to use it that way (for bargaining purposes and to gain economic support) at one time or another, although this is gradually changing as jobs become open to us."

Anyone who is economically and legally dependent on another person, as women traditionally have been, and in the majority of cases still are, is put in a very vulnerable and precarious position when that person expects or demands sex or affection. Although the woman may genuinely want to please the man, still, the fact that she does not feel free *not* to please him, and that she puts his satisfaction before her own and keeps secret her own knowledge of her body, reveals the presence of an element of fear and intimidation. Clearly, if a woman is financially dependent on a man, she is not in a good position to demand equality in bed. Economic dependency, even if you love someone, is a very subtle and corrosive force.

Women who are not married can be economically intimidated in other, more subtle ways. Even a woman who is only on a "date" with a man can be made to feel that she "owes" him sex:

"Sex can be political, when the woman is made to feel obligated, for instance, to pay for a date with sex in exchange for anything."

"I hate Disneyland dating—the old 'I-took-you-here-and-spent-$$$-so-now-you-go-to-bed-with-me.' "

As Dr. Pepper Schwartz, of the University of Washington, has pointed out, even when women are no longer economically dependent, they are still

used to modifying (their sexual) desire to fit their more important needs: food, shelter, protection, and security, and most have ceased to be analytical about their sexual situation. Even when the situation arises that makes them independent of such considerations (personal wealth, a successful career, and a bevy of admirers, etc.) they are so used to having other exigencies define their sexual and marital structure that they do not reevaluate their life style. They believe the myths they have heard about their emotional and sexual needs.

There are also economic pressures on single women to get married—leading to the same financial and legal dependency discussed earlier; as one woman, age twenty-seven, working in an office, explained her situation, "Even with the jobs I can get—and I'm a good secretary—I still can't afford to pay my rent. I'm forced to move in with a man, or else have roommates. Roommates do not give you any privacy, and living with some guy—first one guy and then, after a year or two, another guy, and so on—is a horrible way to live. You feel like an itinerant worker, moving all your belongings from place to place. It's humiliating. So you have the pressure to get married and settle down and forget it. And—(!!) if you are just living with a man on a supposedly equal share-the-rent basis, guess who still gets to clean house and cook? And be loving and affectionate and always ready for sex? And if, God forbid, you just don't feel like it for a while—out you go! So—you wind up thinking you'd be better off married."

As the feminist group the Redstockings put it,

For many women marriage is one of the few forms of employment that is readily available. Not marrying for them could easily mean becoming a domestic or factory worker or going on welfare. To advocate women "liberate themselves" by giving up marriage reflects a strong class bias in automatically excluding the mass of women who have no other means of support but a husband.*

Of course this is not to say that love (for husband and children) cannot also be involved. Unfortunately, however, economic dependency can eventually corrode and subtly undermine the most beautiful feelings, or even go hand in hand with those feelings, leading to a kind of love-hate situation. But marriage could become a *real* love contract (either heterosexual or homosexual) if the laws that make a woman legally dependent were changed and if women had a real chance for economic autonomy.

The negative effect of economics on women's freedom, both sexual and otherwise, is widespread. According to the U.S. Department of Labor, in 1975 women who worked full time year round (40 percent of American women) still earned only about 60 percent of the wages of similarly employed men, and this figure has not increased in the last five years. Women, despite their education and qualifications, are still largely absent from management and non-traditional professional positions. Federal subsidies of child day care centers have been cut back, and job layoffs have affected women more frequently, as they traditionally have more peripheral jobs. This means that most women—whether single or married—are not financially independent.

In other words, as Ellen DuBois, of the State University of New York at Buffalo, has written me,

---

* Dorothy Tennov, in *Prime Time* (a journal "for the liberation of women in the prime of life"), has looked at it another way: Those who recognize that wives who remain in marriage for economic reasons are, in fact, selling sexual services may condemn the practice on the basis of the male-serving edict that there is something wrong with selling sexual services. The thing that is wrong with the wife's situation is not that she gets paid for her services—sexual and others—but that she receives so little for what she provides that she remains dependent.

An erroneous and dangerous assumption is that the only thing that stands between a woman and "satisfactory" sex is her realization of her own physical needs. As an oppressed people, what we women lack is not knowledge . . . but *power*, social power, economic power, physical power. To put it another way, it is not our ignorance that has condemned us to sexual exploitation and dissatisfaction, but our powerlessness.

Lesbianism

"Neither male nor female sexuality is limited by 'genital geography,' and it has been one of the greatest public relations victories of all time to convince us it was. The very naturalness of lesbianism (and homosexuality) is exactly the cause of the strong social and legal rules against it. The basing of our social system on gender difference, biological reproductive function, is barbaric and should be replaced by a system based on affirmation of the individual and support for all life on the planet."

It must be clear by now that female sexuality is physically "pan-sexual," or just "sexual"—certainly not something that is directed at any one type of physical organ to be found in nature. There is no organ especially concocted to fit the clitoral area and the kind of stimulation we generally need for orgasm. From the point of view of physical pleasure, we are free to relate to all the creatures of the planet, according to their individual meaning for us, rather than their specific classification or gender.

Of course it goes without saying that as we move toward a more equitable view of life, the right to love other women will be taken for granted. However, the general villainization of homosexual contacts in our society has a long history. As Kinsey explains:

The general condemnation of homosexuality in our particular culture apparently traces to a series of historical circumstances which had little to do with the protection of the individual or the preservation of the social organization of the day. In Hittite, Chaldean, and early Jewish codes there were no over-all condemnations of such activity, although there were penalties for homosexual activities between persons of particular social status or blood relationships, or homosexual relationships under other particular circumstances, especially when force was involved. The more general condemnation of all homosexual relationships (especially male) originated in Jewish history in about the seventh history B.C., upon the return from the Babylonian exile. Both mouth–genital contacts and homosexual activities had previously been associated with the Jewish religious service, as they had been with the religious services of most of the other peoples of that part of Asia, and just as they have been in many other cultures elsewhere in the world. In the wave of nationalism which was then developing among the Jewish people, there was an attempt to disidentify themselves with their neighbors* by breaking with many of the customs which they had previously shared with them. Many of the Talmudic condemnations were based on the fact that such activities represented the way of the Canaanite, the way of the Chaldean, the way of the pagan, and they were originally condemned as a form of idolatry rather than a sexual crime. Throughout the middle ages homosexuality was associated with heresy. The reform in the custom (the mores) soon, however, became a matter of morals, and finally a question for action under criminal law.

Kinsey (who was originally a biologist) also tells us that other mammals and other animals routinely have lesbian and homosexual relationships:

The impression that infra-human mammals more or less confine themselves to heterosexual activities is a distortion of the fact which appears to have originated in a man-made philosophy, rather than in specific observations of mammalian behavior. Biologists and psychologists who have accepted the doctrine that the only natural function of sex is reproduction have simply ignored the existence of sexual activity which is not reproductive. They have assumed that heterosexual responses are a part of an animal's innate, "instinctive" equipment, and that all other types of sexual activity represent "perversions" of the "normal instincts." Such interpretations are, however, mystical. They do not originate in our knowledge of the physiology of sexual response, and can be maintained only if one assumes that sexual function is in some fashion divorced from the physiologic processes which control other functions of the animal body. It may be true that heterosexual contacts outnumber homosexual contacts in most species of mammals, but it would be hard to demonstrate that this depends upon the "normality" of heterosexual responses, and the "abnormality" of homosexual responses.

Kinsey mentions that lesbian contacts have been observed in such widely separated species as rats, mice, hamsters, guinea pigs, rabbits, porcupines, marten, cattle, antelope, goats, horses, pigs, lions, sheep,

---

* Especially their non-patriarchal neighbors.

monkeys, and chimpanzees. And, he adds, "Every farmer who has raised cattle knows . . . that cows quite regularly mount cows."

The arguments over whether lesbianism and/or homosexuality are biological or psychological in origin (the origin of the "problem," as it is usually put) are still raging in some quarters,* but the "answer" hardly matters any more. Homosexuality, or the desire to be physically intimate with someone of one's own sex at some time, or always, during one's life, can be considered a natural and "normal" variety of life experience. It is "abnormal" only when you posit as "normal" and "healthy" only an interest in reproductive sex. Discussions of why one becomes *heterosexual* would come to the same nonconclusions. To consider all non-reproductive sexual contact "an error of nature" is a very narrow view.

Not being "allowed" to really touch or be in physical contact with anyone other than a sexual partner—since it might "imply" a sexual connection!—is depressing and alienating. Specifically, vis-à-vis women's connection with one another, this ban on physical contact is oppressive and has the effect of separating women. The dynamic works something like this: you may feel a sudden impulse to kiss or hug a friend—or you may feel subtler desires for greater closeness or contact of which you are unaware—which you must stifle and repress. But when a natural impulse is stopped and is not consciously recognized, it can cause feelings of conflict, guilt, and anxiety. Such repression can then lead to half-conscious feelings of rejection, which engender feelings of distrust and dislike for the same person to whom one was originally attracted. This, of course, is a well-known psychological phenomenon, and commonly happens on a subtle level between friends. The point here is that this prohibition on the exchange of physical contact (*of any kind*) between women is bound to increase the level of hostility and distance between them.

One of the best descriptions of how we more or less "unconsciously" select our sexual partners on the basis of gender (and screen out those of the "wrong" gender) has been given by Pepper Schwartz and Philip Blumstein.† To begin with, they explain that given a state of physiological arousal for which an individual has no immediate

* A good summary of the arguments can be found in Edward Brecher's *The Sex Researchers.*
† "Bisexuality: Some Sociological Observations," a paper presented at the Chicago Conference on Bisexual Behavior, October 6, 1973, Department of Sociology, University of Washington.

explanation, "he will 'label' this state and describe his feelings in terms of the cognitions available to him . . ." They continue, "the sources of arousal are likely to be more diverse than the sources to which it is attributed by the most astute laymen," and, "the greater the confidence in, or need for, a heterosexual identity, the more likely that ambiguities will be resolved in a heterosexual direction. When one has strong suspicions about one's homosexuality or has taken on gay identity, then the interpretation is likely to go in the other direction." In other words,

homosexuality—like heterosexuality—becomes self-fulfilling. This is especially so since the free-floating arousal levels early in one's sexual development tend to be channeled and shaped by sexual experience and strengthening sexual identity. So we believe that untapped or uninterpreted homosexual arousal cues tend not to arouse as one takes on more firm heterosexual identity and engages in more heterosexual behavior. Likewise, untapped or uninterpreted heterosexual cues tend not to arouse confirmed homosexuals. Our dichotomous views of our own sexual identity thwart any possibility of bisexuality.

With specific reference to women, Schwartz and Blumstein state that:

Women have a different arousal system from men. Their arousal is a total body response, rather than a genital one. While some women may feel "horny" (i.e., feel sexual tension in the genital area, or lubricate during an exciting encounter), all of these signals are less visible than their counterpart in the male. To put it very simply, a woman can reinterpret her excitement; a man cannot miss noticing his sexual arousal and labeling it as erotic. . . . If a woman has sexual tension in an inappropriate environment such as during a softball game, a mother–child interaction, etc., she has more freedom than a man in how she can label that excitement.

Likewise in female/female relationships, the cues that a woman receives from another woman are more subtle than the cues men give each other. Apropos of our discussion of erection, two women do not have to explain away an erection should one of them get excited while they were having a tête à tête and talking about their sex lives. If they are getting excited, and they want to communicate sexual interest in one another, they have to rely on eye contact, intensified attention, and other kinds of interpersonal connections to convey their meaning. The problem, however, is that these kinds of cues are confusing, they are usually associated with heterosexual negotiation and since they seem inappropriate or unreal in a same sex encounter, may be reinterpreted to mean friendship or non-sexual affection. Women may be afraid to believe—even if they want to—that another woman is giving sexual cues to them. If they were coming from another source their intent would probably be unmistakable; but since they come from what has in the past been an asexual source, the receiver may tend to doubt or reinterpret the most direct of signals.

Because of this obfuscation of cues—and because women are not used to being wooed by other women—nor are they trained to do the aggressive part of sexual pursuance—it may be hypothesized that women rarely activate erotic responses to women simply because they do not realize how often the excitement they feel is mutual and has a possibility of being reciprocated. Furthermore, since no sexual negotiation is apparent, women may not realize or admit to themselves that they have been in a sexual encounter, thereby allowing all such attractions to die out. One final hypothesis along these lines follows this same theme of unapparent, passive aspects in the female sexual tradition. That is, that since women have been taught to eroticize people who eroticize them—i.e., interpret their worth and sexuality by the way men "turned on" to them, many women discover their own sexual feelings when they are approached by a man. When they see someone sexually aroused and interested in them, *then* they decide they might be sexually interested in the other person. To some extent, this seems to be true for both sexes—people start to get sexually aroused when someone begins to show sexual interest, begins aggressive moves and makes the other person feel desirable. Sexual tension begins to build and soon the two people must acknowledge its presence (even if they choose not to act on it). With women, this sexual tension may not get a chance to build because each person is embarrassed, unpracticed and unsure about the validity of the encounter as a sexual experience. Unused to taking the lead (or the responsibility) for such situations, they may back off rather than try to chart something they are unprepared for and unused to. It may be hypothesized that same sex relationships between women will not occur unless at least one person in the dyad is able to take on an aggressive sexual role and dare to make ambiguous cues explicit. If both women are unable to take this role, the relationship may never become articulated.

It is impossible to know what relation there may be between statistics and how many lesbian women there may be in the United States population, since, due to the fear of persecution, no one knows how many lesbians, or bisexuals, there are. Kinsey estimated that perhaps 12 to 13 percent of women had "sexual relations to the point of orgasm" with another woman at some time during their adult lives, and that between 11 and 20 percent of single women and 8 to 10 percent of married women in the sample "were making at least incidental homosexual responses, or making more specific homosexual contacts" between the ages of twenty and thirty-five. In the 1970s Dr. Richard Green, formerly of the University of California (Los Angeles) Gender Identity Research Treatment Program, commented that there may now be an increase in bisexuality and/or lesbianism among women "partly for political reasons"—as one of the ways women can "disassociate themselves from the extraordinary dependency they've had on men all these years."

At the same time, it is important to note that preferences can change during a lifetime, or can change several times; what is called "gender identity" is not so cut and dried as the preceding statistics might seem to imply. As Kinsey explained, there are not two discrete groups, one heterosexual and one homosexual, in other words, the world is not to be divided into sheep and goats. "The living world is a continuum in each and every one of its aspects," and homosexuality and heterosexuality are only the extreme types sitting at the poles of "a rich and varied continuum." In fact, "lesbian," "homosexual," and "heterosexual" should be used as adjectives, not nouns: *people* are not properly described as homosexuals, lesbians, or heterosexuals; rather, *activities* are properly described as homosexual, lesbian, or heterosexual. In other words, it is really only possible to say how many persons have had, at any particular time, a given type of relationship, and that is how the figures in this study should be viewed.

Many more women than do have lesbian sex, said they might be interested in having sex with another woman
One of the most striking points about the answers received to the questionnaires was how frequently, *even though it was not specifically asked*, women brought up the fact that they might be interested in having sexual relations with another woman, or at least were curious:

"I have been married for twelve years. I've never had a physical relationship with a woman, but I feel it would be more satisfying than with a male. I don't know how to relate to another woman physically, as I've never had the opportunity to do so. There is a woman whom I'm attracted to and feel is the same as me but I am afraid to approach her."

"There are times when I feel such a warmth from my best friend that I experience it sexually and almost desire her. But I have never let her know I have this feeling, because it might make her afraid of me."

What is "different" about sexual relations between women is precisely that there is no one institutionalized way of having them, so they can be as inventive and individual as the people involved. Perhaps the two most striking specific differences from most heterosexual relations, as previously defined, were that there were generally more feelings and tenderness, affection and sensitivity, and more orgasms. The higher frequency of orgasm in lesbian sexuality has of course been remarked on by other researchers going at least as far back as Kinsey. Also lesbian sexual relations tend to be longer and to involve more over-all body sensuality, since one orgasm does not automatically signal the end of sexual feeling, as in most of the heterosexual relations described earlier.

Lesbianism can be political

Besides the increased affection and sensitivity and the increased frequency of orgasm, some women felt that sex with another woman could be better because of the more equal relationship possible. Sex with women can be a reaction against men and our second-class status with them in this society:

"Because of my own tremendous conditioning, which I believe is almost universal, it is almost impossible for me to have a truly healthy sexual relationship with a man—probably for any woman."

"I see lesbianism as putting *all* my energies (sexual, political, social, etc.) into women. Sex is a form of comfort and to have sex indiscriminately with males is to give them comfort. I think it should be seriously considered."

"Is sex political? Of course. When I quietly parted from my last male lover (for women) I suddenly, for the first time, moved into my own space, my own time zone, and my own life."

Janis Kelly has had some interesting things to say along these lines in *Sister Love: An Exploration of the Need for Homosexual Experience*:

All heterosexual relationships are corrupted by the imbalance of power between men and women. In order to maintain superiority, males must feed on the emotional care and economic servitude of women. To survive in a male-supremacist social order, women must cripple themselves in order to build the male ego. Due to the stifling effect of this culture and to the damaging roles it enforces, women cannot develop fully in a heterosexual context.

Love relationships between women are more likely to be free of the destructive forces which make [these] defenses necessary. Institutional norms and the restraints of a power-oriented culture have, of course, also influenced women; nevertheless, the domination–subordination patterns women sometimes bring to lesbian relationships cannot overshadow the essential equality of the persons involved. In addition, many of the responses nurtured in females are extremely conducive to non-exploitative interaction. Sensitivity to the feelings and moods of others, care-taking, and gentleness are among the qualities more encouraged in women than in men. . . .

Because men occupy a superior social position and are schooled to covet power over others in order to maintain that position, they can rarely accept others, especially women, as equals. Human contacts must be arranged hierarchically, and women must be on a lower level. Tension is inevitable when a woman refuses to accept this position and must be "put in her place." In contrast, women are able to start from a foundation of equality and devote their energy to growth and creativity rather than to struggling to maintain identities against the destructiveness of the traditional female role.

It is important for women to recognize their own potential for having sexual feelings for other women. If we want to grow strong, we must learn to love, respect, honor, and be attentive to and interested in other women. This includes seeing each other as physically attractive with the possibility of sexual intimacy. As long as we can relate sexually only to men *because they are "men"* (and as long as men can relate only to women because they are "women"), we are dividing the world into the very two classes we are trying to transcend.

Any woman who feels actual horror or revulsion at the thought of kissing or embracing or having physical relations with another woman should re-examine her feelings and attitudes not only about other women, but also about *herself.* A positive attitude toward our bodies and toward touching ourselves and toward any physical contact that might naturally develop with another woman is essential to self-love and accepting our own bodies as good and beautiful. As feminist columnist Jill Johnston has written: ". . . until women see in each other the possibility of a primal commitment which includes sexual love they will be denying themselves the love and value they readily accord to men, thus affirming their own second class status."

The Sexual Revolution

"If the Sexual Revolution implies the attitude that now women are 'free' too, and they can fuck strangers and fuck over the opposite sex, just the way men can, I think it's revolting. Women don't want to be free to adopt the male model of sexuality; they want to be free to find their own."

Women Rebel Against the Sexual Revolution

The "sexual revolution" of the 1960s was a response to long-term social changes that affected the structure of the family and women's role in it. (Contrary to popular opinion, the birth control pill was more a technological response to these same social changes than their cause.) Up until the second half of this century, and throughout most periods of history, a high birth rate has been considered of primary importance by both individuals and society. In social terms, it was thought that the larger the population, the wealthier the society would be, and the stronger the army. Modern technology, however, has ended the need for huge work forces, and nuclear power and technology are far more significant militarily than massive human armies. Large populations are still valuable principally as consumers.

In terms of the individual, large families are no longer the social or economic asset they once were. Children used to add to the family income by working, and they assured the parents of support and protection in their old age. Socially, male children continued the family name, which was felt to be very important, and increased the family's social prestige. Today these assets are considered negligible. Furthermore, children cost a great deal, since their education is prolonged, and after the second or third child, a couple's standing in the community diminishes rather than rises. In addition, most men no longer feel that carrying on the family line is a matter of primary importance—although they may very well enjoy having children and being fathers. But since marriage (in its original form as a property right) had been created so that the father could be sure of his paternity of the child, now that that paternity was no longer so important, marriage (as traditionally defined) was no longer so necessary, and women could be "allowed" sexual "freedom."

This change in women's role was double-edged. In traditional terms, insofar as having many children had become less important, women's status declined. That is, since women had traditionally been seen almost completely in terms of their childbearing role, they themselves as a class became less important and less respected when that role was no longer so important. At the same time, it was said that, now that women were "free" from their old role, they could be "sexually free like men," etc. There was some truth to this idea that new possibilities for female independence *had* opened up. However, as with the slaves after emancipation, becoming independent was easier said than done. In fact, women did not have equal opportunities for education or employment, and so they were stuck in their traditional role of being dependent on men. In spite of the so-called sexual revolution, women (feeling how peripheral, decorative, and expendable they had become to the over-all scheme of things) became more submissive to men than ever. This was even more true *outside* of marriage than inside, since marriage did offer some forms of protection in traditional terms. This increased submissiveness and insecurity was reflected in the child-like, baby-doll fashions of the 1960s—short little-girl dresses, long straight (blond) hair, big innocent (blue) eyes, and of course always looking as young and pretty as possible. The change in men's attitude toward women (from mother to sex object) is summed up in Molly Haskell's title to her book about women in the movies, *From Reverence to Rape*. This situation eventually led to the women's movement of the late 1960s and 1970s, which was now trying to implement some of the positive potentials of the change in women's role, to make women truly independent and free.

Although anti-feminists advise women to give up pretensions to economic independence and return to their traditional role as wives and mothers, for better or worse, fortunately or unfortunately, there is no real way to retreat en masse to our traditional position. Insofar as the importance of childbearing has diminished, women are, so to speak, out of a job. This change has come about over a long period of time, and is not likely to be reversed. Although women are not yet, as a class, financially or socially independent, we can improve our status (or even keep it at present levels) only by going forward and reintegrating ourselves with the world and perhaps, if we find it necessary, changing that world.

In conclusion, what we think of as "sexual freedom"—giving women the "right" to have sex without marriage, and decreasing the emphasis on monogamy—is a function of the decreased importance of childbearing to society, and of paternity to men. Although this change has been labeled "sexual freedom," in fact it has not so far allowed much real freedom for women (or men) to explore their own sexuality; it has merely put pressure on them to have *more* of the same kind of sex. Finally, it is important to remember that *you cannot decree women to be "sexually free" when they are not economically free*; to do so is to put them into a more vulnerable position than ever, and make them into a form of easily available common property.

Pressure on Women to Have Sex: A Critique of the Concept of "Sex Drive"

"I went to a New Year's party with one guy once and crashed there. I said I didn't want to sleep with him and he said I could have the sofa. I felt I should be more relaxed, and I said no, I'd sleep on the floor too. Then he talked me into a corner: Why was I so afraid of touching? Afraid of sex? We didn't have to ball after all, we could just hug and touch. I felt raped even though we never had intercourse; we had oral sex. He didn't know my cunt from a hole in the wall. If this happened to me now I would have acted totally opposite but this was two years ago and I didn't really know that I could actually say no, and not have to prove that I was a 'woman.' "

"Only with my husband. It was a condition of our marriage as it developed, that if I refused him sexually he was insufferable. I think this is a common degradation of women in marriage. But rape is too strong a word, as force was not involved. I felt I was prostituted, being used as a whore, with no regard for my desires. I think it is a barbaric tradition, that men cannot be refused by women in marriage, and this led to my finding my husband sexually repugnant."

How strong is the male "sex drive"?
These quotes graphically illustrate the pressure that is on women to have intercourse, both inside and outside of marriage. One of the

91

worst forms of this pressure comes from the idea that a man's need for "sex" is a strong and urgent "drive," which, if not satisfied, can lead to terrible consequences. As one woman phrased it, "Men being sexual animals, at least to my way of thinking, their bodies drive them to the culmination of sex, the climax, ejaculation, and depositing of their seed. I feel that most of them could gladly do without foreplay. At times I have felt guilty, especially if waiting for me has robbed my partner of some of the intensity of his climax."

This particular stereotype of male sexuality is extremely common-place, and reflects the picture most frequently presented by sex manuals, psychologists, psychiatrists, physicians, men's magazines, and many others. Typically, the male "sex drive" is seen as a constantly surfacing and demanding feeling; as Theodore Reik has expressed it in *The Psychology of Sex Relations*:

. . . the crude sex drive is a biological need which represents the instinct and is conditioned by chemical changes within the organism. The urge is dependent on inner secretions and its aim is the relieving of a physical tension.

The crude sex-urge . . . is entirely incapable of being subli-mated. If it is strongly excited, it needs, in its urgency, an immedi-ate release. It cannot be deflected from its one aim to different aims, or at most can be as little diverted as the need to urinate or as hunger and thirst. It insists on gratification in its original realm.

This glorification of the male "sex drive" and male orgasm "needs" amounts to justifying men in whatever they have to do to get intercourse—even rape—and defines the "normal" male as one who is "hungry" for intercourse. On the other hand, the defi-nition of female sexuality as "passive and receptive" (but, since the sexual revolution, also necessary for a "healthy woman") amounts to telling women to submit to this aggressive male "sex drive." Especially since the 1940s the glorification of male sexuality has often been justified as a kind of natural law of the jungle (the product, we are led to believe, of cave-man hormones), even by some of the most serious social scientists. Actually, the information available does not warrant such conclusions. This idea of male sexual "right" (via biology) is not much more scientifically based than the old idea that kings were monarchs by the grace of god and natural law. Just as kings said that any other political model (like democracy) would be unnatural and would not work, so men say that if women are aggressive sexually (i.e., anything but passive), sex will be unnatural, they will become "impotent," and sex for them will be impossible.

What *is* "sex drive"? Lester A. Kirkendall, in "Towards a Clarification of the Concept of Male Sex Drive," says:

As the term "sex drive" is now used, it has become a blanket term which obscures the components with which we are actually dealing. We should distinguish between sexual capacity, sexual performance, and sexual drive . . . that is, what you can do, what you do do, and what you *want* to do.

Kirkendall explains that although capacity ("what you can do") has a biological base, sex drive ("what you *want* to do") "seems to be very largely a psychologically conditioned component. . . . Sex drive seems to vary considerably from individual to individual, and from time to time in the same individual, and these variations seem related to psychological factors." In other words, sex *drive* (not capacity) is more a function of desires than "needs."*

A further point along this line is that even if a man has a strong physical desire for orgasm—an erection, for example—there is nothing in nature, nothing physical, that impels him to have that orgasm in a vagina. The stimulation he feels is linked to the desire for *orgasm*, and not to any desire for intercourse per se. The physical "urge" a man feels is a desire for further stimulation of the penis, or for orgasm—*not* a desire to penetrate a woman's vagina. There is no "beeper" or sensory device on his penis that makes him seek a vagina in which to put his penis. This pleasurable connection is *learned*, not innate; as mentioned earlier, even chimpanzees must learn to have intercourse, although they masturbate on their own from early childhood. The definition of male sexuality as being "instinctively" drawn to heterosexual intercourse is only another example of the way we define sexuality as reproductive activity.

Finally, there is not even a medical term for the colloquial "blue balls." Contrary to popular opinion, it is no harder on a man not to have an orgasm than on a woman. Men feel no more "pain" than we do. Kinsey gets right to the point:

* For a discussion of possible hormonal influences, see John Money and Anke Ehrhardt's *Man & Woman, Boy & Girl.*

There is a popular opinion that the testes are the sources of the semen which the male ejaculates. The testes are supposed to become swollen with accumulated secretions between the times of sexual activity, and periodic ejaculation is supposed to be necessary in order to relieve these pressures. Many males claim that their testes ache if they do not find regular sources of outlet, and throughout the history of erotic literature and in some psychoanalytic literature the satisfactions of orgasm are considered to depend upon the release of pressures in the "glands"—meaning the testes. Most of these opinions are, however, quite unfounded. The prostate, seminal vesicles, and Cowper's are the only glands which contribute any quantity of material to the semen, and they are the only structures which accumulate secretions which could create pressures that would need to be relieved. Although there is some evidence that the testes may secrete a bit of liquid when the male is erotically aroused, the amount of their secretion is too small to create any pressure. The testes may seem to hurt when there is unrelieved erotic arousal (the so-called stoneache★ of the vernacular), but the pain probably comes from the muscular tensions in the perineal area, and possibly from the tensions in the sperm ducts, especially at the lower ends (the epididymis) where they are wrapped about the testes. Such aches are usually relieved in orgasm because the muscular tensions are relieved—but not because of the release of any pressures which have accumulated in the testes. Exactly similar pains may develop in the groins of the female when sexual arousal is prolonged for some time before there is any release in orgasm.

If a man's desire for intercourse is not shared by a woman, there is no reason why masturbation or other stimulation will not provide him with an equally strong or stronger orgasm, although the psychological satisfaction may not be the same. Or, there is no overriding reason why he must have an orgasm at all. The point is that there is no physically demanding male sex *drive* that forces men to pressure women into intercourse. Women need no longer be intimidated by this argument. As one woman answered, when asked "Have you ever been afraid to say 'no'?", "*No.* This is *my* body, *my* breasts, and *my* cunt, and they are *my* territory and if *anyone*, even my husband, tries to take what I do not wish to give, it's WAR, baby."

★ "Blue-balls."

The Double Standard

Women who did try to be open and share with men, having sex in the new, free way, in all too many cases wound up being disrespected and often hurt—because the double standard still operated.

"I think the sexual revolution is very male-oriented and anti-woman. The idea is that men are telling women they're free to fuck around with whomever they want. But the catch is that the double standard is still employed. A man who has many lovers is 'sowing his oats'; a woman who has many lovers is a 'prostitute' or 'nymphomaniac.' "

"Usually after they know they 'have' me, I get the feeling I am a piece of ass. I feel their hostility and their contempt. The double standard is alive and well."

"Although I live at a college campus which is considered nationwide as a place of avant-garde sexual and intellectual ideas, it is not. Men here still disrespect women who have sex with those they're not 'in love with,' and if a woman cares about her esteem, it is only safe to have sex with either a male who cares about her so he won't make her feel bad and talk about her to other men so they disrespect her—or else with a person no one finds out about (like flings at ski resorts or vacations, etc.). One male, considered a leading radical here, was talking to a supposed female friend of his the day before Halloween. They were invited to a costume party and she, having trouble deciding what to wear, asked him, 'What do you think I should go as?' Very cruelly, he replied, 'Why don't you go as a virgin? I'm sure nobody will recognize you!' "

Be a "good girl"!

Almost all the women who answered these questionnaires had been brought up to be "good girls." And those still living at home were, for the most part, *still* being taught to be "good girls." Girls are still being kept from finding out about, exploring and discovering, their own sexuality—and called "bad girls" when they try. At puberty, girls are given information about their reproductive organs and menstruation, but rarely told about the clitoris!

Sex—disconnected to emotions?

Some of the sexual revolution ideology stated that it was old-fashioned to want to connect sex with feelings—it meant you weren't "hip." Not only marriage but also monogamy and love or even tender feelings were often considered to be something only "neurotic" women wanted. The idea was that "people should spontaneously have sex and not worry about hurting each other, just behave freely and have sex, no strings, anytime with anybody, just for pure physical pleasure." But almost *no* woman in this study wanted that kind of sexual relationship, overwhelmingly, women wanted sex with feeling.

To be told that we should have a regular "appetite" for intercourse does not coincide with how most women feel: periods of greater interest in sex with a partner, for most women, fluctuate according to attraction to a certain individual, and (to a lesser extent) according to the menstrual cycle. Most women* emphasized that the appetite for sex with another person became really intense only in relation to desire for a specific person, although of course they could enjoy sex at any time. What causes the awakening of this intense desire or love for another, specific person is very personal and mysterious.†

"Leaving out love and even commitment for the moment, good sex has to be more than anatomy or even 'psyching' yourself into it. It has to involve a certain amount of chemistry between two people. After a singularly disastrous experience trying to make a sexual relationship work when there was no attraction (just affection), I don't want to try to add sex to my friendships (unless I feel attraction too). I don't understand it in any way but 'chemistry,' but there certainly is such a thing as sexual attraction, which can't be forced into existence."

The Right Not to Have "Sex"

Is sex necessary for health?

Finally, since the arrival of the sexual revolution and its tenet that sex is no longer "serious" (you don't have to fear pregnancy, and marriage

---

* This includes women who do orgasm with their partners as well as women who do not.
† All we really know about our sexuality is that we have a desire for orgasms, and that certain individuals and certain situations stimulate these desires in us more than others. Other primates like chimpanzees become genitally aroused from feelings of frustration or fear, anger, tension, joy, or exuberance, or from playful or affectionate body contact. Arousal, for humans also, is often brought on by tension or frustration, and not only by sexual feelings themselves.

is no longer a requirement), it became "hip" to have a lot of "sex" (intercourse). In fact, we are often told that the sex "drive" must be regularly expressed to maintain "healthy functioning." Many women resented this commercialization and vulgarization of sex—"beds on the sidewalks and pills in the vending machines":

"We are taught that every little twinge is a big sex urge and we must attend to it or we'll be an old maid. I'm getting sick to death of sexuality—everywhere sex sex sex! So what? Sex is not the end all and be all of life. It's very nice but it's not everything!"

"I wish there wouldn't be as much of a 'hype' about sex as there is now. I hate the media's exploitation of sex and women. I would hope that women wouldn't be looked upon as things to look nice and to have sex with. For the most part, women are judged by their potential sexual worth. I would like sex to become more matter of fact, and more personal. In a way, I'd almost like to have back the hush-hush good old days when you just didn't talk about sex. It would not be hidden because it was dirty, but because it was a sweet, private thing."

Unfortunately, the idea that sex is necessary for health has become big business. Magazines, books, television ads using sex (or the happy couple) to sell their product, some psychiatrists, counselors, sex clinics, films, and massage parlors—all have a vested interest in the idea. We are constantly being reminded of sex in one way or another, and subtly coerced into doing it: "Why aren't you doing it? Everybody else is. Get on the bandwagon! You're missing all the fun if you don't!" (And you're probably neurotic and mentally unhealthy.) Many women commented on this, or felt defensive that they did not want to have sex more often:

"I think our culture has made sex over-important. Everyone thinks that everyone else is having a great time fucking all the time and so we all compete against the American myth. Given this, I think that sex in my life has assumed a correct proportion, that is, an expression of love between us; yet, I still feel hung up about the myth sometimes—maybe having sex is less important to me than to others."

"The thing I enjoy most is making love with people I have that 'special' feeling for—this is when it's most satisfying totally, even if it never gets down to real sex—it's still beautiful just holding them and feeling warmth and love with them."

Of course not all sexual activity or physical relations are based on this kind of attraction; some women prefer relationships to be based more on friendship than passion. But they still indicated clearly that their desire for sex with another person is usually based on feelings for another person, and not on a purely mechanical need for "release."*

In fact, there is nothing unusual about spending various periods of one's life without sex

"I am currently celibate. I enjoy it but the society makes it hard to be partnerless sometimes. There are activities I avoid because they will be 'couply.' People often think there's something wrong with you if you're not part of a couple, but being independent is worth it."

"Periods of celibacy can be useful for re-evaluating your life and rediscovering your sexuality—the fallow period before new things can grow. I did it for five years on and off once. By not having to please anyone else, I was able to get really deeply in touch with myself, and develop my understanding of the world—whereas before, always having boyfriends had kept me so narrowly focused on them that I hadn't had time to think about my relationship to the larger scheme of things. I found that giving up physical sex was a small price to pay."

However, other women felt cut off and isolated during periods of celibacy, since sex is almost the only activity in which our society allows us to be close to another human being—since all forms of physical contact are channeled into heterosexual intercourse

"When I go without sex for a while, I begin to crave affection and reaffirmation. I feel closed off from others, and begin to notice an intense need for affection, warmth, and any form of contact with another human being."

"It doesn't seem to bother me physically, but emotionally I tense up. I miss body contact and find it extremely frustrating. There is a special kind of loneliness in being one in a culture that seems to think in terms of pairs."

"I miss feeling wanted and needed, and the body warmth when I wake up. I usually start feeling unattractive and undesirable too—mentally depressed, bored, low-energy. I lose my sense of humor."

Physical contact, "flesh to flesh, warm and tight," is tremendously important, and sex is almost the only way to get it in our culture—after we are "grown up." As one woman explained, "If I was deeply depressed, cold, lonely, even with a stranger sex could be regeneration to me. The closeness gives me a sense that I am not alone, and that life is

* On the other hand, perhaps masturbation and the certainty of orgasm at that time are related more purely to a need for release.

98

not all rough edges after all. It makes me feel loved and special." Another woman said that what she liked best about sex was "the feeling of crazy friendliness it gives, sometimes falsely. And the reassurance, however momentary, of being held. The closeness, intimacy, honesty—and after when you feel alive and happy in a way you never do at any other time."

Conclusion

Finally, what was the ultimate significance of the "sexual revolution" of the 1960s?

Although sexuality is very important, it is questionable whether it is important in and of itself, apart from its meaning in your life as a whole. The increasing emphasis on sex and personal relations as the basic source of happiness and fulfillment is a function of the lessening probability of finding even partial fulfillment through work. In the first place, most people do not have the luxury of being able to choose work that they would like to do; for most people it is a question of finding some way to support themselves as quickly and as best they can, from the very limited options available (unless you have some capital to begin with). Now, added to this, is the fact that since technology and the growth of large corporate business have taken over almost every aspect of life, most jobs have become very repetitive, impersonal, and boring. There is almost no way that most people today can hope to find any real personal fulfillment through the actual work they do. As one woman put it, "Sex* is clearly used as a universal panacea, to keep the masses quiet and stop them from realizing the emptiness, meaninglessness, and alienation of their working lives." It is interesting in this context to note that the sexual revolution came at a time when social and political unrest in the United States was a problem.

Sexuality and sexual relationships can be surrogates for (or obscure our need for) a more satisfying relationship with the larger world—for example, with work. In a way, as long as we accept this schizoid compartmentalization of public and private life, we are abrogating our moral obligation to take an active part in the direction of the

---

* In the same way that women's role has shifted from child-bearer to sex object since the decline in importance of child-bearing, just so the emphasis on personal fulfillment has shifted from family (as a larger group of people) to sexual and romantic love (whether in marriage or not).

99

larger world, and accepting an ethic of powerlessness. Meanwhile, the commercialization and trivialization of sex advances further and further into our private lives and obscures their deeper personal meaning for us. In fact, we haven't had a sexual revolution yet, but we need one.

Toward a New Female Sexuality:
A New Theory of What "Sex" Is

The Future of Intercourse: Sex as Usual?

It must have been clear throughout *The Hite Report on Female Sexuality* how tired women are of the old mechanical pattern of sexual relations, which revolves around male erection, male penetration, and male orgasm. As one woman said, "Cutting an orgasm short doesn't leave me frustrated if I'm masturbating, but I am becoming more and more short-tempered about cutting sex with my husband short just because he is satisfied. Continuing along the same unsatisfying sexual patterns expresses to me a lack of care and concern for me that I am finding unacceptable. It isn't so much cutting an orgasm short and the biological tension that results that hurts—it is an emotional hurt that frustrates me."

In answers to many different questions women mentioned their frustration and annoyance with this pattern, and many wished for something different.

"What would you like to do more often? How would you like to see the usual 'bedroom scene' changed?"
The following types of answers came up over and over again:
"I wish men would be more sensitive rather than acting like a big penis, having an orgasm and that's all. I would say that seventy-five percent of the men I have known knew nothing about a woman except that they had an orgasm and that should be a big treat to me."
"I'd like to change the whole kiss—feel—eat—eat me—fuck routine."

101

Many women felt that this mechanical approach on the part of most men reflected not only a general lack of feeling for them, but also a lack of development of the man's own sensuality and ability to enjoy his own body

"Yes, they enjoy intercourse more, but I think that's conditioning, because men feel that sex play is undignified and revealing. Actually, they can enjoy it as much as we do."

"If a man feels that way, I think of him as childish and undeveloped—he doesn't appreciate the subtleties of sex."

"Yes, men often don't know how to get into play, or just touching, and get hung up on orgasm. But they can learn."

Do women always want intercourse?

Not only were women tired of the old mechanical pattern of "foreplay," penetration, intercourse, and ejaculation, but many also found that *always* having to have intercourse, *knowing* you will have intercourse as a foregone conclusion, is mechanical and boring. If you know in advance that intercourse has to be a part of every heterosexual sexual encounter, there is almost no way the old mechanical pattern of sexual relations can be avoided, since intercourse usually leads to male orgasm, which usually signals the end of "sex." (It would be very interesting to explore whether this needs to be so.) If heterosexual relations are to be de-institutionalized, intercourse must not be a foregone conclusion, or male orgasm during intercourse as the conclusion of "sex" must not be a foregone conclusion. Women must claim the right *not* to have intercourse, *unless they want it*, even when having physical relations with a man. After all, why is it "natural" for a man to expect intercourse to orgasm with or without clitoral stimulation, but treasonable for a woman to expect clitoral stimulation to orgasm without intercourse?

In addition, the kind of change we are talking about here is much deeper than just the idea that "a woman needs an orgasm too."

"Petting," "Foreplay," and Other Pleasures

The term "foreplay" is a very strange one. *What is "foreplay"?* For me to have an orgasm, intercourse must be preceded by foreplay. But I don't like that word because it makes it sound more subordinate than it is." Well, it is common knowledge that "foreplay" is all of the body stimulation prior to, "before," intercourse. There is no "before-play" to speak of in masturbation for most women. "Be-fore" has been retained here because its meaning is so clear, but in general it is important to emphasize that there is no reason why "be-foreplay" must come "be-fore" anything.

The question of what else these activities could be called is interesting. The lack of an appropriate word for them in our language reflects the way our culture has rigidly defined the ways in which we touch each other: only activities surrounding intercourse have been considered legitimate. Thus "clitoral stimulation" and general touching is referred to only as "foreplay," which everyone "knows" precedes intercourse, and which everyone also "knows" will end in male ejaculation. In short, all our terms are geared to a linear progression: "foreplay" is to be followed by "penetration" of the penis into the vagina, and then intercourse (thrusting in and out), followed by male orgasm, and then "rest." If one does not accept this pattern as being what "sex" is, one is left with almost no vocabulary to describe what *could* be alternatives. Of course the *possibility* does exist for many different patterns of sexuality, and many different kinds of physical contact between people that are sensual/sexual, and that do not necessarily have orgasm (or anything else) as their goal.

Would women still want intercourse if they didn't feel obligated to have it? The point is not whether women in *general* would still want to have intercourse, but that it would become a choice, an option, for each *individual* woman. Whether she wanted to have intercourse or not would become her own *choice*, not something she had to do to have physical relations with a man.

Intercourse, as a pleasurable form of physical contact, will always be one of the ways people choose to relate. However, it will not continue to be the *only* way. It will become de-emphasized, one of many alternative possibilities in a whole spectrum of possible physical relations. Heterosexual intercourse is too narrow a definition to remain the only definition of sex for most people most of the time.

Of course, it can only be surmised how much of what we feel during intercourse is real physical pleasure and how much is a product of the glorification of intercourse. Most women would probably still want intercourse sometimes—especially with men for whom they had strong feelings. Some women might like intercourse almost always, while others would almost never want it. Perhaps it could be said that many women might be rather indifferent to intercourse if it were not for feelings toward a particular man.

Three women had stopped having intercourse, but continued sleeping with their partners, with varied reasons and results

"I used to like intercourse but my lovers' insistence on the pattern foreplay/fuck/sleep turned me off to intercourse. I always felt/feel pressured to fuck (are you ready yet?). I started to resent it and now I don't like fucking and I've fucked only once or twice in the past year. I like putting my foot down and trying new ways to get what I want from my lover, but it's created another block, because I've had to stop fucking out of stubbornness and not anything co-operative and mutual, and it seems like communication around this is hard for both of us. However, since I've stopped letting myself be fucked, it's been hard for my lover to ignore my sexual dissatisfaction—which was real easy for him to ignore as long as he was happy. At least now he's started to look for solutions too."

"With my boyfriend of four years, we pretty much stopped fucking, because it just wasn't worth it for me, and he doesn't want me to do it if I don't like it. What with the problems of contraception and no orgasms, it's a waste. We fucked about twice in the past four months. I feel a little guilty about not fucking my boyfriend, but I know I'm right. He still comes, and I do too, and I don't have to worry about pregnancy. It's good this way. I get mad if we fuck and I don't come (and I never have)—I feel 'frigid' and 'out of it' when my partner is ecstatic. I feel silly. I feel like a punching bag."

"I've just come home from vacation all geared up and enthusiastic about being sexually honest, and I ran into a difficulty with my boyfriend. He's been pressing me to go and get a diaphragm, and I have some kind of stigma about it. I thought it over and decided that I didn't want to make an 'official' promotion of sexual intercourse by getting something to make it always possible because I really don't *like* sexual intercourse. I told this to my boyfriend and he felt very highly insulted and made a scene and told me we'd discuss it later. We haven't discussed it yet (two days later) but I have the feeling that in order to continue seeing him there is a prerequisite that I have to have intercourse with him. This is terribly upsetting to me."

A New Kind of Intercourse

Not only are intercourse and male orgasm not necessary in every heterosexual contact, but, in addition, the manner in which intercourse is practiced can change to become more mutual and more varied. It is not necessary for intercourse to be a "male dominant" activity. Intercourse can become a varied and individual practice, which can be done in any way you might create. For example, there are many ways of joining and having intercourse besides male "penetration" and "thrusting." Intercourse need not be as gymnastic as we have usually thought, and it is probable that what we think of as the "natural," physical movements of intercourse are nothing more than "learned" responses. Isn't it possible that men have been told that "mounting and thrusting" is the "right" thing to do, but that they too, if allowed to experiment, would find many other ways they liked to have intercourse?

Although the most common position used for intercourse is the man–above–woman position, there is no physical reason why it should be better for men. As a matter of fact, Masters and Johnson have pointed out that if a man is on the bottom he can receive more orgasmic pleasure, since he is not at the same time involved in physically supporting his body, etc. Furthermore, to call male "mounting and thrusting" natural and "instinctive" is highly questionable. After all, most men masturbate *not* by thrusting but by moving their hands on their penises. What is natural?

In fact, a few women felt the man-on-top position was more political than natural, as evidenced by their replies to "Do you feel that having sex is in any way political?"

However, once again, the point is not to "reverse" the situation but to expand our ideas of what physical relations can be; there is no reason to believe that being on the top is always better than being on the bottom for all women.

Do men need intercourse?

Before we automatically react to the previous section with: "Well, what about men? Don't they *need* intercourse? Won't less intercourse mean less pleasure for men?"—let's re-examine briefly what little we know about male sexuality. There is no basis for saying that men are getting the greatest pleasure they can get from our current model of physical relations, although they are at least having orgasm. Isn't it possible that male sexuality is capable of more, and more in the way of individual variety, than men's sex magazines would have us believe? Are we sure we know what male sexuality is? Books and articles by men have started to appear that question these old stereotypes, and many men—though far too few at present—are beginning to take a fresh look at what they are getting out of their sexual relationships.

Rollo May and Marc Feigen Fasteau, among others, have written that they feel men, by concentrating on achieving orgasm and the *satisfaction* of desire, are in a way missing the whole point of sexual pleasure—which is to *prolong* the pleasure and the feeling of desire, to build it higher and higher. Rollo May:

The pleasure in sex is described by Freud and others as the reduction of tension; in eros, on the contrary, we wish not to be released from the excitement but rather to hang onto it, to bask in it, and even to increase it.

If the importance of female orgasm has been underemphasized, to say the very least, the importance of male orgasm has been greatly overexaggerated. Although orgasm is wonderful, a very large part of the pleasure is building up to the orgasm, as Fasteau wrote:

What the masculine disdain for feeling makes it hard for men to grasp is that the state of desire . . . is one of the best, perhaps *the* best, part of the experience of love.

A woman in this study said something similar to this: "My sexuality has more to do with the desire than with satisfaction. I am not interested in 'satisfaction.' I don't know what it is or why it is considered valuable. I like to be hungry for a person, to desire intimacy and understanding, to be inspired to be loving and to find reciprocation." The real pleasure of sexual relations, in this sense, then, is the prolonging and increasing of desire, not ending it or getting released from it as quickly as possible.

It was recommended in ancient Sanskrit and Hindu literature (and was actually practiced in the New York Oneida Colony, in the nineteenth century) that men could achieve the greatest pleasure by the continual maintenance of high levels of arousal, by refraining from orgasm for long periods of time.

There is no reason why the reintegration of intercourse into the whole spectrum of physical relations should threaten men. Men too can profit by opening up and re-examining their conception of what sexuality is.

Resisting the myth of male "need"

Suppose men won't cooperate in redefining intercourse, or in leaving it out sometimes? What if they still try to follow the same old mechanical pattern of sexual relations? There is no reason why women must help men during intercourse. The fact is, we usually cooperate quite extensively during intercourse in order for the man to be able to orgasm. We move along with his rhythm, keep our legs apart and our bodies in positions that make penetration and thrusting possible, and almost never stop intercourse in midstream unless the man has had his orgasm. We do not *have* to cooperate in these ways with a man if he will not cooperate with us.

Although we do not *have* to, we are taught that if we are anything but helpful (or at least non-interfering) during intercourse, it is tantamount to castrating the man. This is nonsense. Our noncooperation with men in sex is no worse than their noncooperation with us—for example, their using clitoral stimulation as a "foreplay" technique, and withdrawing the stimulation just before orgasm. It is perfectly all right for us to follow the example of one woman who said, "I feel quite confident about ending sexual activity in midstream if it is not working out, or if I begin to drift or feel disinterested." As another woman advised, "Try to get what *you* want and do what *you* feel. (Don't be afraid to act on your most basic, secret, and ultra-secret desires.) If you are not enjoying it in the midst of sex, *say* so. Ladies, you don't have to do anything you don't feel like doing!"

And another woman: "I spent most of my adult life doing what I 'ought'—and having an awful time. It was only when I broke out of that, fairly recently, that sex began to mean anything to me, or feel like anything. And I got no help from the popular culture, or from psychoanalysis, or indeed from anything except something a friend chanced to say, and the women's movement. I would advise women to look to their *own* hearts and bodies, and follow them wherever *they* lead."

Stepping Outside Patriarchal Culture to See How Sexuality Could Be Different★

Touching is Sex Too

Feelings about physical closeness

Besides changing the inevitability and manner of intercourse, what other changes did women emphasize they would like to see in physical relations? One of the most basic changes involves valuing touching and closeness just for their own sakes—rather than only as a prelude to intercourse or orgasm.

"In the best of all possible worlds, sex would be a way of being close, of communing with another person. This would not necessarily mean that we would all have sexual experiences with more people or that I, for example, would be running around bedding down with all our male acquaintances. It might even make it possible for me to have the closeness and affection I need *without* having it lead, inevitably, to sexual intercourse. Perhaps if we all had more people we related to with physical affection and touching, we'd have a generally more loving atmosphere in which to dwell; we wouldn't necessarily feel that every contact points in the direction of intercourse . . . a warning and yet somehow commanding finger . . . so that you don't feel free to take Step A unless you are willing to take Step B, C, D, etc."

"Does having good sex have anything to do with having orgasms?"
Women often said, in answer to this and to many other questions, how much more important body contact and closeness were to them than orgasms per se in sex with a partner. This *could* be accepted purely at face value; however, since women do masturbate for orgasms it is clear that orgasms are also very important to women. The truth is that both

★ See also "The Politics of Intercourse" on page 206.

orgasms *and* close body contact or touching are extremely important to women,* but they have often been forced to get them in separate ways. The important point to realize in reading the answers below is how important touching and body contact are and how undervalued they have been in our model of physical relations.

"I have intense orgasms during masturbation, but intercourse involves a sort of emotional as well as physical satisfaction being with the man I love. Just from the point of view of having an orgasm, masturbation can be just as satisfying, but the rest of my body isn't always satisfied. I still want the rest of my body to be touched and kissed and to feel a warm man next to me."

"Closeness with another person is more important to me than orgasm (which I can have by myself, if necessary). If I had to *choose* between the two, I'd choose touching. I really dig kissing, hugging, fondling, looking at, and feeling the other person."

"Best are the long tender hours of stimulating each other and relaxing before orgasm, then starting again, talking, petting. It is extremely important to me to have this much body contact, and I also like sensual touch games—wrestling is great, and dancing nude and sexy, and also just 'immature cuddling.' A previous lover told me I'd taught him lovemaking was seventy-five percent touching and twenty-five percent intercourse."

"I like to neck on the floor, fully clothed, to music—and play silly games pretending this and that, feeling utterly abandoned!"

"There's something very warm and intimate and very beautiful about lying in the dark with someone, holding them close and talking softly. Frankly, I enjoy it more right now than genital sex, but that could be due to my rather limited experience."

"Sex itself is not terribly important to me, but physical contact in the form of touching, hugs, embraces, caresses, etc. is most important. I am more interested in having that kind of physical contact than sex."

"I *do* feel very strongly that keeping in physical, real physical *touch*, flesh to flesh, with another, or with other human beings, is absolutely necessary to keeping healthy: sane. I *know* that for me it is. That's why I do feel that 'there's more to sex than that,' only nobody's found ways (no biological stain, or recording device) yet to *see* what the effects are of sex, mating, fucking, touching, all that physical stuff—on the people who do

---

*Many other answers to this question did reflect a militancy about getting orgasm, not represented in these quotes. For example: "Having fabulously outrageous sex has to do with having orgasms for me. I *can* have a wonderful sexual experience without orgasm if I am very high emotionally. But sooner or later I feel that I am missing out unless my partner learns to bring me to orgasm."

it together. I feel that there may be subtle neural and chemical interactions set in motion in each partner's body by direct physical contact with the other partner."

The overwhelming number of answers received to this question were just like these; desire for more touching and body contact was more or less universal.

Sometimes it has been implied that petting is "immature"—something people do only when they aren't able to "go all the way." This is not true. Petting has been a major form of sexuality from time immemorial, but, once again, it was condemned in the Judeo-Christian codes unless it was an adjunct to intercourse, and continues in this status up to the present.

Other mammals also engage in a lot of petting and "making out," as Kinsey pointed out:

Among most species of mammals there is, in actuality, a great deal of sex play which never leads to coitus. Most mammals, when sexually aroused, crowd together and nuzzle and explore with their noses, mouths, and feet over each other's bodies. They make lip-to-lip contacts and tongue-to-tongue contacts, and use their mouths to manipulate every part of the companion's body, including the genitalia. . . . The student of mammalian mating behavior, interested in observing coitus in his animal stocks, sometimes may have to wait through hours and days of sex play before he has an opportunity to observe actual coitus, if, indeed, the animals do not finally separate without ever attempting a genital union.

There is no reason why we should not create as many different degrees and kinds of sex as we want—whether or not they lead to orgasm, and whether or not they are genital. If the definition of sexual pleasure is sustaining desire and building arousal higher and higher—not ending it—many possibilities for physical pleasure and for exciting another person open up. The truth is that "sex" is bigger than orgasm and involves any kind of deep physical intimacy one shares with another person. Intense physical contact is one of the most satisfying activities possible—in and of itself.

"In the best of all possible worlds, what would sexuality be like?"

"Sexuality would become just a simple joy and recognition of one's sexual feelings and from there letting all humans define their sexuality as is most comfortable for them at any given time, in any given situation. 'Sexuality' would become an integral part of being, greatly varied and personalized, part of life as a *whole.*"

"Sex would be more nourishing. Self to self, self to others—lots of warmth and involvement and love and touching on all possible levels as a natural expression of body and emotions. Babies, children, pets, old, young, everyone would be cuddled and fondled, touched and encouraged to do so to and for each other and themselves. There would be public rejoicing in the pleasure of affection and the human body."

What kinds of touching do women like?

Sleeping together

"My lover and I are very physical with each other although we don't have sex very often. We sleep naked and intertwined together every night, we shower together and kiss and hug, pat and touch, bite, etc. all the time."

"I really like touching, sleeping next to, and waking up the next morning with the person still there. Holding them. I have slept with two of my close friends like this, and it was wonderful."

"Touching is very important. I sleep cuddled up with my best friend and have for six years, although we do not participate in sexual behavior. (That is her decision, not mine.)"

"I love to embrace and touch completely. I love to curl up back to front together in bed. I intensely enjoy sleeping with my little girl, cuddling with her, stroking her back or her mine."

Pressing together★

"Lying pressed together is a wonderful feeling—a kind of body to body embrace. I like to lie in this position, bodies touching all around, kind of mushing."

"My favorite: deep kissing and pressing of bodies together full length with arms holding tight. Opening my whole mouth to the other person and vice versa."

"I get this kind of swelling feeling in my chest, a feeling like I will

★ Why isn't there any word for this, when it is one of the most important physical activities there is? Full-length body-to-body contact, so important to over-all gratification.

burst with emotion and feeling—and a desire to press them to me and myself to them so tightly—"

"I love it when my husband presses me up against him *real tight*, squeezing me all against him. I like to wrap him up in my body, bury my nose in him, wrestle, kiss, and fuck."

"Until a few years ago, I experienced desire separate from sexual desire: it was an intolerable burning sensation in my chest rather than in my genitals."

"What is most stimulating to me is the closeness of the entire other person. If I can feel any separateness or separation of us, it reduces the excitement. Pressure is the single most important arousal element—generalized, dull (i.e., not sharp), rhythmic pressure. This gets me really excited, and my nipples, clitoris, and genital area go crazy for it. If it keeps up like that, I will have an orgasm."

"Merely lying on top of a desired person will bring me extremely close to orgasm. The only thing required is body movement."

"I like the total immersion of body and mind—if it were possible for the entire surface of my body to be simultaneously very lightly stroked, slow probing kisses all over, tender yet firm—hugging our bodies together and rubbing."

"I like to get in bed and hold each other, flesh to flesh, warm and tight."

"The embrace, which involves the whole body, is important to me. Having my naked body lying against the naked body of my partner—especially my full front touching my partner's full front."

PART THREE

The Hite Report on Men and Male Sexuality

1981

The Ideological Construction of "Male Sexuality" and "Male Psychology"

Research Questionnaire for Men, 1974–1981

Research for this book was done from 1974 to 1981: the following questionnaire was used from 1979 to 1981.

The purpose of this questionnaire is to better understand how men feel about their lives. Since so many of our society's ideas about who men are and who men should be (perhaps made most explicit in "sex") are so stereotyped, it is hard to know what men as individual human beings really feel.

It means so much to us that you will answer, and perhaps help us develop a more positive and caring way of relating to one another.

The results will be published as an extended discussion of the replies, including many quotes, in the same format as *The Hite Report on Female Sexuality*. The replies are anonymous, so don't sign your answers.

It is NOT necessary to answer every single question. Answer only those which interest you, because otherwise you may not have the time to finish. But *please* answer!

We are looking forward to hearing from you. Send answers to S. Hite, F.D.R. Station, Box 5282, New York, New York 10022, U.S.A. THANK YOU.

I. TIME

1. What is the earliest sexual experience you can remember? How old were you?

2. How old were you when you first masturbated? To orgasm? How did you learn—by yourself, from someone else, or from books or movies?

3. At what age did you first orgasm? First ejaculate? Did you

115

orgasm before you were old enough to ejaculate? Did you get intense pleasurable feelings from touching yourself? Have wet dreams?

4. Were you told about sex by your parents? What did they tell you? What did your friends tell you? What did you first hear about menstruation?

5. What were your sexual feelings as you grew up? In childhood? In grade school? In high school?

6. Do you think childhood or teenage sexuality should be repressed? Why or why not? Why *is* it repressed?

7. How has your sex life changed over the years? Does age affect sex? Has your enjoyment of sex changed? Have your attitudes and activities changed?

8. How big a part do sports and exercise play in your overall feeling of physical well-being and pleasure? What sports and exercise do you like? Swimming? Football? Running? Other?

9. How big a part do activities like sunbathing, cuddling up in a bathrobe on the couch, sleeping next to someone's warm body, petting your animals, etc., play in your overall bodily joy? What do you like especially?

10. How big a part does what we generally call "sex" (genital sex) play? Masturbation?

11. How big a part does talking to friends play in your overall feeling of well-being? Do you ever tell your friends how much you care about them?

12. Does home and/or family life play a part in your overall feeling of physical well-being? (This includes *everyone*, of course, not just those who are married.)

13. Do you enjoy touching and holding children? Do you enjoy snuggling with them? Wrestling? Giving them baths? Holding them? Rocking them? Feeding them?

14. Have you ever wished you could be a mother? How did you feel when you found out you couldn't bear children? How did you find out? How do you feel about it now?

15. What do you think of the role of being a father (whether or not you are a father)?

16. Do you enjoy physically caring for another human being, whether child or adult? How do you do it? Do you baby them? Is it fun? Were you prepared by your parents to nurture others?

17. Have you found the warmth and closeness in your life that you want? Where?

18. Would you like more time to yourself?

19. How do you feel about privacy in the bathroom? Do you close the door? Do you sometimes like for your partner to be in the bathroom with you during urination or defecation? Do you like to see your partner urinating, etc.?

II. MASCULINITY

20. What is your age and your background—occupation, education, upbringing, religion, and race, or anything else you consider important?

21. What do you look like? Do you consider yourself handsome, pretty plain, ugly—or no comment? (Please forgive these words!)

22. How would you define masculinity? Are you masculine? How masculine are you?

23. What is the difference between masculine and "macho"? How high or low would you rate yourself on the "macho" scale?

24. What qualities make a man a man? That is, what qualities do you admire in men? Are you proud of your masculinity?

25. What did your father tell you about how to be a man? What did he tell you about women?

26. How can a man distinguish himself today? What is heroic in our time?

27. What can men as a group be proud of today? Ashamed of?

28. What is your biggest worry or problem in general in your life?

29. Is success important? Are you successful? In what way?

30. Do you believe in being ruthless when you have to?

31. Do you often feel hurt or sad when you don't show it? Do you force yourself to behave like a robot? Do you ever *feel* like a robot?

32. How would you feel if you were described as having some-thing—anything—about your behavior or views that was "like a woman's"?

33. Were you ever called a "sissy"? Told to "be a man!"? What was the occasion? How did you feel?

34. Do you envy women's freedom to be gentle or emotional, or to have a temper? Do you envy them the choice of having someone support them, or the seeming lack of pressure on them to make money?

35. Do you have any strong resentments against women, or against ways any women have hurt you?

36. Are there ways in which you feel guilty for how you have behaved toward women, or toward a woman in particular?

37. Do you look at pornography? What kind? Did your father read pornography when you were growing up? Where/when did you see your first "men's magazine"?

38. What is your opinion of pornography you have seen? Do you feel it represents certain elemental truths about how men and women really are—both psychologically and sexually?

39. What do you think of the "sexual revolution"?

40. What do you think of women's liberation? How has it affected your relationships?

41. What do males need from females? What do you get from women that you don't get from men?

42. Do you have more male or female friends? Why?

III. RELATIONSHIPS

43. Do you prefer sex with women, men, or either—or with yourself, or perhaps not at all?

44. Do you think sex is important, or is it overrated? Is it interesting or is too much made of it? What other things in life are more important?

45. Does sex have a spiritual significance for you?

46. Answer *one* of the following:

A. *If you are married*, how many years have you been married? Do you like being married? Why did you get married originally? What is the effect on sex?

Do you love your wife? In what sense? Does she orgasm with you? From what stimulation? If you masturbate, does she know?

Do you believe in monogamy? Why or why not? Have you had/do you have "extramarital" sexual experiences? If so, how many and how long? Are you having one now? What was/is the effect on you as an individual and on your marriage? Did/does your partner know about them?

If you have children, why did you decide to have them? Did you want to be a father? How did you feel when your wife first told you you were having a baby? Do you love your children?

Do you feel you had to give up some things in order to be married and/or have children? Did being married/having children circumscribe your job and career opportunities? How would your life have been different?

B. *If you are divorced*, what are the reasons? How do you feel about it? Also please answer any of the questions above which apply.

C. *If you are homosexual*, please answer any of the previous questions that may apply to you and also: How long have you had physical and emotional relationships with men? How do they compare with relationships with women, if you have had any? Emotionally and physically? Are you involved with more than one man? Do you want to, or do you, live permanently with one man?

D. *If you are "single,"* do you enjoy being single? What are the advantages and disadvantages? Do you plan to marry eventually? What is your sex life like?

E. *If you are still living at home with parents or family*, what rules are set up concerning your sexual and dating activities? Would you like more or less restrictions? Have your parents or relatives discussed sex realistically with you? Where have you gotten most of your knowledge of sex? From friends? Teachers? Books? Sex magazines? Family? Have you had problems getting accurate information on sex? If you have had a sexual relationship, do your parents know? If so, how did they react?

F. *If you have not yet had sex with a partner*, what do you imagine it will be like? Does it interest you, or does too much seem to be made of it? What physical activities have you enjoyed so far?

G. *If you are living with someone*, please answer any of the questions above which apply, and also how long have you been living with them? Would you rather be married? What are your plans for the future?

H. *If you are currently uninterested in sex* (except perhaps for masturbation), how do you like this way of life? How long do you plan to remain "celibate"? How long have you felt this way? Do you think this could be beneficial to other men? Do you find you relate more to nature or your pets or music when you are living alone?

47. Perhaps you do not feel that any of these categories describe your life. If so, please describe yourself in your own way.

LOVE

48. Describe the time you fell the most deeply in love. How did it feel? What happened?

49. Did you ever cry yourself to sleep because of problems with someone you loved? Contemplate suicide? Why?

50. What was the happiest you ever were with someone? The closest? When were you the loneliest?

51 How do your friendships compare with your love relationships?

52 Do you feel you can truly love someone?

53. What are your deepest longings for a relationship with another person?

IV. ORGASM

54. How important are orgasms to you? Can you enjoy sex without an orgasm? Can you enjoy sex if your partner does not have an orgasm?

55. Please describe what an orgasm feels like to you—during the buildup? Before orgasm? During the climax? After? Which moment feels best? How does the very best moment feel?

56. How often *do* you have sex without orgasm? Do you ever feel pressured to have orgasms? If so, when?

57. How does your body react when you are having an orgasm? Tighten up? Move a lot? Stop moving? Go out of control? What happens to your arms and legs? Your face?

58. Do you always ejaculate when you orgasm? How often do you orgasm or experience a sensation close to orgasm without ejaculating? Do you sometimes ejaculate without experiencing orgasm? How often? Or does orgasm *mean* ejaculation? Did you orgasm as a boy before you started ejaculating?

59. Do you have more than one orgasm during sex? Do you ejaculate each time? How do successive orgasms feel? Have you ever continued on to a second orgasm without losing your erection?

60. Is erection necessary for sexual arousal? Have you ever felt sexual without an erection? Did it bother you not to have an erection? What was your partner's reaction?

61. Is it O.K. to have sex with a soft penis? Are you embarrassed to continue sex with a soft penis if you don't have an erection?

62. Are you always aroused when you have an erection, or are there other causes of erection?

63. Do you like feeling aroused for extended periods of time, or do you prefer to go on to orgasm relatively quickly? Could you describe what arousal feels like?

V. MASTURBATION

64. How often do you masturbate? How do you feel about it? Are you pleased? ashamed? satisfied? Are you secretive or open about it?

65. Do you enjoy masturbation? Physically? Emotionally? What do you find satisfying and unsatisfying about masturbation?

66. How do you masturbate? Please give a detailed description. For example, do you hold your penis with your hand and move your hand on your penis, or do you move your whole body—rubbing against something? Is stimulation important at the top or bottom of your penis? Do you mind the wetness of ejaculation? Is there any specific position you like to be in? Are there specific thoughts or fantasies you use?

67. Can you delay your orgasm during masturbation? Does this make it more or less exciting? What specific ways do you use to delay your orgasm?

68. Do you always want an orgasm when you masturbate? Do you ever stop short of orgasm when you masturbate to heighten your sexual feelings? Do you masturbate (but not to orgasm) to arouse yourself before sex? How often?

69. What is the importance of masturbation in your life?

VI. YOUR BODY AND YOUR FEELINGS

70. Do you like the way your genitals look, taste, and smell? Do you like the size and shape of your genitals? Your balls?

71. Are you circumcised? Do you like it, or wish you weren't? Did you, or would you, have your son circumcised?

72. What were your feelings when you found out about circumcision? About your own circumcision? Were you shocked? Pleased? Do you have a physical reaction in your genitals when you think about it?

73. Do you remember anything about the procedure? How old were you?

74. Has circumcision affected your attitude about exposing your penis to others? How? Does having or not having a foreskin affect your sexual activities?

75. Why are men circumcised?

76. Does your partner like your genitals? Has a partner ever commented adversely about your genitals? How? How did you feel about this?

77. Do you like fellatio (oral stimulation of your penis)? Can you orgasm this way always, usually, sometimes, rarely, or never? How often *do* you orgasm this way? How do you like it to be done?

78. Do you like mouth-anal contact?

79. Do you like manual stimulation of your penis by your partner? Do you often orgasm this way? What other parts of your genital area do you like your partner to touch?

80. Do you enjoy masturbating with another person present? Do you like having your partner masturbate him/herself when with you?

81. Do you like (or would you like) to be rectally penetrated? By a finger? By a penis? How does it feel? Do you orgasm this way? Exactly what does anal intercourse feel like—both physically and emotionally?

82. Do you like "foreplay"? What kind of "foreplay" is important to you for *yourself*? How do you like to be touched, and where? Kissed? Petted? Are your breasts sensitive? Your buttocks? Your testicles? Your mouth? Your ears?

83. Do you get enough foreplay from your partner? Does your partner touch and fondle *you* enough?

84. Do you sometimes like making out without having "real sex"? Do you prefer it?

85. Who makes the initial sexual advance? How do you feel if the other person makes the advance? Have you ever wanted the other person to make the advance and not gotten it? Do you feel unloved if your partner never makes the advance? Unwanted?

86. Have you ever approached someone about sex and been refused? How did you feel? Have you ever refused someone else? Why?

87. Are there certain times when you're not interested in sex? Is it O.K. to be celibate? Do you experience periodic highs and lows in your sexual interest? How often?

VII. FEELINGS ABOUT MEN

88. Describe your best male friend. What do you like about spending time with him?

89. Do you belong to, or socialize with, a group of men? What do you enjoy/like about it? What do you do? What do you talk about?

90. Do you value your men friends? Is it important to have male friends—or relatives you are close to? What do you value about their friendship? What do they mean in your life?

91. Were you in the Army or another branch of the military? Did you

like the camaraderie? Did you have any close physical or sexual experiences with men during this time?

92. Do you like sports? Which kinds? Do you enjoy participating in sports with other men? Do you like the closeness with men in these activities?

93. Did you have a best friend in high school or college? What were your feelings for him?

94. Are you or were you close to your father? In what way? What was/is he like? What do you think of him?

95. Describe the man you are or were closest to in your life. In what ways are/were you close? Do/did you spend time together? Why is he valuable to you? Why do you like him?

96. If you have not had a physical or sexual relationship with another man, would you enjoy one?

SEX WITH MEN

97. How old were you when you had your first gay experience?

98. What was the first time you ever had physical contact with a man? Your father? A relative?

99. How is sex with men different from sex with women (if you have had sex with women, or based on what you think it would be like)?

100. What are your favorite things about sex with men? Why would you recommend homosexuality to other men? What are the advantages? Disadvantages?

101. Do you like anal intercourse? Exactly what does it feel like—both physically and emotionally? Do you orgasm this way?

102. Do you like giving a man fellatio? Do you swallow the seminal fluid? Do you like it?

103. Can you orgasm from just lying down together and kissing and rubbing crotches together?

104. Are you in love? In a steady relationship? How many men in your life have you had a sexual relationship with? Do you like monogamy?

105. Is gay "promiscuity" a myth or a reality? Do you prefer emotional closeness or casual sex or both?

106. Would you ever fall in love with a woman (again)? Why or why not?

107. Do people at work know you are gay? Do your parents?

108. Would you take an open stand on gay issues? Are you working for gay liberation? Or do you prefer the adventure of being gay in a straight world, the pleasure of belonging to a secret, elite society?

VIII. FEELINGS ABOUT WOMEN

109. Do you have any close women friends? A sister you are close to?

110. Are you or were you close to your mother? In what way? What was she like? What did you think of her?

111. What things about women in general do you admire? Dislike? What do women contribute to society?

112. What do you think about women's liberation?

113. Are you currently in a relationship with a woman? What is she like? Why do you like her?

SEX WITH WOMEN

114. Has any woman discussed sex and her sexual feelings seriously and openly with you? Did you ask?

115. When did you first learn about the clitoris? What did you hear from other men? From women? From books?

116. Do you like giving clitoral stimulation? Why or why not? When did you first do it? To orgasm? How did it feel? Do you feel comfortable now giving clitoral stimulation?

117. What kind of clitoral stimulation do you give? Please describe how you do it. Describe how you stimulate the clitoris with your hand or finger. Do you do this to orgasm?

118. Does your partner masturbate you to orgasm? How does she do it? If you don't know, would you like her to share that information with you?

119. When did you first hear/realize that most women don't orgasm from intercourse (coitus) alone? What was your original reaction?

120. Do you enjoy cunnilingus with a woman? What do you most dislike about it? Does it depend on your feelings for your partner?

121. Do you get sexually excited by stimulating your partner? Do you enjoy her orgasm? Physically? Emotionally? What aspects of touching, feeling, and kissing your partner(s) do you enjoy most? Least?

122. How do you give the woman an orgasm? Do you prefer the woman to orgasm from coitus?

IX. INTERCOURSE

123. Do you like intercourse (penis/vagina)? Physically? Emotionally? How often do you have intercourse?

124. What position is most satisfying to you? Is this position all right with your partner? What position does she like? Do you like this position?

125. Why do you like intercourse?

126. Do you ever experience physical discomfort during intercourse? Afterwards? Do you ever experience boredom during intercourse?

127. After sex has begun, do you assume intercourse is expected next? Do you assume that every time you have sex, it will include intercourse?

128. Would you be willing to replace intercourse with other activities during some sexual encounters? How often? Or do you *always* want to define sex as intercourse?

129. Does your partner orgasm during sex with you always, usually, sometimes, rarely, or never? During intercourse? During other activities? Which ones?

130. Can you always tell if your partner has an orgasm? How can you tell? Are you ever in doubt? If in doubt, do you ask? If you ask and she says "yes," do you believe her? Do you talk about it?

131. Would you prefer to have sex with a woman who has orgasm from intercourse (coitus) rather than from clitoral stimulation?

When does/do the woman/women you have sex with usually orgasm?

132. How do you feel if a woman stimulates herself to orgasm with you? During intercourse? How do you feel if she uses a vibrator?

133. Do you feel there is something wrong with your "performance," technique, or sensitivity if the woman does not orgasm from intercourse itself? That you're "not *man* enough," or at least that you did not do it right?

134. Does it matter to you if a woman orgasms during sex with you? Do you try to find out what stimulation an individual woman needs to have an orgasm?

135. Who usually orgasms first? You or the woman? During which activity? Do you orgasm when you want to? If not, why?

136. Has a woman ever expressed anxiety or been apologetic to you about how long she takes to orgasm or become ready for intercourse?

137. How do you feel if your partner does not have an orgasm at all, in any way?

138. Can you control when you come to a climax? How long can you hold off without losing your erection? Does it disturb you to lose your erection?

139. Are you embarrassed to have sex with a soft penis (i.e., if you don't get an erection)? Do you stop physical closeness and other activities if you can't have intercourse?

140. Do you ever ejaculate or orgasm "too soon" during intercourse? How long are you talking about? Is this ejaculation/orgasm satisfying to you? When does this happen? Why? Does it bother you?

141. Do you use any particular method to have intercourse longer without orgasming? Does prolonged thrusting dull the sensitivity or feeling of your penis?

142. When should a man ejaculate? Should the woman be consulted? Who decides when sex is over?

143. Do you control which activities sex consists of? Do you control when you come and how you have an orgasm?

144. Do you sometimes have difficulty having an erection at a time you

desire one? When? Why? How often does it happen? What do you do at such times?

145. Do you talk to other men about sex? What do you talk about? Do you or other men tend to brag or exaggerate your exploits with women? Do you share practical information (how-to)? Feelings of insecurity?

146. What are the reasons why many women traditionally have not wanted sex as much as men? What kind of sex do women want most?

X. BIRTH CONTROL

147. What contraceptive methods (birth control) do you use? Who decides what contraception will be used? Which kind do you prefer?

148. Are you aware of the possible side effects of the birth control pill?

149. Have you ever experienced physical discomfort from any form of birth control? Condom? The diaphragm? IUD? Foam? Have you ever used a condom to delay orgasm?

150. Do you feel responsible for discussing birth control before intercourse? If you are having a sexual relationship with a woman, do you protect her from becoming pregnant? Who is responsible if she does become pregnant? Do you ask a woman if she has taken measures to prevent conception before intercourse?

151. Do you fear impregnating someone? Does the possibility of pregnancy cause you problems in a sexual relationship?

152. Have you ever been a party to an unwanted pregnancy? What did you do about it?

153. Are you in favor of abortion? Have you ever impregnated a woman who subsequently had an abortion? Have you ever been involved in helping a woman secure an abortion? Did you share the expenses? Go with her? What was the outcome?

154. Do you have a vasectomy? (Do you have children?) How has having a vasectomy affected your sexual activities? What do your partners think about it? Have you ever wished to have it reversed? Would you recommend it to other men?

155. Do you know what vasectomy involves? Would you be willing to get one, and under what circumstances?

156. Have you ever witnessed childbirth?

XI. VIOLENCE

157. Are you interested in violent sex? Has violence been part of a sexual relationship you had? What kind? How did you feel about it?

158. Have you ever been excited by a physical struggle or combat, or a fight—with a man or woman? Please describe.

159. Have you ever deliberately struck or hurt your lover? Why? What effect did it have on the relationship? Did you feel good when you did it?

160. Are you interested in bondage? Spanking? Why or why not? How does it feel?

161. Is it fun to force someone to your will?

162. Do you find kissing feet sexual? Golden showers?

163. Would you or have you had a sexual relationship with a very young person? How did you feel about it?

164. How do you define rape? Is it disturbing to you? How? How not? Where do you draw the line between consent and rape?

165. Have you ever raped a woman? If not, have you ever *wanted* to rape a woman? Why?

166. Have you ever pressured a woman to have sex with you, when she didn't seem to want to? How did you do it? Did you have a line? Did it succeed? Did you enjoy sex?

167. Is being forceful with your partner fun for you in sex? Do you usually control your partner during sexual activities? How do you develop the sexual relationship in the direction you desire? Is it easy to remain in charge of the situation?

168. If there is a power relationship involved in sex, who has the most power—you or your partner?

169. Is sex political?

A. Why did you answer this questionnaire?

B. Did you read *The Hite Report on Female Sexuality*?

C. Do you think other men will be as honest as you were in answering this questionnaire? How honest were you?

D. Please add anything you would like to say that was not mentioned.

E. Are you happy with your life, or do you want to change it?

The Creation of Male Psychology

Growing Up Male

"I used to go hunting with my dad for four or five years, during my boyhood. Unfortunately, I have always been a very poor marksman (my hands shake too much). I gave up hunting after an incident in which my dad and I were duck hunting in a boat with some other men. I had just brought down a duck, and we paddled the boat over to pick it up. As we reached it, I was astonished and delighted to find it still alive and looking well. It seemed so cute and attractive I envisioned taking it home with me, nursing it back to health, and keeping it for a pet. One of the men picked it up and proceeded to beat its brains out over the side of the boat."

The tragedy of the father/son relationship

"All the time I was growing up, it was funny—I was closer to my mother than my father, she was the one who was more loving—but I knew it was my father's opinion of me that counted, it was his approval that I really wanted. Why? I don't know. But I'm still that way, in a sense: I love my wife, very much, and we are happy together—but to be really happy, I want more than anything to be part of the world of men and to be recognized by other men as a man and successful."

In a very real sense, relationships between men are "what matters" to men in a patriarchal society—even more so than male–female relations. Men look to other men for approval, acceptance, validation, and respect. Men see other men as the arbiters of what is real, the guardians of wisdom, the holders and wielders of power.

But are men able to be close to each other in our society? What do men learn from their fathers about being men? Paradoxically, even though men regard one another as "who is important" most are afraid to become too close. "Feelings" for other men are supposed to be expressed only casually, and should not go beyond admiration and respect. Thus, men's relationships with one another tend to be based on an acceptance of mutually understood roles and positions, a belonging to the group, rather than on intimate personal discussion of the details of their individual lives and feelings. As one man put it, "We are comrades more than friends." Our culture simultaneously glorifies and severely limits men's relationships, even relationships between fathers and sons. Still, men often feel a deep sense of affinity and comradeship with other men.

When asked, "Are you or were you close to your father? When you were a child, were you physically close (affectionate)?" almost no men said they had been or were close to their fathers:

"He was always busy. He was a quiet man of few words, though extremely witty, and articulate—and very loving and affectionate, which slowly disappeared as I got older to eventually become a formal, stiff, cold relationship."

"Not particularly. We played sports, talked politics. I can talk to him about nonpersonal subjects, but we are not personally close."

Most men were not able to talk to their fathers:

"He is a very quiet and simple man, I guess the fact that he is quiet never allowed me to talk to him as much as I would have liked. As a child we were pretty close because he did things with me that I enjoyed, like baseball, football, etc. We would pass time together rather than talk."

"I've never said anything important to my father."

Even physical relationships with their fathers as very young children seemed to have been off limits to many men; when asked whether they had been physically close to their fathers as children, very few could remember being carried or cuddled by their fathers—although they often remembered being spanked or punished.

Some men described wanting more affection:

"During my childhood, my relationships with my parents were unpredictable and insecure. I always felt that my father wanted me continually to prove my feelings and loyalty, but I felt that I couldn't rely on my parents to come through for me. I think that I learned early that boys don't show affection, and hence stopped being affectionate with my mother also at an early age. Now I see physical affection as a sign of assurance, trust, etc.—the opposite of unreliability. But I feel uncomfortable with it, I'm afraid to reach out and give it—I think it looks inappropriate, too feminine, silly. Maybe this is why I don't connect sex with feelings much—it seems too nerve-racking and I don't feel comfortable with it."

These were some of the saddest stories I have ever heard from men:

the poignant tone of missing something, longing for something—a deeply lonely feeling—emerged in man after man. Surprisingly most said that there had been no father–son talks; that they had learned only from example and disapproval or condemnation and ridicule when they did something "wrong." As one put it, "We didn't do much together, he said I played baseball like a girl."

Most also had not spent a lot of time doing things with their fathers: "We did not really attend sports events together or play much except to kick a soccer ball around occasionally. Because of the nature of his business, we were not able to spend much time together except when we were on vacation . . . I don't remember much about those trips."

One man said what was probably true for many: "I discovered the male role more from watching James Cagney, Humphrey Bogart, and James Bond than from my father. At least, a male as I would *like* to be."

Thus, the testing grounds for masculine identity, according to men in the study, are:

1. Most men said there had been great pressure on them as boys to be interested in and participate in sports, and compete with other boys in physical strength—competitive type sports.
2. There was also pressure to have "made it" sexually—penetrated a girl!
3. On the other hand, there was pressure not to play with or associate with girls, not to have girls as "friends."
4. Hunting was another testing ground of "masculinity" or toughness.
5. Fraternities and clubs also often involved initiation ceremonies designed to test "manhood"—to see if the applicant could withstand humiliation or "teasing."

One man probably articulated what many men had missed and longed for, when he said, "I think a relationship between a father and son is one of the most, if not THE most, important in society today. Yet it is probably the most troubled. A father/son relationship must not be fraught with hatred and a tense tyrant–subject relationship; this will ultimately destroy one or the other or both. It must be a wide open relationship in which the man will give of himself and of his love so that his son will become the man he wants to become."

It is impossible not to sympathize with men as they describe their childhoods, filled with the pain of trying to conform to the male role, which demanded complete obedience, strength (or the appearance of it), intense competition, success, and control. This usually was taught by a father who seemed very distant, due to his *own* attempt to comply with the stereotypical male role, which pictures the father as always stable, never showing "weakness" (i.e., feelings), or "burdening" his family with his worries. As one man put it, "My father told me: work hard, never complain, and don't spend all your time with your mother. If I cried, he was humiliated and told me to be a man—or go to my room and stay there until I got control of myself. Other than that, I hardly knew him."

Masculinity and Gender Conformity

The main lesson boys learn about how to be male is to stay in control—especially of emotions, but also of information, of friendliness, not to be too effusive, to keep a cynical eye peeled for others' motives, to look out for number one. A man should look, act and behave like other men.

"Men should not hurt, cry, openly display affection, or react to emotion in another. I feel embarrassed when someone shows strong or tender emotions. I feel embarrassed for him."

Boys brought up to be "tough" and not show pain or be emotional often continue to cover over feelings later in life. Most men say they did cover over feelings especially of pain or frustration—or even great happiness or enthusiasm—lest they be teased:

"I was raised to conceal my actual emotions and to display whatever emotion I believed was most appropriate, to maintain or achieve control of a social situation. Since age forty I have been learning to kick the habit."

"Men are trained at an early age to disregard any and every emotion, and *be strong*. You take someone like that and they wonder why they don't and can't express feelings. Not only that, they are supposed to be a cross between John Wayne, the Chase Manhattan Bank, and Hugh Hefner. We are only human, for christsake."

Strangely (or perhaps not so strangely) most men never quite feel they match these rules: the majority of men, when asked their opinion on any topic, will soon respond, "But don't ask me, I'm not really typical, so my opinion may not be valuable or valid." Although on one level most men accept traditional definitions of masculinity, on another they doubt whether they can ever completely "measure up."

Underneath the outward conformity necessary for personal survival (in most cases), there often lurks a man who feels he is not really quite "what a man should be."

Some men, when asked how they would define masculinity, expressed a kind of rebellion against the rules:

"They say masculinity is someone who thinks he is superior to the opposite sex. That masculinity is easily defined by muscle, or masculinity is someone who never cries, is always tough. Let's face it, I'm so full of the 'masculinity' crap, it is sickening. I consider myself 1/4 masculine, 1/4 feminine (oh, if those jocks could hear me now), and 1/2 fighting for something in between. I cry when I feel like it, yet there is pressure to not cry ('Young men don't cry'), but then I tell myself, the hell with everyone else, I feel sad and crying is the only way. The other part of me says, 'Boy, you are a real sissy crying, you are showing a weak character.' The other part (feminine) says, 'Who ever claimed that if a man cries, he is weak? It takes a stronger person (man) to cry, you know.' That kind of thing I'm fighting, not daily, yet the questions are always there. The answers, I am trying to find them."

But even when men rebel against male stereotypes, as in James Dean's film heroes, they then fulfill the other male stereotype of the "bad boy"—as in the Billy Joel song "Uptown Girl" with her "downtown boy", or the Warren Beatty film character "Bugsy."

Learning to be "tough" and stay in control of emotions puts men in a difficult situation when trying to express love or negotiate a relationship with a woman, the whole "male" role value system is antithetical to the role a person needs for a warm and generous, emotive and empathetic relationship—a relationship in which the Number One Rule is: don't try to dominate the other person. Men would usually not try to do this in a friendship with another man, but as "a man" not "dominating" a woman could seem "unmasculine." And there lies the rub—the dilemma for a man in love with a woman.

In addition to "male" upbringing, the twentieth century's increased insistence that a man's nature is to be "rational" (not spiritual or emotional) has turned many men's lives into an emotional desert. There is no longer much trace of the Greek or Renaissance ideal of a balance between reason and the passions:* the success of the Industrial Revolution in the early part of this century created an extreme fixation on "science," which came to mean that men should be as efficient,

---

* Teaching men to obey reason, not feelings, also has roots in Biblical tradition: the ultimate lesson to men to deny their own individual desires and feelings, and to follow laws, rules, and orders unflinchingly, is the story of Abraham on the mountain preparing to kill (sacrifice) his own son, in order to follow the will of God the Father. No more wrenching story of a man learning to kill his own feelings can be found.

mentally and physically, as machines.* But this can play havoc with men's emotional relationships†—and eventually with men's ability to be creative and to have a human perspective on their work.

---

* This is reflected even in men's clothing: eighteenth-century men's clothing was ornate and flowing, whether the man was rich or poor; twentieth-century men's clothing is generally utilitarian and symmetrical, square in shape, resembling somewhat the cutout figures used to represent statistical tables in children's grade-school textbooks.

† Not only with women but also with men. Most men did not have a close male friend with whom they could talk intimately. It also inhibited men's relationships with *themselves*—their ability to know themselves.

Love, Male Psychology, and Male Identity

Do Men Believe in Love?

Descriptions of being in love—the following written by two younger men—often imply that intense feelings of love are bad, that being in love with a woman is a bad experience, a mistake that makes them weak. Thus, most men determined, after such an early experience in their lives, to define "real love" as something less passionately involving.

Love stories from men

"When she finally broke it off it was as if I had died. It was the only time in my life that I ever cried myself to sleep at night, and this I did frequently. I did not actually consciously think about suicide but I considered myself already dead. A greater emptiness and sense of loss I have not known. Since that time I have not been able to love a woman with such utter abandonment. I just haven't been able to do it. This happened twelve years ago and I can still feel the pain. If I were to see her right now I know my heart would jump into my throat."

"There is the good kind of love, but then there is the *other* kind, the kind that can't or won't work for whatever reasons. The reasons don't make sense. *Nothing* makes sense. It's not like a form of mental illness, it *is* a mental illness—something completely unexpected, even unwanted. Who in hell would *want* to feel jealous? Or possessive? Or greedy to usurp another's time? But that's all part of it. The dark emotions *do* exist, and all the peace, sex, dope shit will never change that . . . *never*. Whole men will always be able to feel these things. A half-man can't. The dark emotions have a *right* to exist *because they are there*. I want this person so much it makes me feel guilty for wanting too much—guilty and *bad*. But this is what keeps me going, oddly enough. It's what I

137

live for and think about every day. I think that maybe today it will all work, even though I know that this is foolishness. And *that* makes me feel *bad* too. Makes me feel wrong, like I'm feeling something I'm not supposed to because it isn't shared, but I feel anyway, in *spite* of what I am *supposed* to be allowed to feel.

"Well, this is Confession City, so I'll tell you that occasionally I cry myself to sleep over it, or in the middle of the day I think about her with other men, laughing at my needs. Once in a while I have to hold down a crying jag because I'm at work, but it happens then too. But normally, I don't try to hold the crying jags back. Holding a crying jag back is worse than letting it happen and getting it over with. I know it won't last forever (the present crying jag, that is). I get the crying jags when I cannot be consoled, 'never' *is a very long time* and the thought of it hurts like hell, there are no easy answers: I can't be consoled, nothing does any good, I feel worthless—like shit, and all these things make me mad, mad that someone has this power over me against my better judgment. Against My Will. Mind rape, the kind that women do.

"I have had thoughts of suicide, of my two arms opening up like vaginas with the blood flowing out and, with it, my life and the pain. But I have never picked up the knife. There is always one little bit of brain left during these bouts with the Black Thoughts that says, 'No.' That little bit of brain paralyzes my ability to move toward the cutlery. It has saved my life more than once. I'm a survivor. The Black Thoughts can come around during a crying jag, or in just silently thinking about 'it' and what just exactly 'it' is and what 'it' is doing to *me*. I tell these things here because it is necessary for men to know that it happens, that a man can be *that* weak and *that* vulnerable and know *that* capacity for hurting. *And that crazy*, because that's just exactly what it is: crazy. But knowing that won't make it go away either. This kind of craziness isn't in the textbooks."

Most Men Don't Marry the Women They Most Passionately Love

"Dad's idea of a man was someone who hunted, fished, played sports, etc. Love was not to be taken seriously or given free rein in your life."

Traditionally, men have been taught not to take love that seriously—not to "let a woman run your life." But as we have just seen, men do fall in love, and experience all the feelings of ecstasy and abandon, all the happiness that goes with it—for at least two weeks. At this point, many men unfortunately become very confused and apprehensive. Being brought up not to let themselves be "out of control," or "overly emotional," men mistrust the excitement, the rush, thinking that feeling that much cannot be good, cannot be relied on, is not "rational"—and therefore not "masculine" and "strong."

Men's comments about these feelings are quite illuminating. "To be in love," as one man in his early twenties writes, "is to be uncomfortable because you are out of control, you do things you wouldn't normally do. Women are more willing to be dependent, or part of another person, than a man who wants to keep a separation, keep himself for himself, who fears losing his independence. Of course, one does sometimes start to fall in love, but you can always stop it before it's too late. It will be nice in the future if they invent a pill to neutralize you if you fall in love—to alleviate your dis-ease!"

Most men are so uncomfortable with feelings of love, desire/need and vulnerability, that they do not marry the woman they are most "in love" with. Distrusting the feelings they run from their own emotional openness, and furthermore, are proud that they "made the right decision," "didn't let their feelings carry them away" and "stayed in control"—made a "rational decision." They are proud and feel they did the right thing, marrying "more sensibly."

And yet this, added to the fact that most men are brought up not to respect women—other than as mothers or mothering-type helping figures—puts most marriages in a very vulnerable, problematic position. An additional problem is most men's training not to talk about feelings or to solve emotional problems by discussing them, talking them out: most men's reaction to a dispute would be to retain "manly" objectivity by going for a walk, etc., expecting the air to have cleared on their return, and to feel proud of this solution, since they had not "lost control."

Men and marriage

Many men in this study said that they were deeply frustrated, angry, or disappointed with their emotional relationships with women, at the same time that they treasured these relationships as providing the happiest and most intimate moments of their lives. Many married men were so dissatisfied with their relationships that they resorted to outside sexual encounters to "make the marriage workable."

Most men had not married the women they most passionately loved. Most men did not feel comfortable being deeply in love. Although they sounded very similar to women when they spoke of the first wonderful feelings of falling in love, very soon thereafter many began to feel uncomfortable, anxious, even trapped—and wanted to withdraw. Most men felt very out of control of their emotions when they were in love, not reasonable and "rational," and most men did not like this feeling: men have been taught that the worst thing possible is to be out of control, to be "overly emotional," as this behavior is "womanly" (uncool).

Thus, being in love, a man begins to feel out of control, "unmanly," and even worse, he begins to feel that he is controlled by the woman—that is, he would do anything to please her, he is afraid of her displeasure, and so he is "dominated" by her. This is an intolerable situation. Add to this the idea that most men still believe on some level that there are two kinds of women: "good," motherly women, and "bad," sexy women. The man, feeling very attracted when falling in love, is sure that he should not let himself go into his love, trust in it, and count on her. At this point, he tends to pull back, to try to provoke a fight or find a problem in the relationship, in order to regain his former stance in life, his "control." He looks for, or believes he should look for, someone more "stable," someone who doesn't put him in a constant position of rethinking his life. Most men described this as a "rational" decision and took pride in having acted wisely, remaining cool and collected, and "using their heads"—even though they missed their lost love.

Most of the men in these marriages were not monogamous as we shall see. Most marriages based on this "rational" idea tended to develop a pattern (at least in the man) of extramarital sex unknown to the woman—or, since there was such emotional distance in the marriage anyway, sometimes the wife did know but just did not care, since she herself had little interest in sex with her husband. These ("traditional") marriages, while not close in the romantic sense, could often be long-term: if reasons other than love were the basis of the marriage in the first place, it was not necessary to maintain a high level of communication, intimacy, or understanding to ensure continuation of the marriage. "Newer," more equal, marriages in which emotional closeness and equality between the man and woman were goals, tended to be more monogamous and also to have quite different sexual patterns.

Men, Marriage, and Monogamy*

The majority of marriages were not based on the kind of emotional intensity, the feeling of being "in love," seen in answers in the preceding section—at least as men described their feelings about their marriages and their wives. But most men said they definitely loved their wives and had no intention of leaving them, even though most also had sex outside of their marriages, unknown to their wives.

Most men had sex outside their marriages

"Do you like extended periods of monogamy? Why or why not? Have you had 'extramarital' sexual experiences? If so, how many and how long? Did/does your partner know about them? What was/is the effect on you as an individual and on your marriage?"
The great majority of married men were not monogamous. Seventy-two percent of men married two years or more had had sex outside of marriage: the overwhelming majority did not tell their wives, at least at the time. By far, the most typical answers to this question were like the following:

"I have been married eighteen years. I like it, very much. We have a very good sexual relationship—I could not ask for a better sex life. I believe in monogamy. It is the moral and the religious thing to do. My outside sex has been unknown to my wife. It had no effect on my marriage. The only problem is it costs too much money to support a family and a girlfriend."

"Married to the same woman thirty-nine years. Never more affection and pleasure than this morning. As far as extramarital, yes. Unknown to my wife. It has broadened my understanding of life."

"Married seven years. I greatly enjoy being married. Marriage has given me a regular sex partner and opened more doors for us sexually. I love my wife very much. My love has gone from one of selfish, possessive love to a feeling of need, sharing, communication, protectiveness, and mutual enjoyment of our child and life. I do not believe in total monogamy. I feel that there are times in every person's

---

* Many more single (never-married) men were in favor of monogamy than married men; in fact, the majority of single men planned to be monogamous in their marriages, or were currently monogamous in their (non-living-together) relationship. Is this a reaction to the "sexual revolution," and the lives of their parents, or are younger men more idealistic—or both? Or had married men also intended to be monogamous before they were married?

life when they need outside input, even to the extent of intercourse, to renew their sexual feelings and stimulate their fantasies. I feel that it can improve the marriage relationship under the present circumstances. I have had ten 'extramarital' experiences and they were of the one-time type. I do not now have one planned. I feel that these experiences greatly increased my sexual feelings for a while and added to my passion with my wife."

"Eight years. I don't like being married. I'm still married because of our kid. I've had affairs and they were very satisfying to me. They were unknown to my wife. At first I was bitter, to be out in the street doing something which I thought I would be doing home with my wife. But I've resigned myself to her being as she is, and I try not to make comparisons between the women in my affairs and my wife. I just enjoy them. Even prostitutes."

Why?

The most frequent reason men gave for having sex outside their marriages was sexual rejection by their wives, or the boring nature of repeated sex with the same person in marriage. But since these two statements practically cancel each other out, are there other reasons? Why do men need to bolster their marriages on a continuing basis like this? It would seem that there may be hidden tensions or anger between men and women which focus on sex.

Does sex automatically become boring in marriage, or in a long relationship? Is the constant repetition of certain activities with one person inevitably less interesting as time passes? One way to answer this is to ask, is it less interesting to have dinner and a conversation with a friend you have known for twenty years, than with a friend you have known for one? Obviously, it depends on the friend, and on the status of your relationship at that particular time. But usually one can talk more deeply to an old and good friend than to a new one—although there is fun and excitement in discovering a new person.

Part of the reason for the "inevitable boringness" of sex in many of the marriages of men in this book is the fact that they have frequently shied away from marrying the women with whom they were most in love, the women who most excited them, to whom they felt the most open and emotionally vulnerable. Men have tended to base their marriages on practicalities, more on a "rational" feeling of being "in control" over their lives, being able to foresee a stable and predictable future—than on a feeling of being overwhelmed by the sudden beauty (in manner and thought, in a total sense, not just physically) of another. But to be so totally in control is boring, eventually.

Another reason repeated sex with the same person may become "boring" has to do with the repetitive nature of the way we define sex—i.e., as "foreplay," followed by "vaginal penetration," and ending with intercourse and male orgasm in the vagina. This was discussed in *The Hite Report on Female Sexuality* on women's sexuality, and will be discussed in the following chapters. If the definition of sex is constantly static and filled with performance pressures, perhaps the only way to find variety is to change partners.

In some ways, also, the alienation that has been built into marriages, due to the inequality between men and women legislated by our society, can also lead to a feeling of "boredom"—as boredom often represents built-up and unexpressed anger, rage, or hopelessness. Men often feel this rage against their wives, and marriages often contain decade-long cold wars. Most men's reaction to this situation is to search secretly for an interim relationship outside of the marriage. But men seeking emotional intimacy and fulfillment through sex—first with one partner, then another, as a pattern throughout a marriage—were not, in this study, very happy in the end because of it. Much more rewarding was, as some men did, to seek out the causes of the "boredom" or lack of closeness, whether they were bottled up anger or something else. To deny that there are problems, to describe "male sexuality" as if it were a mechanical "drive," with a built-in need for "variety," as if men were inevitably "biologically programmed" to go from "blossom to blossom" spreading their "pollen," is only a way to increasing loneliness and isolation.

Men's Anger at Women

Are there other reasons for men's extramarital sex? Let's return to our question about why men so frequently seek sexual relationships outside of marriage. In one sense, it can be said that perhaps many men see it as their "right"—something they are privileged to do when they feel like it; in fact, some men may even feel pressured to have extramarital sex by a culture that implies that all "real men" do it. Other reasons include maintaining a separate identity or individuality, getting affection or an ego boost when needed, or getting out of a marriage they want to end.

But the main reason for most extramarital sex, the reason most men give, was that it "makes the marriage workable"—that without these affairs, they would not be able to continue in the marriage. And, in fact, some of the longest marriages did seem to have survived in just this way.

But why *were* these marriages "unworkable"? Is lack of sex, or "boring" sex the reason,* or is the trouble men so often describe as sexual merely a reflection of larger unresolved issues in the relationship? Are these unresolved or unacknowledged issues unique to every relationship, or are there also larger culturally created problems between men and women? Of course, there are always individual conflicts or problems unique to any two people that can lead to fighting or alienated feelings; but there are also problems common to many couples, problems which therefore take on a larger meaning.

On one level, many men find that they cannot reconcile in their own minds the idea of loving their wives as the mothers of their children (and the woman who has, in a sense, the role of "mothering"—taking care of, feeding—them), and seeing her as a sexual being. Many men, raised to think of the mother as asexual or sexually taboo, find that they begin to have similar feelings about their wives, soon after marriage or after children arrive.

But another, perhaps more hidden or underlying reason, is unexpressed or unrecognized anger. In fact, many men's extramarital affairs, kept secret from their wives, can be seen as an escape valve—a way of secretly or unconsciously expressing anger at their wives, "getting even," "showing her"—a kind of private revenge that does not on the surface disturb the relationship, but gives a feeling of relief, allowing one to return refreshed, feeling more loving than ever, now that the anger has been expressed.

What, underneath it all, are men angry about? Were there any underlying themes in the complaints men presented—any complaints which re-emerged again and again, which could be, on a larger scale, an underlying cause of much of the anger? Or was most of this anger hidden, even unrecognized? In fact, in many, many replies, hidden anger, guilt and ambivalence that men seemed to feel about women are blocking relationships, especially long-term relationships.

All too often, men learned from their fathers' attitudes toward their mothers to see women as weak and overly emotional, dependent, able to gain "power" only by relying on psychological domination and

---

* See chapter 3 of *The Hite Report on Male Sexuality* for a discussion of what sex means to men, what they need from it, and what they get out of it.

manipulation, using men for their own economic advantage. As one man put it, "My father taught me (by implication) that women are traps and burdens, but the best that's available for overcoming loneliness." It is remarkable, given these views—and sadly, the fact that, due to cultural and economic pressures on women, these stereotypes have, at times, been true—that any relationships between men and women have ever managed to succeed.

Men's perception of women as weak

But why does men seeing women basically as "sex partners" or mothers, or looking down on them as generally weak and inferior, make men angry with women? The first reason is that this makes men feel guilty and conflicted in their loyalties, and angry with women for making them feel guilty:

"Since she loves me so much, I feel guilty that maybe I don't love her as much. She really looks up to me. Sometimes I feel like she worships me. This makes me feel funny. I know that as a man it is my duty to help her, but sometimes I feel annoyed with her. Why can't she stand on her own two feet?"

"I can't help looking down on women. You can get anything you want from them by telling them they are 'special.' They love to be told they are 'special.' "

"I guess what makes me maddest about women is when they lack pride, underestimate themselves, and are over-careful. When I see a woman with intelligence and abilities take a passive role in life because she lacks self-confidence, it upsets me and I tend to become critical."

A great deal of the alienation between men and women is caused by men's knowledge, on some level, of their superior, privileged class status over women—or at least the difference in status. This is an unspoken issue, too emotionally charged to discuss in most cases, whose existence is taken for granted between most men and women, but which has a diffused effect over the entire relationship. Although men felt somewhat free to voice these feelings about their mothers, and to recognize their mothers' subordinate position vis-à-vis their fathers—often calling them "weak"—many men did not feel free to express, or perhaps even recognize, some of these same feelings about their own wives and lovers.

A further problem is economics. Since society has kept women economically, socially, and even emotionally dependent on men, it is no wonder that men sometimes feel "trapped" in marriage. And yet, most men do not explicitly connect problems with the social and legal role assigned women (or their own role as "caretaker") and their own feeling of lack of satisfaction in marriage, or suffocation. Most seem to feel that their problems in their own marriage related to their wife as an individual, i.e., she was being unreasonable and making too many demands—or that she was not responding with a sufficient amount of affection (gratitude?) by participating in more frequent sex, etc. Or she was not being "giving" enough. Thus, men felt perfectly justified in going outside the marriage for sex and pleasure, since they felt they were being cheated inside the marriage.

However—even though most men did not connect society's assigning women a second-class or dependent role with their own feelings of dissatisfaction, accompanied by their endless search for a gratifying "sexual" relationship with a woman—a majority did recognize the bad effect that being supported or dependent could have on one's spirit. When asked, "Do you envy women the choice of having someone support them, the seeming lack of pressure on them to make money?" almost no men said they envied women, and most stated strongly that they would *not* like to be supported by someone else.

The Status of Men's Relationships With Women

The traditional marriage, in which the man controlled the money, while the woman's domain was the house, was the type of marriage most likely to include a pattern of extramarital sex for the man.* Newer marriages, struggling to create more equal relationships, were more likely to be monogamous—with the partners also being more likely to end the marriage if the closeness dissolved, rather than patching it up with outside sex. But "newer" marriages were not necessarily between younger men and women, by any means. A more equal marriage could be something a couple of any age might strive for.

The happiest men in this study were those with the closest, most

---

* Studies have implied that women's extramarital sex is somewhat less; many men have outside sex with unmarried women. Actually, women's traditional patterns of extramarital sex are largely unknown.

functioning relationships with women—that is, a minority of (in most cases, married) men. Trying to live by the male code, being totally self-sufficient, emotionally and economically, always *providing* shelter and food (or sex and orgasms), never receiving or needing anything, never needing a woman's love more than she needs the man's—all this hurts and stunts men.

Some men were beginning to see how their own welfare is tied up with women's fight to restructure their lives and relationships for the better—to redefine themselves above and beyond the traditional confines of "femininity." "Masculinity" can be just as much of a pressure on men as an enforced "femininity" can be on women.

But one of the deepest problems still prevalent in many men's minds is the connection they made between money and sex with women. Most men believed that women were somehow for sale. When asked, "How do you feel about paying a woman for sex?" meaning in prostitution, many answered, "You always pay anyway"—explaining that whether it is in marriage where the man provides support in return for (what he considers should be) domestic and sexual services, childrearing—or on a date, in which the man pays for dinner, expecting sex in return, he is always paying. Many said that it was more honest, and more of a bargain, to actually pay a woman outright. In fact, the number one reason given by most men for being angry with women was financial support, mentioning frequently that you can't trust women, that women often "use" men to get financial support. Many men feel they can never be sure that a woman loves them just for themselves—as many men said, "Maybe she is just staying with me as a meal ticket."

The most unfortunate part of all this is that most men did not accept the women's movement, which could change things. If women had equal rights with men, equal access to jobs and education, and equal pay then men would not have to fear that women loved them only for their money or for financial support. Most men gave lip service to women's rights, saying that women should be"equal," but disapproved of most of the ways that this could be brought about. Most were afraid that women's liberation would mean less love: if women got equal rights, and especially if they were financially independent, they would not love men any more. Most men did not seem to feel secure that they were worthy of love on a deeper level. And most men did not want to give up their so-called masculine privileges, even though these "privileges" had not made them particularly happy. Perhaps the less happy some men are, the more they cling, paradoxically, to the very ideas and beliefs that have left them so unfulfilled.

Are things changing? Do men want to redefine their relationships with women?

Are most men changing their view of the world—and who they are in that world—or is it true to say "the more things change, the more they remain the same"?

The inequalities between men's and women's traditional roles have placed a tremendous burden on relationships between men and women, often creating an adversary, distrusting situation. If individuals were free to choose their role in a relationship, to create new types of relationships with each other, and especially more equal relationships, there would be less need for distrust and more mutual respect and communication possible.

Unfortunately, our society has kept women in a secondary position, economically and socially, and so most women remain dependent on men.* Traditionally, a woman with children had to depend on the good will of her husband for her and her children's support. This may have created a subtle pressure on her to fear her husband, and to cater to his wishes, no matter what her own feelings—thus inhibiting a free and spontaneous relationship between equals.

Clearly, men have cause to be insecure about women's motives in loving them in a society in which women are dependent on men's good will and financial support for survival. Thus, keeping women economically dependent places men in a position in which they may sometimes wonder if they are loved for themselves or because they are, as one man put it, "a meal ticket." This is a tragic consequence of the system as we have known it—both women and men have had, in many ways, to distrust each other, and this distrust can permeate even deep and committed relationships.

And yet, many men in this study did not see the relevance to them of the women's movement; they did not see the connection between their own feelings of being trapped and alienated—in their role in marriage, in their jobs, in their lifestyle, their lack of closeness—and the critique of society and relationships which the women's movement poses, the suggestions the women's movement has made for improving things. Many men tended to see the women's movement more as "women complaining, raising a ruckus" than understanding how both men and women, working to change and restructure their relationships (and the

---

* According to the U.S. Bureau of Labor statistics, women in 1980 still earned only 59 percent of what men earn for the same work.

family), could make increased happiness for both. In fact, many men were angry that now women might be "getting ahead," because their own lives had often left them feeling unappreciated, unsatisfied, angry, and stifled.

What do men think of women's liberation?

"I think women's liberation is great. It has not affected any of my relationships."

"A man and woman can't live and love each other as husband and wife unless the man is the head of the house and the wife considers her husband as the master over her in everything."

"I can't respect women, because why did they *let* themselves be subjugated, owned and ruled?"

"I think it's important to mention the guilt I sometimes feel very acutely when I realize the privileges I enjoy as opposed to what the majority of women enjoy. I think of all the hidden ways that this privilege is handed to me by the culture in which I live, and the ways women are shortchanged of those same privileges. It makes me uncomfortable to be given extra points for being a white, middle-class male with an education, but the ingredient that provides the most credence in this society is gender."

Many of the answers to the question "What do you think about women's liberation?" brought out a huge amount of anger at women, or anger with men's own situation, their own role in society and tre-mendous lack of fulfillment. Many men felt that now, with the women's movement and the emphasis on women achieving more independence and equality, they were being falsely maligned and misunderstood:

"All I ever hear about these days is how brutal men are, how women are always getting fucked over by men, and how the sisterhood is gonna go it alone. Well, men get the same kind of shit, and I do not like being put in a category. I'm no better or no worse than anyone else, regardless of gender. Just like a woman, I want to be loved and give love in return."

"There seems to be a growing stereotype of what bastards men are. Although I suppose some do live up to this stereotype, I know many men who don't (including, I believe, myself). I don't like this trend and find it similar to the black backlash against all whites once they achieved greater control over their lives . . . alienating even those whites who had fought alongside them for equal opportunities, etc. Some men are stronger feminists than many women. Why condemn all of us? Society has dictated not only to women the roles they should play but also to men. Men have been stereotyped and enslaved into following traditional approaches to life just as much as women, and the more moderate feminists are willing to accept this and seem to be turning towards a cooperation with men in changing society."

Many answers seemed to imply that the women's movement is merely something having to do with women's "self-esteem," rather than being a fundamental critique of the society and both men's and women's roles in it, and therefore something to which men must address themselves directly, as it involves a basic readjustment in "their" world:*

"The 'movement' has not affected my relationships because the women I like do things as individuals, not as part of movements. However, if some subtle change in the general atmosphere has helped them to reach a more open state, that's good. Most, though, still want the man to take the initiative in the early stages of dating and sex. So it has not changed my relationships."

"I feel that it has helped my wife."

"Women's liberation provides a medium of support for women who can't otherwise feel good about their womanhood. As such it has its benefits to our society."

A minority of men, still misunderstanding it, said they were totally against women's liberation:

"It stinks. Women should be feminine, but with equal rights. American women should make men feel like men, not competitors."

"I believe men and women are not equal. They each have their own jobs in life. Let me explain. First of all, a woman can have a child, a man cannot. He doesn't even have to be there for conception. A sperm bank can do that. A woman's skeleton matures faster than a man's. Women have faster reaction times in general. The list is endless in comparing men and women. They were each put on this earth with all their differences. However, if men and women stopped competing with each other it would be a better world."

"It made women feel like they can do it all, as if they don't need men to keep up a house. I think being pregnant should be the woman's natural desire."

"I think it's the worst thing that ever happened to women and their relations with men."

"Ridiculous."

* But they *have*—it's fundamentalism!

150

"I don't like it. The vital role women play as mothers who mold the future generation has been de-emphasized. We are on a self-destruction course. If you think we have a lot of crazies now—you ain't seen nothing. Day care centers are sadly run by people who raise children as a business. The children are second-class children, they are entitled to more. Up with Mother Power. It's all marketing and media hype. If some women want to work in this cold, often boring life outside the home, fine. But never degrade the role of the mother. Also, some women are getting socially aggressive. I'm flattered and respond—but if they didn't make advances to me I probably wouldn't go after them, therefore after the initial thrill is over I dump them, and I got a depressed liberated broad to deal with."

"Women just need to sound off. The greatest people alive have been men, including Jesus Christ Himself. *No woman has yet lived* and been great enough to be the Daughter of God! Print it!"

"A farcical gyration of dykes. It has afforded me many laughs."

But the largest number of men said they were "in favor of women's liberation, BUT"; these answers also continued to misunderstand the ideas of the women's movement in the most fundamental ways, or frequently to give a very shallow interpretation of the women's movement:

"Women need equal rights but not as a man."

"It's O.K. but I wouldn't want a woman for a boss."

"It is righting some wrongs, but also causing disruptions in established patterns which have been beneficial to society."

"Women's liberation is a just cause when it pursues equality of opportunity in life, and the desire to be judged as a person first, not on a prejudicial basis. But the women's movement is unjust when it chooses anti-male attitudes instead of the pursuit of justice. Anti-male is no better than anti-female."

"I'm in favor of it when it comes to getting rid of discrimination, but it's overblown. Women have always been able to get what they want."

"I think that women's liberation is good and healthy, but there has been some backlash and reversal of roles, so that women, in action if not vocally, say, 'O.K., I'm wearing the pants now; you grovel.' Any slaves are bound to take some revenge when they have overcome the odds; it's human nature, but it's not pleasant for me as a man."

"I am all for women being equal, but nothing they or I can do will change biological differences. It is wrong when women 'want to be men,' and I feel sorry for those who do. The world would be a miserable place if most men and women were not happy to be what they are. But basically I am open-minded and want to be fair, so I can't say I'm against women's liberation, but women's liberation turns me off when it becomes hatred of things masculine."

"I am grateful for their telling how I've unthinkingly been insensitive to women's needs. They've made me aware of my own inflated male ego, which has caused me to make an ass of myself more than once. But I happen to be fairly handsome and have been used as a sex object on a number of occasions, so I get sick of hearing that 'women are treated as sex objects.' That whole game is a *two-way* street. I'm also turned off by all the unthinking propaganda. I also don't like it when women close their own eyes to their own nagging bitchiness, hypocrisy, cheating, castration complexes, superficiality, etc."

A Time of Change For Men—Troubled Waters For Men

Many men today—men of every age, not just younger men—are privately anguished over how to define masculinity, what it means to be a man. The majority feel an enormous amount of pressure and frustration in their lives, but usually focus on women as the cause of it, rather than the values of the society we live in. Most men, also, feel that they cannot talk to other men about their frustrations with "masculinity"—because to do so might make them look less "masculine" to other men, as if they couldn't "make it" as a man.

While masculinity as currently defined has good points, such as grooming of men to face life with fortitude, knowledge, and skill, it also unfortunately teaches men to deny their emotional sides to such a degree that they wind up feeling isolated and upset about their personal relationships—or cynical about them, saying that emotional relationships are a woman's domain, something not too important in their lives.

The men in this study who most accepted traditional stereotypes of masculinity were those who were most unhappy with their lives. There has been a built-in contradiction between the so-called male lifestyle and human closeness. Lack of emotionality and closeness makes men feel isolated, angry, and cynical. Men today are faced with the rather formidable choice of either continuing to live their lives as in the past, feeling torn apart by constantly having to suppress and deny their own needs (and suffering with their early death rate and illnesses)—and creating something new.

Men want to be close to women to express their emotional lives. This is especially true since, as we have seen, men learned from their fathers that closeness, personal talks, and affection were not an appropriate part of a relationship with another man; men feel they can only express this part of themselves with a woman—and even then, all too many men have mixed feelings, believing that these feelings, these needs, represent weakness, needs they should not have.

Most men are cautious about falling in love. Men's first feelings on falling in love were as joyous and ecstatic as women's—in fact, this is one of the only parts of this book which could have been written by women—but after their initial feelings of happiness (and erotic attraction), most men ironically backed off or distrusted their feelings, the very feelings that had given them such pleasure. In fact, most men distrusted these feelings so much that the majority of marriages were not based on this kind of emotional intensity—at least as men in this study described their feelings about their marriages and their wives. Most men did not marry the women they had been most "in love" with, although they emphasize that they love their wives and do not want to leave them, even when they are having regular sex with someone they care about outside the marriage.

Deconstructing Intercourse and the Definition of Male Sexuality

Is "Male Sexuality" Socially Constructed?

Is there any difference between how individual men feel about their sexuality and themselves as men—and how the culture says they should feel? It is important to ask what *can* sex and sexual relationships be? What do we want to make them?

"Male" sexuality is central to the definition of masculinity—and masculinity is central to the world-view of the entire culture—in a sense, *is* the culture. Therefore, what we are looking at here is far more than male sexuality, it is a way of life, the world itself, a culture in microcosm. To discuss sex is to discuss our most basic views of who we are, what we want life to be, and what kind of a society we believe in.

What is "male sexuality"?

Intercourse is one of—if not *the*—basic ingredient of sex for most men: in fact, the overwhelming majority of men studied did not want to have sex that did not culminate in intercourse and male orgasm. Why is what we know as "male sexuality" so identified with intercourse? Is it for reasons of physical pleasure, or are other, more symbolic, cultural forces at work? Intercourse is such a dominant symbol of our society that its actual identity has hardly been studied, and the right questions not asked. The standard interpretation of male sexuality says that intercourse is the greatest pleasure a man can have. And yet, isn't this a bit simplistic?

The old mechanistic definition of male sexuality as basically a question of getting an erection, penetrating the woman, and reaching orgasm is in large part a reproductive pattern created and perpetuated by our culture—not an inevitable reaction to the "male sex drive." Men are more complicated than that, and male sexuality is just as much tied

154

to emotions as is female sexuality. Is it possible the men are missing out on a large part of their sexuality/sensuality, and their enjoyment, by so totally equating sex and intercourse?

Is Men's Focus on Coitus "Natural," or Part of a Socially Constructed Ideology?*

Why do men want intercourse? Is intercourse necessary to sex?

Most men liked intercourse. However, the reasons are surprising. It is often repeated—in fact, almost universally assumed—that what men like/want from intercourse is their orgasm. And yet, as men point out over and over, they can easily have an orgasm from their own stimulation (and often even a stronger one†); what men want from intercourse is something else:

"I like intercourse more psychologically than physically. I get a lot of *physical* pleasure from intercourse, but I can also get that from masturbating. The physical feeling of moving my penis back and forth inside my lover is pleasurable, but probably not as intense as a good hand job or fellatio combined with hands. Psychologically, though, there's much to want—the anticipation of putting my penis inside my lover, knowing I'm going to be surrounded by her, warmed by the inside of her. Then when I first slowly enter her, I want the instant to last and last. I like to stop moving, just lie there, and think and feel, 'This is happening to me. This is so neat. I feel so good.' "

Boys are brought up to equate intercourse with manhood:

"I felt (and still do, to a lesser extent) incredible pressure on me to prove my manhood by screwing women. This pressure made it harder on me to meet women and have sexual relations with them. I had to do it; if I didn't there was something wrong with me. Also, it was supposedly so great, look what I was missing. This pressure bred its own miserable rationales, e.g., 'women always want it, even when they say "no." ' Thus, I had *no* excuses. If I couldn't find a woman to fuck, it

---

* If coitus is really the basic expression of men's "sexual drive," why does society need so many laws and religious injunctions to insist that this is the only "right" way for them to have sex?
† Also found by Masters and Johnson in their work, *Human Sexual Response.*

was my fault I was a failure. I feel this pressure helped retard my sexual growth and experience and placed undue importance on fucking."

The culture has taught men and women that intercourse symbolizes masculinity and male identity; the historical reason for this (to create a social system that would maximize reproduction) has long been forgotten, but the symbol continues to be glorified. That is, in a patriarchal society, intercourse (or the erect penis, ready for intercourse) *symbolizes* masculinity. More specifically, just as the erect penis symbolizes masculinity, intercourse symbolizes the *acceptance* of the erect penis—i.e., the validation of masculinity by both the individual woman and the entire culture. How much of men's desire for, and identification with, intercourse is due to a culture which tells men that this is what they *should* want?

Some men did not answer whether they liked intercourse, or why, but simply stated that intercourse is what men do—the natural and inevitable expression of "instinctive" male "sex drive"
"Sex identifies me to myself as a man; sex admits me to full citizenship in my species and my world. Without sex I would regard myself as somewhat less than a man and somewhat less than a person."

"I feel that our Creator made men with a penis and women with a vagina for a reason, and that's for intercourse."

"Being a healthy male, sex is very important to me. The purpose of sex is a normal function of the human mind and body."

Many men's answers seem to suggest that they are not sure how often they would like to have intercourse, but that they are fairly sure that they should be having it more often than they are, or that other men are having it more than they are. There is also a vague sense of disquiet in some answers in which men say that it is not theirs to choose how often they will have intercourse, that at any moment the woman/women may "shut them out" and refuse to have intercourse with them.

In fact, the cultural pressure on men to have frequent intercourse is based on a purely mechanical definition of masculinity, in which the desire/"need" for intercourse is related solely to a man's supposed inner hormonal cycles, or some other mysterious "innate" sexual urges. Of course, how often a man has or wants to have an orgasm is a separate matter from how often he has or wants to have intercourse.

In fact, it is possible that our culture has pushed men to "want" intercourse more than they, without this pressure, might. Certainly it is possible to have sex without having intercourse. And certainly, men have the right to go without sex entirely or not have sex with a partner (celibacy), if they want, as almost all men in fact do for certain (more or less brief) periods of their lives. Men should not be made to feel that they "have to" have sex/intercourse to prove they are men or for any other reason.

Erection and patriarchal definitions of self

In a culture which says a man is not "a man" unless he likes/wants intercourse, of course a man who "cannot" have intercourse (does not get an erection) sees himself as "less than a man." The demeaning term "impotent" has usually been applied to lack of erection, and means, of course, "lack of power"—i.e., lack of ability to impregnate a woman, the basic "power" of patriarchy. Many beautiful types of closeness have been given second-class status by a social structure which once wanted and needed to increase reproduction. Even though the idea is now so antiquated that birth control is practiced almost universally, we still insist on describing a man without an erection as "impotent," a failure—rather than seeing the whole human being, and the appropriateness of many degrees of physical arousal.

Of course, erection and intercourse are pleasurable to both men and women; however, it is one thing if a man cannot get an erection when he desires one, and another when he feels he *must* produce one. In fact, a man need not have an erection to give a woman an orgasm, since orgasm in women is usually created by manual or oral stimulation of the clitoral and vulval areas—or at least not by friction of the penis on the inner vaginal walls.* The need for erection to "satisfy a woman" has been greatly overemphasized. And most men fear "impotence" more because they think they will appear unmanly, or a failure, than because of fear of loss of pleasure.

The cultural emphasis on erection, which leads to an ever-present fear of lack of erection, forces most men to become focused on getting and maintaining an erection during sex. This in turn forces the activities to revolve around the erection, influencing the timing and sequence of events. Physical relations could develop a more spontaneous feeling if the importance of erection were greatly de-emphasized. Older men, who *may* have trouble achieving or maintaining an erection (but not always), have been ridiculed and made to feel "less than men" by society; in fact,

---

* Although a minority of women do orgasm during intercourse itself, as they explain in *The Hite Report on Female Sexuality*, this is most often due to friction between the two pubic areas or other such exterior contact, which can sometimes accompany penetration.

often their diversification and rethinking of sexual pleasure has made them "better" lovers than younger men.

And some men did in fact feel repulsed by the vulgarization of their sexuality—i.e., cultural/advertising images of how "a real man is just naturally crazy for sex." Many men voiced a strong reaction against some of the ideas of the "sexual revolution," including the idea that men should want/have sex and intercourse at any time or place, not needing an emotional relationship or feelings as the context for sex:

"It's depressing. I don't usually have sex just for lust, it's more spiritual. I'm old-fashioned, romantic. I'm a dreamer, I guess."

"I hate the sexification of everything in which oppressive sex roles are just more visible and blatant, and everybody goes around acting terribly sexy and fucking each other's brains out, and sex is openly alluded to in aspirin commercials and toothpaste promos, etc. I think that's sometimes called the sexual revolution and I hate it."

The pressure on men to be "sexual" and to have frequent sex has been particularly strong during the last twenty years, or perhaps especially since the 40s and World War II, with the increasing equation of masculinity with aggressive characteristics. As mentioned elsewhere, in Victorian times men were often urged (by doctors and others) not to have sex and orgasm too often, lest they drain themselves of their "vital fluids" and become weak. Today just the opposite is urged. The idea of a male "biological need" for penetration and intercourse, an aggressive, "animalistic" "sex drive" was incorporated into the movement for "sexual freedom" known as the "sexual revolution."

Male "sex drive" as an ideological construct

The term "male sex drive" is part of the larger reproductive ideology of our patriarchal society; there is no biological or physical proof of a male "sex drive" for *intercourse*. Although both male and female do have a need (or "drive") for orgasm from time to time, there is no evidence that men biologically "need" vaginas in which to orgasm, or that there is anything hormonal or "instinctual" which drives men toward women or vaginas.

Many kinds of physical contact are enjoyed by the other mammals just as frequently as or more frequently than coitus, which is practiced only when females are in estrus. Most mammals spend more time on grooming and petting each other than they do on specifically sexual (genital) contact, as many primate researchers have described. Mammals and other animals also masturbate and quite commonly have homosexual relations. Among the animals for whom these activities have been recorded are the rat, chinchilla, rabbit, porcupine, squirrel, ferret, horse, cow, elephant, dog, baboon, monkey, chimpanzee, and many others.

Our culture seems to assume that since (theoretically) sexual feelings are provided by nature to ensure reproduction, therefore intercourse is (or should be) "instinctive" behavior. Yet when one looks at other animals it is obvious that other forms of touching and genital sexuality are just as "instinctive." Masturbation may even be a more natural behavior than intercourse, since chimpanzees brought up in isolation have no idea how to have intercourse, but do masturbate almost from birth.

And finally, if (as is so frequently asserted) intercourse really is "instinctive" and all else "unnatural," why do we need laws and social institutions that both glorify and require intercourse (especially in marriage), while setting up grave penalties and taboos against other forms of sexuality?

Built-in "Inadequacy" For Men

A constant source of anxiety among men is whether they continue intercourse long enough, remaining erect, or whether they reach orgasm "too soon." (Most men, although they sometimes used the term "premature ejaculation," did not in fact refer to its standard clinical meaning—i.e., orgasm before or just at the moment of penetration—but rather referred to very varied amounts of time of intercourse. In fact, most men who expressed this concern felt that this was probably the reason why a woman might not reach orgasm during intercourse with them; this thinking is inaccurate, however, as discussed in *The Hite Report on Female Sexuality*.

Seventy-four percent of the men who answered expressed concern over whether they continued intercourse long enough:

"Sadly, so far, I have been climaxing too soon to suit me. I can't control it. And I feel as though I haven't really done much for my partner even though I do try to continue stimulation somehow. I consider it a failed test of virility."

The popular media are constantly warning men against "coming too soon," insisting that this is the cause of most women not having orgasm from intercourse (coitus). Thus most men feel it is their duty to the woman to have intercourse for as long as possible, so that the woman can have a chance to orgasm too. However, the results of *The Hite Report on Female Sexuality* suggest that this is a fallacy, since whether a woman has an orgasm is usually not related to length of intercourse. In fact, most women do not orgasm simply as a result of intercourse; and the minority of women who do, do so not so much from long thrusting as from individually created ways of getting specific clitoral stimulation during intercourse.

But the amount of pressure on men has been enormous. Even the term "premature ejaculation" is negative, giving a man the implicit message that no matter when he orgasms it may be too soon, "premature," unwanted, or out of place. Men have been getting a double message: on the one hand they are told that it is very "virile" to become erect and excited and thrust home to orgasm; on the other hand, they are told not to orgasm "too soon." Since most men get rather good stimulation during thrusting, this provides a contradiction—leaving most men feeling slightly uneasy, guilty, and inadequate.

Although extending intercourse can be a pleasure in itself for both men and women, this guilt is unnecessary—as long as women's needs are acknowledged in a realistic manner at some time during sex, or any special needs of women desiring to orgasm during intercourse are fulfilled in a mutually agreeable fashion.

Pressure to "make her come"

Closely linked with the traditional pressure on men to maintain long erection and thrusting during intercourse is the idea that it is a man's role to "give" the woman an orgasm during intercourse. Just as the man has traditionally been considered the "provider" economically—the man should "bring home the bacon" or buy the house—he has also been given the role of "providing" the woman with sexual satisfaction. A "real man" should "make her come."

In addition to the pressure created by this role, this idea also often puts the man in a no-win situation since the information he has been given—that thrusting during intercourse should bring a woman to orgasm—is faulty. This places him in a vulnerable position, leaving him to doubt his masculinity whenever female orgasm does not occur, and also possibly pressuring the woman to fake orgasms. Thus this needless pressure alienates men and women, as each blames the other when expectations are not met.

"Do you feel there is something wrong with your 'performance,' technique, or sensitivity if the woman does not orgasm from intercourse itself? That you're 'not man enough'?"
A few men insisted women never fail to orgasm with them:

"Are you kidding? I never had a complaint."

"I never have failed a woman yet to achieve orgasm."

"Never had the problem."

"Experience has shown that if a woman can't orgasm with me, she can't with anybody. I have brought out the first orgasm in several."

But the overwhelming majority of men realized that women often did not orgasm during intercourse, and found this a source of pressure. Many felt it was their fault:

"If anything goes wrong, I'm blamed for it. Girls always seem to just lie there and say, 'O.K., make it happen.' I feel an immense pressure to perform and feel that it's all up to me."

This pressure to orgasm from intercourse has been very oppressive to women, and has often led to faking orgasms. And, in fact, although men here say that they do not feel guilty there is a tone of defensiveness. The unrealistic goal of women reaching orgasm simply from the rubbing of the penis in the vagina has placed undue pressure on both men and women, and left both vulnerable and defensive before each other—creating, all too often, an adversary situation.

Expanding the Definition of Male Sexual Identity

Would Men Like to Diversify Their Sexuality Beyond Intercourse?

Although intercourse is still the cornerstone of our definition of sex, perhaps we are in a period of rethinking and transition. Why should men feel that if they don't want intercourse, they are not "real men"? That only by having intercourse will they have "true sex"? Most men have felt resentment at the many pressures on them to perform, but have rarely revolted against the pressure on them to have intercourse itself—a pressure which makes having intercourse during sex more an inevitability than a choice, or something spontaneously desired.

Without the cultural insistence that intercourse *is* sex, and that it is the most desirable activity in the world and especially that a *man* should always want intercourse, how important would intercourse be to sex? Would it remain the dominant activity of sex, or would it become simply one of many possible ways of relating, something done sometimes and not other times?

This is not to suggest that intercourse is not often a great, powerful experience. But as one man said, "Unless the woman and I are both really desiring intercourse in particular with each other, then the lovemaking act tends to become a dull ritual. Sometimes I think it should be saved for special times."

Does defining sex as intercourse to orgasm inhibit men's sensuality?

There was a strong feeling expressed by many men in this study that they would like to diversify their sexual activities. When discussing sexual activities other than intercourse, many replies sounded much freer and more spontaneous. It was almost as if, when talking of less symbolically charged activities, a burden had been lifted, a tension released, and a new expansiveness and enthusiasm filled them.

Hidden Pleasures for Men: Forbidden Male Eroticism

Masturbation

"I have more or less two sex lives, one with my wife and one with myself. I have masturbated for many years, but I now enjoy masturbation very much with no guilt (that I can consciously identify). I hope to discuss this with my wife someday, but free as I think I am with her, I can't bring myself to that point yet. I get pleasures that are deeply solitary, 'forbidden' so to say, from masturbating, that are different from person-to-person lovemaking. I make love to myself. Most men won't admit that. But it's been a gradual lessening of guilt. I still have, in fact they're stronger, definite religious feelings. But I have now accommodated my religious feelings with my sexuality, and no area is more important here than masturbation. I find masturbation very healthy to my sexuality. I'm more in tune with my body and a better lover as a result of feeling freer, less guilty."

Do most men masturbate?
When asked, "How often do you masturbate?" 98 percent of men, whether married or single, with or without an otherwise active sex life, said they made masturbation a regular part of their lives:
"I have masturbated since I can remember—began probably around eight or ten. Now at thirty-five I masturbate on the average of four times a week. It almost always leads to orgasm because I stick to it until it does."

Most boys begin masturbating between the ages of ten and twelve. It is surprising to note that most girls begin masturbating at an earlier age than do boys, opposite of what has been assumed in the past. Most girls begin to masturbate between the ages of five and ten, rarely later, although sometimes earlier. Finally, many more boys learned to masturbate from other boys than girls did from each other. In fact, almost none of the women who participated in *The Hite Report on Female Sexuality* had learned from other girls or talked to other girls about masturbation.

How do men masturbate? What do men do when alone that they rarely tell anyone else?

The question "How do you masturbate?" brought out some of the longest and most specific answers of any of the replies. This is important material because there is very little general understanding of some of the things men enjoy, particularly the importance of anal and scrotal stimulation. Men uninhibitedly touch themselves in many ways during masturbation that they do not feel free to do or ask for during sex with a partner. In addition, many men's answers contain a great sense of freedom, fun, and pleasure.

Twenty-four percent of the men who answered sometimes included anal penetration in their masturbation; another 23 percent also often used exterior anal stimulation:

"I use the middle finger of my left hand to massage my prostate gland in the anus while masturbating my penis with my right hand."

"Sometimes while in the shower I slip one or two (or more) fingers of my left hand up my rectum and move them, usually in a wriggling motion, while I stroke my penis with the right hand. I move my fingers towards the front of my body while they are inside of me, because it feels best there (maybe that's where the prostate is). The orgasm, a crashing, intense one, is centered in my body where the fingers were moving. (There is very little sensation in my penis.) When I come, I can feel something swelling against my fingers. It's kind of exciting. I've tried using anal stimulation alone, but it seems that I can't orgasm without stroking my penis too."*

"I spread my legs wide, bend the knees and draw my thighs up to my chest and play with my asshole while masturbating. I get tremendously excited fingering my ass. Sometimes I dildo myself with whatever's available. I masturbate my ass until I can't stand it any longer then grip my penis and jack to orgasm."

"Foreplay," touching, and affection

Stereotypes of male sexuality say that what men want from sex is their orgasm, especially through intercourse—and that they find "foreplay" something more necessary to "get the woman ready" than something they want for themselves. Is this true?

---

* This sounds very similar to descriptions women gave of feeling extreme pleasure from vaginal stimulation, feeling almost, almost, almost as if they would reach orgasm, but not being quite able to get there without clitoral stimulation.

"What kind of foreplay is important to you for yourself? Do you like to be embraced? Kissed? Petted?"

"Those special little spots are from the bottom of my ear down my neck, eye contact, my breast, my stomach, around the genital area, the small of my back, the back of my knees, down the inside of my thighs and my toes. My testicles are very sensitive. My mouth is perhaps the greatest turn-on in foreplay as I am very aroused by touching lips together or French kissing, etc. But I hate someone to put their tongue in my ear or kiss it, etc."

While a few men stated that affection and touching would be very enjoyable without leading to sex, some men are beginning to change:

"We are often affectionate, even in the presence of our children. Moreover, since we sleep together nude, we cuddle at night when we go to bed and in the morning when we wake up. This is our 'way of life'—in a sense; it sort of sets the stage so that when either of us feels the need, urge, or desire for more intimacy (sexual intercourse and orgasm) we read each other's body signals and just 'drift into' (spontaneously) more pleasure tension—right on through to orgasm. For the majority of times, physical affection and touching are sufficient."

"Physical affection and touching are *essential* in really good sex, but even more important in daily life. They convey much more than words can, and are very important in a really satisfying relationship."

Anal stimulation by a partner

"I never really understood how a woman could let a man enter her until I was entered myself. I enjoyed the feeling. It's an experience or a feeling, a state that most men never have. To be penetrated is very different from penetrating. I realize now that this applies equally well to nonsexual things. To let someone into your life, into your heart, into your fears and desires is a quality that is much more highly developed in women. Perhaps this difference in men is what makes it difficult for men to love. I know my fear of love is like a fear of letting in."

Anal penetration and stimulation is an important subject which has received almost no attention in the literature of sex research. And yet, it is a real chance for men to have another, completely different type of experience.

Although anal penetration is usually thought of as a homosexual activity, with the anus being used only as a substitute for the vagina, in fact receiving anal stimulation or penetration by a finger is an important activity for many men. Most men, of either heterosexual or homosexual experience, who have tried being penetrated said they enjoyed it: it brought feelings of deep pleasure and fulfillment. The main characteristic of being penetrated described by men was an extreme feeling of emotional passion—followed by a feeling of peace and satisfaction. Many men said that orgasm, when accompanied by anal stimulation, could be physically exquisite.

Why, physiologically speaking, does being penetrated and stimulated anally feel good to men? There are two possible reasons. First, the feeling of being penetrated itself is rewarding. In fact, many men described the pleasurable feeling of being penetrated (whether by a finger or a penis) in words similar to those used by women to describe the pleasure of vaginal penetration—feeling "full," "complete," and emotionally satisfied. Penetrating and being penetrated can be important emotional statements from one person to another.

THE PENILE SYSTEM
THE PARTS OF THE PENIS ARE UNDERLINED
THE PENIS IS IN A NON AROUSED STATE

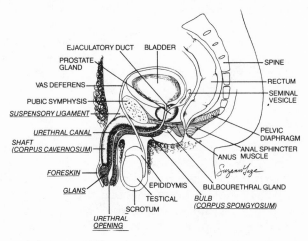

A second reason is that men's prostate gland is located just inside (approximately two inches) the anal opening. Stimulation of this gland can cause a man to orgasm, if done properly. However, most anal penetration does not stimulate the prostate directly, since it is necessary, once inside the anal canal, to press against the anterior wall of the anus and down slightly to locate it (it may feel about one inch in diameter), and then continue concentrating the stimulation there to bring on orgasm. Most anal penetration, whether by a finger or a penis, passes over this gland and only stimulates it slightly and indirectly. This explains, perhaps, why so many men say that the feeling of being penetrated anally is one of being almost, almost, almost ready to orgasm. This is also interesting in light of a similar phenomenon with regard to vaginal penetration: that is, that during intercourse for most women, the clitoris is almost, but not quite, stimulated sufficiently for orgasm, giving women a feeling that they could almost orgasm—almost. But the feelings in both cases are often beautiful beyond description, and quite inimitable.

Many men enjoyed a woman penetrating their anus with a finger or other small object, and described great feelings of pleasure:

"When my girl goes down on me or when she is on top during intercourse, she reaches over or under and puts her finger about one or two inches up my rectum and makes low round movements. it drives me crazy. I never thought I would tell anyone this but I'm trying to be as honest as possible."

"I enjoy rectal penetration by a finger . . . the most intense orgasms I recall were by either oral or genital contact coupled with finger penetration . . . it feels like a delicious pain, an openness, a vulnerability, a focusing of all my energy and desire."

Emotional feelings during anal stimulation

"Is anal intercourse more satisfying physically or emotionally? Probably emotionally, although I feel somewhat strange admitting that. Because after the act is complete what I remember most vividly and savor long afterward was the union, the tenderness, and the language that was established between my partner and myself. The good physical feeling derives more from the close physical contact with my partner."

"It feels like the other person is 'with in' me. I only let people I love fuck me. It is like someone physically putting their love in me."

"It makes me feel joined and part of the man I am with, having him inside me. This is an act with my body which I give the right to very few—it is my way of showing total trust and unity with the lover and a time when I can enjoy the feeling of total passivity and what society terms femininity. It is that feeling of masculinity and femininity combined which makes me feel complete inside my body and mind."

"I feel like I'm wanting a person in me. I mean deep like in soul or something."

"It's a feeling of surrender, but I know I won't be hurt by my lover. It's a feeling of fullness and power in my lover."

Toward a New Male Sexuality

Men loved almost all of the activities in this chapter, and felt that they did not get enough of them—including fellatio, being stimulated and caressed on their penis, testicles, and anus, perhaps masturbating with a partner, and general foreplay and touching. Perhaps many men would like to end the focus on intercourse as being "*the* sex act," but cultural pressures (both internal and external) are such that they feel that they have no right to do so, as "men."

Many men seemed to feel on a gut level that somehow they were missing out—and yet our culture's prescriptions about sexuality (and "masculinity") have been so strong, that only a few have been able to go past them and follow their own feelings, create their own personal sexuality.

Most men in this study did not want to be penetrated, either physically or emotionally—and yet *did* want it. Just as in love and marriage men believe they will be happy dominating the relationship, controlling it, rather than risking their guts to a more equal, give-and-take relationship—just so in traditional sex men say they want to penetrate the other, thrust, be in charge, in control, and define the end of sex, the goal, as their orgasm, and yet they long for the opposite, to be out of control, also dominated by the other. To control something, whether it be sex or a relationship, is boring in the long run. And yet most men *do* want to be in deeper contact—to feel more—to not only take, but also be penetrated and taken.

What would this kind of sex be like? "Sexuality" as we know it has usually had orgasm as its object; but sensuality, being without an object, would allow you to go beyond the bounds of everyday existence to experience an end to rational awareness, a losing of the "self"—to feel, to be, in a pure state, to renew yourself, to reach a stage of intensity, letting layers of feeling penetrate deeper and deeper, until you feel yourself transformed. As Isolde sings to Tristan, as they are making love, she wishes "to live and die in eternal night—in the heaving swell, in the resounding echoes, in the universal stream of the world breath, to drown, to founder, unconscious, in utmost rapture."

Passion is one of the most beautiful parts of all sensuality—the desire to possess, to take, to ravish and be ravished, penetrate and be penetrated. But is physical love real love? While love is caring, love is also passion and desire, the desire to belong to, mingle with, be inside of another. Part of love is a sheer physical feeling—a desire not only to have orgasm or "sex," but to lie close while sleeping together, to inhale the breath of the other, to press chests (and souls) together as tightly, as closely, as possible; to lie feeling the other breathe as they sleep, their breath grazing your cheek and mingling with your own breath; to smell their body, caress their mouth with your tongue as if it were your own mouth, know the smell and taste of their genitals—to feel with your finger inside them, to caress the opening of their buttocks. What is love? Love is talking and understanding and counting on and being counted on, but love is also the deepest intermingling of bodies. In a way, body memory of a loved one is stronger and lasts longer than all the other memories.

Men Encounter Female Orgasm

Doubts, Questions, and Lack of Information About Women's Orgasms

What is the cause of women's seeming lack of interest in sex? Of what many men called women's "passivity" during sex? Certainly it is not any innate biological difference from men in desire for orgasm* or desire for closeness and touching. Nor is it, for the most part, "Victorian upbringing," although this was the reason usually ascribed to it by men. Nor is it related in older women to "menopause," since this does not in any way reduce or end women's sexual feelings.

Let's look at one of the most obvious explanations—an explanation which has been emerging gradually over the last ten years: that is, that most women's need for specific (non-coital) clitoral stimulation to orgasm is frequently not recognized—so that many women never or only irregularly orgasm during sex with men. This cultural denial of women's sexual needs reflects the larger social system in which women have been given second-class status for hundreds of years, and is part of a larger problem between men and women.

How has this affected men? How has women's lack of orgasm, or the irregularity of their orgasms, made men feel? How has it put pressures on men? Increased tensions between men and women? And how is this new information, and possibly women's new active role, being accepted and integrated—or not being integrated—into sex?

Most men who answered the questionnaire experienced a great deal of insecurity and confusion over knowing when—or whether—a woman had had an orgasm. (The overwhelming majority were looking for this orgasm during intercourse.) In fact, most men had great doubts about whether, or how frequently, women had orgasms with them; 61 percent of the men who answered said they usually could not tell when a woman had an orgasm, or could not be sure.

* Most women masturbate to orgasm very regularly, especially when not reaching orgasm with a partner; just because women's desire for orgasm has often been hidden from society does not mean it is any less than men's.

170

Most men still assume women should orgasm from intercourse and lack information about the clitoris

"I always assumed there was something wrong with them if they couldn't orgasm with each intercourse without clitoral stimulation. That prejudice dies hard. Although now I know what the truth is, doubts still remain just below rational consciousness."

"One weekend my wife sent the kids off to their grandparents' house, and then she told me she had something to tell me. Well, what it was was that she didn't have orgasms the way I thought she did, that she didn't mean to hurt me, that she had really loved having sex with me all those years, but she just hadn't been honest. I was flabbergasted, I didn't know what to say. We started talking and she told me just how she did orgasm, and then I couldn't believe my eyes, she showed me how she did it. I have never been the same since, I mean for the better. I fell in love with her all over again, or anyway, I got a case of the hots for her that didn't quiet down for about six months. She was *much* more interested in sex than before. I learned how to make her come with my hand and we started specializing in weekend-long sex sessions. It was just too much. Bliss. Heaven. I was ready to die."

"When I first read that women needed stimulation on their clitoris, and didn't usually orgasm with the penis, I thought, but what about all those women who had orgasms with me? Then I realized maybe they didn't really have orgasms, maybe they were just excited *with me*. I usually said something like "Was it good?" and they would say yeah—but maybe they didn't orgasm at all. That thought really shoots my ego down. Why don't they tell men? Why put men in such a stupid position? It made me feel like a fool, not knowing all those years, and acting like such a big jock. Were the women laughing at me behind my back? Or feeling sorry for me, or thinking I was stupid? Did other men treat them different? It's all just too hard to believe."

Most men (61 percent of the study) do not know, or are not sure, when a woman has an orgasm. Much of this uncertainty is due to the fact that men have wrongly been taught that woman should orgasm from the thrusting of the penis, and have been told very little about clitoral stimulation, and so are looking for women's orgasm at the wrong time. The fact is that only approximately 30 percent of women do orgasm from intercourse itself★ (usually from pubic area contact, rather than

★ This figure reflects the answers of 3,019 women in *The Hite Report on Female Sexuality*.

171

thrusting per se); on the other hand, most women orgasm easily from more direct clitoral stimulation.

In spite of this, most men still assume women should orgasm from simple thrusting during intercourse, and would greatly prefer that they do.

"Would you prefer to have sex with a woman who has orgasm from intercourse (coitus), rather than clitoral stimulation? When does your partner usually orgasm?"

Most men still assume women should/would orgasm from simple intercourse (coitus):*

"If she didn't come during intercourse I would wonder why she didn't."

"Some women will not orgasm from intercourse. Either they do not know how to make themselves orgasm or they do not want to. I feel a woman should orgasm during intercourse. She should try all different positions till she finds one that is best for her. If a woman can have fantasies when she is having intercourse and learn how to enjoy each movement, she will find that she will orgasm. I have taught this to many women with good results. Of course, the man has to know how to fuck."

"A lot of women have trouble reaching a climax. Some women should have surgery or go to a psychiatrist. I went with four women in a row that had to have manual stimulation to reach a climax. I was a little bit shaky, wondering if the entire sex had gone to pot."

"I believe that a woman's emotions play a large part in whether she has an orgasm. If I am tender and careful to be attentive to her during intercourse and still she doesn't have an orgasm, then the problem is in her head. She either doesn't love me enough or is preoccupied with something that's bothering her or something. If she wants to be orgasmic, I believe that a woman can be."

And the overwhelming majority of men† preferred the woman to orgasm from intercourse/coitus:

"I prefer to have sex with a woman who orgasms from intercourse to a woman who only orgasms from clitoral stimulation."

"I like it if she gets off when I do; I feel like that is the most 'natural' and free way for me."

---

* Answers seen here include men of all ages, points of view and backgrounds; younger and older men alike were just as likely to expect women to orgasm from intercourse, and to be unfamiliar with giving clitoral stimulation to orgasm.
† Of those who understood the question.

"I prefer intercourse because during intercourse you get the idea that you're both thoroughly involved at the same time."

"Coitus, because I want to feel her orgasm on my penis. Also, I think her orgasm would be more violent and all-encompassing."

"Coitus because otherwise it seems too one-sided."

But most men in this study had not had the actual experience of giving a woman an orgasm from specific clitoral stimulation, and thus were answering theoretically.

An almost equally large number answered "either" or "both." Often they included the phrases "I don't care how she has orgasms—either way," or "It doesn't matter to me how she does it," or "Any way she wants to." These statements seemed to indicate less a willingness to try anything than a kind of lack of knowledge, or frustration with the "problem" of women's orgasms—or lack of interest. Perhaps it was easier for these men to say something like "It doesn't matter to me as long as she gets pleasure," than to really distinguish what it is their partners specifically require:

"It doesn't really matter—any way they want to get off is fine with me."

"It doesn't make much difference to me."

"It doesn't matter to me. They usually come during intercourse."

"I have only had intercourse with my wife. I don't care how she has orgasm, she can have it any way she wants to. If my wife wants to stimulate herself with a freight train she has my blessing. I will even be the conductor. But if my wife does not orgasm during intercourse I do not feel bad. In fact, I like it better when she does not orgasm because she will be warmer next time. She is best when she orgasms about once a week."

"I enjoy the freedom of stimulation in any manner. I dislike any limitations."

"I don't really prefer any certain way for the woman to get off. I don't think that much about whether she is getting off but I do what I can to make the experience the most exhilarating for the both of us."

"It doesn't matter to me. I prefer to have sex with women that are sexually uninhibited, with open minds, and have clear thoughts about themselves and their sexuality."

"Who cares? As long as she gets as much pleasure from me as I get from her, it shouldn't matter."

"It doesn't really matter to me where she gets her orgasmic sensations."

And several men said they would prefer "both"—as long as her orgasm during intercourse was the grand finale:

"I prefer a woman who has both. The best times are when I can create at least a couple of clitoral orgasms before we begin to have intercourse and then be able to make her climax vaginally three or four times."

"The woman who has orgasm first from clitoral, then again during intercourse with my orgasm is the best."

However, some men who gave "both" as their answer indicated a more complete understanding of the alternatives:

"Sometimes I would prefer to have her orgasm from intercourse rather than from clitoral stimulation, but not always. It's a different sort of enjoyment. When she orgasms from intercourse, I have to exercise more self-discipline. However, it does cause contractions in her vagina which give me a good deal of pleasure, as well as her body movements just prior to orgasm. But if she orgasms from clitoral stimulation, I can then fuck at my own speed knowing that she is not depending on me to last a certain length of time. Also when she has her orgasm prior to my entry, it makes her very loose and slippery and sensual, which I like."

"I don't feel it is very important whether the woman has orgasm from intercourse or clitoral stimulation. Most of the women I have known have had orgasms more readily, and apparently with as much pleasure, from clitoral stimulation. I get a big kick out of stimulating a woman to orgasm with my hand. Orgasm during actual intercourse is also nice. If I stimulate a woman with my hand during sex, it often is the case that the woman can experience more than one orgasm. If she only has orgasm during intercourse, it often excites me to the point of orgasm too, and the woman then has less chance of multiple orgasms, my potential for frequent orgasms being very small."

Many men avoided answering this question directly, often discussing the importance of feelings, while ignoring the issue of how the woman actually did orgasm:

"The partner's type of stimulation is not as important as that there be mutual physical satisfaction and love."

"How she orgasms is not as important as if she feels love in the act."

"This is a tricky question. Let's just say that I'll do whatever my partner needs to have done for an orgasm. I'm one of those fools who links sex and love as much as possible—in other words, I try just to make love to women I care a lot about—so giving a woman an orgasm is more important than the process of doing so. In summation of all this, I really don't have a preference."

"I prefer to have sex with a woman who has knowledge of how to stimulate me and no hang-ups about any part of her own anatomy."

"I guess it doesn't matter how they do it as long as they do it with me."

"The question is whether she had pleasure from going to bed with me and not whether she had an orgasm."

"I enjoy intercourse with a woman who also enjoys inter-course—however that is accomplished."

Others expressed confusion over whether intercourse itself actually provides indirect clitoral stimulation for the woman:*

"Why separate orgasm from intercourse from orgasm from clitoral stimulation? Can't coitus also stimulate the clitoris? I do not really have a preference anyway—I want to give a woman what she wants, and as I observe orgasm, I can't tell any difference. Nearly all women can orgasm from finger/tongue stimulation directly to the clitoris. Some have a very hard time reaching orgasm from straight coitus."

"I try to have my woman get off first during foreplay, then intercourse; both are clitoral stimulation just by different means—or am I mistaken? If they have an orgasm at all, I'm happy."

"Aren't they the same? Isn't *that* question settled yet?"

Or held the misconception that it did:†

"I believe clitoral stimulation is the only way a woman can reach orgasm. What most people feel is coital stimulation is really a very gentle and indirect clitoral stimulation."

A few men used the phrase "She gets clitoral stimulation from my penis," with no explanation given as to what the writer meant, or as to how this might be true—implying a possible misunderstanding of female anatomy:

"During intercourse I never had a woman stimulate herself other than to rub her clitoris against my inserted penis."

---

* For a discussion of the differences between *The Hite Report on Female Sexuality* and Masters and Johnson on this issue, see *The Hite Report on Female Sexuality*, chapter 3. Basically, Masters and Johnson have said that women should get sufficient indirect clitoral stimulation from the penis's traction on the skin surrounding the vagina, which is indirectly connected to the skin covering the clitoris, to reach orgasm; however, *The Hite Report on Female Sexuality*, based on a much larger sample, found that, in practice, this was not effective for the large majority of women, who need more direct clitoral stimulation for orgasm.
† Women in *The Hite Report on Female Sexuality* who had orgasm during intercourse without the addition of manual clitoral stimulation usually got the needed clitoral stimulation from friction on their mons, in contact with the man's pubic area, and not from simple thrusting inside the vagina.

"I believe that a woman who has coitus orgasm can be easier stimulated to orgasm than one who has clitoral orgasm because of the location of the penis in the vaginal tract."

"Standing up against a wall allows the woman to get more stimulation of her clitoris. As the penis goes into the vagina the outer lips are pulled down and in slightly. This allows the swollen clitoris to contact the top of the penis and thereby stimulate the woman. However, if the woman is shorter than the man, he must either bend slightly at the knees or she must stand in a little higher on some support."

"All orgasms are from the clitoris. My penis comes in consistent contact with my wife's clitoris so she's really getting clitoral stimulation as part of our intercourse."

One man commented:
"Some women like to rub the shaft of the penis against their clitoris as I move in and out, but that is agonizing because it bends the shaft where it isn't supposed to bend."

However, the fact that these methods can work for some women in some situations does not imply that all women "should" be able to make them work. For example, a great many women can orgasm only with their legs and thighs together.

Most men who had done clitoral stimulation clearly thought of the clitoris as something there to fall back on if nothing else worked; for a woman to have an orgasm from clitoral stimulation was second best.

Many also said, surprisingly, that they would still prefer the woman to orgasm from coitus—even though this was not the case or would be impossible!

Other men, however, clearly expressed that—since it is the woman's anatomy!—it is the woman, not the man, who has the right to a preference:

"Whatever my wife wants is best. *She's* what I want."

"I love whatever she loves. I love *her*, not a 'type' of woman who orgasms from one thing or another."

"No preferences. You have to find what each woman prefers. I would simply adjust."

"Her choice."

"No preference. Trying out new ideas means more pleasure."

"My goal is to please her, who cares where she operates from."

"Whatever *she* likes best."

"I believe that it is the woman's right to have orgasm in whatever way she wants. For too long men have dictated what the 'right' way for a woman to act should be. Sex should be for mutual pleasure and should involve sharing. Each partner should get the maximum out of it that is possible. If a woman prefers clitoral stimulation, then it is her right to expect it."

A few men did say that not only is clitoral stimulation necessary but that they also enjoyed it:

"Clitoral stimulation is enjoyable because I can be 100 percent aware of what is happening to her—preceding, during, and after her orgasm—without having my orgasm distract me from my attention to her."

"I enjoy stimulating the clitoris and bringing on orgasm manually."★

Conclusion

There was an unfortunate tendency in some of the answers to this question to hope or assume, if the respondent was aware of the statistics of *The Hite Report on Female Sexuality*, that his partner was among the 30 percent of women who do get clitoral stimulation during intercourse (adequate to orgasm)—and a further tendency to believe that the most "mature" and "best" women are naturally among the 30 percent.

How did men feel when they first understood women's need for clitoral stimulation as separate from coitus?
Some men told how they had felt when they first realized that (contrary to cultural stereotypes) clitoral stimulation was more important for most women's orgasms than intercourse itself—that intercourse did not actually lead to orgasm for most women:

"I used to think I understood feminine sexuality—you know, I was gentle, patient, understanding, etc.—if they 'couldn't' orgasm, it was 'O.K.,' I let them get on top during intercourse and *everything* (a real sport, wasn't I?). Anyway, now I see that the sensitivity I had that I thought was about 90 percent was more like 10 percent." (Age twenty-two.)

"I guess I had personally observed in my own experience that the clitoris was the place of excitement in the female; I know that on many occasions I knocked myself out thrusting in the female with little effect. There was something wrong, but I must admit I was crestfallen when I

★ These statements are included here because, even though they seem unremarkable, they were very rare.

finally became aware that what I had suspected was true—male thrusting of the penis in the female vagina is not what we males thought it was." (Age thirty-eight.)

"I didn't feel good when I heard it. I didn't feel good for them, like a car with a defect that the dealer wouldn't fix. You're stuck with it and have to work around it. Or don't drive. (Age thirty.)

"The other day a friend of mine told me that I was making a mistake expecting women to orgasm during intercourse with me, and that I should try to stimulate them some other way. This was radical news to me. It was odd, talking about it with another man like that. I have never really talked about sex with another man before, except the usual stories, etc. I wonder what he thought of my reaction, or if he thought I should have known or what. Anyway, I'm glad he told me." (Age thirty-one.)

"Through almost eleven years of marriage, I believed that orgasm through intercourse was the rule rather than the exception. I 'knew' that the clitoris was part of the female orgasm process—nothing more. In the last year a lover entered my life (I am still married) and it is with her and through reading *The Hite Report* that I began to understand the function of the clitoris and the importance of manual stimulation. It has opened up a whole new side of sexuality, an addition." (Age forty.)

Certain men had accepted the information with relief and a sense of pleasure—especially when it confirmed their own personal experience or when they thought that the "problem" had been their fault:

"My wife has never orgasmed from intercourse. I used to feel that something was wrong with my technique or with my wife's frame of mind (mental block). Now all that is gone and forgotten. She can always orgasm from clitoral stimulation, so we are not missing something." (Age forty-six.)

"I can't believe we have been deceived so long about the penis–vagina orgasm. I am sure my wife (and I) would have developed much more sensibly if we had known this fact thirty-five years ago. I often felt sad and puzzled that she did not orgasm from intercourse. I was relieved to find out that this is normal." (Age fifty-seven.)

One man had worried at first that the news that women needed more clitoral stimulation would mean even more work for him, and even more pressure to perform ("give the woman an orgasm"):

"At first I was worried because I thought this would mean more responsibility for me, that women needed more stimulation, not that it would make things easier in the long run. But that's how it worked out, really, because I don't have to strain so much during intercourse for a result that's impossible anyway—and besides, sometimes she helps me with her hand on top of mine stimulating her clitoris. I'm glad I learned." (Age forty-six.)

Some men voiced the difficulties of changing:

"I feel a great resistance in myself to the idea that a woman really needs direct clitoral or mons stimulation to orgasm. She *should* be able to orgasm during intercourse—that is what men have always said. And yet, if it isn't true, it isn't true. I know I should accept it, but it's really a revolutionary change in all my assumptions (and the way I've always behaved). I have to force myself to believe it. And yet, how egotistical can I be, with my very own love telling me it is so? Change is hard."

"It's a bit worrying to think of women not enjoying intercourse as we do—hope they're not going to lock us out of their vaginas forever. Still, the facts of female physiology can't be denied, even if they're not as men might wish. As Martin Luther declared: 'There I stand. I can do no other.' "

One man was grappling with the information and its implications—wondering how the woman felt about intercourse and how he himself should feel about it—and in the process rethinking his own definition of sex:

"First of all my partner, my wife, has never orgasmed during intercourse, or in my presence, while nearly every time we have had intercourse, I have come to orgasm and ejaculation. Never! Here is the way I feel about it. Besides expecting to orgasm during sexual intercourse, I rejoice in the fact that I can orgasm during intercourse. I consider orgasm during masturbation and during intercourse as two different types of orgasm: masturbatory orgasm, for me, is a selfish orgasm, a self-love orgasm, all for myself. Orgasm during intercourse, to me, is a mutual orgasm, that is, I feel that I have not brought myself to 'come,' but also that my wife has helped me to 'come.' The fact I am enjoying the physical contact and closeness with her, the fact she has allowed me to penetrate her, make love to her, is an intricate/intimate articulation of the fact my orgasm is in part a gift from her. To me, emotionally and psychologically, this is ultimate, this kind of orgasm means so much more to me than my own masturbatory orgasm. This is how I feel I am.

"But I feel bothered I cannot bring her to orgasm during a mutual experience of lovemaking and intercourse. I do *not* feel bothered because I feel responsible to bring her to 'come,' or that 'it is my job.' I have transcended this expectation. She is entitled to her orgasms as I am (masturbatorily). But, because I feel so much ecstasy when I have come

179

while having coitus with her, I feel that I can be a part of an orgasm with her. I want to give or bring her to orgasm. Can you sympathize or empathize with me? When I come and she does not, I feel one-sided about the orgasmic ecstasy: I feel I have reached a plateau she has not, which does make me feel alone in ecstasy, sometimes lonely. I desire my body, myself, and my lovemaking to be in part hers, for her, the gift of myself to her.

"Since we are both aware of *The Hite Report on Female Sexuality*, my wife no longer feels the pressure or feels inferior about not being able to 'come' with me. Now, I feel good about this fact and more realistic about the reality of female orgasm. However, this fact does not exonerate my desire to be a part of her orgasm, especially in the knowledge of who I am to her.

"As for helping my wife (if she wants it) to come before or after I come, I feel all game and willing to participate in this. But she feels a bit embarrassed to stimulate herself 'in front of me.' This is O.K. What I wish to make clear is that I am quite willing to help her come, in whatever manner it takes."

A popular response was to say that the woman's orgasm is her own responsibility:

"It's her business. She is responsible for her own orgasms."

"I offer everything. If she doesn't accept, I'm clean."

"It's her decision."

"The problem would be more hers than mine. She needs to know what turns her on."

"It's not my problem. It's up to her."

"I consider myself ultimately responsible for providing my own orgasms. To be hard-nosed about it, I frankly consider a woman ultimately responsible for hers too. None of my relationships has ever been so lacking in respect, tenderness, and diplomacy that we degenerated to fighting about orgasms, but if it did happen, and I was accused of 'being not man enough,' I would counter righteously that it takes two, and it is more than likely that she wasn't woman enough."

Conclusion

These slightly defensive or hostile answers are certainly correct in one sense—that everyone does, finally, make his or her own orgasm. However, a woman's situation is different from that of a man. To

180

imply that women are not taking their fair share of responsibility for what goes on overlooks the fact that most "sex" is still carried on according to the old rules—that is, the woman is supposed to orgasm from intercourse, intercourse *is* sex, it is assumed that intercourse will be included, and that the man has the right to the appropriate stimulation for his orgasm, i.e., intercourse. The man has society behind him, encouraging him to have his orgasm, but the woman has society telling her that what she needs—i.e., clitoral stimulation to orgasm, usually in the form of manual or oral stimulation—is not "normal," or that she has no right to assert herself. In other words, our pattern of sex does not put men in the position of having to ask for the stimulation they need; it is clear that "sex" should end with intercourse and male orgasm, whereas women must request "special" ("extra") stimulation, and/or stimulation not related to intercourse. As one man put it, "If the woman needs some special stimulation, she should let the guy know."

In summary, many men were very annoyed with women for not having orgasm more frequently or more easily during sex—feeling, "Why are women being so difficult? They could orgasm if they wanted to, if they would just try a little harder, or if they were not being overly emotionally complicated—why are they trying to make men feel bad?"—not realizing that it is the lack of adequate clitoral stimulation in traditional "sex" that makes orgasm difficult for most women, and not esoteric reasons. There was a great sense of annoyance, anger, and hostility in these answers—*why* are women so difficult after all?

"Women should speak up"
Other men felt the situation was the woman's fault in the sense that the woman should tell the man what she needs—and should especially speak up about her need for clitoral stimulation outside of intercourse—although here again, many answers seemed still to imply that the woman would speak up about some particular preferences *during* intercourse. Men were frequently angry if they felt women wouldn't tell them what they wanted:

"There is something wrong with me only if a woman lets me know that she can orgasm if I do a certain thing, and I refuse to do it. Nothing works all the time for everyone, and I'm not going to stake my manhood on my ability to read minds."

"I would prefer she would tell me anything she wants rather than dead silence."

"It's her fault. I'm not a mind reader. She has to tell me what to do."

"I would help, if she would just *tell* me. It *really* pisses me off to

181

think that a girl would tell me she had come when she hadn't and wanted to. Hell, that's what I'm there for!"

"If I have anything to say about it, I pretty well know what it takes for a woman to orgasm *before* I climb into bed with her. If she plays games, is consistently noncommittal, and won't talk straight about it, then I think she gets what she deserves; if she can verbalize a little about where she's at, then we'll probably do O.K. Women who are scared to tell a guy where they're at are usually too timid for me to really open up with either. I wish I knew what they were scared of."

"If I ever make love to another woman, I will insist that she express her feelings freely and tell me what she really wants. Then it's up to me to act on what she says."

"It's the woman's fault for *not telling*!"

"I assume that if she's not satisfied she'll tell me. But again, just try to find a woman this open—I think it's almost impossible. This is why I'm sick and tired of women's libbers telling everybody that men just like to 'love 'em and leave 'em.' This is bullshit. The truth is that women avoid being controlled by men by being secretive and unpredictable."

"Many women indicated that they could not even suggest that their male partner was not satisfying them because if they did he would just *fall apart*. I felt a little insulted by that. I'm a big boy. If I'm not stimulating your clitoris correctly or whatever, tell me. I can handle that. I think most men can."

"So much of what women seem to think about men seems so blatantly unfair. It seems that women have only recently discovered the nature and depth of their own sexuality with the feminist movement, discovering for the first time what they share and where they're completely individual. Yet women are angry at men for not understanding their sexuality already (we're supposed always to be the competent, skilful, knowledgeable ones, right? And if we're not, we're less masculine, right?) as if men should be experts at something about women that even women didn't know!"

Feelings of alienation, blame, guilt, and anger were created in many men when the woman didn't orgasm

"How do you feel if the woman you are with does not have an orgasm at all in any way?"
Doubts about how or if women were having orgasms frequently made men feel uncomfortable, guilty, inadequate, or defensive during

sex—although some men said that they didn't care whether a woman had orgasms or not, since women's orgasms were not that important. But most men, still assuming women should orgasm during intercourse, all too often wound up feeling alienated, and either blaming themselves or blaming women for not achieving what really is very difficult or impossible to achieve.

Men had many ways of expressing this discomfort:

I accept it, but it is as if a part of her is not allowing itself to open to me.

Like a doctor who loses a patient on the surgery table.

Inadequate, a poor lover, a failure.

Sorry for her.

Pity her.

Depressed, disappointed. Feelings of self-hatred.

She says it's O.K., but I worry.

Disappointed with her.

Like I'm in bed with a cold dead fish.

Not concerned.

There's no point in making love.

A selfish pig.

With my first wife, I became indifferent.

Sensitive and hurt.

I feel parasitic or unexciting.

Disappointed because there was no mutuality.

Disgusted if it's a pattern.

Surprise—what was all that noise about?—uncertainty, disappointment. Does she mind? What did I do wrong? What should I have done? But she seems O.K.

Angry.

Defeated.

Lousy, but I don't worry about it.

I would lose interest in her.

Growing disillusionment.

Sorry—she helped me even though she didn't want it.

Disappointed for her—not for me!

I used to feel rejected.

Sorry for her—I ask what she likes for next time.

It's nicer if she does; it makes the air clearer after.

Lack of women's orgasm, mainly due to cultural imperatives which insist women should orgasm when men do, has been an unspoken source of alienation between men and women over the years. As one man put it, "I feel more respect for her and myself if I don't feel I am cheating her out of an orgasm—or I guess the word is 'using' her, since I have an orgasm and she doesn't. I feel relieved to be with an equal." And another man said, "I have been married for sixteen years. My wife reaches orgasm only with some difficulty. I have been trying all means of helping her gain confidence and relaxation during intercourse, but I believe that there is a shade of jealousy in her mind about my easy satisfaction."

All this could lead to feelings of guilt and negativity:

"I feel inadequate. Sometimes I wonder just how good a sex partner I am. But I guess we all have those doubts."

"I feel I am at fault.'

"It's something I have done wrong."

"I have not done enough or the 'right' thing."

"I let her down."

"I failed her."

"I must be inadequate."

Men and the Clitoris:
A Moment in History

Men's Feelings About Giving a Woman
Clitoral Stimulation to Orgasm

In 1976, women's need for clitoral stimulation to orgasm (not coincidental to intercourse) became a public issue. For many men, this was the first time they encountered these facts. How did they react to this new information?

What were men's general attitudes toward the clitoris? When men were asked, "How do you feel about the clitoris?" many answers included jokes or satirical remarks:

"How do I feel about the clitoris? I feel in awe of the little bugger. It's gotten so much publicity and become the focal point of so much rancor that I have the urge to salute it when I see it."

"A woman's clitoris is the greatest thing since the mop—other questions redundant."

In many other answers, the importance of the clitoris was brought into question by the frequent use of diminutives:*

"A woman's clitoris is a wonderful little thing."

"The clitoris is a mysterious little 'love button.' "

"I think it is cute as it peeps out from its hiding place. Sometimes girls call it the 'tickle button.' "

"Big surprises come in little packages."

"Cute little devil."

But there were enthusiastic and positive remarks too—some beautiful and serious, others containing some of the diminutives and

---

* The exterior clitoris as we know it is only a part of a very large internal clitoral network. See the drawing on page 65.

humorous phrases mentioned before:

"It is the primary erotic center of her body, tender and sensitive, and has to be treated with great care and emotion."

"It's just as important to her as my penis is to me."

"Beautiful, stimulating, the most sensual part of a woman's body."

"The clitoris is the blasting cap on a stick of dynamite. It is the trigger mechanism which puts everything else into motion."

"The clitoris is the center of her emotional sexuality, and once I have it under my finger or tongue, I know she's mine!"

"Wonderful organ."

"It's the most important part of the vulva. A man that has loved a woman and cares for her knows these things."

"It amazes me. It's the center of my wife's entire sexual being. Every square micron must be packed with nerve endings because of her reaction when I touch it or even get near it."

"It's the area where I come most in contact with her sexual feelings."

"An amazing thing, because it's so hidden but has such a powerful effect on women."

"Very beautiful and mysterious."

A few men professed complete neutrality:

"What do I think about it? Nothing really."

"I never really felt anything about it emotionally."

"O.K., I guess."

"Nothing special."

"No particular feeling. I know where it is after medical anatomy courses."

"It is just a part of her that I caress now and then, but nothing to rave over."

"If that is the point she wants stimulated, I will stimulate it. But I don't have any special feeling about it any more than I have any special feeling about any other body part that isn't in plain sight. It's like asking me how I feel about her liver."

Others had had no experience, or bad experiences:

"She won't let me touch it."

"My wife says my finger hurts it."

"The clitoris is a strange thing to me. It protrudes."

"I could never find my wife's. She doesn't seem to have one."

"I'm not sure what the clitoris is."

And one man said:

MEN AND THE CLITORIS: A MOMENT IN HISTORY

"I have no feelings about it. She shouldn't have one."

When men were asked, "What does the clitoris look like?" there was a wide range of replies—many containing elements of discomfort and unfamiliarity, and sometimes hostility, again often using diminutives:

A small hooded pink bump which enlarges on arousal.

It looks like a tiny worm which needs sunlight . . .very pale.

It looks good and tasty.

When the hood is pulled back, it looks like a red pea coming out of its shell.

Like the tip of a male cat's penis.

It looks like a funny little critter peeping out of its house.

Pink and easily mistaken for another part if you are not careful.

A small pink mound.

A tiny titty jelly bean (I like the red ones).

Like a grapefruit seed in a translucent veil of tissue.

A shiny translucent pimple.

Small, round, pink, and sensitive.

Beautiful. A pearly little head. I have not seen it as illustrated in books.

Like a dog's penis.

Anything from an unnoticeable rise to a swollen mound.

Cute nubbin about an inch or so that's pink and smooth and tender —not fully developed. Concealed as a hard lump beneath the skin.

A small nipple—that's why I love to suck it.

It looks like a woman's helmet or something similar at the tip.

Why, it looks like a clitoris, of course.

But most men said they had never actually seen the clitoris:

"Never seen one in real life."

"Only seen them in books."

"I've never seen one because the lights are off or my eyes are closed."

"The clitoris remains somewhat of a mystery to me. I know what it is and where it is located from pictures and descriptions in my biology classes, but I have never been shown a girl's clitoris and I'm not sure I could find a girl's clitoris if I had to."

"I learned long ago that the top of a woman's cunt was very sensitive to touch from hand or tongue when she was aroused, but I had no idea of the location or name of the clitoris before reading about it. And I have never seen it."

"I've seen diagrams and photos but not my partner's clitoris—she admonished me not to 'play doctor.' Instead we have operated by verbal feedback, i.e., 'further up . . . a little to the right.' This seems to work O.K."

"The clitoris swells and is easier to find as a woman becomes aroused. But I have never turned on the lights, sat back, and examined one, so I am unclear about the exact description."

"I was never told about the clitoris, nor about the shape of a woman's vulva (apart from there being a hole there). Nor did I hear where the urethra was. So I've had some difficulty in finding my way in on various occasions. I haven't seen it or examined it in detail, but believe I know where it is. Just inside the top of the main slit. Incredibly high up in fact, right out of the region that I used to consider as cunt."

"I don't know much about a woman's clitoris, but I'd like to know more. I don't know exactly where it is or what exactly it looks like. It's never been important to any of my lovers yet."

"I know where it's supposed to be according to the books but she's apparently fully hooded and it is never exposed. At the slightest pressure it rolls sideways and gets lost again."

And most men of every age said they had gotten most of their information out of books:

"I have only learned about the clitoris from books on sexuality. No women have ever shared any information on their clitoris or masturbatory style with me." (Age twenty-five.)

"I took a course in college that filled me in about some of the intimacies of marriage, but real awareness about the clitoris came only in the last ten years when I picked up a book about it. No woman has ever *shown* me her clitoris. I took the liberty to explore my wife, once, not knowing if she would even approve." (Age fifty.)

"I learned about the clitoris from pornographic books." (Age thirty.)

"I read about it recently in some anatomy literature." (Age seventy-four.)

"I first heard the word 'clitoris' on the radio, and then looked it up in a few books. I was surprised to find that so important a part of human anatomy and sexuality existed, that was spoken of so little." (Age twenty-eight.)

"I read in a book that it was the center of sexual stimulation for a woman and that its manipulation is necessary for her orgasm. (Age thirty-two.)

"From texts I've tried to learn best how to stimulate it, especially with my tongue." (Age thirty-eight.)

"Until I read about it recently (my wife gave me a book), I didn't realize the importance of the clitoris, I just thought of powerful thrusting intercourse as the thing a woman would like." (Age sixty-two.)

"I read in a book in college that the clitoris was anatomically synonymous with the glans penis. I got the impression that it was much more 'like a penis' than it turned out to be. I thought it would be much bigger (longer) than it actually is." (Age thirty-three.)

When asked, "Where is the clitoris?," although most men knew basically where it is, many of the answers were rather vague. The most common answer was: "At the top of the vagina." It is unlikely that most men think the clitoris is inside the vagina; are these men using the word "vagina" to mean "vulva"?

"High up on her vagina."
"Just above the vagina."
"Right at the top of the vagina."
"It's between the lips above the vaginal opening."
"Centered just above the vaginal opening."
"Under the hood/sheath in front of/top of the vagina."
"Very top edge of the vagina."
"Top of the vaginal opening."

Clearer descriptions included the following:
"It's near the top of the 'crack.'"
"It's higher up than one would think—and farther away from the vagina."
"It's at the upper end of the outer lips, near the pelvic bone."
"It's above the vagina toward the belly button."
"At the top (pubic bone) end of the vagina."
"It's under the V-shaped hood in front of the vagina (I hope)."
"It's at the upper corner of the genitals. When it's stimulated, it hides under its hood."
"Right above the pee hole."
"At the base of the mons, sandwiched between several folds of flesh."
"Hiding under the covers above the vagina."

Also notable is the emotional reaction this question created in some men:
"I could give an average location in centimeters from the top of the vagina, etc., but there are many more questions I could better spend the time on."
"I would rather show than tell."
"In the illustration on page 6 of 'Sex for Third Graders.'"
"Sure ain't in her nose."

A few men said they did not know for sure:
"I have never separated the clitoris from the whole genital area."
"To tell the truth, I am not quite sure where a woman's clitoris is."
"I was performing cunnilingus one time and all of a sudden I stopped and said to my girlfriend, 'Where the heck is your clitoris anyway?' I think

SIMILARITIES BETWEEN CLITORIS AND PENIS ANATOMY

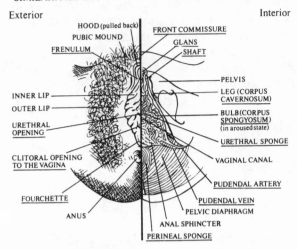

Exterior   Interior

HOOD (pulled back)
PUBIC MOUND
FRENULUM

FRONT COMMISSURE
GLANS
SHAFT

INNER LIP
OUTER LIP
URETHRAL OPENING

PELVIS
LEG (CORPUS CAVERNOSUM)
BULB (CORPUS SPONGYOSUM) (in aroused state)
URETHRAL SPONGE

CLITORAL OPENING TO THE VAGINA

VAGINAL CANAL

PUDENDAL ARTERY

FOURCHETTE
ANUS

PUDENDAL VEIN
PELVIC DIAPHRAGM
ANAL SPHINCTER
PERINEAL SPONGE

The clitoral system during arousal

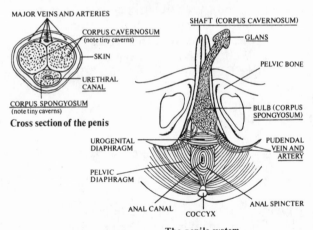

MAJOR VEINS AND ARTERIES

CORPUS CAVERNOSUM (note tiny caverns)
SKIN
URETHRAL CANAL

CORPUS SPONGYOSUM (note tiny caverns)
Cross section of the penis

SHAFT (CORPUS CAVERNOSUM)
GLANS
PELVIC BONE
BULB (CORPUS SPONGYOSUM)

UROGENITAL DIAPHRAGM
PELVIC DIAPHRAGM

PUDENDAL VEIN AND ARTERY

ANAL CANAL
COCCYX
ANAL SPINCTER

The penile system

From an original by Suzann Gage

There is a widespread misunderstanding of women's sexual anatomy. What we usually think of as the "clitoris" is simply the exterior part of a larger interior structure. The extent of this interior clitoral network is quite large—comparable to the size of the penis and testicles in men. Inside the penis there are two cavernous bulbs the length of the shaft that fill with blood and thus cause erection. These same two cavernous bulbs exist in the female; however, in the female they are separate, each extending on one side of the vulva, beginning at the pubic area (the exterior clitoris) and going back on either side of the vagina. During arousal they fill with blood and cause the entire area to swell: this is why a woman's vulva becomes swollen and puffy, pleasurably sensitive to the touch. When orgasm occurs, the blood is sent out of these structures in waves by muscle contractions. In other words, the clitoral system is similar in size to the penis, but the clitoral system is interior, while the penis is exterior. Both systems are the same in the early embryo.

190

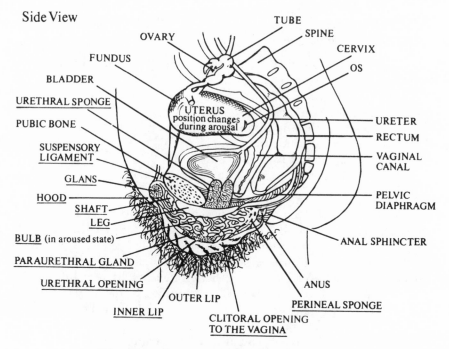

Side View

TUBE
SPINE
OVARY
CERVIX
FUNDUS
OS
BLADDER
URETHRAL SPONGE
UTERUS
position changes
during arousal
PUBIC BONE
URETER
RECTUM
SUSPENSORY
LIGAMENT
VAGINAL
CANAL
GLANS
HOOD
PELVIC
DIAPHRAGM
SHAFT
LEG
BULB (in aroused state)
ANAL SPHINCTER
PARAURETHRAL GLAND
URETHRAL OPENING
ANUS
OUTER LIP
INNER LIP
PERINEAL SPONGE
CLITORAL OPENING
TO THE VAGINA

The clitoral system during arousal

If men could understand the similarities of their structures to those of women, they could understand clitoral stimulation much more easily. For example, most men need stimulation at the top of their penis for orgasm, even though they feel the orgasm basically at the base of the penis and inside their bodies: stimulation at the sensitive tip and around the rim leads to sensations deeper inside the body. In the same way, stimulation of the exterior clitoral area causes sensations deeper in the body and vaginal area, culminating in orgasm.
From an original by Suzann Gage

191

she was a little embarrassed and just gave one-word answers, 'higher,' 'lower,' while I prodded with my finger. All of a sudden she said 'there.' I looked to see where my finger was, but I couldn't see anything special. I still don't know where it is."

And some men truly did not know where it was, stating that it was inside the vagina:
"It is inside the vagina."
"It is deep down inside."
"Between the lips up inside the vaginal opening."
"An inch or so inside the vagina."
"In the vagina just past the folds of skin."
"Just inside her pussy."

And some further comments:
"How do I feel about a woman's clitoris? Curious. I want to know what she feels as I stimulate it in different ways. I know where it should be, and where it has been on some partners, but I can't always find it with my fingers. With partners who don't like cunnilingus, I feel funny going down there to look for it, although I eventually resort to that if I can't feel it. In the partner who *did* like cunnilingus (the only one whose genitals I've had a really good close look at), it was a small mound about 3/8 inch in diameter and equally high. Red."

"I feel that feminine genitals are quite complicated, and it took me a long time, when I began to have sex, to find out exactly where everything was. It sounds silly, but it's true. I bet many men cannot really describe what a cunt is like. In college, I had a good school friend who insisted—joking, more or less—that in spite of having made love quite a few times, he had never found a clitoris, and suspected they didn't exist."

How do men feel about stimulating a woman clitorally by hand?

"I hate to admit it, but my wife's way of having orgasm used to really irritate me in the beginning. She always clenches her legs together, sometimes even twists them together while I am supposed to rub her clitoris. After all I had heard about a woman spreading her legs meaning she wants you, I felt that this was a rejection, and really, that there was something 'weird' about her. It took a couple of years before we could talk about this. In the beginning, I just did what I thought she wanted, but I really resented it, and gradually I began to do it less and less enthusiastically, I guess. Finally, we had a fight about it. She said she thought I resented her orgasms, and I said I thought she was being selfish when she had them. She didn't need me at all. I wasn't involved, I wasn't inside her, and I wasn't getting stimulated (although I have to admit that sometimes it was a pretty sexy situation, with her doing all that moaning and groaning, writhing and getting hot and sweaty, saying she loved me and grabbing me after—wow, very passionate kisses). Anyway, I still resented it. She was very hurt that I didn't enjoy her orgasms, and didn't want to have sex for a while. That got me started thinking, what was the point of sex anyway? It's taken me a long time to begin to accept that this is how she (women?) has orgasm, and that it doesn't mean that there is anything wrong with me because she doesn't do it during intercourse. I mean, I know rationally that this is it, clitoral stimulation, and I really dig it, but at the same time, the myth of how it should be is still there."

Most men who had tried it expressed doubts about their expertise at giving manual clitoral stimulation. When asked, "Do you feel knowledgeable and comfortable stimulating a woman clitorally? How do you feel while giving clitoral stimulation with your hand?" most mentioned feelings of discomfort and said that getting feedback from the woman was essential:

"I don't feel sublimely confident when dealing with a clitoris; the orgasm seems very picky about what it likes and what it doesn't like, and it's hard to know, until you get to know a girl pretty well, just what the right thing is."

"Sometimes I can't find a woman's clitoris. I am either constantly getting lost—or the damn thing moves around a lot."★

"I feel knowledgeable about touching a clitoris up to a point (get it?), and then I want her to communicate to me what she likes. I'm no mind reader, and different women like different pressures and motions, although I find that they often are so glad to have their joy button get any attention at all that they go up the walls."

"I don't think I'm doing it right. I've talked about it with the other guys, but all I hear are stories about 'sticking-your-whole-god-damn-fist-up-there' while 'she-was-getting-wet-to-her-ankles' crap."

"It's exciting to stimulate a woman clitorally and see her sexual arousal. My girlfriend told me I was too rough sometimes. I was never too gentle, or then she didn't say anything."

★ Once again, these replies were much more likely to contain jokes than answers relating to intercourse or other topics.

"Generally I feel knowledgeable about touching it, but some differ *so* radically in preferences that one can never be sure."

"After ten years my wife finally conceded to letting me touch her, but was very embarrassed in those days but not today. I enjoy giving my wife stimulation, but I have to keep myself stimulated too with my other hand because she cannot hold my penis during her stimulation—it distracts her and she can't come."

A few men said they felt they were doing something "abnormal" that they should not need to do. A few connected manual clitoral stimulation with "teenage" behavior, calling it a high school activity, or adolescent behavior, something they had done only before intercourse was possible. Still, in 1981, according to my data, most men had never given a woman an orgasm with manual clitoral stimulation!

When asked, "Do you get sexually excited by stimulating your partner? Do you enjoy her orgasm physically? Emotionally?," many men were very enthusiastic, and commented on how much they enjoyed stimulating their partner to orgasm in this way. Some said it was great, even to stimulate her to multiple orgasms:

"How do I feel? Proud!"

"It's an ego trip."

"I feel flattered."

"It boosts my ego."

"It's fun . . ."

How do men feel about a woman stimulating herself?

But can a woman also stimulate herself manually while she is with a man? In the same way that men said that women often don't give them the correct manual stimulation of their penis, isn't it difficult for one person (especially of the opposite sex) to know just how to stimulate another? Although learning to do just that with a specific partner can be very loving and exciting, it is also very important for men and women to feel that they can stimulate themselves during sex with a partner. This can be an extremely intimate activity, while at the same time removing many frustrations and pressures from both the woman and the man.

"How do you feel if a woman stimulates herself to orgasm with you? During intercourse?"

Most men had never experienced a woman stimulating herself (manually) while close to them; for most men, having the woman give herself an orgasm was a new idea. As one man said, "No woman has ever shown me how or even admitted to masturbation."

In fact, many men were shocked by the idea that their partner could masturbate to orgasm at all, even when alone; most men did not know how (or if) she did it. When asked, "Does your partner masturbate to orgasm? How? If you don't know, would you like her to share this information with you?" many gave answers similar to the following:

"No. I don't think so."

"No. Yes."

"Yes—when alone."

"I don't think she ever has."

"Can't answer."

"Don't know or care—probably on rare occasions."

"She and I orgasm together if possible but I have a tough time holding mine."

Many men did not like the idea of the woman stimulating herself while with them:

"It's O.K. if she has to, but I would feel let down that I can't please her."

"I would feel inadequate if she did that."

"There would be a tinge of personal failure."

"It has never happened. I would feel very threatened."

"I would resent it."

"I hope it never happens. I would get up and leave."

"I feel very uncomfortable when she masturbates while I watch. I feel left out, an audience, unimportant, merely an afterthought on her part."

"Maybe *deep* inside my male ego would be wounded. It would depend on if there is malicious intent."

"It would be like I didn't satisfy her."

"Why does she need me?"

And many had mixed feelings about it:

"It's O.K., provided it does not lead to a sense of separateness between us, or inadequacy on my part."

"It's good—but I would also feel slightly inadequate and hurt."

"It's O.K. if she uses my cock."

"It's not much fun being pushed out of the way, but I don't mind having expert guidance. And who more expert than the recipient?"

"It wouldn't hurt my ego but it would disturb me if she climaxed that way only."

"Great if she's willing to disclose this to me. I feel strange—happy that she'll reach orgasm, but unhappy because I'm not doing it to her liking."

"I don't feel too bad, as long as I'm the *mental* stimulation."

"I might feel left out; somewhat undesirable, unattractive, inadequate. However, if the woman lets me know that she is doing it not because of my failure but because at this time it is necessary to meet her needs, I feel better."

"If I am feeling O.K. about myself, I feel O.K. when a woman reaches orgasm by stimulating herself on me. When I'm not feeling O.K., I tend to feel used."

And mixed feelings about their partner using a vibrator, too:

"I'd rather she came without a vibrator."

"A vibrator is cancerous, probably."

"Anything to make her come."

"It's not the end of the world if she stimulates herself, especially if she uses her own imagination to do it. I don't think I'd be crazy about her using a vibrator though."

"I only feel no good if she needs a vibrator to orgasm."

"Clitoral stimulation is O.K. but it's carrying it too far when she uses a vibrator!"

"I am very happy she does not use one."

"Something about vibrators bothers me, but I don't complain to the one person I know who likes to incorporate one into the act."

"If a woman stimulates herself to orgasm with me, I feel cheated. I would like to bring her to orgasm, and if I'm not, why am I her lover? Vibrators are for shit as far as I'm concerned."

But a few men expressed an open attitude toward trying one:

"I intend to buy a vibrator to see if we can enhance our sex life. I hear they're great."

"I never experienced it, but I would enjoy watching her use a vibrator."

"I would not mind my partner using a vibrator if I also took part, e.g., manipulating or helping manipulate the vibrator while kissing and fondling her breasts, etc."

"We don't have vibrators etc. as we don't know a reliable place to get any, but I would enjoy it."

And a few men enjoyed the use of the vibrator by a woman:

"I love to watch her body spasmodically orgasm while she uses her vibrator."

"My lover does not orgasm from intercourse—but we do many

things together besides intercourse. It is very exciting to masturbate together. She has orgasms when she wants to—she just grabs the vibrator."

"I really loved using the vibrator we had on my lover, as I could give her intense orgasms that way."

"Fine, anytime. If she uses it, then she can use it on me, it feels good. It doesn't make me feel unmasculine."

"One woman uses a vibrator during intercourse. I am thrilled, frankly, that she is so into sex. She apologizes, and I have to keep supporting her, encouraging her. The nitwit. It's like me eating a whole meal, and her feeling she must nibble."

Men's feelings about cunnilingus

Although most men liked cunnilingus, and were more familiar with it than manual stimulation, it was not a major way of giving women clitoral stimulation *to orgasm*. Only 32 percent of the men who answered said that they usually continued cunnilingus until the woman reached orgasm, with most others ignoring this part of the question.

However, most men were extremely enthusiastic about cunnilingus. For just over half of the men who answered who enjoyed sex with women, cunnilingus was the second most popular sexual activity, after intercourse. But a large number of men felt squeamish about cunnilingus—including many of those who were enthusiastic about it. There were very few in-between opinions about cunnilingus, and the answers show a much greater emotional reaction than those to almost any other subject.

Although most men thought of cunnilingus as "foreplay," they felt more comfortable with this form of clitoral stimulation than with manual clitoral stimulation. In fact, when asked about "clitoral stimulation," most men began discussing oral sex, not mentioning manual stimulation unless it was specifically referred to by the question. Still, the form of cunnilingus practiced by most men did not include much specific clitoral stimulation, but was more likely to concentrate on the general vulva and/or vaginal opening, rather than the clitoris. While this can be very pleasurable, both physically and emotionally, and even preferable to many women, lack of precise clitoral stimulation for orgasm is a drawback if no other provision is made for the woman's orgasm during sex.

"Do you enjoy cunnilingus with a woman? What do you like and/or dislike about it?"

Many men were extremely enthusiastic about cunnilingus:

"More than anything else I enjoy oral sex. If my partner wants, I will eat her all day long. I feel very happy, content, secure, and loving doing so. I adore the texture, feel, and taste, and also the lovely way a woman seems to respond while being eaten. The women I have had oral sex with seem to relax and very much enjoy being eaten. We both seem to have very good feelings about oral sex. There seems to be a very open feeling between us."

"Oral sex with a woman is my favorite of all. I feel a great closeness, a deep intimacy burying my face in that dark secret place. I feel that she trusts me fully. I love to look up and see her eyes closed and her face contorted in exquisite agony. I love my face drenched in her secretions, and her clit dancing under my tongue and her rocking hard and arching her back. And especially her moaning, screaming, raising her arms above her head so I can see her armpits. I love the convulsive motions of her coming. I love it when it's over and I keep my face between her legs and it gets dry and sticky and our skin pulls when it peels apart."

Others were ambivalent about the taste and smell:

"Sometimes the smell is bad but human beings can get used to anything."

"Her hair smells like urine."

"My wife repels me four out of five times. Sometimes her genitals smell like a chicken dinner."

"First you sniff it, if you wouldn't lick it, don't lick it."

"I recall one girl in my teens who smelled so terrible that from just fingering her I vomited."

Or that they smelled very strong:

"Some gals smell strong at first but if you just get going, it's like eating Limburger cheese. Smells rough but tastes great."

"As the taste and smell are strong, I sometimes have to be slightly deliberate about first contact, but no more so than when eating, say, a particularly ripe cheese or unusual fruit, drink, spice, etc.—once you get a good sniff or taste, then whatever the initial apprehensions, it's enjoyable. And anyway, it's her."

"Occasionally during a woman's cycle the smell is more of a turn-off than a turn-on initially. If I 'kiss' her anyway the smell soon becomes a turn-on."

Of course, yeast infections could disrupt the natural smell:

"Several minor vaginal infections, including trichomonas, produce an off odor. I'm confident that I can diagnose trichomonas by the odor-flavor."

"Once in a while she's had some sort of vaginal infection that produces a strong and definitely unpleasant smell, an odor of old sweat and decaying fish. I don't like it. She understands . . . but I've never found a way to tell her that without making her feel hurt. I wish I could say, 'Hey, you've got that symptom again,' without making it sound like a moral accusation."

Some men hadn't decided yet:

"Female genitals are fragrant. Taste wonderful and my only complaint is a really, really raunchy crotch that hasn't been washed. But it's not really a true complaint since I've never experienced one—I just think that if someone didn't wash for two weeks it would smell foul."

"What I dislike is that some women have an offensive—well, not really offensive but strange—smell. I'm still trying to get used to it."

But some men had none of these negative associations:

"Many men and women find a woman's sex to be unclean in some way. I enjoy showing the woman that not only do I find her sex not unclean, but in fact I find it extremely delightful."

"Would you believe that some women are reluctant to engage in such an activity since a lot of them have hang-ups and prehistoric beliefs that they smell bad? Usually my partner showers before the activity and it smells clean and tastes great with all the woman juices."

"Many women have a tendency to push your face away from their genitals as though they feel they've done something wrong or smell bad. It is hard to convince them that I enjoy the smell and taste—and I do."

"My wife cleans too much."

"For me, cunnilingus is beautiful but only when the woman enjoys it. Some get pretty freaked out about it. The smell and taste is something exquisite. It can get a bit raunchy at times, but on the other hand, a freshly scrubbed cunt can be pretty tasteless, and lose a lot of appeal."

Some men emphasized that they liked the taste very much:

"Darndest thing: women taste so sweet down there. Without using anything added. Just reasonably clean. It's really nice."

"Tastes and smells always excite me. Tastes vary—sometimes they are sweet and sometimes a little salty or tangy."

"The taste is a very plain taste with just a slight distinctness which I like and which also arouses me."

"Most are sweet and creamy."

"I love the way my wife's genitals taste and smell, the way her pussy looks and feels, the heat and velvety wetness of it."

"I like, in fact, just adore, the taste of women's genitals."

In fact, of men who mentioned "feminine-hygiene sprays" or flavored creams, most said they did not like them:

"Women taste great (if clean and if they're not using any of those hygiene sprays). Their odor is a definite sexual turn-on and the taste is superb."

"All the women I've gone with have been clean and washed. I like the natural woman taste and smell and do not like the use of the 'vaginal mouthwash' sometimes advertised."

"I generally like the smell of women's genitals—I like the smell of sweat too. I don't believe in all this hype about anti-perspirants, etc. All that advertising serves to separate people from each other, makes them think they stink and are ugly, and uses sexuality for profit."

And other men emphasized that they liked the smells:

"The taste is faintly salty; there's a delicate smell that's very distinctive, but I can't describe it. I like it. Sometimes I've gotten it on my fingers and long afterwards I can hold them to my nose and still get a trace of that lovely scent."

"Smells (the healthy ones) have become increasingly attractive to me with age."

"The taste is good but not as exciting as the smell."

Are women's genitals "clean"?

Although many men liked cunnilingus very much, almost half of those who answered were also preoccupied with whether the woman or the woman's genitals were "clean":

"I'm learning more and more to enjoy cunnilingus. It's been hard to do—I have uncomfortable feelings about oozing. I was raised clean clean clean. I like to take a shower after sex."

"If I want to have oral sex with a gal, I am saying to her, 'You are clean.'"

"I'm still kind of squeamish about cunnilingus, and still think of female genitalia as dirty. Most of my earliest sexual experiences were with women whose genitals *were* dirty and really did smell awful. I sometimes enjoy oral sex with women when I first establish that they're clean. I like the musky, sweet smell of a woman and get some pleasure from cunnilingus for myself, but mainly get into it to please the woman."

"My partner usually washes just before or at least a few hours before and is either tasteless or pleasantly scented. Stale, unwashed female genitals taste and smell bad to me."

"How does one ask a woman politely to wash?"

"Female cunt is not good-looking but I love it, every inch of it, if it is clean."

"My wife keeps very clean."

"Clean. I do not have the deviant's taste for stale accumulations, the same as I do not care for stinky armpits or for kissing a lip corrupted by a runny nose, or dirty hair, etc."

"I like everything about oral sex with my lover-wife as long as she has secretly showered (I like my partners 'clean')—taste, smell, texture, the pleasure it gives her, the turn-on to me."

"I think women usually consider their pubic area 'unclean, smelly, dirty, slimy, etc.' Pardon me, but I would rather make that distinction. If I find a distasteful (no pun intended) situation, I'll suggest an erotic, arousing shower together."

"I only like it after a bath. I don't like the taste of urine or stale secretions. Or the smell of feces. But a clean pussy tastes good, believe me!"

"Sometimes the smell can be a little strong, but that's nothing that a quick washing won't take care of. This is a delicate point of etiquette: how do you tell a woman that you'd be only too glad to eat her out for the next hour and a half, if she wants, if she'd only go and use a touch of soap and water? I've only said it to one woman, a *very* good friend who was very candid and verbal about sex, and even she got a little offended, though she said she understood it in the spirit in which I had said it—trying to be helpful, not to offend."

"I appreciate it *if* the genitals on a woman are not filthy!"

Closely associated with this were comments that women's genitals smelled bad:

"You can rub and scrub and clean it well, but you can't get rid of that codfish smell."

Conclusion

One of men's most frequent "buts" about the vagina and vulva is related to whether the woman is clean or has washed recently. While the fact that all bodies need bathing rather regularly would seem to go without saying, no men mentioned the necessity for brushing teeth regularly to make kissing pleasant. The fact that so many men saw fit to stress this point with regard to women's vulvas seems to reflect the influence of the age-old patriarchal view of female sexuality (and women) as being "dirty," "nasty," or "not quite nice." Each child still learns this in the story of Adam and Eve: it was Eve's sexuality and "desire for carnal knowledge" which ruined the Garden of Eden and for which men and women are still being punished—especially women, who are told that they must henceforth bring forth children in pain and suffering. And of course women who are overtly sexual are often punished by society's double standard, which still categorizes women as "good women" and "bad women."

Unfortunately, for centuries in our society, women's sexuality has been considered "dirty": a sensual, sexual woman is a "tramp," "dirty," "filthy," and so on, whereas a sexual man is very masculine, admirable. The vulva, of which women are taught to be ashamed (the medical term for the vulva is "pudendum," a Latin word meaning "of which one ought to be ashamed"), has been hidden away for so long that few people really know what it looks like. The general impression many men have is of a dark wet place with an unfamiliar smell, a kind of unknown space into which the penis ventures courageously. One of the early triumphs of the women's movement was to reclaim the beauty, strength, and dignity of women's bodies for women, and to emphasize that it is women who own women's bodies, and not men. Women for the first time felt that they had the right to explore their own bodies and look inside them. With a mirror and a light and a plastic speculum a woman could see her interior, suddenly finding it to be a beautiful glossy pink, clean and dazzling—as opposed to the dark and unpleasant place she might have been led to believe she would find.

Perhaps men who still feel they are affected by these stereotypes about women's genitals can overcome them by also looking inside a vagina once, with someone they care about. Some men have seen their wife's or partner's vagina during a joint physical examination, conducted by a gynecologist or sex therapist. This technique was originated by Drs. Leon and Shirley Zussman, and has had excellent results.

A few men commented on cunnilingus during menstruation:

"I like the warmth and moisture of my partner's genitals, and I enjoy the very pleasant odor of them. The only time I do not like cunnilingus is during her period, although I have done it and was surprised that I could not tell the difference in taste or odor."

"I love the smell of my lover's vagina while she is menstruating. I want her to menstruate in my mouth and on my face—it tastes so sexy and smells so good."

"The smell and taste of a menstruating vagina does not appeal to me, though I have never tasted one."

"Some women have a psychological hang-up of feeling dirty during this time. Why should they? Aren't they proud to have such sophisticated bodies? Aren't they proud that they are women?"

"As I grew up I was led to believe that this was the time of the month when a woman discharged all the poison and disease germs from her womb. I know better now, but still am hung up about it."

"Menstruation makes little difference to me. Oral sex with a tampon in place is just the same as when she is not menstruating. Without a tampon, I reserve the right to refuse but that is unlikely."

"I feel more 'afraid' of the vagina at that time. I'm less likely to play with it, to touch it or feel it. I rule out oral sex completely. She is hornier when menstruating. I will not hesitate to have intercourse."

"I ate one girl who later said she was menstruating at the time, but I guess I was too wrapped up in it to care. Blood, blood, I had enough of it on me in Vietnam not to worry about it."

"How do women's genitals look?"
Not only were there misgivings about whether women's genitals were "clean," but also many men had ambivalent feelings about the looks of women's vulvas. On the other hand, some men liked them very much and offered beautiful descriptions. The range of answers covered every attitude imaginable:

"Objectively ugly. But they turn me on."

"A ripe peach cut halfway across by a knife."

"Like lips."

"They look forbidden."

"Better than men's."

"I dislike the hair. A beautiful face and 'raw flesh' is a horrible mismatch."

"I wish they were dry. I dislike the loose lips."

"Moisture bothers me. It looks like the skin of an old woman on a young one."

"Female genitals are shaped to do the job intended."

"Gorgeous."

"They look O.K., I guess. Certainly no sillier than a penis."

"They look mysterious."

"Inviting."

"They look hairy, sensual, puffy, excited, red, and full."

"A pretty furry pet animal."

"Ugly but appealing and nice to touch."

"Like a damp rose, petals blossoming."

"Strange and compelling, inviting and ripe for explorations."

Some men, in longer answers, described why they liked the looks:

"I love my wife's genitals. They look big, pink, wet, warm, ready for fun, ready to respond to me, mysterious, powerful, something to explore. Wow!"

"I think women's genitals are about as lovely as something on this earth can get. I love the way they taste and smell. There have been some genitals about which I held a near-religious feeling; this was because they were attached to women for whom I felt a deep love."

"I think a woman's—my friend's when I peeled off her pants— genitalia are so beautifully shaped and designed! What was very nice was that her pubic hair was very blond and the moon shone in the window as I put my head between her legs."

How clitoral stimulation affects men's happiness

Is clitoral stimulation (whether by hand or mouth) something that men "should" learn to do because women need it, women "demand" it—or is clitoral stimulation an erotic and beautiful activity, as valuable and intense as intercourse? Is it pleasurable for men?

Most men know that women do not orgasm regularly during intercourse with them—and this often makes them feel insecure, defensive or "inadequate." There was an undertone of anger and frustration in many of the answers: "What's wrong with women that they have such difficulty having orgasm?" Or, "When she doesn't have orgasm during intercourse, I feel like I've ripped her off. I wonder whether I should be sticking myself in her, or not. What's in it for her? Is this some sort of martyr shtick?"

And yet, as we have seen, though most men realize that women do not orgasm with them regularly during intercourse, most still also assume women *should* orgasm from simple intercourse. Most men have very little understanding of women's need for clitoral stimulation outside of intercourse.

The stereotype in our society that says that women have a "problem" having orgasm is false: it is not women that have a "problem" having orgasm, but society that has a problem accepting how women do orgasm.

The Politics of Intercourse

What Is "Male Sexuality"?

Once again, we must ask, what *is* "male sexuality"? Is it intercourse? Why is it so closely identified with intercourse? Have men missed the boat because of the total focus our society teaches them to have on intercourse, on an always aggressive, dominating, goal-oriented definition of their sexuality?

To always assume that "sex" equals "foreplay," followed by "vaginal penetration" (why not call it "penile enfolding"?), and ending with male orgasm in the vagina—even if now clitoral stimulation to orgasm is included before intercourse—means that sex will still be focused on intercourse and retain its overly structured definition.

Defining sex as basically intercourse holds men back from getting to know and appreciate their own sensuality, forcing them into an unneccessary, anxious preoccupation with erection: focusing on (what he believes to be) his responsibility to achieve erection and perform coitus, "to perform his duties as a man," tends to cut off many men's erotic responses before they even get started. For example, many men cut short "foreplay" and physical affection because they are afraid they may lose their erection—which they have been taught is necessary to enjoy sex (and which it would be "shameful" to lose). But men could reach much higher peaks of feeling and arousal if they did not feel anxious about how they "should" behave sexually, and if they did not focus so much on reaching orgasm.

Men's denial of their great sensuality is significant because it is part of the overall denial by men of their feelings and emotions: a "real man," it is said, should learn to always be "in control" of his emotions. Thus the traditional definition of masculinity tries to close men off from their full capacity to feel joy, sadness, love, the world, life.

Men have everything to gain from leaving behind the old mechanical

206

definition of "male sexuality" and at the same time developing a greater appreciation of their great sensuality, their own capacity for enjoyment and expression. Men's experience of their own bodies has been cut off and limited, falsified, by the culture's insistence that "male sexuality" is a simple mechanistic drive for intercourse.

"Sex" could be un-defined to become something with infinite variety, not always including intercourse or even orgasm (for either person). It can become part of an individual vocabulary of many ways to relate physically—including activities which express anger, tenderness, passion, and/or love, depending on the current feelings of the two people—a way of expressing a thousand different feelings, saying a thousand different things.

Can men imagine a new conception of male sexuality and sensuality not necessarily focused on intercourse or orgasm? Would men like to diversify and expand, eroticize their sexuality—become less constantly active, sometimes more passive, more receptive? Have most men ever experienced sex as less orgasm and more passion?

What does sex mean to men?

Why do they want intercourse? Why is it so important to them? Not only are men encouraged to want intercourse by a culture that says that this is how "men" behave, but also men are left little other choice of ways to be truly close and intimate with other human beings. Men are brought up not to be "sissies," to control their feelings, and to be dominant insofar as possible in every situation. Only in "sex" are men encouraged to "let their hair down" and be tender, affectionate, passionate, or "out of control." Only through "sex" are men encouraged to relate emotionally to women. If men are cut off from each other—first from their fathers, by the "rules" of male behavior, and then later, following that example, from their friends, at least in the sense of being able to talk intimately and show affection—then men must turn to women for close companionship. But at the same time, they are "supposed to" dominate those women. It is in this confused atmosphere that men and women experience "sex." Even more confusing, it is in the moments of sexual intimacy that most men feel most free to talk about their feelings, problems, hopes, and dreams. This, in combination with the need we all have for close, warm body contact, can make a sexual connection with a woman almost the most important need a man has. And the central focus of that sexual connection is intercourse—only intercourse, perhaps, has the symbolic overtones

207

to make this connection deep enough. But the symbolism has both a positive and negative aspect.

Origins of the definition of sex as intercourse

In fact, the current definition of "sex"—basically, "foreplay" followed by intercourse and ending with male orgasm in the vagina as the "right" way to have sex—has not always been the definition of sex. Everything we think of as "male sexuality" is in very large part a reflection of the values and needs of the society we live in, and the culture we have inherited. The definition of sex as we know it was begun approximately twenty-five hundred years ago for the purpose of increasing reproduction. It was at this time that the Hebrew tribes returned from the Babylonian exile, a small, struggling group. These tribes passed a law, the first such law we know of, saying that henceforth, all sexual activities other than heterosexual intercourse would be illegal. The Old Testament constantly warned against other forms of sexuality, including "spilling one's seed" (masturbation), oral sex, and the sexual practices of the "heathens" (surrounding tribes), especially the Babylonians. This officially promoted focus on reproductive activities (and glorification of intercourse) was important for the small tribes, since only through increasing their population could they become more powerful, consolidating their hold on their territory, cultivating and harvesting more crops, and maintaining a larger army to defend themselves.

This definition of sex also reflected a new male ascendancy in society, in that henceforth, the children were to belong (along with their wives) to the fathers (or husbands), which had not previously been the case. The Hebrew tribes (possibly influenced by traditions of invading Indo-European or Aryan tribes) were organized with a patriarchal social structure—that is, ruled by men: women and children were owned (legally) by an individual man (husband or father), who in turn owed his allegiance (legally) to a male king, who in turn owed his allegiance to a male priesthood and a male god. But the Babylonians, like many other societies of the time, for example the Canaanites, did not worship one male god, or even one god; furthermore, many of the gods they did worship were female, and indeed it was women who were the priests. Queens in these societies were frequently more powerful or as powerful as kings—going back to an earlier nonpatriarchal tradition, which was probably very widespread throughout the entire Middle East at that time, and even more widespread during an earlier period.

The exact nature of this tradition is still a matter of debate,* but many scholars now agree that, based on archaeological and written evidence, very early periods of history—often called "prehistory"— had quite a different form of social organization from our own. Some scholars refer to these early societies as "matriarchies," although very little is known in the popular culture about them; other feminist scholars have objected to the term "matriarchy," since it implies that these societies were the simple reverse of "patriarchy," that is, that women owned the children and ruled men, rather than having a more complex tradition of their own, possibly more egalitarian. However, although there was a great variety of social organizations among these groups, it does seem clear that women were held in higher esteem than men, and that women were usually in charge in general of the temples and distribution of food and goods. Whether women also were warriors is not known—although many goddesses were addressed as warrior-goddesses. But these societies were certainly not male dominated. And the "sex" (i.e., physical relations between individuals) and family structure were in all probability quite different in these early forms of social organization than in the later patriarchal structure.

Following is a simplified version of some hypotheses of the changes which seemed to have taken place over a period of a thousand or more years, perhaps sometime around 8000 to 5000 B.C.†

The very earliest societies may have worshiped/venerated women because it was thought that only women could bring forth new life. In very early societies, much earlier than the Babylonians or the Egyptians, some scholars believe that the relationship between intercourse and pregnancy was not known, and so the male role in reproduction was unknown. Additionally, the earliest families we know of did not consist of the mother, father, and child as we know them today, but rather a group that included the mother, sisters, brothers, aunts, uncles, and children; children could be brought up by various members of the group—the biological mother having had the choice of whether to

* Books related to this subject include *Egypt and Chaldea*, by W. Boscawen (London: Harper, 1894); *Ancient Israel*, by Roland DeVaux (London: Darton, Longman & Todd, 1965); *The Lost World of Elam*, by Walther Hinz (New York: New York University Press, 1973); *The Splendor that Was Egypt*, by Margaret Murray (London: Sidgwick & Jackson, 1949); *When God Was a Woman*, by Merlin Stone (New York: Dial Press, 1976); and *Prehistory and the Beginning of Civilization*, by Jacquetta Hawkes and Sir Leonard Woolley. Also helpful is the extensive bibliography contained in *When God Was a Woman*.
† At present, we do not know the exact dates of the changeover from pre-patriarchy, or "matriarchy," but we do know that the struggles went on for many years, even centuries, and in many separate locations.

"stay at home" with the child or not. In other words, there has not always been the close tie between the biological mother and child (nor the father and child) we consider "natural" today; children of many mothers mixed together and were brought up by many members of the group. In fact, the concept of private property may not yet have existed, or may have been very weak or unimportant to the society; certainly children were not "owned."

It has been theorized that when the male contribution to childbearing became known, possibly around 10,000 or more years ago (this knowledge coming at different times to different societies), there began a gradual shift to more male involvement in religious functions, and gradually to the system of patriarchal social order in which men now are almost entirely dominant. Scholars are only slowly piecing together fragments of records to understand what happened in these early times; much remains to be understood. However, some scholars see the Old Testament as, among other things, representing the story of the early patriarchal struggle against goddess worship and female-oriented societies, and the transition to a male-dominated, "one-god" society. The history of Greece, also, and the chronological changes in Greek mythology, have been seen as representing a changeover in thinking from goddess worship to God ascendancy.* A similar change from the ascendancy of queens to the ascendancy of kings can be seen in several centuries of early Egyptian history. The transition from Cretan culture to later Mycenaean/mainland Greek culture is another example. However, these interpretations, while steadily gaining adherents, are far from orthodox. On the other hand, scholars generally agree on a recent revision of the extent of our fully human ("civilized") history: according to latest estimate, complex human societies existed as far back as 40,000 years—quite an increase over what had previously been thought.

What was the role of intercourse in pre-patriarchal or "matriarchal" societies? Even in early patriarchal or transitional times, intercourse was not thought of romantically, or in terms of being the greatest physical pleasure there is, more pleasurable than other forms of intimacy and sexuality, but basically was practiced for reproduction; this was true, for example, in most periods of Greek and Roman history. What must sex and physical relations have been like even earlier, then, 20,000 or 40,000 years ago, when it may have been believed (at least for some time) that women became pregnant simply by lying in the moonlight? When intercourse was not an especially noted symbol in the society?

* See Jane Harrison, *Prologomena to the Study of Greek Religion*, Cambridge, 1903, and E. A. Butterworth, *Some Traces of the Pre-Olympian World*, Berlin and New York, De Gruyter, 1966.

Were sexual feelings tied to religious ("fertility") group activities, rather than "romantic" personal activities? Or were sexual feelings and orgasm linked to "romantic" personal feelings, while fertility activities (whatever they may have been) linked to group or religious activities? There is some evidence that the latter may have been the case, but we honestly do not know what people did.*

But to return to the present, it must now be clear how completely sex as we know it is tied to our own history and social organization. This definition has come down to us from the early Judeo-Christian laws,† which became, in fact, the civil code of the entire West, and whose laws are still basically those of our present civil code; in addition, old church laws are still enforced by many churches today. For example, the Catholic Church says that women should not use birth control, since the purpose of sex is reproduction, and since women should make their bodies available to their husbands for this purpose at all times; and further, that the fathers will own the children. It is also important to note that other societies, like those of Japan, China, India, and the Arab world, once they became patriarchal, also defined sex in much the same way—that is, regulated physical relations so that maximum reproduction, with the children being owned by the father, is the rule;‡ in other words, the reproductive definition of sexuality is an inherent part of a patriarchal society—i.e., in order for men to control a society, it has been essential for men to control reproduction and to own the children.

But sexuality today is changing—probably largely due to the fundamental changes brought about by the industrial revolution. Increasing population is not as necessary to the power of a society as it once was, since we now have very large populations and even more importantly, machines (and computers) can now do much of the work large populations once performed, from farming to defending a country. Therefore, as society feels it no longer needs to encourage reproduction to the extent that it once did, birth control is becoming more and more

* However, women then, as today, must have known about the importance of the clitoris, since, as discussed in *The Hite Report on Female Sexuality*, women in the twentieth century, without being given any information whatsoever on how, begin to masturbate quite early in their lives; for the great majority of women this has meant manual clitoral stimulation. Therefore it is logical to assume that if women do this "instinctively" today, women must also have done this then, and known that this was a pleasurable area to have stimulated. Was this sublimation part of sexual institutions or customs at that time? Was masturbation considered private? What other activities were considered important?

† These laws may have stemmed from certain Indo-European or Aryan ideologies—the same ideologies which influenced early religion in Iran, Turkey, and India.

acceptable (legal), and male ownership of children (and marriage) less crucial, with "living together" arrangements more accepted.

However, this change has not yet deeply affected our idea of what "sex" is or could be. Even though we frequently use birth control, we still generally follow the traditional reproductive definition of physical relations, centered on intercourse. But, as seen in this book, some men are beginning to question the assumptions of our culture about "male sexuality" and our definition of sex: even though the issues are just beginning to surface, there is a gut feeling on the part of most men that something is wrong—that although there are beautiful elements to sex as we know it, somehow there are unnecessary problems, too.

The Traditional Meaning of Intercourse: The Politics of Intercourse

How much of men's desire for intercourse is due to our culture's insistence that all men "should" seek and want intercourse, that it is "natural" for men; and how much is due to an individual man's desire to have intercourse with a particular woman, for his own personal reasons? We can never know exactly. But it does seem clear that, without the accompanying cultural symbolism and pressures, intercourse would become a matter of choice during sexual activities, not the sine qua non, or denouement toward which all sexual activities move, which it now is. This is not to say, of course, that men and women will not continue to enjoy intercourse with each other when they want, but simply that sex could be more enjoyable for both people if intercourse were not a "requirement"—if intercourse were a choice and not a given. Sex does not always have to include intercourse, and sex would become much freer if intercourse were not always its focus.

Intercourse is at once one of the most beautiful and at the same time most oppressive and exploitative acts of our society. It has been symbolic of men's ownership of women, as just described, for approximately the last three thousand years. It is the central symbol of patriarchal society; without it, there could be no patriarchy. Intercourse culminating in male orgasm in the vagina is the sublime moment during which the male contribution to reproduction takes place. This is the reason for its glorification. And as such, men *must* love it; intercourse is a celebration of "male" patriarchal culture.

Surely the definition of sex as we know it (that is, intercourse) is guaranteed to make a man feel that his needs are serious, worthwhile, and important—at least his need for orgasm and his need for stimulation of the penis to reach that orgasm. This fact is so obvious that it is usually overlooked, or taken as a "given," a simple "biological" imperative. However, our definition of sex is, to a large extent, culturally, and not biologically, created. Women's need for orgasm and for specific clitoral stimulation to reach that orgasm is not honored or respected in the traditional definition of sex. Certainly it is not enshrined within an institution, as is male orgasm. Although perhaps the institution we know as "sex" was created to lead to male orgasm in the vagina not because of male dominance but only because of the society's desire to increase reproduction, nevertheless, the man himself, as eventual owner of the child (should pregnancy occur) and of the woman, must surely feel secure in the knowledge that this ritual honors him and enshrines and venerates his orgasm. Thus men feel that their orgasm during intercourse is *good*. However, men usually do not attribute creation of the institution to man-made society; they look, rather, to biological or religious sources—i.e., "It's just the way things are," or, as one man said, "Intercourse is a heavenly blessing which God created for man."

In addition, this cultural institution, this symbolic rite, is aided and attended to by another person, a woman. If male orgasm is the sacrament here, the woman functions as the priest. This woman not only gives the man a sense of being accepted and desirable on an individual personal level, but also gives him a further sense of acceptance by joining in and catering to the sequence of events which culminates in his orgasm. This woman, with perhaps varying degrees of enthusiasm, but almost never with withdrawal once "sex" (the ritual sequence of events), and especially intercourse, has begun, helps him along toward his orgasm and a sense of pleasure.

Both men and women feel that this is woman's role. And yet most women still do not feel that they have a similar automatic right to clitoral stimulation to orgasm—and even less do they feel they have the right to touch or stimulate themselves to orgasm—and still less do they feel they have the right to insist that men cater to their needs (especially if the woman is not also catering to the man's needs). Why does our society consider it perfectly acceptable to assume that "sex" can be defined as intercourse to male orgasm "every time," with clitoral stimulation to female orgasm included only "sometimes" or not at all—while considering it outrageous to define "sex" as clitoral stimulation to female orgasm "every time" if it almost never or only rarely included also penis stimulation/intercourse to male orgasm?

In addition, in traditional intercourse, the man was on top of the woman, adding to the symbolic impact of his culturally decreed superiority. Also, the fact that he almost always had an orgasm and she did not further encouraged him to think of himself as superior, more successful, healthier, and more sexual (more fully evolved, as some contemporary psychiatrists have recently asserted)—as opposed to the "weaker" woman, who was not able to have a similar climax (despite the fact that she almost certainly was not getting the right stimulation).

In other words, during traditional intercourse, the ancient patriarchal symbolism of the man on top comes to the fore: the man on top, "taking" his pleasure, the whole force of the social structure behind him, telling him that what he is doing is Good, Right, and that he is a Strong Male—with the woman looking up into his eyes, not resisting and hopefully celebrating these feelings with him, saying yes, you are great.

And there is yet another point: the symbolic acceptance of the sperm by the woman. As the woman accepts the semen, she accepts an intimate part of the man and, at least symbolically, she accepts the idea of carrying the child for him. Intercourse in patriarchy, as we remember, means power because a man can say, "I own this woman. I can make her pregnant." This was equated with power in early patriarchy, because earlier societies had not known the connection between intercourse (sperm) and pregnancy; they thought women reproduced by themselves. After this connection was discovered, the erect penis gradually became the dominant symbol in society that it remains today. Before this, the female body, and especially the vulva and breasts (as seen in the thousands of "fertility goddess statues" that have been unearthed) was the primary symbol.

This is not to say, of course, that intercourse does not feel good to both women and men in its own right. However, superimposed on these basic feelings is an enormous cultural symbolism which has become so ingrained in all our minds, both male and female, that it is hard for us to be sure just why we do like intercourse.

Another implication of patriarchal ideology is that intercourse makes a male a man before other men; intercourse is a form of male bonding. Boys are told that they cannot have intercourse; only men can. Thus intercourse becomes a test of status and dominance through which males prove their membership in the male group—not only the first time, but over and over. One basic definition of a man is "one who has intercourse with women." Why is this? Would this be a test of "masculinity" (whatever that may be) in a society which did not hold reproduction as a primary value? Historically speaking, men's identification with intercourse (and the emphasis on "performance") grew out of a social system which wanted more soldiers and farmers. In fact, for quite a long time, intercourse was not connected with love or romantic love, nor was it even considered necessarily the main thing a "man" would want to do: Greek men, for example, often seemed quite happy having sex among themselves—considering intercourse with their wives a duty necessary basically only for procreation. No doubt this was the way the wife viewed it as well, since her orgasm was not a consideration. (Was she having orgasms through masturbation? Or with her women acquaintances with whom she spent the day? No one knows.) And even earlier, Hebrew men had to be admonished in the Old Testament not to "spill their seed"—i.e., masturbate—or practice sodomy, but instead to have *vaginal intercourse*. This implies that they may have found it more pleasurable or convenient to masturbate or to have other sex for orgasm, and that in fact this may have been their custom.

In patriarchal society, then, intercourse for a man has the whole force of a society's approval behind it: he is doing what the entire society says he should be praised for doing, and the woman's acceptance of him functions as a symbol of the acceptance of him by the entire social order—and especially by other men. However, intercourse does not bestow the same feeling of social acceptance upon women; the meaning of sex/intercourse for women is quite different. Although the woman, as agent for the society (fulfilling her socially dictated role as nurturer, helper), is bestowing acceptance and approval (and the stimulation for male orgasm) on the man, she is frequently not getting any of these in return. In addition, society does not praise *her* for having intercourse. Her orgasm is not enshrined, and she may be looked down on by the man for having "given herself." This is another issue, one which was covered in *The Hite Report on Female Sexuality*—but it is well to keep in mind how differently our culture has chosen to reward the two sexes for the same activity.

Still, women do enjoy intercourse, and women and men do often transcend these cultural meanings in their personal lives. Although intercourse has been a symbol of masculinity and male power, it need not continue to be. As women gain equality—economic, social, and legal—intercourse can lose these exploitative connotations to become once more a simple thing of beauty and freedom—and above all, a choice.

Finally, the point here is not that men are wrong for liking and wanting intercourse, but that they should be freed from feeling that they must have intercourse to have true sex—and to be "real" men. It would be senseless to "blame" anyone, either men or women, for traditional and stereotyped attitudes and behaviors which we all learn every day and endlessly hear repeated around us. The point now is to re-examine the part intercourse plays in our lives, to reassess our personal definitions of sex, and try to create more individual, and more equal, forms of physical relations.

In fact, it may be, on some level, just this cultural catering to men during intercourse which also makes men feel uncomfortable, uneasy, and ambivalent about it. Do they want to feel the object of so much unequal attention? Do men want to feel that the success or failure of the whole ritual rests on their performance? The ideal of masculinity glorifies men at the same time that it would dehumanize them.

Women's Resistance to Sex and Intercourse: Political, Not "Neurotic"

Many men are frustrated and dissatisfied with sex with women, or have profoundly mixed feelings about it, even while they say they want more. The reasons for this are deep and very ancient—but not unchangeable—in that they are tied to the basic social structure: the society has created a great inequality and separation between the sexes, which originally involved a struggle over the control of reproduction, and which now permeates almost every aspect of sexual relations between men and women. These attitudes are only slowly beginning to change.

Why aren't many women enthusiastic about sex with men more frequently? First, because women feel exploited sexually: they must help the man have his orgasm but must not take/make the stimulation they need for their own. Given our definition of sex, the fact that men usually want sex more often than women should come as no surprise. Sex provides efficiently for male orgasm, and inefficiently and irregularly for female orgasm; sex is defined so that the woman expects to help the man orgasm every time, but the man is not realistically informed about how to help the woman orgasm, and the woman is told it is wrong to stimulate herself. Therefore, should we be surprised that men want sex more often than women do? Sex as we know it is a "male"-defined* activity, and women, in not showing enthusiasm for many aspects of it, are displaying resistance to participating in an institution which they do not have an equal part in creating.

* That is, defined by patriarchal ("male") ideology.

And yet most men have believed that they were doing "what a man should" by performing intercourse, and that a woman should orgasm from their thrusting. They were taught that providing a woman with intercourse, especially for an extended period of time, would give her what she wanted and needed. However, somehow men have known on some level that it didn't, and this has led to deep, unspoken feelings of discomfort, alienation and guilt—which were often manifested as distrust of women's motives for having sex, and anger at women for not speaking up and being "honest" about sex.

Where did the belief arise that women should orgasm from intercourse? The institution we know as "sex"—"foreplay" to intercourse ending with male orgasm—was first legislated into existence as the only acceptable form of sexual expression approximately 2,500 years ago, for purposes of increasing reproduction. But it did not take on the connotations we give it today until much later; intercourse was not always considered a romantic activity during which women were supposed to orgasm. In the late nineteenth century, in fact, women were considered vulgar if they did. However, in the early part of our century, with the increasing discussion of the rights of women, women's orgasm was begun to be considered important. Perhaps it seemed logical, in the beginning, to assume that women should orgasm from the same activity from which men orgasmed,* especially since participation in this activity was glorified as being a form of "natural law."

In addition, women's interior clitoral anatomy had not yet been studied. However, it was known that women did masturbate to orgasm clitorally and generally not with vaginal penetration. Refusal to accept women's testimony (how they stimulated themselves) was characteristic of the general attitude toward women as second-class in a male-dominated society: women were advised to learn to orgasm "the right way"—from vaginal penetration—and thus conform to supposed "male sexuality" needs, women's role being that of "helpmate." When, however, this often did not work in practice, who was to blame? Who was flawed? Was it women, or men, or both? Although generally it has been women who were considered inherently flawed or inadequate, in fact many men felt that *they* were to blame—that there was something deeply wrong with them or their penis when the woman did not orgasm. This oppressive expectation, then, has led to needless suffering, self-examination, and accusations between men and women.

Tragically, although most women have known how to stimulate

---

* Of course, men orgasm from other forms of stimulation too, but the "acceptable" time for men to orgasm was during intercourse.

themselves to orgasm easily during masturbation, they have not felt free to explain the stimulation they needed to men, or to stimulate themselves during sex with men. Being dependent on men, economically,* socially, and politically, has kept women silent: women have not felt that they had the right to challenge the society's definition of sex or to assert their own needs and forms of sexual expression.

But on another level, women have been resistant to intercourse because intercourse has not been a choice. The legal structure in which women were owned by either their fathers or their husbands included (and still includes in many countries today) the provision that a man has a right to intercourse with his wife on demand; there was (is) no such thing as "rape" in marriage. Further, many women have felt unable to protect themselves against pregnancy by using birth control, when it was (is) against the rules of the state or church.† Thus, in a very real sense, women had no rights over their own bodies, as their husbands controlled them; and therefore many women, feeling that their husbands could do with them whatever they pleased, and that any attempt at resistance or influence was futile, developed very passive and/or hostile attitudes about sexual relationships: they would participate in sex, but only when they had to, and would not be any more active during it than necessary.

Thus, intercourse, far from being a simple pleasurable activity, has for centuries symbolized and celebrated male domination and ownership of women, children, and society. Conversely, it also symbolizes female subservience, or being owned. A woman, in having intercourse, especially in the traditional position with the woman on the bottom, helping the man have an orgasm, but not having one herself, was reminded of her position vis-à-vis the man. It is obvious, in this context, why many men would feel much more drawn toward participating in this institution than would women.

Many women's resistance to "sex"—far from being simply negative "conditioning" about sex—can also be seen as a large-scale and healthy resistance to being dominated, and to their bodies being owned. Saying

---

* The 1980 census report showed that still, for every $1.00 a man makes, a woman makes only $.59 for equal work. This gap has also been evident in U.S. Bureau of Labor statistics for many years. The amount women earn proportionately has not been increasing.
† Today, women in some countries have the right to use birth control, but the forms available often make it difficult or dangerous; furthermore, the tradition of women's availability to men for orgasm inside the vagina is continued in the idea that the woman should have the entire responsibility for using birth control, and that she should use a form which does not interfere with the man's pleasure—invisible, if possible. As one man remarked, "Why, in all the movies or sex magazines, don't they ever show the problem of birth control? They make it too romantic."

no to "sex" has become, for many women, a way of maintaining dignity and integrity, and some control over their own identity.

A basic cause of many women's resistance to sex/intercourse is emotional alienation. If women feel that men think of them as second-class, and value them only as "helpmates" and sexual partners, this is likely to lead to emotional alienation within the relationship—giving yet more cause for women's passive resistance (in the Gandhian sense) to having sex. One man embodied these attitudes quite clearly: "My wife is not perhaps the woman one might dream up, but she's steady, dependable, and consistent. She's the mother of my four kids, and in my own way I love her, even though she doesn't like sex too much. She doesn't initiate oral sex spontaneously, or intercourse either. She says the reason is because I don't show her enough kindness and affection throughout the day. She says if I did she'd be more active sexually. These things are not so bad that I can't live with them, but after twenty-seven years of marriage, they bug me if I don't watch out."

Another man commented on men's actions: "Most men are only attentive to women when they want sex, and women know it. From my experience as a minister listening to married women describe their sexual problems, men spend their time, energy, and interest elsewhere—then expect the women to want them when it's time for sex. This hurts the women considerably."

This emotional alienation can be directly traced to the inequality created by society in giving men rights and privileges over women, and is aggravated by bringing up men and women with different psychological attitudes, and rewarding them for different types of behavior. Owning (or having the tradition of owning) women can lead men to have attitudes of condescension toward women, while valuing other men more. But if a woman is valued only sexually, sex (or not having sex) can be her only power. If a man only expresses a real desire to spend time with a woman when he wants her to have sex with him, is it any wonder that a woman often says no? In a society in which women are dependent on men, and in which men sometimes seem only to "need" women for sex, saying no is many women's only chance to gain recognition as an individual, or have some control in the relationship.*

---

* As one man put it, "As a male, there is no question, we are always in control once she consents to love-making. We have the dick, that's all there is to it! We are the fucker and she is the fuckee. At the same time, in this society, the woman has the final choice as to sex or no sex. She can deny us (and herself) or she can engage in sex."

How do men feel about all of this. Men often feel very angry with women who never initiate sex and too often don't want sex. But this anger has an undertone of alienation, guilt, and insecurity: men feel instinctively on some level that sex does not involve an equal sharing, especially when they are having an orgasm and the woman does not—and this puts them on the defensive. As one man remarked, "I feel more respect for her and myself if I don't feel I am cheating her of an orgasm—or I guess the word is 'using' her, since I have an orgasm and she doesn't. I feel relieved to be with an equal." But many men covered this feeling over by bragging, accepting their "aggressiveness" as inherently "male," and insisting that they were only behaving as their "natures" compelled them to.

Although many men are very angry with women and suffer profound discomfort due to women's "passivity" regarding sex—possibly because of buried feelings of guilt and defensiveness, knowing that somehow women are being exploited—most men do not overtly connect this with the need for improving women's status. Most men prefer to think that the problem is simply a lingering vestige of "Victorian morality"—and further to believe that somehow women can be sexually "free" even though they are not also economically and politically free.

Men are encouraged to accept this "difference" between men and women, and not to question it. Although many men instinctively feel uneasy on some level about what is going on, they are told by society that this is "just the way things are." Even though many men feel that by their having an orgasm and the woman not, they are exploiting the woman, that the situation is unfair, or that the woman is somehow in an inferior position, they are told that it is men's "nature" to continue wanting intercourse and having orgasm, and that whether the woman does or not is "her own problem." Men's reaction to this is often to become alienated from women, to feel "different," superior, uncomfortable, hostile or insecure with them. But, they may still wonder, do women really accept their less privileged status, or are women angry?

Men are faced with the dilemma of either believing that (1) women are built differently from men, and do not always need orgasm to be satisfied, and further that women in fact do not mind simply watching/helping the man have an orgasm while they do not; or (2) that women can indeed orgasm (through masturbation, for example) but that they have been oppressed economically and socially into a position in which they have been forced to accede to men's wishes in sex, and that women have a hidden residue of anger at men for this. In other words, either women are innately unequal, or women have been forced to submit. These are not pleasant options from which men may choose. If a man believes (1), he must accept the idea that women are somehow fundamentally different from men in their basic humanity. This point of view was implied by Freud's famous question, "What do women want?", which seemed to say that what women want is so fundamentally different from what men want, that it is mysterious and unfathomable. If a man accepts this position, then his ability to be truly close to a woman is quite limited, as he feels himself so different from her.* Their relationship may be quite distant and formal, as each views the other as truly "other." On the other hand, if a man believes (2), he is in a much better position for achieving a close and fulfilling relationship with a woman, even though he may have to re-examine how sexuality is defined, and re-think the basis of male–female relationships. But this process can lead to much greater fulfillment and happiness for a man in his own sexuality and life.

* Not only sexually, but also in what he wants out of life; he may feel he is more aggressive and demanding of life in general, in his career, etc., than women—who are "naturally" content with home and security. This can make him feel alienated, emotionally unconnected, isolated, and angry.

Rape, Sexual Violence, and Pornography

Sexual Violence in the Culture

Where do pressuring women into sex, rape (of various kinds), paying women for sex (either outright, or as many men said, in marriage or on dates), and buying women in pornography fit into men's lives—if they do? Are they things only "abnormal" men are involved with, or do they in some way involve and affect all men's lives and relationships with women, because they somehow involve the basic underpinnings of the entire social structure?

If sex/intercourse has traditionally been the basic symbol of male domination and ownership of women (whether or not an individual man may feel this at any given time), rape and paying women for sex, or buying women through pornography, are basic extensions of this ideology—not biologic "urges" or part of a physical male "sex drive." It is what "sex" means to men that makes them sometimes want to rape or buy women, not a desire for orgasm or sexual sharing.

The general culture—in movies, books, jokes, and popular sayings—reinforces the idea that men "get" or "take" sex from women, men "have" women, men conquer and possess women, women say "no" but mean yes, women "give in" to men—and "penetration" is the symbol of this victory. Men, brought up to feel that a vital part of being a male is to orgasm in a vagina, often resent women's "power" to withhold this "male need" from them—not realizing that this is in many ways the only "power" left to many women. It is this dynamic that in part sometimes leads men to say that women are "more powerful" than men.

In fact, the model of sex as we know it has even been called the "rape model" of sex. If men have more power, money, and privilege than women, can the definition of "sex" change? Won't forcing women into sex (intercourse), either physically through rape, or financially through paying a woman or buying pornography, continue its appeal, due to its meaning? Arguably a real and profound change may occur. Right now, in many ways "fucking" and physical rape stand as an overwhelming metaphor for the rape—physical, emotional, and spiritual—of an entire gender by our culture.

Rape

Do men want to rape women?

"Sometimes I've found myself getting excited watching a show in which a man is planning a rape. It bothered me that I was being aroused by it. I'm not sure I understand why."

"I have often wanted to rape a woman, and I fantasize about it a lot. But the idea disturbs me because it runs counter to my sense of mutual respect, humanism, feminism, etc. I'm really anxious to see what other men feel about rape."

What does the physical rape of a woman mean to men? Is the desire sexual? A form of hostility and anger? Or a way to reassert an injured "masculine pride"?

Many men think of rape as a way of putting a woman "back in her place"—this was a man's right. Others say women are "asking for it," the implication being that women have no right to be sexual unless it leads to intercourse with men, and that men have the right to control women's sexuality:

"I've seen a lot of women who seem to be asking for it . . . just as a person with a fistful of money is asking for robbery by flaunting his money, especially in a gin mill or dark alley. I also feel sympathy for women. After all, when someone wants to protect one's money from being stolen, the money can be placed in a bank. But how does a woman protect her body from being raped? I wish I knew. A little more prudence, I guess. I'm glad I'm a man."

"There is the provocation of 'dry hustling.' Dry hustling is making oneself available for sex and then withdrawing or withholding it. The brassiere-less woman in a public place is a dry hustler. The bra-less look is attractive. It is supposed to be. *And it is a provocation.*"

A few say rape is justified by the male "sex drive" and the "failure" of women to meet that "need." Underlying this point of view is the idea, strong in our culture and in all patriarchal cultures, that men own women's bodies. As one man said, "She is mine. I have a right to orgasm

223

through intercourse. God gave me the right when he made women for men." A man should not have to masturbate for orgasm when sexual desire is not mutual, according to this point of view; he should have his orgasm through a woman at all times (only an orgasm had through intercourse with a woman is legitimate), and it is a woman's duty at all times to help him do this.

Also implicit in many of the replies is the idea that a woman denying a man sex is somehow denying his manhood and that by raping a woman a man is re-asserting his masculinity—not only with the woman but in his own mind:

"Once I was going with a woman (in high school) and she would not let me have sex. All my friends had done it with their girlfriends, and even did it with us when we went out on double dates and parked together after. I got to feel like a real reject. I could have lied to them about it, but then my girlfriend would have found out, and they probably wouldn't have believed me anyway, since I couldn't have described the feeling. This made me so angry I felt like raping her. Finally, without anybody knowing, I picked up a streetwalker and had intercourse. This did a lot for my feeling of confidence in my own masculinity. Soon after, I broke up with my girlfriend and started going with somebody else who would go all the way. Then I could tell the guys, and I felt like one of the group again."

One man writes about his desire to rape being connected to the teachings of the culture:

"It's pretty obvious that I have some hostility toward women that started way back—they have something I want, and I'm a 'bad boy' for wanting it—they're excluding me—they have a secret—they have a sex organ, but dirty little boys don't get any, etc., etc., ad nauseam. I have become aware of these feelings and know when they are active; when I feel them, I back off whatever situation is causing them and find something else to do."

One man describes chillingly his generalized feeling of rejection—feeling left out of what "everyone else" is enjoying, what other men are having:

"I have certainly wanted to. Usually this desire comes after I have been rejected by a very attractive woman, e.g., at the office. Then I fantasize following her, putting a gun to her head (I own a revolver), and asking her something like 'Now tell me who you want to go to bed with.' In recent months, I have become more sympathetic toward rapists, because I see in myself the other side of the sexual revolution: it is all well and good for the Beautiful People to decide to bring their fantasies out of the closet and talk about the joys of sex in public—it is another to be tantalized day after day by the sight of beautiful women you desire but can't have. Apparently every one of them is experiencing the wildest sexual pleasures and fulfillment, because the media are everywhere saying so."

The image of a rapist appeals to some men, who identify it with being strong and virile, passionate and powerful:

"I don't think I could. But I have been sort of impressed by people who pulled off what seemed to be an especially brilliant or daring rape."

"I have fantasies of doing it, as a form of 'proving' to the woman that I am really all 'man,' able to get and keep a hard-on and use it to force myself on her, whether she wants me or not."

Some men even write that all "real" men have a desire to rape women because this is part of a male's innate makeup (a "natural" animal instinct★):

"Why do I want to rape women? Because I am basically, as a male, a predator and all women look to men like prey. I fantasize about the expression on a woman's face when I 'capture' her and she realizes she cannot escape. It's like I won, I own her."

"Rape behavior in males today probably exists because it has been selected for (this would take precedence over selection by females) in the Darwinian model of natural selection; as much as our contemporary society despises the rapist, we must admit that in man's history the rapist's genes were naturally selected because the behavior had survival value."†

A few men wonder why they don't have these feelings, and if they are "abnormal":

"I have never raped a woman, or wanted to. In this I guess I am somewhat odd. Most of my friends talk about rape a lot and fantasize about it. The whole idea leaves me cold."

In fact, despite the seeming secret admiration of some men for rapists as the ultimate "man," strong and powerful, the reality is usually just the opposite: it is the man with the lowest self-esteem who is most likely to rape women or pressure them for sex—the man who does not see

---

★ This is inaccurate, since animals do not rape. The implication in this answer is that rape is a "natural instinct," which only "civilization" can overcome. In fact, it is our "civilization" which has created the concept and encouraged it.
† Darwin's theory concerned selection between different species, not within species. This is a misunderstanding and misuse of the concept of "survival of the fittest."

himself as strong and powerful, the man who feels the most rejected, the most like a "loser."

The loner-rapist who becomes violent is becoming more and more a common figure in our society—unfortunately:

"I am single, never married, never lived with a woman, and I am so alone that I am slowly going crazy. I am fifty pounds overweight, work as a clerk in a welfare office and as a security guard at nights. I find going out to meet women very frustrating. Going to dances and no one wanting to dance with me gets me pissed. I get very depressed and antisocial. I have a perverse but vicarious thrill in other people (usually men) who go berserk in public places and kill innocent bystanders, such as David Berkowitz (Son of Sam). When I was in college, I wanted to shoot good-looking coeds on campus with a concealed automatic pistol. They never look at me or acknowledge my humanity, so maybe I'm not good enough for them. I think they're afraid I'm going to rape them. I would never rape a woman because I don't think I could convince them I'm serious, they'd probably scream and I would run. Berkowitz's strategy was more direct, hostile, vengeful, and up-front. I admire Berkowitz, Son of Sam, for what he did."

The story of a rapist

"I am twenty-three. I am at present incarcerated here at the State Medical Facility prison for rape. I have been incarcerated for approximately four years.

"I turned myself in to the authorities after my fourth successful (if it can be properly termed as such) rape, I couldn't stand the pressure or the worry that I might seriously hurt or kill my next victim. I have since been in various therapy sessions, and am still attempting to glue my thoughts, feelings, and ideas to a more suitable state that is more acceptable to myself and society.

"I sincerely hope you can find that my feelings are honest, as I did my best. I'd like to say this before going on to the questions, that a rapist is tagged a Mentally Disordered Sex Offender (M.D.S.O.), but it's a question not so much of a sickness, but comparable to a building block. In most of our childhoods, we start learning and experiencing life, and it's our responsibility to build correctly foundational morals. If incidents happen, trauma, accidents, whatever, that tears down one's blocks, he must put it back together. I believe that when my 'blocks' were kicked over, I put them back up incorrectly and in a disordered fashion. It took twenty years to try and gain enough confidence and self-respect to try and reorder and rebuild my 'blocks.' An M.D.S.O. is not a diseased animal, but someone who has to get a thing straightened out in his own life and head before he can live acceptably to his peers.

"I'm presently a nurse's aide in this facility's hospital, specializing in emergency aid and the intensive care unit for the last two years. I have a G.E.D. with only tenth-grade backing.

"I was brought up in a broken home before my mother remarried my stepfather. I'm the oldest of five children. I suffered disrespect for myself, and feelings of guilt and helplessness since my father's divorcing when I was five, and have lived my life being a phony to get people's attention.

"I have raped women (four rapes with one attempt) for two major reasons: (1) to gain a feeling of absolute control over a woman I felt rejected me, and (2) to prove I was as worthless as my inner turmoil made me believe I was. A lot more is involved, but that's the basic cause for my acts. The acts themselves were frightening to both myself and my victim. I felt like I only wanted to be accepted, to have her say she understood me, I just didn't have enough on the ball, or the confidence to ask, or try and build the relationship because I had myself doomed in my own head towards rejection.

"When I was refused sex before, I usually felt rejected and then anger, and get pissed off to the point I feel justified to rape her and degrade her. I'm now at the point that I still feel rejection, but I try to understand women have their preferences, as I do, and they have desires and likes, as we all do.

"When I raped, I felt a commitment to finish intercourse after initiating my approach, though I didn't want sex (I was after that feeling of utter control and domination over someone else), but I felt I had to finish what I started. In normal sex with a willing partner, I usually desire intercourse, and I also like to just hold and hug and lightly pet with those women in my life I feel close to without the actual sex act, or having to go on to intercourse.

"I used to ejaculate immediately (three to five seconds after penetration) if the intercourse was forced on my partner. I feel this happened because when I'm forcing sex, I'm not into the act of sex, but only out to prove I can control my victim, and also to increase my inadequate feelings about myself. It used to bother me so much that the confusing act would in itself cause me to rape for a fourth time, eventually forcing me to turn myself in for help. I now have routed out most of my inadequacies to the point of I now realize I no longer have to be phony, which helps my self-confidence and allows me to be a bit more open with my relationships.

"I felt very inadequate and powerless when I raped. Most often and as often as I can feel powerful, I'll try and achieve the feeling. The point where I feel most powerful during non-forced sex is at the point I keep up my foreplay until they beg for me to enter them. I feel like I'm very much in absolute control.

"I would still like to live my fantasy in sex. I would like to have a partner who is at first unwilling (young; between fifteen and twenty-six) but is soon aroused by my tongue until she asks for my penis.

"My first sex experience was also the first time I was very aware of orgasm, I was nine and my partner thirteen. She dared me to first kiss her, and she manipulated me until I was performing intercourse. All I can recall is that when I came, I felt like a part of me had just left and went into her, and I neither understood it or wanted it. I was very much afraid someone (my mother) would discover its absence and hate me. I was extremely confused and very frightened.

"I had sex with a hooker once, and it was a mess. We did it in a motel room with her four kids not more than three feet away watching TV. I was feeling greatly inadequate, afraid, and guilty, plus I didn't have the agreed-upon price (ten dollars). This was when I was fifteen, my last of three previous sexual encounters before I met my wife in high school.

"I was still living at home with my family when my wife first came into my life during our high school days and it was simply assumed and accepted we were having sex. We never really discussed this until the question of marriage and children cropped up two years after we had been together. So we are common law. We have a seven-year relationship that has been broken up in pieces of time by army service and my present four-year incarceration period. I much like my long-standing relationship, am at this time in it, very much in love and comfortable and proud to have this woman who's lived with my mistakes and still loves me. Our sex is varied and pleasing, we know more or less just what we both want and how we need to express our sexual needs.

"I've had extramarital experiences and my wife has had two known to me. She knows of all of mine now, but didn't at the times they occurred, with the exceptions of when we were separated or traveling, or in the Army. At the time I felt I was being cute, with no regard to my wife's feelings, sometimes hoping she'll find out and force an issue. When she discovered my affairs and my rapes, she was very much hurt, confused, and very willing to accept *her* actions as the reasons I raped.

"I don't think I ever trusted myself with love enough to let it affect me until these last three years. I just used my wife for our first five years, I suspected and was wary of her reasons for loving me until two years ago when we started talking about fears and inhibitions we were trying to avoid concerning ourselves. After that, it seemed I just accepted her. By that I mean I didn't suspect her motives, I respect them. I don't worry about her leaving me. If it happens, I hope it's with a man she can be happier with. With this growth, my feelings for my family and friends is larger and a lot more comfortable.

"I've cried out front and without hindrance just these last three years. Also over my wife's and my near breakup, over a close friend's inability to express himself and his bottled-up emotions. I've never thought of suicide, and I consider it to be a weakness, and a very selfish act. Even when I turned myself in, I did it to stop hurting others and from tearing myself and my wife up further and to get help with my problem.

"Before, my wife and I only had a fairly content sexual relationship, with nothing else about it truly understood. Since I've started feeling good about myself, we've been talking a little more openly, and about our feelings and wants more than just saying mundane day-to-day talk. I think my first rape was sexually satisfying because it was one of my fantasies and it worked out, and because it was an on-the-spot encounter and I didn't have to communicate, or trust this woman, just have sex with her and no other responsibility.

"Now I have enough confidence and trust in my wife to tell her absolutely everything I feel or think or want, and don't worry about her rejecting me (my biggest fear is rejection), or laughing at me. Sometimes I don't feel my wife is as open with her feelings and thoughts as I'd like her to be, and she has difficulty expressing herself from what I feel she may be afraid I won't understand. She also can't bring herself to trust me as fully as I'd like for her to, due to my past actions and behavior. Hopefully she'll learn to trust and respect the changes I've tried to make in these last four years.

"I believe my sex life now will be completely altered from what it had been six years ago. I'm not into 'just sticking it in until I bust' no longer. I have to bring out my partner's fulfillment to enjoy my own. I no longer have the desire to 'take' my partner, she now has to be willing in order for me to gain my pleasure. I no longer feel women were made just to please me, but are individuals I must work with and for to gain their respect. I feel I've grown and matured in the past four years of incarceration to the point that I'm content with myself, which seems to reflect to my loved ones. I feel I have a great deal to offer now, it just hasn't been asked of me yet.

"I've gone those four years with no more sex than fantasy and masturbation. Not including the first nine years of my life, this is the longest I've abstained from sex. I sure as hell don't like it.

"I answered these questions because I felt a present need to express my feelings and to see if I could be honest with myself. I wanted to do it in a way I wouldn't be laughed at or misunderstood by assholes. I think, too, I secretly want a pat on the back. I also hope people will see that some rapists aren't just animals, but just confused and tightly locked up in their own fantasy worlds. As a whole, if a person has the balls to answer these honestly and openly, he may find quite a few surprises and insights. I found it an eye opener and I used it to get a little feeling out, it made me back up and take another look at aspects of sex that I had taken for granted."

Of course, rape can happen in less "dramatic" ways, in daily life; some men admit they have raped a woman—but "only my wife":

"Only my wife once, after about fifteen years of marriage from frustration and anger when she wouldn't verbalize with me. Once was too much."

"I would never think of taking it by force—except from my wife. I don't think I could get it up in a rape situation. It so appalls me that I couldn't do it. I have forced myself on my wife when she has repeatedly refused me and has led me to believe I could have some then closed up."

Other men describe using their positions of power to pressure a woman into sex or acceptance of an inappropriate situation at work:

"She was an employee and I was the 'boss.' I don't think this is the only reason why she had sex with me, but it was an influencing factor. *Maybe* she felt that intercourse with me would give her some security in her job, but only maybe."

"I have raped a woman, but never by beating her or that type. Rape by exorcism, firing her off the job, or not giving her a contract in business, etc."

But a large minority of men stress they would not even think about raping a woman, because they want the woman to want to be involved; rape would not satisfy their desire to be wanted and accepted:

"If the woman doesn't want me, I don't want her."

"It would not be at all self-assuring to have to force my attentions on a female. It's a woman's affections that I want—not just her body. I'd rather masturbate than have sex without affection."

One man whose wife had been raped describes his opposition to rape:

"My wife was a rape victim when she was nineteen. A good part of our marriage so far has consisted of my, and our, attempts to pick up the pieces. The idea of rape is a complete and total turn-off to me;

even the pseudo-rape sequences in X-rated movies fill me with the vilest hate. I sincerely believe (intend) that I would without hesitation kill any man who ever again touched my wife with this unspeakable atrocity. I at moments imagine my wife's screams on that night several years ago—I'm afraid that all the anxiety I've ever felt for the victim (my wife), I would unleash on a man if I heard a woman's call for help. It is my belief now, and she agrees, that this is a good part of the reason we cannot seem to get to a normal sexual functioning level in our marriage.

"She is a beautiful and intelligent girl, and it infuriates me to see all the ways that it has put kinks into her personality. She is afraid to be by herself, even somewhat in our house. She seems to want to be as unobtrusive as possible all the time. This whole rape fixation in the porno industry is a big bring-down for both of us . . . and at moments I wonder whether it is good that women's rape fantasies are stressed so frequently in the men's magazines, as they are. I mean, how many animals are there around?"

Pornography and the Definition of "Male Sexuality"

What is the reason for pornography's increasing importance in our society? According to *Forbes* magazine, by 1978, sex was a larger business than the record and film industries combined, amounting to $4 billion a year. Why do men use and look at pornography? Is it for sexual stimulation or male bonding and identification? What "turns men on" about pornography? Is it because of the viewing of female nudity or sexual activities? Or because of the fantasies of male power that accompany the viewing?

Certainly we all—men and women—have a right to see and read about intimate relationships between people—and in this way, to make more sense of our own lives and feelings. But pornography as we know it does not for the most part serve this purpose. In fact, much of pornography shows a woman submitting to a stronger, threatening, perhaps hostile and violent male.* Even in "soft-core" pornography, in which a woman is alone on the page, perhaps making eye contact with the viewer but almost always in a "come and get me" pose, the woman

---

* Pornography much more frequently shows women rather than men being dominated, tortured, and humiliated. Sadism against women is a cultural theme for the West which goes back to the "witch" burnings of the Middle Ages during which several million women were killed.

is being dominated too—not by a man in the picture, but directly by the viewer, who can use her in any way he pleases. Pornography as we know it—as, indeed, sex itself—is a reflection of society, with women often being used for men's pleasure. The fact that men dominate women in most of these pictures is such a commonplace that it is not seen as remarkable.

Pornography also reinforces in men the idea that all women can be bought; as one man said, "Pornography is a cheap way of buying a woman." Pornography does not glorify women; most men have contempt for the women they see on the pages, no matter how beautiful. A common form of using pornography is for men to look at it together in a group and to make comments about the women. This is a form of male bonding and reinforces the idea of male ownership of women.* Pornography reminds one of slave markets and slave auctions: each man can appraise, select, and buy the body that suits him. House slaves are the younger, "prettier" women, while field slaves are the hard workers—domestics or wives. The economic pressures on women, especially poor women, to sell their bodies in this way are great.

The continued spread of pornography will make relationships between men and women much slower to change, because pornography reinforces in men so many of the old and stereotyped attitudes to women and toward themselves that have done so much damage—both to women and men—already. This is true just as much of pornography that shows the woman/women dominating men as it is of depictions of men dominating women, since this is only a role reversal and still centers on the same definitions of sex involving all the issues we have discussed in this book so far. Pornography keeps men believing women are the way they want women to be, or have been told women are (either submissive or dominant, "bitchy"), and fortifies men's belief in their own sex role. Men, reading and looking at pornography, know they are sharing in something other men see, and assume therefore that this is what all "real men" want, identify with, and enjoy.

* Most men do not look at pornography with a woman, as most women do not like the way women are portrayed in pornography. Also, men looking at pornography together also find that it is another way of proclaiming one's masculinity for other men to see, and a way for men to have sexual feelings together while still focused on a "heterosexual" object.

Sex and Love Between Men

Homosexuality and Close Male Friendship

What is a close male friendship? There is no word in the language which recognizes this possibility—or for that matter the possibility of close friendships between women. The only word available to "describe" men's strong feelings or important relationships with each other is "homosexual." And yet this word is tied to an outdated view of the world which defines people by the gender of their sexual preference or their function in reproductive sex.

If we lived in a non-patriarchal, non-reproductively focused society, it is likely that the terms "heterosexual" and "homosexual" would be rather obscure and infrequently used. Kinsey pointed out in his works on male and female sexuality that the terms "heterosexual" and "homosexual" should be used not as nouns but as adjectives, and that they should be used to describe activities, not people. Other than that, these words have no meaning. And even used as adjectives referring to activities, the words are vague, since as we have seen in previous chapters, many activities can be shared by either sex and are not gender-specific. Additionally, some men do not fit into either "category," as they like to have sex with both men and women. For them, the word "bisexual" has been devised, but this word is rather unpleasant; in fact, wouldn't the word "sexual" be sufficient for all of these categories?

"Homosexuality" is an anti-word—that is, it is known basically as the opposite of "heterosexuality." But the word "heterosexual" is hardly ever used to describe a person; a man is simply assumed to be "heterosexual" unless the prefix "homosexual" (i.e., "deviant") is placed before his name. The whole viewpoint which makes a fetish of gender is out of date. It developed out of the definition of "sex" as reproductive activity.

There is a need for many more subtle descriptive and personal terms

233

in our vocabularies. What is a "homosexual" act? In one way, men are having sex with other men when they share pornography and discuss how they "have" sex with women, or go to topless bars together. They are enjoying sex together and joining in a form of sexually related bonding. Is caring for another man "homosexual"? In some ways, as we have seen earlier, it is considered even less manly to embrace or kiss a man than to have sex with him. Why can't men be close and affectionate? In fact, not only can men *not* touch each other and be close physically, even just as friends, but also they are not allowed to share real emotional intimacy, in most cases. A large part of the problem is our language—or lack of it—and the ever-present fear of being labelled "homosexual." And yet, many men seemed to express a longing for men to see each other in a new way, to relate to each other differently, become more open, close, and honest with each other.

Love stories between men

"I was almost seventeen years old when I first fell deeply in love. The intensity and the depth of the feeling frightened and overwhelmed me. At the time I was working as a cashier in a large supermarket. I enjoyed the work and enjoyed the close contact with people, especially the employees. After work we often got together and went bowling or played pool, etc. I was especially attracted to one of the fellows and we double-dated. It was on one of these double dates that I started having sexual fantasies. While he was making love to a girl in the back seat, I thought of him while I was kissing my girl in the front seat and wondered what it would feel like to be made love to by him. After the date I asked him to spend the night at my house and he accepted. I knew that something was happening to me but I wasn't sure what. After he fell asleep I got up, put my clothes on, and went to a nearby church. I knelt there and prayed, begging God for guidance. I cried, dried my tears, and returned home to bed and the strangest, most enduring relationship of my life began. I was surprised when he responded to me sexually and I discovered what his kisses were like. I was in a state of shock at what had happened to me when I realized I was in love.

"We both had feelings of guilt and fought the relationship. We stopped double-dating and avoided each other like the plague. Once or twice I visited the places that he frequented and remained in the background watching him. After a stint in the armed forces we got together one night. The feelings were still there but I had developed some self-control and we touched and kissed and that was it. After that we got together about twice a month for several years, but didn't touch. I always remember the magnetism of his body chemistry in relation to mine."

"Does feeling deeply in love really need description? I felt that the most important thing in my life was the happiness of the person I loved. I subordinated my own feelings and interests to the objective of my love's happiness. I felt (no doubt irrationally) that had it been necessary I might as well have sacrificed my very life for the preservation of my love. My whole experience for a couple of years was suffused with this all-important passion. What happened? The person I loved, who had reciprocated my feelings at first, grew less interested in me and by the end of three years of living together he was not any longer in love with me at all. It was a heartbreaking crisis for me, and the emotional agony and scars from that experience have left me permanently and clearly altered in my personality. I have never since had the same emotional capacity that I had before this experience. It is as though a part of my emotional capacity had been burned right out of my body or amputated. Eventually after many months I slowly resumed living. I have never, however, in the ten years since, been able to shed a single tear over anything. As I said, it is as if a part of my emotional capacity had been removed . . . cauterized away. I am basically a happy person. Only rarely do I feel a slight depression, but after that episode I think it must have been three years before I had a week when I could look at myself and say honestly, 'I am happy this week.' "

"The most deeply in love I have been was when I was nineteen, with someone I lived with for six years. There was a sexual attraction, but beyond this there was a sense of 'comfortability,' a tremendously joyful feeling of well-being. I don't like the gay term 'lover'; to me that denotes something risqué, spurious, without depth. This was a partnership, an equal sharing where we both used our talents to complement the other and shared the day-to-day responsibilities of living. There was no 'he' or 'she,' simply two people who happened to be male and who happened to fully enjoy and respect each other. I do not recall that either of us felt any need to be jealous even when one or the other would seek a sexual encounter outside. We were honest in our relationships with others as well as each other. I believe that the honesty in our relationship gave it a tremendous amount of security.

I have never known such a sense of well-being or happiness since that time."

"I have been deeply in love twice . . . both times with straight men who loved me also but could not totally express that feeling, sexually or otherwise. I have kept close contact with both and have continued to love them, one for seventeen years and the other for fourteen. The two times I was in love it hit me like an electric shock—like having a bolt of lightning hit me. I knew at that instant that this was going to be 'the one.' I was relatively speechless and fumbled for words. I became flustered. I was enormously aroused sexually although not aware of having an erection. The first time the fellow touched my hand (by circumstance, not intentionally), it was so intense it was almost painful."

Of course, not all gay men honor love:
"Essentially what I have to say about relationships is that I don't want one. I enjoy my life. But when somebody falls out of the sky and strikes up the harmonious chord, well, what can you do? Honor it.

"Two nights ago I went to bed with a man who had never been to bed with a man before. I loved it. We were sitting there at the bar talking about how hard it is growing up male, and then I started yapping about growing up gay, and then suddenly he said. 'Would you like to make love to me?' Honest. Perfect. So we went to his house and I kept giving him every out, in case he didn't really mean it, but he did, and we did, and he was Great. No hesitation, no bad ideas (mutual fellatio is what seemed natural to him)—and I was surprised because I would have expected some reluctance on the part of a first-timer to suck. Wrong-o. And he always referred to it as 'making love,' which, yes, is different. If I take him at face value—I mean, what he told me—he is exactly the kind of new man this society needs. Quiet; open; affectionate; articulate; and incidentally, a hell of a looker.

"I guess I can't really explain this without telling you the whole thing about Jim, the nineteen-year-old hustler who committed suicide in New York. He was pushy as hell, and loud and demanding, and scared. He became a liberated faggot at age fourteen in a small town. He needed support desperately, so I'd feed him dinner and kiss him goodbye at the door as he went out to work the streets. Then he'd come home about two and make me walk to the Quik-Trip for burritos. Ick. But then he really did drive me crazy, too; by the time he left we just said, 'Later,' by which I meant give yourself a couple of years. Six months later—when I was having a fling with another farm-boy fairy with adjustment problems—he called up and said I have to come back. Now. I said nah, you don't mean now. He said please and I said no. So then a couple of weeks later he calls late one night and talks for a while, clearly drunk, asking for phone numbers, desperate to talk, and maybe not to me. He called back at some outrageous hour the next morning and told me stories and read a poem and laughed a lot and then got kinda spooky, but not more so than a lot of other times, saying 'remember this conversation' (which I don't quite), but anyway we both knew that he was dying and he did a few hours later. Why was it love? A lot of it is energy, I guess. The energy flow between us, the amount of respect—respect—that can be expressed meaningfully. I come off sounding real hard when I talk about him because it was such a ludicrous situation. We thought we were the latest thing from MGM Productions. I gave him two oak trees in a small pot. His abandoned pet mice came to die on my dining-room rug—two floors below their home—after he left. After he died I felt stood up.

"I am happiest with strangers. I mean, none of these relationships was really balanced right sexually. So I really get into one terrific night. No phone numbers. Although—honorable mention goes to the two-week man who moved. Haven't heard from him since, but sleeping with him was a real treat. Couldn't go to sleep because he grinds his teeth; the noise was deafening, so I'd lie next to him and try to massage his jaw. Once he asked me to rub my stubbly chin on the nape of his neck. Good details, even if the big picture turned out to be not so attractive.

"My friends are permanent. Sex partners come and go. So do lovers. Love? Oh my. Really, it's like the ocean, it just goes on and on.

"Every sexual act I've performed was illegal. Am I pissed? Do you wonder if I'm pissed?

"Questions I have to ask myself: How much of my desire to fuck men is based on hostility? How far have I pushed myself *not* to become the upright Baptist Masons man I was born to be? How much further to go? And what *do* all those men think about themselves?

"Observation: Most straight men like me. They'll open doors or pat my ass or just any crazy thing because (I think) they're intrigued by my apparent 'decadence.' I don't mind.

"Gee, why did I answer? Well, gay men have a responsibility to help change the patterns, to ensure personal freedom and mass survival. Ain't gonna be easy. The Facts of Life, they used to say."

In our society, despite all the recent publicity regarding gay rights, there is still an enormous amount of prejudice, and gay men must, for the most part, hide their feelings. As one man put it unforgettably, "In our society you can go to war and kill a guy, but God help you if you're caught in bed with one."

Another man describes the history in his lifetime of prejudice against homosexuality:

"I see no reason for homosexuality to be taboo. But like a lot of other things it just did not fit into the society. Before World War II, I can remember when mentally retarded children were kept in hiding from the public eye. When these children were big enough to cause a lot of trouble, they were taken to the *insane asylum* (as it was called then) and some of them were never seen again by the people who knew them. A homosexual was considered the same as mentally retarded except worse."

The view that heterosexuality is the only "natural" form of sexuality and the only basis for the family, can be questioned on historical grounds. The earliest families were not the nuclear, "heterosexual" family as we know it, but included the mother, sisters and brothers, aunts, uncles, and so on in a loose grouping. There was no "father," and the relationship between mother and child was nowhere near as primary as we believe it to be today—in fact, sometimes children, mothers, and sisters became confused as to whose child was whose. However, it was not considered to be an important issue, as each would receive nurturance from various members of the group or from whichever members felt most sympathetic to one another. Indeed, for centuries the role of intercourse in causing pregnancy was not known. During these centuries, the clan-family was a viable social institution whose demise came only with the changeover to patriarchy and male ownership of children around 8000–5000 B.C.

Then, even in classical Greece, male homosexuality (we do not know about lesbianism) was a standard way of life, men having to be admonished by public decree to have sex with their wives at least three times a month, to ensure procreation. Sex with boys was the "norm," as is well documented. It might be interesting to speculate at another time what "the home of democracy" and homosexuality as an accepted institution had in common.

PART FOUR

1987: Women and Love: A Cultural Revolution in Progress

The Hite Report on Love, Passion, and Emotional Violence

Research Questionnaire for Women on Emotions, 1981–1987

The purpose of this questionnaire is to hear women's points of view on questions that were unanswered in the original *Hite Report on Female Sexuality*. For example, how women feel about love, relationships, marriage, and monogamy were not covered, due to lack of funds. We would very much like to hear your thoughts and opinions on these subjects now, as well as anything else you would like to add. The results will be published as a large-scale discussion of what was said, with many quotes.

The questionnaire is anonymous, so do not sign it. *It is not necessary to answer every question!* There are seven headings; feel free to skip around and answer only those sections or questions you choose. Also, you may answer on a tape cassette, if you prefer. Use as much additional paper as you need.

Send your answers to Shere Hite, P.O. Box 5282, F.D.R. Station, New York, N.Y. 10022.

HELLO!

1. Who are you? What is your own description of yourself?

2. What makes you feel happiest, the most alive? Your work? Your love relationship? A hobby or second career? Music? Going places (travel, concerts, dinner with friends)? Your children? Family? How happy are you, on a scale of one to ten?

3. What do you want most from life?

4. What was your greatest achievement personally to date?

241

5. What was the biggest emotional upset or disturbance you ever had to face—the greatest crisis, the thing you needed the most courage to get through?

6. Are you in love? Who is the person you are closest to?

7. What is your favourite way to "waste time"?

GROWING UP FEMALE

8. As a child were you close to your mother? Your father? Did they love you? What did you like most and least about them?

9. Was your mother affectionate with you? Did she speak sweetly to you? Sing to you? Bathe you and do your hair? Were there any clashes between you? When was she angriest? What do you think of her today? Do you like to spend time with her?

10. Was your father affectionate? How? Did you talk? Go places together? Did you like him? Fear him? Respect him? What did you argue about? What do you think of him today?

11. Were your parents affectionate together in front of you? Did they argue? What did you learn from your father was the proper attitude toward your mother? What did you learn from your mother was the proper attitude toward your father?

12. Did your mother show you how to be "feminine"—act like a girl or a "lady"? Did you and your mother do things your brothers or father did not do, and vice versa? How would you define femininity?

13. Were you (are you) a "tomboy"? Was it fun? Were you warned against acting too rough, playing "boys'" games, not acting "ladylike"? Were you urged to be a "good girl"? Were you rebellious?

14. Did you masturbate as a child? How old were you when you started? Did your parents know? Your friends?

15. What did/do you dislike about high school? Was/is there a lot of pressure to conform, be like everyone else? Dress a certain way? Be popular? To be a virgin, or to have had sex?

16. Did/do you have a best friend? Did you spend the night at each other's houses? Talk on the phone? What about? Go out together? Are you still in touch?

17. How did you feel when you started dating? When you first kissed? Made out? Had sex? Did you discuss any of this with your parents? Friends?

FALLING IN LOVE

18. Are you "in love" now? How can you tell?

19. How would you define love? Is love the thing you work at in a relationship over a period of time, or is it the strong feeling you feel right from the beginning, for no known reason?

20. To live with someone, is it more important to be "in love" or to love them? What is the difference between being "in love" and loving someone?

21. When, with whom, were you most deeply in love? Were you happy? What was it like? Did the relationship last? Was this when you felt the most passionate?

22. Did you ever cry yourself to sleep because of problems with someone you loved? Why? Contemplate suicide? When were you the loneliest?

23. When were you the happiest with someone?

24. Do you like being in love? Is it a condition of pleasure or pain? Learning? Enlightenment? Joy? Ambivalent feelings? Frustration? How important is it?

25. What are your favorite love stories, in books or films?

YOUR CURRENT RELATIONSHIP

26. Are you in a relationship now? For how long? Do you live together? Are you married? Do you have children?

27. What is the most important part of this relationship, the reason you want it? Is it love, passion, sexual intimacy, economics, daily companionship, or the long-term value of a family relationship? Other?

28. Are you happy with the relationship? Inspired? What do you like most and least about it? Can you imagine spending the rest of your life in it? Is your partner happy?

29. Are you "in love"? Or do you love them, more than being "in love"? What kind of love do you feel?

30. Do you love your partner as much as s/he loves you? More? Does one of you need the other more? Do you feel loved?

31. What is the biggest problem in your relationship? How would you like to change things, if you could?

32. What do you enjoy doing together the most? Talking? Having sex? Being affectionate? Daily life? Sharing children? Hobbies? Going out? Other?

33. How does your partner act toward you in intimate moments? Does your partner tell you s/he loves you? That you are wonderful and beautiful? Very sexually desirable? Talk tenderly to you? Use baby talk? Sex talk? How do you feel?

34. What things does your partner most often criticize about you? What do you most often criticize about him/her?

35. What is the worst thing your partner has ever done to you? The worst thing you have ever done to him/her?

36. Is it easy to talk? Who talks more? Would you like more intimate talk—about feelings, reactions, and problems? Future plans and dreams?

37. Does the relationship fill your deepest needs for closeness with another person? Or are there some parts of yourself that you can't share? That aren't accepted or understood? Or do you prefer not to share every part of yourself?

38. Is the kind of love you are giving and receiving now the kind you most want? Have you seen another type in a friend's relationship or a movie or novel that you would find more satisfying?

39. Is this relationship important to you? How important? The center of your life? An important addition to your relationship with yourself and/or your work? Or merely peripheral—pleasant, but lacking somehow? What would make you leave it?

40. What are the practical arrangements? Who does the dishes? Makes the beds? Does the cooking? Takes care of the children? What is daily life like? Do you sleep in the same bed? Take baths or showers together?

41. Do you share the money? Who controls the money? Do you both

work outside the home? Who pays the rent or mortgage? Buys the groceries? How do you feel about the financial arrangements? Do they affect the relationship?

42. What is the best way you have found to make a relationship work?

43. If you are married, how long have you been married? Do you like it? What is the best part of being married? The worst? Before you got married, did you expect it to be like it is?

44. Why did you decide to get married? Because of love? Sex? Social pressures? Economic pressures? Pregnancy? Companionship? To have children? A home life? Emotional security? Was it a hard decision? Whose idea was it? How long had you known each other?

45. How did you feel immediately after you got married? Elated? Worried? Did your feelings for him change? His actions toward you?

46. If you have children, do you like having them? What was having your children like? Was your husband there?

47. How did you feel when you first knew you were pregnant? How did your lover/husband react? After the child was born? Does he take as much part in child rearing as you?

48. Would your life have been different if you had not had children? How? Would you do it over again?

49. Which is more important: Your job? Your love relationship? Your children? Yourself, having time for yourself?

50. Do you believe in monogamy? Have you/are you having sex outside the relationship? Known to your partner? How do you feel about it? What is it/was it giving you?

51. What was your original reason? Were you in love? Was there a lack of understanding or closeness at home? A desire to experiment sexually? Anger? Long absence? Other? Is/was the affair serious?

52. Do you think your partner is having sex with anyone else now? In the past? How do you feel about this? Do you want your partner to be monogamous? Do you want to know if s/he is not?

53. Would you have sex outside the relationship in the future? Tell your partner?

54. Have you ever dated someone married? Did you mind that s/he was married? Did you want them to get divorced, and marry you?

55. Describe the biggest (or most recent) fight you had with your husband or lover.

56. What do you most frequently fight about? Who usually wins (if anybody)? How do you feel during? After?

57. How do conflicts or arguments usually get resolved—or at least ended? Who usually says they're sorry first after a fight? Who initiates talking over the problem? Making up?

58. Describe the time recently you were most happy with your lover, most joyous.

BEING SINGLE

59. Do you like being "single"—whether you are single now or were in the past? Why are you single?

60. What are the advantages of being single? Disadvantages? Do you like going out alone, to a party, restaurant, or shopping, etc? Or do you sometimes get the impression people think there is something wrong with you when you are not in a couple? Do some people envy you for being single?

61. What is your sex life like? Do you enjoy periods of no sex with another person?

62. Is it easy or difficult to meet someone you like and are attracted to, and whom you respect?

63. Do you think most men today want to be married? Do single men find it difficult to accept the idea of marriage at first? Do they tend to avoid commitment? Do you think men today are less committed?

BREAKING UP/GETTING A DIVORCE

64. If you have ever gotten divorced, or broken up with someone important, what was it like? Who wanted to break up—you or the other person? Why?

65. Were you glad or did you have regrets? Did you feel like a failure, or did you feel freer—or both? Did you hate the other person? Cry a lot? Or feel relieved, that now you could start living again?

66. How did you get over it, if you didn't want to break up? How

long did it take? Did you talk to friends? Hide from them? Work harder?

67. While breaking up, what did you feel was the most permanent, solid thing in your life? Your parents or relatives? Friends? Children? Your work? Yourself?

68. Was there a time at which you gave up on love relationships as not being very important? You preferred to put more energy into work or children? You revised your definitions of what kind of love was important? Or have you always put love relationships first in your life?

69. Have you ever lost a loved one through death? What do you miss most about the person? Was a part of you not sorry? Did you feel deserted? Free? Did you grieve?

SPECIAL PROBLEMS IN RELATIONSHIPS

70. Did you enter therapy to try to solve personal problems related to your love relationships? What were they? Did therapy help? What were your conclusions?

71. Do you sometimes think you pick the "wrong" lovers? What kinds of lovers do you pick?

72. Are you jealous? Of friendships? Career? Other women? Men?

73. Did you ever grow to hate a lover? Act violently? Scream? Hit them? Did a lover ever strike you, or beat you? What were the circumstances?

74. Have you ever loved someone who hurt you deeply, in spite of what had happened, and in spite of your desire not to love them any longer?

75. Who usually breaks up the relationship first—you or the other person?

76. Do you sometimes find you have to employ a "streak of manipulative coldness"—keep your distance, keep things "cool"?

77. Have you ever pretended you cared less than you did? That s/he was less important than they were? Put up a front? Did it work?

78. Are you afraid of clinging? Making someone feel tied down, "unfree"? Did you ever feel you were too emotionally dependent?

Are men afraid of women's dependency? If you tell a man you love him, will he feel tied down?

79. Did you ever have a nagging fear of losing someone's love, or being deserted? That the other person would grow tired of you?

80. Do you ever feel you have "unhealthy" needs and cravings for love and affection? As one woman put it, "My love has usually been too blind, too desperate."

81. How do you feel if someone is very emotionally dependent on *you* in a relationship? Needs you more? Complains that you don't love him enough?

82. Have you ever felt that you were "owned" or suffocated, held down, in a relationship, so that you wanted out?

83. Do you think men take love and falling in love as seriously as women do—if they do? What part does it play in men's lives? Are men more emotionally dependent, or women?

84. Were you ever financially dependent on a man you lived with? Was this a problem? How did/do you feel about it? Did/does it affect the relationship?

85. How do you think men feel about women working outside the home? If you work, and are married/living with someone, how does he feel about it? Does he share the housework?

86. Does your husband/lover see you as an equal? Or are there times when he seems to treat you as an inferior? Leave you out of the decisions? Act superior?

87. How do most men you know feel about the women's movement? How does your husband/lover feel about it?

SEXUALITY

88. What is sex with your partner (or in general) usually like? Do you enjoy it? Do you usually orgasm? During which activity? What is the worst thing about sex? The best?

89. Has your sexuality, or your style of relating sexually, changed over the last few years? In what way?

90. Have you read *The Hite Report on Female Sexuality*? Which ideas do you most agree with? Disagree?

91. Which is the easiest way for you to orgasm: Through masturbation? Clitoral stimulation by hand from your partner? Oral sex? Intercourse (vaginal penetration)? With a vibrator?

92. If you orgasm during vaginal penetration, how do you usually do it? (a) By added clitoral stimulation from your partner? Please explain. (b) By your own clitoral stimulation/masturbation during penetration? (c) By being on top and rubbing against your partner? (d) Friction of the penis inside the vagina, without other stimulation? (e) Other? Please describe.

93. When did you first orgasm—during sex with a partner, or masturbation? (a) Did you discover masturbation on your own, or did you read about it? How old were you? How did you feel? Did your parents know about it? Friends? (b) When you had your first orgasm with another person, which activity was it during? Did you learn to make it happen, or did it happen without trying?

94. Have you ever masturbated with a partner? During intercourse? During general caresses? Was it hard to do the first time? How did you feel? What was his/her reaction? Do you have to have your legs together or apart for orgasm?

95. Have you told a woman friend you don't orgasm from intercourse (if you don't)? Explained your sex life in detail to her? What did you say? How did she react?

96. Have you told a man you don't orgasm from intercourse (if you don't)? What did he say? Did you tell him most women don't? How did you feel?

97. Have you talked with your mother, sister, or daughters about some of these things? Do they know if you masturbate? Do you know if they do? What else have you talked about? What would you like to talk about?

98. If you prefer sex with women, how did you come to this point of view? If you prefer sex with men, how did you come to this point of view? Have you always felt this way? What do you like best about sex with women/men?

99. Does sex with the same partner change over the years? Does it become boring, or more pleasurable? Or does it depend on how the relationship goes?

100. Is there a contradiction between sexual passion and a more

long-term stable relationship? Do you have to choose? Do the daily details of living conflict with, or make difficult, feelings of passion?

101. When do you feel most passionate? How does it feel? Craving? Do you become more aggressive? Or want to be taken?

102. Do you usually like to be more passive or active, dominant, during sex?

103. Do you like exploring a man's body? His chest? Penis and testicles? Anus and buttocks? Have you ever penetrated a man's anus with your finger? How did you feel about this? How do you feel about giving him oral sex? Do most men/does he like you to do this—or is he shy and uncomfortable?

104. Do you like, or would you like to try, exploring a woman's body? Her breasts? Her clitoris? Her vulva? Vagina? Anus and buttocks? How do you feel about giving her oral sex? Do you like the taste and smell? Do most women like you to do this, or feel shy and uncomfortable? Do you like penetrating a woman's vagina? Anus?

105. Do you like to be stimulated vaginally? Penetrated? By a finger? Penis? Dildo? What do you like and dislike about it?

106. Do you like to be stimulated/penetrated anally? By a finger? Penis? Dildo? How does it feel, and why do you like or dislike it?

107. Do you like oral sex to be done to you? What do you think about how you look and smell? What does the other person usually seem to think? How about menstruation? Do you orgasm this way.

108. Can your partner stimulate you with his/her hand or finger on your clitoris? To orgasm? How does it feel? Do you have to guide his/her hand?

109. Have you shown someone how to masturbate you—that is, how to stimulate you to orgasm with their hand? Do most men offer clitoral stimulation by hand or mouth for orgasm, without being asked?

110. Do you use fantasies to help you orgasm? During sex? During masturbation? Which fantasies?

111. Do you feel pressured into sex? Into liking sex? Why? To be loving? To be "hip"? Have you ever been raped? Was this an important experience? How did you feel? Whom did you tell?

112. Do you like rough sex? What do you think of bondage-discipline? Spanking? Sadomasochism? Have you ever experienced them? Fantasized about them? Had rape fantasies? What were they like?

113. What do you think of pornography? Do you look at it? How did you feel when you first saw it? What does pornography tell you about what it means to be a woman?

114. Does your partner look at pornography? What kind? Men's magazines? Videotapes? How do you feel about this?

115. Do you use birth control? What kind? What are its advantages and disadvantages? Do you think men should be involved in birth control?

116. Have you ever had an abortion? Why did you decide to have it? How did you feel after you had it?

FRIENDSHIPS BETWEEN WOMEN

117. What is or has been your most important relationship with a woman in your life? Describe the woman you have loved the most. Hated the most.

118. What do you like about your closest woman friend? What do you do together? When do you see each other? Has she helped you through difficult times, and vice versa? How do you feel when you are together—do you have a good time? How much time do you spend together, or talking on the telephone? What does she do that you like least?

119. Were you close to your mother? Did she work outside the home, or was she a full-time mother and homemaker? Did you like her? Admire her? How did you feel about her taste in clothing? Are you like her?

120. Do you have a daughter? How do you feel about her? Have you talked to her about menstruation and sexuality? What did you say? What did she say?

121. What things about women in general do you admire? Which well-known women have contributed most to our society?

122. What do you think about the women's movement? Do you consider yourself a feminist, or in favor of the women's movement?

251

123. Have your feelings about the women's movement and its ideas affected your life?

124. Do you enjoy being "feminine"? How would you describe "femininity"? Do you enjoy beautiful clothing? Dresses and lingerie? Do you spend time on your hair and makeup? How do you feel about the way you look? How "feminine" are you?

125. How do you feel about getting older?

126. If you could say just one thing to other women today, what would you tell them?

127. What do you think is the biggest problem in the United States today?

THANK YOU

Please give the following statistical information:

a. What is your age? b. What is your racial background? Ethnic? c. What is your total amount of schooling? d. What was the approximate total income of your household before taxes in the past year? e. What kind of work do you do (inside or outside the home)? f. Where did you obtain this questionnaire?

Redefining the Emotions Known as "Love":

A Cultural Revolution in Progress

Women are in the midst of a dramatic shift. While most women say that, *theoretically*, love should be the most important part of life, most women (both married and single) also say that *their* love relationship is not the center of *their* life. The majority of women also say that they are still hoping they will have a greater, deeper, better love "yet to come." And so it seems that women now are very ambivalent: most want a deep love relationship and think it should be the most important thing in life; however, most have found it almost impossible to get love to work the way they *want*. Most women find they have to face a daily stream of identity-challenging behaviors from the men in their lives; increasingly they are solving this dilemma by reordering their priorities and making love with men less important than before.

If women say they can no longer emotionally afford to put love relationships with men first in their lives, does this mean that women, in "giving up on love," are taking on "male" values? Have we decided that the "male" model is right in its tradition of making love only part of life, less important than work, career, identity, pride in "being a man"? Or are women keeping their belief in love, just putting their hopes for this with men away for a while, protecting themselves until such time as the men in their lives can relate as equals to them?

Many women are creating a third alternative: they say love can continue to be the basis of one's value system, but its object can be changed. Many women are diversifying their love, still believing in love, but finding other objects to exchange it with, such as friends, children, lovers—even embellishing their work, and the people they come in contact with, with more caring and loving. Though women may be sad not to have the degree of closeness and intimacy with men that they would like, and some are giving up on *ever* having it, and look

253

back with deep regret and longing, many also definitely relish this new diversity, with its new opportunities.

What Happens to Love?

"Initially, being in love is fun but something happens and it becomes frustrating, painful, and disappointing. What is the thing that happens?"

"I try to open him up. I want to talk about our relationship, feelings and problems, and develop solutions or compromises. He is quiet, so I have to initiate it and drag it out of him. I usually work the hardest to resolve the problem. Sometimes, when he finds it hard to express himself, he withdraws. Without communicating, how can you solve anything?"

"Although I find that I'm funny, sarcastic, and energetic when in mixed groups, 'the life of the party'—when my boyfriend's there . . . boom. I'm very quiet. Almost like I don't want to steal his 'spotlight.' Am I alone in this?"

"My father was somewhat affectionate, as much as he knew how to be—you know, that masculine way, by being insulting."

"When I was three or four, my mother was already teaching me to *see* dust and other people's feelings. ('Don't bother your father, he's tired.') Men don't learn the same sensitivity."

"Generally I like least about men their tendency to bottle up their thoughts and emotions so that you have to use all your energy trying to get them to speak out and share their inner selves."

"I don't know if my short relationships with men are at all typical. The main thing that struck me was that there was virtually no discussion of anyone's feelings. Most men seem to see women as women, never as people. Things that I kept finding myself doing/feeling around men: Feeling like they were the important ones. Feeling too big, in all ways. Too tall, too large, said too much, felt too much, occupied more space than I had a right to. Wanting to please them. Wanting to appear femininely pretty."

"I was so hurt by the emotional abuse that I can't even talk about it now. Funny how feminists always get excited about physical abuse. Me too. If he'd ever hit me I would have walked out forever. Emotionally is something different . . . but the sick cycle of lashing out and then being repentant, and of finally in the end giving the emotional 'gifts,' is the same. It is sick, sick, sick, but when you are in the middle of it, it is hard to see, hard to get the perspective. You keep giving, simply the fact that you have invested so much makes it harder to give up."

"I am fighting with him all the time to preserve our relationship. He is happier when I never bring anything up. But if I don't, I feel unhappy, because emotional issues are never discussed—and I feel isolated, at a distance, alone. If we can't really be together, I'd rather leave the relationship. He probably doesn't realize this, because when I try to discuss things, he acts very put upon and martyred, or bitchy—certainly he shows no serious attempt to listen (although I am always there for him). He just seems to want to get any discussion over as quickly as possible, saying as little as possible. But later, when he's ready to cuddle in bed and have sex, he doesn't expect me to be distant because of his previous attitude. He doesn't realize it's all connected for me—wanting to have sex is, for me, connected to our warmth and closeness."

"If I tell him there's something he is doing that's bothering me, he'll say, 'Well, that's just the way I am.' But if he doesn't like something about me, I'm supposed to change. Then I worry about it a lot, trying to figure out if he's right, if there's something wrong with me. I spend a lot of energy trying to keep track of the relationship—knowing what kind of a mood he's in, asking him how he is feeling, keep things going, in touch. I know he loves me, but he just doesn't seem to have the same needs—he'll rarely ask me about the same things. When I try to explain this, he doesn't understand what 'the problem' is."

"To me, being involved with another person means asking them about things they have expressed concern over, giving them a chance to talk about things they are wondering about, being *with* them emotionally, to toss around whatever's on their mind that day, if they're worried or if they're excited about something. My friends and I do this all the time, but my husband never seems to do this with me. When I ask him, finally, to ask me how I'm feeling about something I've told him about, it is like pulling teeth to get him to do it even a little bit. And he never brings up the things later that I said were on my mind. It's so frustrating. He often tells me he loves me, and I believe he does, but why isn't he more interested in what's on my mind?"

Where is Love?

Strangely, hauntingly, most women in this study—whether married, single, or divorced, of all ages—say they have not yet found the love they are looking for, that they hope their greatest love is yet to come:

"My family, it is O.K. But I think I will never find what I truly want in love. My greatest love was too unstable, too much hurt. I am still looking for the love I need to share in my life and I hope I have time for it to come later."

"I have not found what I need in love and family. This gives me a desperate feeling in the pit of my stomach. I am losing faith and hope of realizing it in my lifetime."

"I have not as yet been able to give the love I would like to give, neither have I received it. Since I come from a broken home, maybe I don't know how. I would like to have a love that is openly expressed without fear of rejection."

Most women, no matter how frustrating their relationship, or how clearly they see the difficulty of coming to a real, mutual recognition with a man they love, still hope for, long for, love. As one woman says, love keeps returning to us, resurfacing perhaps as some kind of key: "In some way which I cannot find the words for yet, romantic love contains the key toward my identity—toward discovering myself, my inner being." Many women feel this way. Why? Perhaps women are right to come back, to try again and again to make love work or understand why it does not.

Cultural change, then, is something we are all in together now, as at night when we go home and try to accommodate our needs to his *but* still insist that he meet us halfway; or when we talk to our friends; or when we work at a standard job but try to do it our own way. In this manner we are all changing society, developing a new consensus of what is valid philosophically as a way to live.

There is nothing that can stop this process—it is the mental development of each and every one of us every day. Why at this time in history are *women* so important to this process—in fact, the driving force behind change? Perhaps because of the economic independence we have just achieved—but really, who can say? Historically, there may be many reasons, but history is also funny like that: a cause or an idea may lie dormant—as "freedom" and "individuality" did within the Christian tradition for centuries, all of a sudden to blossom during the eighteenth century as the Enlightenment—whose philosophical and political concepts within only fifty years became so widely held that they completely overturned the old order. The new watchwords became "liberty, equality, fraternity," and "the rights of man."

We are in another of those times—a time of fundamental change. Only this time the "revolution" is coming from women. It is such a sea change in consciousness—whether women consider themselves individually "conservative" or "liberal" in the old sense—that it has already progressed beyond the possibility of forgetting.

We are living through history. We have a chance to be dynamic actors and we are doing this—both well-known women and "unknown" women everywhere. We are taking our place on the stage, and history will judge us for the progress we make—both for ourselves and for the world.

The Emotional Contract: Injustice Built Into the System

Women are Questioning the Emotional Arrangements in Their Lives

Despite the rhetoric of the "sexual revolution" that insists women and men are now equal, women say that subtle but extremely painful (and powerful) forms of discrimination are still built into the very structure of relationships, lodged in the smallest wedges of daily interaction.

What women describe is an entrenched, largely unrecognized system of emotional discrimination—a system whose subterranean roots are entwined so deeply in the psyche of the culture that it underlies our entire social structure. As many women point out, the incidents that upset them can be small—and yet these incidents are troubling because they reflect an overall attitude, are part of a fabric of denial of women as complete human beings.

How does one begin to name and demonstrate a pattern that has had no name for so long—these subtle interactions and subliminal messages that are much more deadly to love than arguing over money or children?

The emotional contract in relationships hasn't really been looked at yet, as we are doing here: it is the core of a relationship—the implicit understanding between two people about how each should behave in a relationship, how each expects the other to express her or his emotions, how each interprets the emotional outcries and silences of the other. These tender and often brief moments are the lifeblood of the emotional closeness between two people, and small misunderstandings can lead to a chain reaction, ending empathy between the two—even though they may remain "married" or "together." But this emotional interaction is troubled by an unclear, demeaning, and gender-oriented set of subliminal attitudes, assumptions interwoven into our ideas of who men and women are. We believe that women are "loving and giving" and men are "doers," that one has more rights than the other.

258

Thus the emotional contract contains psychological stereotypes which put women at a disadvantage, and give men preferential treatment, superior psychological status that is built into the system, into the tiniest crevices of our minds. It is the fundamental cause of the problems between women and men in love relationships.

What is Emotional Equality?

One woman describes what it *isn't*:

"Like today, R. just turned his back on me while I was talking to him, thinking that would be the end of it. Was he surprised when I grabbed him by the arm and jerked him around! I could tell he wanted to really hit me, but he didn't. Then he said something like, 'You can't make me do anything you want. I don't take orders from you.' I suppose that refers to the chores I asked him to do. He could help me a *little*—like maybe screw in a light bulb without being asked. If I ask him, he says, 'Oh, I didn't notice it.' I can't believe it. Incredibly juvenile. Men can get away with it, because they run things. Or they think they can. But if women would stick together and not put up with this stuff, we could change it. If England could run the whole world for a time, and David could beat Goliath, we as women can get ourselves out of this hole and end the stupidity of the whole male thing."

The signs of this unequal emotional "contract"—the unspoken assumptions, the word choices—are thrown at women every day in a thousand ways. Indeed, these patterns are so subtle and accepted, coloring everything, that they make discussion of the "problem" almost impossible, and arguments seem circular. As one woman put it, "There are no words, to begin with, and when you *do* use words, they are viewed by men through a reversing telescope (when they are heard at all)—taking what I said for something totally NOT what I meant."

Another woman describes this dilemma in a typical "non-conversation" about an issue she is trying to discuss:

"If we go out, we always end up going out with his friends and not mine. If I tell him this, he says, that's not true, my friends are just around more. I say, so why don't you make an effort to get to know my friends better—they're important to me. Him, totally missing my point: well, you know how it is when I hang out with the boys. How do I explain to him that it bothers me that I can't explain to him *why*

259

it bothers me that his friends are more important than my friends—or that he seems to be saying that his friends are BETTER than my friends. That's it—he really thinks his friends are better! But I can't tell him that, because then he'll say, no they're not, I don't think that. And then we're at a dead end."

Lack of emotional equality is the fundamental stumbling block to love in relationships. Furthermore, the underlying inequalities are so taken for granted—often not even consciously noticed, built into the culture—that women can become angry without knowing exactly why. As one young woman says, "I wonder if our relationship could get better, because I resent him and don't know why. I feel on the defensive a lot."

The purpose here is to unravel some of the traditional assumptions in relationships, to see more clearly what is going on, and build a new framework for understanding the dynamics of love relationships.

Everyday Language as a Tool of Ideology: Emotional Aggression Against Women

Names—what things are called, which feelings are given "reality" by having words that refer to them (and which are not)—are among the most powerful tools of a society for carrying on and reinforcing its ideology. In the case of gender, words embedded in the language act as hidden, subliminal attacks and value judgments, often leading to irrational interpretations of behavior.

The language that exists dictates, in a way, what "reality" will consist of, what parts of oneself one can let exist, tell others about. For this reason, we need to find new terms for women's experiences which may have been misnamed, inadequately named, or negatively named. For example, terming women "emotionally needy" or "overly emotional"—with "male" behavior considered to be the norm—is not an objective description of women's qualities. To reverse the point of view, one might call "male" behavior "emotionally repressed," and "female" behavior "gloriously expressive." But in our society, non-communicative "male" behavior is more generally seen as something like "heroically in control."

The frequent use of words and phrases with built-in gender insults for women (words that have special meaning when used for/about women) creates an atmosphere of emotional intimidation, which weighs just as heavily on women as economic intimidation has. Through using this vocabulary, subtly, often unconsciously, and in a socially acceptable way, many men bully women emotionally, and thus control relationships. The implied threat often is that if the woman "complains" too much, or wants a better relationship (is "demanding" or "nagging")—she will be unlovable and therefore a man will leave her.

One woman says poignantly, "I remember my father calling my mother a whore because she wasn't tidy enough in the kitchen." Also relevant here is the phrase, "Treat her like a lady"—which implies that, at any moment, if the woman doesn't behave "right," she can be turned against, treated without respect, called the opposite, "a bitch."

Or consider the common use of diminutives when referring to women, and the tendency to see women's achievements as "good" rather than "great" (women are "brilliant," but almost never "geniuses"). Women can be counselors or advice-givers, but not philosophers. People belittle women also by using their first names, though they have just been introduced, or worse, by calling them "dear" and "honey," even when they are complete strangers. In a similar situation, a man would probably be addressed as "Mr. Smith"; at least he would never be called "dear."

Even compliments can refer to women's lesser status. Most women like to hear things such as "I think you're beautiful. You're so pretty . . ." And men too like to hear, "You're so handsome, so attractive . . ." And yet, as one woman puts it, "The thing I like least about men is that they judge you like you're a goddam cow at the county fair. I wonder how they would feel if we started judging them like that, telling them to their faces how we rated their looks! They say things like that about me and other women as we pass by on the street all the time. What gives them the right to be the judges, anyway???"

Verbal clichés and assumptions: being "insisting" and being "demanding"

Gender-biased remarks—such as the statements often made to women: "I think you've got a complex," as a retort to any "complaint" a woman might have about a man's treatment of her—are so intertwined with the language we use to discuss our emotional relationships with one another, and to describe our feelings, that even in the midst of "trying to talk," a woman can find herself being unconsciously (?) put down by the "caring" or even "solicitous" (condescending) responses of others, especially of men. For example, the word "sensitive," with its two meanings, illustrates the sexism of words as they are often applied to women's behavior: to be "sensitive" to the world and others is good, but to be a "sensitive" woman (i.e., a woman who is always having her feelings hurt) is bad.

Another frequent retort made by men, referred to over and over by women in this study, occurs when a woman has just described her injured feelings in a relationship and the reply is: "I'm sorry you feel that way." This, rather than opening up the topic for discussion and serious consideration, places the burden for the "feelings" on the other person, and no responsibility on the person spoken to for trying to understand those feelings. In other words, the man has no emotional responsibility in the relationship. Do men who say things like this realize they are being emotionally destructive? Or do they simply believe they are right, that women *are* too "emotionally demanding" and "difficult," and that it is the proper role of men to make sure women don't "go too far" and "dominate" a relationship? In any case, men often use this and similar statements to end a conversation, turn a cold shoulder, rather than examine in more depth what a woman is trying to express. It is a form of emotional violence—the cutting off of communication—and is very harmful to relationships.

Many women, of course, have interiorized second-class values about themselves and each other, such as in the put-down of herself contained in one woman's response to being asked if she can talk easily to her husband: "If I want to whine, moan and groan, and be dramatic, I'd best talk to a woman friend. My husband comes from a place of analyzing and being rational. I need a little drama." In this book itself, one could characterize what women are saying about their relationships as "Women often *complain* that . . ." rather than, "Women often *report* that . . ." The gender-biased choice of verbs is one we might all make unconsciously, not realizing the implications.

"Teasing" and other "fun" put-downs

One of the most frustrating aspects of the stereotyped put-downs women live with is that they frequently crop up in conversation "in passing." They are so enmeshed in the larger conversation that it would seem disruptive and "out of proportion" to stop the discussion to point them out. Women often find such built-in, loaded words offensive, but not to such an extent that they want to risk being called "obnoxious" or "aggressive" by making an issue out of them. On the other hand, this leaves the woman to swallow the thing said, and even worse, to seem to be condoning both it and the assumptions (hardly noticed by the speaker) it embodies.

These comments can be subtle and almost "unretortable," according to most women:

"I hate it when men say something to the effect of 'Isn't that just like a woman,' or 'All women are like that.' I feel we deserve to be judged on a one-to-one basis, not as part of a vague mob. It is the main thing I am trying to correct in my attitude toward men. Whenever I catch myself saying, 'You men are all alike,' I stop and try to see the man as himself, not as a group. Also I hate it when a man I like calls me his 'old lady,' 'broad,' or 'the little woman.' "

Even more subtle may be the put-downs contained in what is *not* said. For example, the way the language celebrates masculinity—with the traditional cry of delight on the birth of a male child, "It's a *boy!*" There is no equivalent cry of delight when it is a girl, although many people are thrilled to have girls. However, the fact that one phrase is standard, and no equivalent other phrase is, carries a significant message to women and men every time they hear it, whether they recognize it or not: boys are more valuable than girls.

Ninety-five percent of women in this study say this atmosphere—"men are more important," "men are the ones who matter"—is still all around us even now, twenty years into the current women's movement:

"Men in relationships I have seen always wanted to control or at least feel their own power—and it seeps in no matter how subtle it is. The hardest part is, just like sexism has poisoned us all in very subtle ways, it can be tedious and troublesome to remember that everyone else is wrong about a very important part of your nature—sort of like keeping the ghosts out by locking the door and then finding they still get in through the cracks"

Sexist vocabulary: "being left"

Many, perhaps most, people display a subtle gender bias in their choice of the adjectives they apply to behavior, depending on whether it is a man or a woman's behavior they are describing: people may watch a man do exactly the same thing they watch a woman do—argue with a taxi driver over the fare, for example—and characterize what they have seen in a totally different way. The man may be seen as "righteous," as not a fool, not letting himself be taken; the woman may be seen as argumentative, loud, "bitchy," aggressive, and so on.

263

Value judgments built into words used to describe women

Many particularly ideologically laden words and phrases relate to the supposedly "dependent" nature of women in relationships. "Being left" almost always refers to a woman "being left"—with the implication that now the woman is sad and alone, rejected. It is usually assumed, when marriages break up, that it was the man who wanted to leave, although according to this study, it is usually women who decide to do so. "Deserted" and "abandoned" are other words with similar connotations applied almost exclusively to women. It does not fit in with beliefs about men's superior status to think that women could be the less "needy" ones.

Another related stereotype is the idea that women have difficulty accepting men's departure because they fear "being left"; this is said to be a woman's "syndrome," part of women's "psychology," its origin existing in women's "nature," i.e., women are biologically dependent on men because of becoming pregnant and needing men to stay and protect them and their babies. (But in other societies women bond together, or the clan takes care of mother and child.) In fact, needing men's support is not something which grows out of women's "innate" or "biological" psychology. Rather, in our society, it is more likely that women have sometimes felt uncomfortable about men's departures because of economic dependence—and because of men's non-communicative attitudes, which leave women feeling emotionally uneasy, unclear about what will happen next.

Emotional harassment

Emotional harassment or a put-down can be a pattern in a relationship—but even more importantly, it is a pattern in society, a pattern which is socially acceptable. Therefore, it can happen at any moment, when a woman is least expecting it—a kind of emotional terrorism. (Unfortunately, "teasing" is also one of the few ways women are allowed to express anger at men, so that one finds it a common pattern on TV sitcoms, such as *The Jeffersons*; the result is a bantering to see who can ridicule the other's remark first.) Men may feel much more social credibility when "teasing" women, since this has been legitimized by society's seeing women as less, or "foolish," for a very long time. A notorious example of this "accepted" teasing or poking fun at women was White House chief of staff Donald Regan's statement in 1986 that women would not really be interested in the problems of South Africa, for they are more interested in diamond bracelets.

Emotional Violence

There are more extreme cases of emotional harassment which amount to emotional violence (for which the perpetrator need never answer, will never be called to justice):

"My ex-husband destroyed my confidence in myself. I remember once he wanted me to make a soup like his mother, so I spent all afternoon shopping and preparing it from scratch. Then he came home, and when he tasted it, he said that I put too much paprika in it and flushed the whole thing down the toilet and then slapped me. You can't just start living again after many experiences like that."

"In my sixth month of my first pregnancy I was spotting and the doctor put me to bed. That night my husband insisted on having intercourse. The next day I went to the hospital and gave birth to my first child prematurely, who weighed only one pound fourteen ounces, but who survived. I'm sure I would have given birth [prematurely] anyway, but I felt very hurt by that for a long time."

"We had been going together for six months, and told each other how much we loved each other. Then I realized I was pregnant, and bought one of those home tests. I was nervous about taking it, and before doing it, I told him. I said, "You won't believe this, darling, but I think I'm pregnant.' After a while he said, 'How can I be sure it's mine?' "

"Years ago, when I was pregnant with my second baby, we had gone to a dance. I was sick, exhausted, and a number of other things, and had gone only because I didn't want to be a party pooper and spoil his fun. I made the best of a totally miserable evening, but by 1:30 a.m. I had had it and told him that I wasn't feeling well, had not been all evening (he didn't even notice), and could we please leave now. He agreed and I got my coat and stood by the door while he table-hopped and said goodbye for another forty-five minutes. I finally left without him, in tears. This leads to the worst thing that I ever did to him . . . I took the car out of the parking lot, and by this time I was furious. He was leaving the building as I drove down the street, so I swerved the car to run him over, just missing him. I drove like a maniac for three blocks, then parked the car and got hold of myself. I almost left him that night when I got home. I started to pack and we had a terrible argument. I didn't leave him, and now I'm glad I didn't. It was uncharacteristic of him to be so thoughtless, and uncharacteristic of me to react the way I did."

"I was very hurt that he just left without a word. I thought we should have been able to talk about it. I thought he knew me well enough to know I would not create a scene. He was my first real love and everything was so good. It had taken me a long time to put myself back together, and to accept the fact that I will never see him again."

Emotional harassment and put-downs of women (those many small layers of habit, verbal and non-verbal cues—no *one* of which one would want to start a fight about, or if one did, one might be called "hysterical") are more or less a pattern in society—and in many women's personal love relationships, so that a remark can be made at any moment, when a woman is least expecting it. This amounts to a kind of emotional terrorism.

Women are blackmailed into silence by the labels which wait for them if they do "complain" (i.e., women are "nagging" or "difficult"). Thus, an individual woman, no matter how strong or aware, living with these stereotypes over a period of time, can find her will steadily, slowly eroded, her self-esteem becoming something to be fought for, piece by piece, day by day, in an unending, uphill battle. Popular magazines say it is *her* problem, not men's or the society's problem.

Gender-biased attitudes are particularly harmful in a deep, intimate personal relationship. If the butcher or a salesperson makes a demeaning remark (which, as every woman knows, can always happen), it is one thing: something unpleasant, but something one can overlook as coming from a prejudiced person. But if the person one loves, is closest to, and depends on for one's most intimate contact with humanity makes such a remark—that is another matter. And this seems to be, in case after case, exactly what is happening. It is possible that many men have no idea what they are doing. Most do seem to be quite unaware of the residual stereotypes they hold. They think, "Oh, this is just Mary, she is like that. She had a childhood that . . ." Or, "She is a specialist with children, who cannot understand all that I, having been in the world so long, can know . . ." and so on.

If these attitudes were blatantly expressed they would be easier to fight. But the subtle distancing and harassment that have been accepted for millennia not as "put-downs" but as just describing "how women are," are very difficult to deal with, and their effects are insidious.

What is the answer then? For women to keep putting in disproportionate amounts of time in relationships with men to explain all of this (over and over), and also to rebuild their own damaged self-esteem? Or are women giving up some of their belief in the importance of love, deciding to stop investing so much energy in "love," adopting a "male" point of view, placing love second after work or career? Women could easily decide to take this route as the path of least resistance, unless equality, openness, and emotional support become traits men choose to develop in themselves—so that women can share a highly developed inner emotional world with men, without winding up feeling burned out and terribly lonely.

266

The pattern of alienation

One woman describes her increasing alienation:

"He doesn't care if I climax or not, but only is interested in his own ability to be satisfied, mostly because he is not knowledgeable and he doesn't want to become knowledgeable. This would make him look like less of a man to himself, I suppose. So I think he is a chickenshit and a bore and I've told him so. I suppose trying to be honest is the worst thing I ever did to him, yelling at him. (He loves it too, though, because then he looks like the knight in white armor and I look like the whore/screamer.) I finally explode and say all the wrong things in front of anybody, mostly the children. I talk and he does nothing. He doesn't listen. He has a short attention span and no desire to change. I would have shared all of myself if only I were loved, but I've tried and been rejected for it. It is hard to share with a person who just doesn't talk to you."

Many women know they are not getting equal emotional support, esteem, or respect in their relationships. And yet it can be difficult to describe definitively to a man just how he is projecting diminishing attitudes. Some of the ways this happens are so subtle in their expression that, while a woman may wind up feeling frustrated and on the defensive, she can find it almost impossible to say just why: pointing to the subtle thing said or done would look petty, like overreacting. But taken all together, it is no surprise when even one of these incidents can set off a major fight—or, more typically, another round of alienation which never gets resolved. These little incidents cut away at the relationship, making women angry and finally causing love to dwindle down to a mere modest toleration.

Does fighting, bringing up the issues, work? Do women change their relationships this way?

Most women wind up screaming or shouting at men from time to time because they so often feel they can't be heard, that men don't hear them. Since women generally have such low credibility in the culture, men often do not hear them objectively, justly.

Do men make an effort to understand women, to talk with them? Not usually, according to the women in this study—and the statistics on the number of women taking tranquilizers and consulting psychologists also attest to the fact that women are having a rough time constructing mutually satisfying personal relationships.

Negotiating for respect and understanding in a relationship is important, something which possibly could be accomplished with grace and good humor. But if men are satisfied with the status quo in relationships, and women are not, what should women do? What should a woman do when there are frequent subtle indications of condescension toward her because of her gender, and mentioning these to a man once or twice does not suffice to change his attitude?

The issues women are bringing up may appear on the surface to be "petty," but the pattern of condescension that is provoking women is so widespread that women are forced to fight back, even on this level. And yet, individual fighting back doesn't always work, because men don't understand what it is women are trying to point out to them. Perhaps it will be necessary for women to change the status of women as a whole before gaining enough respect and dignity to make it possible for their love relationships to survive.

Anger Against Men is Forbidden

One woman makes an excellent point about where we *should* direct our anger, and why we don't:

"Depression is, for me, taking out my anger on myself because it's too scary to face up to the real person who is making me angry. If you have been taught by your parents that you are worthless, it is then easier to consider self-destructive acts and behavior than to fight back against the people who you think are better than you. You don't know that you have any rights."

Anger unexpressed can become a fog which pervades everything, leading to a perpetual low-level anxiety. Indeed, women's frustration and/or anger is responsible in large part for much of the psychological counseling, tranquilizers, and so on women use.* And yet, it is considered almost treasonous for a woman to say she is angry with men or with "male" culture—either for personal reasons or for larger social reasons (i.e., because men still do not share their social and political power equally with women).

---

* Statistically, in the United States twice as many women go to psychiatrists, psychologists, and counselors as men; this figure has not changed since the 1950s, despite monumental feminist works, including "Psychology Constructs the Female" by Naomi Weisstein, works by Shulamith Firestone, and *Women and Madness* by Phyllis Chesler.

In the 1880s, Freud gave his fiancée cocaine for her "nerves." Perhaps it was Freud himself, or her position in the general society with its limitations for her, that gave her "nerves." Also, in Spanish culture women are well known for having *"nervios"*; in our own, as noted, women are by far the largest consumers of tranquilizers, so that it could be said that a large percentage of the female population is chemically pacified.

In fact, anger against men is the most *verboten* feeling a woman can have. A woman who says she is angry at men, or, even more, at "male" culture or the "male" system, is frequently labeled a "crazy lady," a "man-hater," or "hysterical," "needing a psychologist," and so on. To be seen as freaks, being made outcasts or pariahs, is the unspoken threat to which so many women react by saying—as one sees frequently in magazine articles, etc., when women worry they cannot keep up with all that is expected of them, i.e., maintain their looks, make men desire them and now, earn money too—that they fear their fate will be to become a "bag lady." Even though we joke about this, it is significant: we wonder if there is really a place in society for us, especially as older women. We cannot afford *psychologically* to be mad at men because we fear we may wind up as outcasts.

Women's Way of Fighting: Non-Violent Resistance

While the initial impulse might be to say, well, why don't women get even with men? revolt?—the matter is more complicated than that. Women don't take violent revenge on individual men (or society) because not to do so is in accord with their most basic values.

Most women, as we have seen, do not believe in fighting back on men's terms (although they could—i.e., be cold and distant, less interested in "hearing" and understanding the other person, or on a larger level, undertake terroristic actions to influence government policy, etc.); most feel it would be unethical to fight men "male" style, beneath them. Instead, most prefer a stance of non-violent resistance for which they deserve respect. However, some would not give women credit but put women down as not "smart," as too "stupid" to fight and get their own way—saying that women are "peaceful" only because they are afraid or have been "brainwashed" not to fight back. But women do fight back in arguments, and stand up for themselves, as seen; and increasingly they fight back by leaving unsatisfying relationships: 90 percent of the high number of divorces in the United States are initiated and carried through by women.

Is not fighting a basic "female" value because this is what women have been taught?* Or because women believe in these values? Women

* And taught by whom? Taught by a "social structure" which would deform them? Or by an historic tradition handed down by their mothers, aunts, grandmothers, and so on? This poses interesting questions not yet adequately addressed in the literature.

have tried, during the last ten to twenty years, to take on new values, i.e., women have experimented with not connecting love and sex, with repressing their emotions, and with taking jobs out of the home. The only values of the recent years of experimentation they seem to have taken firmly to heart are those of independence defined as having jobs, incomes of their own, and as being able to express oneself, be complete, a person in one's own right, not only as attached to a man. But women seem to have firmly rejected the "male" culture's belief in expressing less love in personal life. And when they fail to convince men they love to join them in *their* value system, they are likely to begin expressing nurturing and enthusiasm for their work and for their friends—nurturing and enthusiasm that were once reserved for their husbands and families.

Men should not fear women's anger; they should welcome it

Men should not fear women's anger. After all, it is right to express anger at injustice. If we state clearly what the problems are, then we have a chance to think clearly about strategies for change. For men to simply ignore the problem of the status of women in society, and/or problems in relationships, or think of them as "women's issues" and turn their attention to other matters, rather than making an effort to do something about the situation, will only make the problem worse. Women "bring up issues," and men fall silent, hoping the "problem" will go away—which only makes women angrier and the problem worse. It could be said that women's so-called passive nature is just a screen for women's fury*—which is channeled in the wrong direction (against women) but could turn to become a positive force for society.

But it is not only anger women are expressing here: what we hear woman after woman describe is a mixture of anger and sadness: anger and frustration at not being able to get through to a man with their love, their hearts, their selves; and sadness that most men just will not see what is happening, so that women watch as the love fades and the dreams slowly die.

* As the acceptance of Freudian "explanations" of women's nature at the turn of the century was a way of "explaining away" the women's movement of that time, according to Shulamith Firestone in *The Dialectic of Sex*.

Does Therapy Help? Why Therapy Is Often Harmful to Women

"There came a time (about two years ago) when I realized that the pain of my romances was essentially the same pain and conflict I experienced in dealing with my mother and that I was using romance as a way of dealing with my mother, of trying to be separate—individual."

The situations described here—violence and aggression in the emotional contract—involve large *social* issues; they are not something one person can or should have to fight alone. Although it is productive to understand one's own personal history and personality, to come away from "therapy" without it having been acknowledged that the culture has a strong hand in *creating* these situations is extremely unfortunate. After all, women will have to continue dealing with society's messages about women's status and "characteristics"; what tools would a therapy, which does not acknowledge the existence of this gender bias in the culture, give to a woman to help her go on with her life?*

Even worse, some schools of therapy seem to blame women as a general principle by labeling their *socially* created problems with gender-biased and blaming phrases, such as "masochistic," "dependent," and so on—completely ignoring the concrete phenomenon of most women's economic dependency during most of the twentieth century (encouraged by the culture) and the effects this has had on women's (and men's) "psychologies." A new psycho-cultural therapy should be developed.

Some types of therapy and psychoanalysis also seem to believe that women have no right to "complain"—that a woman's "complaining" is a sign of a woman having a problem (rather than the society having a problem, i.e., trying to discover whether there is a reality in the woman's relationship causing this; this means, again, that women have no right to name things):

"In early marriage I felt ganged up against by the man/woman therapy team trying to help J. and me solve our problems. It always seemed that I was neurotic and he was not. Fine help. Finally I met up with a Jungian analyst who was very helpful in getting me to sort out my relationship with my parents, but he also as much as turned to J. and said, 'You are suffering from the existential alienation of modern man,' and to me said, 'You are neurotic.' I ultimately quit, and not until I discovered feminism and consciousness raising did I begin to sort out

* Only a smug "Don't bug me, don't bring your troubles to me; go get therapy" attitude—because this will fit women into the "male" world?

my feelings about therapy, aided by Chesler's *Women and Madness* and others. I learned a lot but it *did not help me at all.*"

However, some forms of counseling are more progressive. Another woman describes a very good experience she had with an unusual therapist, who did not deny the reality of gender bias against women in society, and took her anger against "male" society into realistic account:

"Therapy can be wonderful—with the right therapist. At the point when I was in despair after the breakup of my affair after my marriage, I needed a therapist—and after trying two I didn't like, I found one who proved just right. I knew he would be right when he suggested at the initial session that if I really would prefer a woman therapist, he'd help me find one.

"We worked together for nearly three years—I say 'worked together' very much on purpose, for I felt very much an equal in the relationship—perhaps the only relationship with any man in which I've really felt an equal. My initial 'love relationship problem' faded, and most of the therapy delved into the causes for my tendency toward depressions—which basically has to do with my frequent feeling of helplessness to be equal to men in the world as it exists. This starting from the birth of my brother and being reinforced at every point in my life. I could never be outstanding enough in anything I did to be taken as seriously as men were—it is a fight I will fight all the rest of my life.

"Therapy helped me understand that this is the structure of our social milieu, and that I do not lack something essential. Thanks to the therapy, and to my own strengths, I understand now that I don't have to be perfect and invulnerable. I see some of my hang-ups and realize that I'll never get over some of them. I know that, as a woman playwright in a world where men pull the puppet and purse strings, I will have to work twice as hard as men and there will be a lot of unfairness and enormous frustrations. I won't like it one bit, but mostly I won't think my failures are because there is something inherently wrong with *me.* Therapy went a long way beyond curing a 'broken heart.'"

Women's Complaints About Private Life Are Political and Should Be Taken Seriously—Not Trivialized and Individually "Psychologized" Away

This study shows that most women are not in love relationships they consider to be anywhere near what they would like. Ninety-five percent of the married women in this study want to make basic changes in their marriages, and 84 percent of single women say that love relationships with men are more often than not filled with anxiety, fear of being "un-cool" (by wanting commitment), and so on.

Woman after woman says she is putting enormous amounts of energy into trying to make her relationship work—but that the man doesn't seem to be putting in the same effort. This makes women even more alienated, frustrated, and often angry.

Many women lie in bed at night, knowing things could be so much better, wondering how to reach the man sleeping next to them, or wondering why a man they love doesn't call—or how to get out of a relationship although they can't really explain just why they don't like it. So many women lie there thinking, "It's too bad that things are like this . . . Why can't they change?"

Women have been "complaining" about love relationships for some time, at least since Freud, but these complaints have rarely been taken seriously. What women say is going on has rarely been given full credibility, instead being discounted as "women bitching and moaning" and so on. Society blames women's feelings of frustration with men on women's "psychology"—not on the fact that most women have a legitimate complaint, i.e., that they live with discrimination, even in love relationships.

It is usually implied that if a woman is having problems, the problem is with the *woman*—with her outdated values, "demanding" behaviors, "neediness," upbringing, "dependency," and so forth. Women daily hear themselves referred to as "messed up," "masochistic," or "neurotic" if they step the least bit out of line, and some part of them wonders if it could be true. They wonder, "Do I send out vibrations that attract the 'wrong men,' " or they fault themselves for not recognizing or disengaging quickly enough from "destructive" relationships. Alternately, women worry that they may not be patient *enough*, understanding enough, expect too much, are too "idealistic." But are women really doing something wrong?

Women Recreate Female Psychology: 4,500 Women Speak*

Is It Women's Values Which Should Change—or Men's?

There are many assumptions about acceptable behavior in the traditional emotional contract. The one most frequently noted is that women's role is to be loving and "mothering," non-"demanding." Less frequently noted is the role that the ideology gives to men: that of being "dominant," of "starring" in relationships, and of being the active "doers" in charge of the world. These assumptions are built into the culture—into language and psychological theories and philosophy—and are based on an underlying set of beliefs which we call here the "male" ideology.

If women want to love men, but men have little practice in loving in the sense that women mean (nor are most men busily engaged in trying to cultivate these characteristics in themselves), then women's desire to have equal, non-competitive, nurturing relationships puts women in an awkward position. The advice that is often offered to them now as to how to relieve their "discomfort" is to stop loving so much.

Should women stop loving "too much" (if you can't beat 'em, join 'em)—or do women now expect men to change and become more loving?

* This is 4,447 more than Freud heard—but then, why should women know as much about women as Freud?!!

Do women "love too much"? Or do men love too little?

Women's belief in giving and nurturing is very controversial. Women have been criticized in recent years, first by some in the women's movement and later by "advice books," for being "too loving," too giving, too nurturing, obsessed with "romance." The theory has been that women rely too much on love for their fulfillment in life, that women "cling" because they are brought up to be psychologically "dependent," even that women are "crippled" psychologically(!). If women would only give up these behaviors and stop loving "too much," be more "like men," they would find that they would be happier, they wouldn't have so many problems with love.

Women have a lot to say about this, and in fact are in the midst of an important historic debate within themselves about it, as we see throughout this research. In particular, individual women everywhere now are engaged in redefining love for themselves. Too much giving without receiving, non-reciprocal giving, or constantly being belittled by someone one loves, can eventually threaten one's personality and identity—or at least one's ability to express that identity. But to become competitive and aggressive, critical rather than positive, this is not the alternative most women would like.

What they are struggling with is one of the most important issues of our times: how to love, how to restore feeling and emotionality to life, while not letting oneself be done in by those who would take advantage of a person who is less aggressive, more nurturing and giving.

Many women in this study express anger at the ridicule so often addressed to them for their interest in love: instead of women loving less, women ask, why can't men love more, be more emotionally supportive and involved? Why must it always be *women* who change? And what kinds of love are we talking about anyway?

Masochism or Heroism? A New View of "Female Psychology": Goodbye to Freud and Assorted Others

If women feel "needy" and "insecure," looking for reassurances that men love them, it is said that this is a sign of women's "biological" character or of some innate fear of "being left," resulting from the fact that they get pregnant and "must" have a man to take care of them at this vulnerable time.* But are not women's feelings a logical reaction to the fact that many men are treating women as if they indeed do *not* love them, no matter what they say—at least not according to women's definition of love?

If a woman complains of bad treatment from a man (and it is always part-time bad treatment, not full-time, which adds to the confusion), she is apt to be told she is a "masochist," and she must "like it"—i.e., "if you don't like it, why do you stay and take it?" But this is "blaming the victim": for a social structure in which women have been brought up and are still brought up to make love the wellspring of their identity in life, to then put down women for being "too focused on love," "obsessed with love," and so on is astonishing. Women are being blamed for doing what the social situation asks of them.

And women do this in the confusing context of having to love individually those of a "superior" group socially: men. In other words, women are told to focus love on a group—men—whose status is "above" their own. Being told they should love people of a "superior" group automatically proposes that women be "martyrs," in that they must give to those who do not give as much back, those who do not spend time changing society to make women's status equal.

This makes the labeling of women as "masochistic" particularly ironic and even sadistic: women are told to love men, who (as a group) are "above" them, then told to endure men's condescending or superior behavior (because men "don't mean it," and "really love you")—and when women do this, and still keep on loving, they are rewarded by being called "masochistic"! And so women are told it is their own fault if their status in society doesn't change: "Why don't you change it if you don't like it?," they are taunted, aggressively. These are baiting remarks.

Perhaps another way to look at women's and men's situation would be in terms of a family in which there are two young children who have a fight. One hits the other, who begins crying. Now the family has the option of labeling the second one a "crybaby" or the first one "mean" and "aggressive."

In our society/family, men are constantly being psychologically aggressive with women, but rarely are men called to account for this:

* This is often "supported" on "biological" grounds: that is, since women become pregnant and need men to take care of them, they are somehow hormonally, psychologically disposed to being "dependent" on men. Logic of nature is "unarguable" according to its adherents. However, one could argue that if society were constructed differently (as it has been in many times and places), maternal clans, mothers, uncles and brothers, female lovers and friends, could protect pregnant women, and later the baby, as they have done and do in some societies—and to a great extent, even in our own.

instead, society criticizes women for being "too emotional," too easily upset, too needful of reassurances of love, too obsessed with "romance." People rarely think to criticize the man involved, to try to get him to change, because our mind-set is focused on women as "the problem child," the "problem gender." And so women live with the frustration of an unfair social setup, finding that they can only really talk to one another about it.

Instead of being called "masochists," why aren't women admired for their loyalty?

Women in unhappy love relationships are often courageous in trying to see a bad relationship through, trying to help the one they love, remaining loyal even when the other person is difficult, but this behavior is almost never seen as heroic. Instead women are often put down or called "masochists" ("clinging," "too needy," or "despicable females who only want something") for staying. Would men be admired for the same behavior? Or are men, like Lord Byron, or Rod Stewart, perhaps, seen as great romantic heroes when love is unrequited or doesn't work out?

This is an example of how what women do is frequently seen as inferior to what men do: women are rarely characterized as gallant and brave for questing after love; woman as the love hero and seeker is almost never glorified. She is seen as a victim—or stupid, perhaps.

Women also, in some of these relationships, are making a positive statement, in that they are not *reacting* to what the man does, but expressing their *own* view of the potential and relevance of the relationship, their *own* feelings. *They* are defining the situation.

A love affair that is non-stable is not a failure, necessarily, if it gives us poetry and beauty: this may be what we want. It may not be that we are 'picking the wrong men." But in these situations, we are usually made to feel bad by society. ("It didn't work out! She can't get her life in order!") Society has penalized women severely when they do not form permanent alliances with men.

Women in this study *do* make themselves leave men they love, even while still loving them—if they need to. But sometimes there is a real reason for staying—for a while. What if we pledge our souls, and then are "betrayed," hurt, or the person we love changes? This does not mean we should not have pledged our souls, should not have loved. Isn't it better at least to make what we feel real for the time it is real—even if it breaks up? It is good to have the capacity to believe in the reality of another's love.

Women's Rebellion vs. Patriarchal Definitions of Female Identity: Culture Creates Psychology*

The standard understanding of women's psychology is thus inaccurate, and standard judgments of women by the "male" system are wrong—or lacking in subtlety, to say the least. Certainly the 4,500 women here express better than Freud who women are.†

The "male" ideological structure (since it is the dominant ideology) extends into the farthest recesses of the psyches of both women and men, as seen here and in the previous study on men. Women who want to love are all too often forced into compromise after compromise with a culture that sees them as emotionally inferior or"different." Furthermore they must overlook this time and again, appear not to see how they come second, how their thoughts and points of view are disregarded—or even receive no attention at all, being perceived by men as less important than work, friends, football on TV, and so on. For their patience, they are frequently seen as "wimps" or "martyrs," as "non-assertive," "easy," and so on.

A woman faced with a daily lack of communication and lack of respect often feels a loss of dignity: she is placed in a position of having to choose either leaving the relationship and being "alone" (but *is* one more alone?) or staying and living with this pattern of subtle belittling and condescension. The outward symptom of her inner struggle to maintain dignity and self-respect is usually bickering and small daily hostilities, silences—or feeling emotionally "insecure." But although bickering can be "normal" in human relationships, in our world it is more frequent and bitter than need be, because female–male relationships are "political"—i.e., the stereotyped way of seeing female psychology is to see women as "emotionally unstable" or "irrational" and to give women less credibility, place them constantly on the defensive and in a secondary role.

---

* Bruno Bettelheim, in his writing on concentration camps during World War II, showed clearly that psychology can change within days of a person's being placed in a totally new environment with a totally new set of rules—i.e., people who were proud become humble and fearful, and so on. Thus, while childhood upbringing is important, even more important is the constant cultural messages we are all receiving all the time about "who we are."

Professor Naomi Weisstein, of S.U.N.Y., has also written "Psychology Creates the Female," a landmark theoretical treatise on this subject.

† Women's behavior in love relationships has long been interpreted by "studies" done from a "male" ideological perspective. As Simone de Beauvoir explained in 1984, "Although I admire Freud . . . I find that in the case of women, as he said himself, there's a dark continent; he understood nothing of what women want. Anyone who wants to work on women has to break completely with Freud." (Interview by Helene Wenzel, published in *The Women's Review of Books*, July 1985.)

How does the psychological position women are put in by "male" behavior patterns seen in this section relate to so-called normal behavior? By the terms of traditional "social science," if the majority of people display certain feelings, this makes those feelings "normal behavior" in that group, and therefore "how people/women are"—i.e., if women love "men who hurt them," women are "masochists."

And yet, if one takes an historical and philosophical perspective, one can see these behaviors quite another way—i.e., as logical responses to the specific cultural setup. Indeed, if we are to lift ourselves out of the forest, to see our alternatives, to understand, have visions and make plans, we must take this broader perspective, see the current situation between women and men as only the creation of the larger overall ideology or set of beliefs—the "male ideology."

Patriarchal smears: standard theories of women's psychology are wrong and harmful*

Women's statements and descriptions of their experiences here have clear and pressing implications: changes in the way women are seen should be immediate. Women must no longer be "defined" and "judged" through the lens of a culture which for centuries has barely seen them as "second-class" psychologically, certainly as less than the standard of "normality." Data must be looked at from a new standpoint. The myriad findings and statements here from women's testimony (and there are other women scholars engaged in this work) present the field of psychology with a wealth of basic new information—information which must be seen in terms of a new philosophy. Psychology currently has little vocabulary which can encompass the real form of women's thinking and psychology: it is, in general, very unfamiliar with women's culture, and should begin immediately to try to familiarize itself with the literature of this different cultural perspective.

* Much if not most of the theory of female psychology is a distortion, built on small, selective samples, with authoritarian research principles leaving only one voice to judge, name, and describe the others.

Men's double message to women, not women's "lack of self-esteem," makes women feel "insecure"

The "psychology of women," women's "human nature," is not inherently passive, "martyrish," "masochistic," complaining, and so on—but these characteristics, when they occur, are usually part of the logical reaction of an individual to the subliminal attacks of the "male" ideology.

If men withhold equal companionship with women, distance themselves emotionally (the one less vulnerable has more power . . .); and if men aggressively harass and trivialize women in relationships, and then turn to those same women looking for love, affection, and understanding, believing that the women should "be there" for them (as well as provide domestic services such as cooking and housekeeping)—what effect must this have on women?

What effect would such contradictory behavior have on anyone? That is, how *should* we react to being with someone who, on the one hand, frequently acts emotionally distant and inaccessible, even ridiculing you or not listening—and then, on the other, at times turns to you expecting love and affection, saying he loves you?

If a woman loves a man, and he says he loves her (even though exhibiting the two-sided behavior just described), she may feel off balance and disoriented—though probably she will want to stay and "make it work." But which is the "real" other person? she may wonder. The one who loves her, or the one who is distant and ridiculing? How can she break through that distance, when it occurs, to the "good parts"? So she tries to "bring up the issues," and keeps on trying, but often goes through an agony of frustration at the cruelty and emotional coldness she encounters along the way.

A note on the popular epithet, "Women lack self-esteem"

Do women, as is so often heard, have "low self-esteem"—or is this to "blame the victim"?

In fact, women are doing quite well, considering all the propaganda coming their way that they aren't worth as much as men. But there is great social pressure on women to prove this "self-esteem" by becoming as aggressive and aloof as many men. One woman's statement portrays this new equation of aggressiveness with having a sense of self: "It seems to me that many women—myself included—don't have the sense of self that men are trained to have. Men don't have to feel badly if they hurt someone; they are supposed to beat up other people, in a way—even their mothers probably told them, 'Go back to the schoolyard and beat him up, whoever gives you a hard time,' and are always pushed to win in all competitions. This makes for the difference in women's rules and men's rules."

But do women really undervalue themselves as much as is popularly suggested—or is it just that women refuse to behave aggressively and give up their beliefs in nurturing and loving as the right and proper ways to be, still hoping that men will join their system, and learn how to be more nurturing too?

Most women do, as we have seen, try harder to make relationships work; indeed, they stay even in the face of the most adverse circumstances. Then they may be put down for this! (They are also put down for leaving.) But isn't this loyalty admirable? Isn't this what men should be doing too—i.e., putting more effort into understanding and caring for the other person, even when the other seems to be going through some sort of unintelligible hard time?

Being Single: Women and Autonomy

How the Emotional Contract Applies to the Dating Scenario

Reading what women have said—despite the sense of humor and strength in so many of their statements—leaves one with a very poignant feeling: why does it often have to be so hard? Many women say they are emotionally worn out from all of this—but almost all still want to try, to keep searching, to make it work. Is it because love is a basic human hunger? Or are women brought up to focus so much on men's love as "their destiny" that no matter what their experiences with men, they still believe they must find a way for this dream to work? That other dreams are not as valid?*

It is ironic that the place women are going for love, to get love, is the very place from which it is hardest to get, according to women—because of the way men in this culture are conditioned, what "masculinity means." This is very sad, as woman after woman struggles to draw a man out, to develop emotional companionship to go along with more or less instant physical intimacy. Most find the going difficult. For every two steps forward, they go one step back. Although while lying in bed together at night, they may break through and talk, the next day the atmosphere is often changed back to a silent ambiguity.

"Love is a battlefield"†

Single women are having to have relationships with men who have grown up with images of the Marlboro man (the idealized "loner") and single male movie heroes, men who don't want to commit themselves and who believe in "freedom"—freedom from relationships

---

* Also, of course, there is great pressure on women—a feeling (after age twenty-eight or so) that this is the only basic way to fit into society; most women feel that there will be no place for them in society after their twenties if they don't "find someone" and get married.
† As the hit rock video by Pat Benatar says.

with women. Thus, when most men are *in* relationships, they act ambivalently. This puts women emotionally on the defensive. The rules are: "don't cling," "don't ask for monogamy," "there is something wrong with you if you feel insecure," etc.

Women are defined by the "male" ideology as needing men more than men need women. This puts women in a vulnerable position psychologically with men—women must "catch" men, not seem too "needy" of a relationship, not "complain" about men's lack of emotional support or condescension, bad manners, and so on.

There is an undercurrent in most dating relationships of this unstated imbalance of power status between women and men—i.e., the so-called desirability of females vs. the desirability of males. The suspense in a relationship for a woman hovers around the question "Is it love, or is he just using you?" Women have a realistic fear of being tricked—then being left to end up feeling taken, yet emotionally open and still loving. Meeting men and having sex/friendships with men becomes a minefield, often filled with traumas, perhaps also with some pleasant surprises, but almost always involving the terror of never knowing what to expect next. Indeed, women often want to get married sometimes just to escape all the put-downs, the endless "looking" and "trying out," the doubts and fears of single life. In fact, it is the "male" ideology and double standard that makes it dangerous to "fall in love," not women's "need" to know someone for a long time and "learn to care" as the only way to have a good experience.

How many compromises should a woman make?

One woman offers her thoughts about what is going on in the whole singles area:

"In a desperation to get the supposed security of having a man, single women may hurt their own self-esteem. They cater to what they feel the man wants, while completely ignoring their own needs, which are reasonable and correct. For example, they are having sex with men after just a date, hoping the man will love and be close to them, marry them, and it doesn't even work. The tragedy is how much women are hurt along the way. Women are answering to men's needs, believing that men's ideology about marriage and love is correct, not being true to themselves. They're afraid to be rejected if they state their real hopes and dreams—and try to be 'loose' the way the 'male' culture is. But they should have more belief in themselves. Their ideas have dignity and depth and profundity. *Women* should set the standards, and not listen to 'male' standards."

Many women are really torn over whether they are making the right choices, whether they have the "right" feelings about love, whether they are assessing clearly what is happening in their lives: "Sometimes I'm depressed or sad for a short while after leaving a lover. The first few times, I thought I might die, but I guess I'm getting used to it. It seems the older I get, the easier the break-ups become. I'm not sure how great that is, and it depresses me, all this long string of love affairs—even if some of them are 'good friends' later. What does it mean?"

Many women's relationships are miserable, even degrading (though no one wants to say so)—and many men treat women condescendingly—so casually that they may drop a woman at any time, proposition another, talk of love but never feel obliged to discuss the pros and cons of commitments or their plans for the future. There is very little idea of team sharing; the "lone hero" version of the "male" ideology does not stop to consider women as having equal rights. Hence, women's pride can be whittled away during the course of their relationships with men.

Women frequently feel they are being "fucked over," not only physically but also emotionally, by men who reflect the values of a culture which is trying to persuade women to take on the "male" ideology (even though it does not value sex and love in the way most women feel they should be valued), and even though it tends to see many of women's beliefs as laughable or "psychologically defective."

Many women still take all this, even though they know what is going on, because they feel they have no choice: feel every woman "has" to get married eventually; and also, being asked out by men, paid attention to by men, it is natural that a woman would eventually fall in love with one—and then the cycle begins.

All of this can lead to what one woman described as "relationship burnout": "I do believe love involves problems for many women. Just by the mere fact that loving requires a tremendous amount of work and energy—on an ongoing basis. This could lead to 'relationship burnout.' (I just made up this term!)"

Patterns in Single Relationships

"You want to forget the feeling of being so hurt and just go on—like in a break-up—but is life serious? Does one event imply thinking about it, and changing your view of life? Or can you just forget and cover everything over?"

The whole scenario—a woman feeling, when meeting someone or starting a relationship, that if she doesn't sleep with him relatively quickly, he may never call her again; but if she does sleep with him, he may not take her seriously or treat her respectfully and may never call again anyway—puts women in an impossible position. Even worse, it never allows a woman to be the "judge" of a relationship: women hardly have a chance to think about what they actually feel, because they are so busy having to deal with the man's prejudices, stereotypes, and possible condescending remarks. She has to judge situations in an atmosphere which makes the man a possible adversary: he trying to "get" something, she wondering if she is being "had" or not.

The "male" pattern of no-holds-barred competition and aggression has become much harsher during recent years in the "singles world," and that pressure on single women to try to appease men and fit in with their system has become stronger. Women in the "singles scene" often rightly feel anxiety about whether men will drop or dump them—the man first acting loving, then leaving and acting unfriendly, then later returning to act loving again (meanwhile hotly denying any wrongdoing, and wondering why she is "so unstable and frequently demanding to know if he loves her or if he is only there for sex"). How can women love men in this atmosphere?

Men's trashy behavior and bad manners

Men's casual treatment of women in single relationships seems to be becoming more hostile and confrontational; the wild impoliteness of many men in the "dating scene" documented here seems to represent an enormous increase over previous years. The rudeness at times amounts to a flagrant show of male power and contempt: since a woman is so "powerless," it cannot hurt a man to be rude to her or treat her callously.

In the world of non-committed, fluctuating relationships, men's leaving immediately after sex, not calling, calling at random times, keeping unpredictable schedules, but still expecting the woman to be available, are all standard behaviors—so that a woman often finds it hard to enjoy a relationship—or even to know if she is in a relationship or what the status is. The attitude of "I deserve a woman to love me and be nice to me, but I don't have to be nice back" has become very widespread. As one woman asks, "Are they afraid and nervous, or did someone tell them it's macho to be mean?" Many men seem to have leaped mentally from the 1950s' attitude that women who are not playing the role of mothers/Marys are "bad girls" to a post-"sexual revolution" attitude that since most women now have sex before marriage, and furthermore work outside the home, most women are "bad girls" who deserve to be treated roughly, or however one wants—"they deserve what they get" because they gave up being put on pedestals when they went out into the "male world." Chivalry, they say, was extra-special treatment (naturally they do not usually recognize the special treatment women give men—i.e., listening to men's opinions as if they are more important, being there emotionally for them, etc.); in some instances, as we have seen, they do not even treat women they have slept with with the same amount of respect and politeness that they would a business associate.

The seduction scenario (emotional violence)

Many men have a pattern of giving a woman a lot of attention until she is interested and involved, has come to trust them and enjoy them—then changing, coming and going (both physically and emotionally) casually, irregularly (having established their territory?). If a woman "complains" she may be reminded by the man, "I'm happy, why are you making waves?", with an undertone of "Now, don't start being a neurotic, clinging woman on me. I thought you were different." Thus, men's behavior, while provoking a realistic response in women, i.e., women are wondering what is going on and trying to find out—comes off seeming "neutral": the man is "not doing anything." In these situations, men often then accuse women of "attacking them for no reason." In fact, the man is practicing a form of passive aggression.

Do men go through this process of flirtation, seduction, saying "beautiful things" only for "conquest"? No, it is also because they want the adulation, the affection, and the understanding that women give.

It is hardly surprising that many women feel very angry and unsettled about these situations. While they may know that in fact it is the whole weight of the system against them that they are feeling, and that the system is unjust to do this—still, for an individual who has just been called names or had all her assumptions challenged by her "boyfriend," this knowledge is not too helpful.

Nor is it perhaps surprising that, by contrast with single life now, men's commitment in marriage can look more civilized to single women than what they are experiencing. As one woman puts it, "It's all a jungle—but maybe at least if you're married, it's a private jungle."*

* To look at it more cynically, "male" culture has caused the harassment of women sexually with the "sexual revolution," putting women down for being "too sexual" outside of marriage at the same time that it urges women to be sexual (on male terms)—then offered "protection" inside marriage if women give up this idea of "freedom"—like a "Mafia" shakedown.

Men's manipulation of power in "singles" relationships: the emotional contract writ large

The psychological imbalance many men set up in single relationships often leads women to wind up asking themselves, "Is everything all right with him? Does he still love me? What is his mood today?"—not "Is everything all right with me? How am I? Do I want this kind of relationship?" After all, women are used to men's setting the rules, declaring what reality is, with women being expected to make the adjustments in *their* lives. Even if they realize how outrageous the situation is, they still feel they should stay, due to the heavy social pressure to "have a man."

Ironically, in non-married relationships, it often seems now that men are even *more* in charge, have more power, than they do in marriage (ironically, since feminists fought against men's ownership of women in marriage). This is because in single relationships, in addition to the usual subtle gender put-downs, emotional harassment, and not being listened to, the man here has the ace in the hole of total privatization of the relationship: his staying or leaving will never be judged publicly—as it will be if he divorces.

On another level, if a man can be "in love" with a woman, deeply, and still treat her with disrespect, even be macho and cruel—does a woman want a man like this? But what if *most* men are like this? (And most men *are* brought up to see women as "second," "different" fundamentally, more emotional, not as "rational," etc.) Should a woman take a man she loves and who loves her, and try to fight it through with him, to get him to see her as an equal, change his thinking, learn about emotional sharing, etc.? Or is this a job which may never succeed, and which may take up more of her time and energy than it should?

Women's growing disrespect for men with these behaviors

Perhaps women have great courage in not being afraid to keep on trying to love in the face of all this. But at the same time, more and more women are becoming exasperated with men's behavior, often losing their respect for men. In fact, women are becoming increasingly restive, increasingly concerned with changing this situation, perhaps leaving. Individual women everywhere are asking, why does it have to be like this? *Does* it have to be like this? What is behind this system? Isn't another system possible?

Actually, single women are doing quite well, despite all these circumstances. They very much enjoy their lives in general, being on their own—their work, their friends, even some of the playing around with men. Even when hurt and upset, they often display a marvelous sense of humor in the face of it all—mixed with wrath.

In fact, it is just this thinking going on in women's lives, combined with women's growing economic self-sufficiency and their happiness with friends, that is creating the new philosophical outlook, the new vision of what life can be, that is beginning to emerge, as woman after woman comes to the conclusion that there is something wrong with the system, not with her. On another level, women are coming to see that it is not even so much a problem with the individual men they know, but that somehow men too are caught up in an unreasonable set of beliefs which twists their lives and causes them to behave in truncated and distorted fashions. This system grasps men so tightly that many become lonely and desperate, finally losing "control": it is almost always men who are reported to have committed violent crimes. It is likely that women do not become violent because their system, "women's" culture, allows for talking things out. But men feel they have no place to turn, that they are not allowed any place to turn—except perhaps to sex, through which they can at least get physical affection. (Thus rape is often a way for men to try to make a statement to themselves about themselves and the attention they are angry they are not receiving.) The "male" system hurts men and closes them off from others, and yet men continue to believe in it, to defend its "values" no matter what. Why?

A New Politico-Historical Analysis of "Male Psychology"

Does the great amount of emotional violence by men in relationships with women imply a sort of vague unrest men feel with their lives *in general*? Are men the "winners" in the system of "male dominance" that they are supposed to be? What we see men expressing here (against women, where it is easiest) is a kind of fury, a nervousness that might indicate a feeling on men's part that things are not in fact going well, that men are not getting the rewards they were promised by the system, meant to get. Perhaps men are finding their world now somewhat frightening and unsatisfying, particularly with jobs often scarce and the future uncertain in a world where one is now expected to change jobs or careers several times in a lifetime. Even the once guaranteed love from women may be taken away, as men are expected to see women as equals, to "watch every little thing one says around them." Maybe men can no longer expect women to "be there," "be nice," ready to be caretakers, to make a home, etc. No longer is there a promise that there will be someone there, someone at "home" waiting. It is possible that how men treat women is a stage on which men are acting out their general feelings about life, themselves, and the future.

As Jacob Bronowski has stated, "Perhaps we have dehumanized ourselves and others with World War II and the bomb."* "Masculinity" has undergone a great change since World War II, a toughening. Is it possible that the collective male psyche in America somehow felt uncomfortable with war, with learning to believe it was right to kill—and so dealt with its guilt by glorifying it, glorifying the tough, brutal loner, the jungle fighter—the man who could "take it," "do what he had to do"—as a way of absorbing the shock of collective responsibility for the violence and death which was the price of victory? This style has remained popular; yet not all men "buy into" this brutalized idea of masculinity. What makes them different, what keeps them safe from this desensitizing process?

Dating Men: Fun or Russian Roulette?

Women's training to be loving and giving makes dating very lopsided in terms of the needs of the two parties. Alienated, unscrupulous men and boys who want to feel very "masculine," who have been taught that their "hormones" propel them to have intercourse with women, and that this makes them "real men," take advantage of women's desire to love and be giving, to push for sex.

Some men say, "Well, don't women enjoy sex too, just as much as men? Therefore, the man is not taking advantage of the woman, he is giving her something she needs as much as he does—even if temporarily." But while sometimes women are at a point in their lives when they enjoy experimenting and having "adventures," it is quite clear that most women, for most of their lives, prefer sex in a context of feelings and respect.

Women should not have to choose between being sexual and not being sexual; nor should women have to define their sexuality

---

* Public Television series, "The Ascent of Man," with Professor Jacob Bronowski host.

under such pressure and negativity from men. Instead women and men should challenge the reigning ideology—i.e., the version of the "male" culture which decrees that "boys will be boys," closing a blind eye to many boys' "hit and run" or "shopping" attitudes toward girls—the same "male" culture which looks down on teenage girls for getting abortions, but does not think that the missing boys who probably pushed for intercourse are also "villains"/victims, now set up for emotional confusion and alienation too. Sex is not bad; treating another person with disrespect is.

Is looking for lots of "sex" "natural"? Are women "brainwashed"—or are men "dehumanized"?

Is monogamous love, and/or a desire for marriage, a "natural" tendency which men have been taught to repress? Or are multiple sexual relationships "natural," and do women typically avoid them only because they are brought up to be prudes and "good girls"? (Or because people call them "sluts" otherwise?)

The presumption is usually that what men do, think, or feel is "natural," that if only women would give up their "hang-ups," they would naturally be "like men" too. The assumption since the "sexual revolution" has therefore almost universally been that women would—and should—change their values and sexual behavior to be more like men, i.e., to have sex more outside of marriage and have it not mean so much. This thinking assumes that the "male" system is biologically ordained, and the "female" system is "acculturated"—that women are "held back" because of the fear of getting pregnant and other historical reasons.

But is there any logical reason for believing that "promiscuity" is "natural"? (After all, men are taught to "go after sex.") Even if it might be "natural" (to start with that as an assumption), to value "having sex" over having a very emotional love (and wanting to be monogamous) is not a belief system most women would want to take on. Most women would say here that it is men who should change and begin to understand the connection of sex with feelings, understand that the body and spirit may not be separate after all.

The Right to be Single: Most Women Love to Spend Time Alone

"I find that being single is a time I take quantum leaps in self-development. It seems to release a surge of creative energy in me. I think I am a better person for the time I spend alone."

Although living alone is supposed to be lonely, most women love to spend time alone, have time to themselves. Many women can be themselves when alone in a more complete way than at any other time.

More women mention feeling lonely inside a non-close relationship than they ever do being single (almost no women mention feeling alone because of being single). Women say, over and over, that they have many good women friends, sometimes friends of a lifetime, and that their communication with them is the closest of their lives. Being single and trying out different relationships can be "lonely" because of the ups and downs, the lack of stability, and the constant "starting over." While breaking up or being in a bad relationship can be depressing, actually being "alone" is not, according to women here.

Most women in this study, single or married, say they would like to have *more* time alone. When asked, "What is your favorite activity for yourself, your favorite way to waste time?" the overwhelming majority of women chose activities that were solitary—such as taking a bath, reading a book, going for a long walk, perhaps with their dogs, having time to just sit and have a cup of tea, etc.

When asked, "What is your favorite way to waste time? Please yourself?" 92 percent of women mention activities they do alone:

"I love to play music and dance. I love to read, I read a lot, and I love movies. I love to sit around by myself and space out, I call it. That kind of time is very important, very, very important to me."

One woman describes her single life after years of marriage and motherhood:

"The disadvantage of blessed singleness is that I live in what I call Noah's Ark. It used to be called a 'bedroom town,' a place for commuting husbands to keep their wives and children, but now is a corporate headquarters town. When you go downtown at noon and the streets are crawling with squads of men in their dull business suits who practically knock you into the gutter in their arrogance.

"Between being a suburb of families and patriarchal corporate headquarters, there is little social life for a single old woman. (I'm sixty-two now.) I have few friends. But I'm not lonely or unhappy. For

291

the most part, I feel contented—that is, when I am not driven because I'm not accomplishing.

"After taking the drastic, terrifying step of no longer kowtowing to my husband, I recognized him as a brutalizing monster. But at the time, he seemed better than most and everyone said to me, 'You're so lucky.' Romantic 'love' is a myth conjured up in our society to keep women enslaved—always looking for a mate in order to feel 'human.' The concept is enforced by Hollywood patriarchal moguls, admen, and the like—the male brotherhood.

"For my second job, the YWCA job counselor tore up my paper when she saw my only credentials outside of housework were the past ten years of volunteer work. No matter how I'd couch it, it would come out the same.

'Eventually, I had to get a renter to keep afloat. This turned out to be the biggest break for me. He moved in with his computer, and soon began teaching me with infinite patience to use it—so well that I am now doing a free-lance indexing paid job. I am enjoying this experience the most of anything since 1978. I keep thinking I should learn faster and do more. I don't know any woman with as sophisticated equipment as this, or with the knowledge that he and his friends have. It's fun knowing him.

"After raising five children to adulthood and independence, I entered the job market for the first time at fifty-six and I am surviving—'making it'! My goals are to retain my home, remain financially independent, and start making enough money to do things like go to shows and concerts, travel and take vacations. I can see it's all within my grasp now—in just a year or two, I will have it all—and I can be proud of having done it myself."

The stereotype of being "old and alone" is basically inaccurate: in this study, 81 percent of single women over sixty-five like their lives very much (even if they could use a little more money): most enjoy their friends, their work, their gardens, lovers, in fact all facets of life. In fact, many women say they feel *happier* when "old and alone."

Painful Love Affairs in the Dating Scene

Is it worth having a less intense relationship, just to avoid the pain of volatile ups and downs?

Emotional uncertainty in relationships: one woman describes her feeling of frustration, confusion, and love, all mixed together, as she experiences a great deal of ambiguity in the man she loves:

"I have a constant feeling of never being satisfied for some reason. Either he's not calling, or when he's calling, it's not romantic, and so on. . . . When I try to talk to him, really talk to him, I feel like I just can't get through—except sometimes, when *he* wants to talk, he'll say the loveliest things. Other times, he just won't respond and/or doesn't want to make love, and I never know why.

"It seems to revolve around a constant question of should I be asking myself, 'Is everything all right in terms of him (does he still love me)?' or 'Is everything all right in terms of *me*? How am *I*?' If I am unhappy a lot, and he won't talk to me about the problems or resolve the issues, should I say, 'Well, everything is really O.K. because he's O.K. and he's still there and still loves me? Or should I say, 'This relationship is terrible and I will leave it because he is not making me happy'? Loving him makes it difficult to leave him.

"Should I want to help him open up more, or should I worry about myself and break up with him? Or maybe I should become pregnant and solve the whole question of what will become of us (I'm sure he'd never want me to have an abortion).

"But he keeps saying these condescending remarks, like I was a little girl or something. I found myself trying to write him a note to explain my feelings to him the other day. I wrote it late one night. The next morning I looked at it and it started out, 'I know that you think of me as complicated and crazy, but I just want to explain to you . . .' I couldn't believe I had written that, and just put myself down! What a macho view he has, like *Gaslight*, the movie, to imply there is anything wrong with my thinking! You know, the movie with Ingrid Bergman and Charles Boyer made a long time ago, where he tries to convince her she is losing her mind, by making the lights flicker and claiming they are not, that it's all in her mind? The idea is that men are the norm, I guess, and women are the deviants. But it starts subtly—I would have been outraged three months ago if anyone had implied I was 'complicated and crazy'—but it happens gradually, you lose your self-esteem and belief in yourself gradually. Now all that seems apparent to me is that I want to be alone and strong again. I say that now, but . . .

"The problem is that first he says he's vulnerable and in love—then later he denies it or doesn't act like it, acts cold. I ask myself, 'Is the goal this man at any cost?' It's almost as if someone is egging me on to go into the deep end of the pool—and then when I get there (with my emotions) and really fall in love, trust him, he says, 'What? Why me?' I've been so scared all the way, thinking to myself, no matter what happened, giving him the benefit of the doubt, 'Let me trust, let me trust,' not letting myself believe the negative signals, thinking he was just insecure or reacting to something I had done in my *own* effort to seem invulnerable—I've always been so afraid, wondering, 'Will somebody stay?' A relationship like ours where there is no commitment yet means anybody can pull out whenever they want—but I have tried not to believe that would be the case, to believe we are building something more valuable, more permanent, even though he has not said so.

"Maybe this whole relationship has been a big mistake on my part. I feel less strong. Instead of working on my career, I am obsessed with our phone calls and meetings. I feel weak. Why does love have to make you feel weak? Does it? It all turns into a game of strategy. It always feels like he is in control. But who knows, maybe he feels like *I* am in control, he feels just as vulnerable as I do. Oh, here I go again obsessing about this relationship. I am so angry at myself that I have lost myself in this love affair.

"How to judge the situation is so hard: is he afraid to love, or does he really not love *me*? It's all so one-sided, I feel sometimes. Then sometimes I think he loves me, but he would never marry me—you know the way I mean? And *if* he loves me, why does he leave me so often? Does he really have to spend so much time at work? If we were married, it would give me a base to know he really did care and love me in some special way; just the way we are, although he calls me every day, I always wonder and feel very insecure. Everything seems to be on his terms—he tells me when he can come and see me. I tried doing the same thing to him and being busy at work a lot, but it didn't bother him at all, it just hurt me because I missed him.

"Why do I want somebody who is not making me happy? His low and trivializing opinion of women comes out in bits and snatches. But other times are really great, and he can be so charming and so much fun, and then say some really beautiful things. He's not that great in bed, however, I must admit.

"My mother has counseled me the following way: She said, when I complained I couldn't get through to him about what was bothering me about the relationship, 'It is easy to speak with a friend, but not with a man. With a man, you become silent. You have to find your own liberty inside—and then you can be with a man. No matter how free and strong you are, when you are with a man, you start thinking how *he* feels, lose any self, any center. You feel he's not completely yours—especially if you are creative. You want to be comforted by a man. Men want a woman who looks good, is brilliant, but still will be dominated.' I couldn't believe she told me these things. I guess, as Laurence Olivier once remarked in one of his films, 'No matter what they tell you, you really *are* on your own out there. Completely and totally alone.' I guess this is why people become mediocre—safety in following the flock.

"Anyway, there's something about the setup with men that's so unfair. It's O.K. if *men* bring up commitment, but not if we do. So—life isn't fair, love relationships with men aren't fair—but I still want one! But how do I get him??? Do I have to play a game and wait for him? Should I appear strong and independent, or do I have to seem to *need* him??? I feel so depressed, but there's no reason! I'm starting to be insecure, and worse, to show him my insecurities. It's not knowing what's going to happen with us, and I really care."

Often women who go into therapy to try to figure out why their love lives aren't working decide to rid themselves of a desire for romantic love, to make themselves more "rational," stifle so-called unrealistic expectations, and concentrate on more stable and friendly day-to-day relationships.

One woman, after having had a rather disastrous experience of being "in love," decided to develop a more low-key relationship with a man she loves less, but feels will be stable and with whom she can work it out:

"In the last three years, I have made a major change, removing myself from a self-destructive relationship. The man I lived with wouldn't marry me, always accused me of not really liking his daughter (who lived with us, or should I say, I lived with them). I constantly cleaned up after her, took care of her, talked to her after school, fed her, etc. Once he even hit me because she said I had been mean to her while he was out. Part of the time I lived there, I wasn't working, so I was financially dependent, and this was demeaning too. I mean, I felt like a real Cinderella. But I was crazy about him, I always liked sex with him, he was very sexy. It took me ages to leave. Even after I had gotten a degree, I still wanted to be with him, and also by that time, I was pretty low, so it was hard to get up enough belief in myself to make the move.

"Perhaps my biggest achievement so far has been to enter analysis, and to form a different relationship, with a special friend. We enjoy a wonderful sex life together. We have both had terrible hurts in the past and run away from each other, but he is very understanding.

"I consider myself a feminist. I think the women's movement helped me feel like I am less alone with my problems. I am still raging at the double messages in society, at discrimination, at sexism, at churches that cripple people sexually, etc. Mostly, I rage now at people who treat me like dirt. I think it's all right to rage, but I also want to learn to love—myself and everyone else."

Practicality Versus the Soul: Must Every Relationship End with the "Perfectly Adjusted Heterosexual Couple"?

Is "happiness" always the goal in a love relationship? There is a case to be made for not having to have every love fit into some socially approved scheme of the perfect household and the Perfectly Adjusted Heterosexual Couple. All relationships are not tryouts for "marriage"!

Sometimes women decide to stay in a relationship because no matter how great the pain, their love is real, and feeling it, expressing it, gives them more pleasure, more of a feeling of being themselves, alive, than being stable and "normal." As one woman says, "I would go out of my way for my boyfriend, and love makes it seem not out of the way. This is the first time that I have felt like this. My two previous boyfriends loved me more than I loved them. I felt guilty when they would talk about our future together with happiness in their eyes and I felt doubt."

Is following an impractical "great love" a mistake?

What is a good relationship? Is it getting along? Companionship? Feeling great passion? Closeness? Being there? Actually, a relationship can be very unstable, or even unhappy, and still provide a kind of nourishment for the soul, or somehow open up doors in one's mind that didn't exist before.

As one woman puts it, "He is the one I want to love. Some other relationships might be easier, or more talkative, but I don't *love* them. I love him for the unique person he is—I love a person, not a relationship. I'm not looking for a person to give me the best relationship there is, I'm looking for a person I feel connected to."

Being "obsessed" with love has at times been labeled "neurotic" behavior, as if only "rationality" is acceptable; and yet, even the Greeks accepted "divine madness" as a good. And, not even thinking in these extremes, it is undoubtedly true that people at times feel a connection beyond words.

But are women too prone to seek after the "great love," too easily led by their feelings, too likely to continue loving when it is not "rational"? And is this thirst for love somehow reflective of our thirst for approval and love, nurturance, from a society which hardly welcomed our birth as it did those of our brothers—a society which does not give much approval or encouragement to women, except in the secondary role of helping males?

Love as a Passion of the Soul

Or perhaps our quest for love is also a hidden form of love for ourselves—*we* are not supposed to love ourselves, so we hunger to find a *man* who can, to certify that love—to get the love we feel we cannot give ourselves. In a way, perhaps, our quest for love is a sublimation of the spiritual ecstasy of the self, being one with that self. Is that why we may find it so hard to leave a man with whom we are "in love," even if the relationship becomes more negative?

Is love our emancipator or our oppressor? Love is, after all, the prescribed lifestyle for women, *the* lifestyle for women. "Love" can be very oppressive and manipulative, and drain women incredibly—although it should not be like this—which has led many feminists to say that as women we should "throw off our chains," and "stop having sex with our oppressors," give up romance with men. But *feeling* love is not the culprit, *we* are not "weak," "masochistic," and "silly"—rather, it is the cultural context, the genderizing of society, that makes love "wrong," makes masochistic situations so common in the emotional contract.

Male Alienation and Brutalization

It is the "male" ideology that tells boys that a boy becomes a man when he first "has" a woman—i.e., has intercourse/penetrates a woman—and that a man stays more of a man the more often he continues to do so. Other aspects of this "male" credo include "the more sex, the better," "shopping around is natural," "nature made men to disseminate their semen to the widest possible sample" (as in *The King and I*: "Bee must go from blossom to blossom," etc.). The corollary to this kind of attitude (wherein "getting some"—i.e., penetration—is still "scoring," "getting it over on so-and-so," "having her") is the idea that all women "want a man," need to "catch a man," "trap" one into marriage. So there is a built-in, never acknowledged game going on: he trying to "get some," she trying to "get him to care"—and he fleeing as if "caring" were a fate worse than death.

The "male" philosophy has tended to see sex as a simple biological pleasure, indeed, to endorse this view of it. Men have put an enormous amount of pressure on women to have "sex." Women find this pressure and this philosophy, for the most part, mechanical and insensitive, making erotic and sensual interaction almost impossible. Men have called women who say "no" to sex when there are no feelings involved "hung up" or "Victorian" (1960s) or "anti-male," "man haters" (1970s and 1980s). Even in "serious" academic journals, these theories have consistently been proposed or assumed—i.e., that women historically have been "brainwashed" to be "good girls" and for this reason are afraid to like sex, especially sex without love—"the way men (in their more grown-up way?) do."

Rather than seeing women's philosophy as just as valid as their own, a topic for research or philosophical debate between two equal, differing cultural perspectives, requiring thought and analysis, many men ridicule women's point of view as nonsense, both personally and in articles. Whether the prospect of getting AIDS will change this behavior has yet to be seen; 1987 research for this study shows a surprising apathy with regard to changing behavior—although everyone agrees they "ought to."

Where did the double standard come from? Adam and Eve as early propaganda

Why does the "male" ideology have to make such an extreme fetish of gender division? Many theorists have pointed to the obvious; that only through controlling women's sexuality and reproduction can men have inheritance pass through them—i.e., have a male-dominated society. Without strict rules and regulations regarding gender behavior (especially for women), men could not be sure that the children women were bearing were their own, claim them as their legal property, have rights over them. This is why such continuous cultural reinforcement of "what sexuality is" is necessary. (Is it possible that gender division has not always been the fundamental principle of society—or that the genders were not always defined in the ways they are now?)

But there is another way of looking at the Adam and Eve story than that usually seen by historians. Could it be that one of its messages—a message now unseen, but clear to those of early times—was exactly this: *to focus attention on gender division as the fundamental principle of a new social order* and to establish the basic "personality traits" of these two "original beings" as the prototypes for future society? These personality traits may not have been standard for the two genders at that time. Certainly Adam and Eve are the earliest symbol known of the double standard and negative attitudes toward women in Western thought.*

And symbols and pictures of Adam and Eve continue to be used in advertising and design, appearing constantly all around us, reminding us of Eve's "wickedness," that she caused our "downfall," our being expelled from the Garden of Eden. Women were supposedly responsible for "original sin," and we are still reminded of our "basic natures"—thus making us try even harder to be "good," show we are "trustworthy," so as to be accepted by society, be loved. It is no surprise that something as old in Western tradition, in patriarchal tradition, as the dichotomy between "bad" women and "good" women† has not been ended by the mere twenty years of women's challenging male domination. Or even by the last hundred years since the end of women's legal ownership by husbands and fathers, since the dichotomy—and there is, of course, no such dichotomy for men—has ancient roots entwined in the foundations of our culture.

---

* Other creation stories, with some similar themes, are found in surrounding cultures around 3000 B.C., such as in Sumerian texts, etc.; some may be older.
† See Professor Wendy Doniger O'Flaherty's work for the documentation of this split in classical Indian culture, in the Rig Vedas; that culture, like ours, was also based in large part on the ideology and social structure of Indo-European tribes; indeed we have an extremely important common cultural heritage, which is, however, generally unmentioned.

The New Fundamentalist Religions: Reinforcing the Double Standard and Seduction Scenario

Has the religious revival movement made any change in the widespread male acceptance of the double standard? Not really. The movement puts great pressure on women to "realize" their natural desire for children, to be mothers, and to put the needs of the children and family/father *first*. Women who are not married or mothers are asked to re-examine their reasons and listen carefully to those who know better about what is "right" in life. In addition, the religious version of the "male" ideology usually expects women to make sacrifices in marriage and love relationships that men are almost never asked to make.

There are, in fact, two sides to the double standard: the playboy version—"all women are for sex, let's take them"; and the religious version—"all women should be in the home, mothers." In other words, the double standard is part of the "male" ideology, which is so enmeshed in all aspects of our lives. This is why the double standard did not disappear with the "sexual revolution," and why it has not yet disappeared even with the strides made by the women's movement.*

Moreover, while it certainly does not endorse the "playboy" mentality, the "born again" movement has produced very little propaganda exhorting boys not to see girls either as "targets" from which to get sex or as "mothers"—i.e., service people—especially compared to the amount of propaganda directed at women to say "no," and stressing the values of motherhood and subordination to one's family. And most parts of the revivalist religious movement also clearly state that although husband and wife are a team, in the final analysis the man must lead—in traditional, patriarchal fashion. As Jerry Falwell put it in 1986 on television, "The man is the spiritual fountainhead of the family—the leader." In other words, the "good old days" are simply the old, unequal, oppressed days women have been struggling to get choices out of, to escape from.

Still, the atmosphere in a family-oriented philosophy, even a hierarchically organized one, can be felt as an improvement for a woman emerging from the singles arena of the "sexual revolution," wherein sex is seen as a biological urge not to be denied or interfered

---

* Of course, not all men agree with the playboy game plan regarding sex, or with the religious revival movement's version of the proper way of life for women either. There is a vigorous minority of men of every political persuasion who do not see themselves in either the men-are-beasts-who-want-women's-bodies idea of who men are, or the men-marry-mothers-only school of thought. Some of these interesting men appear in *The Hite Report on Men and Male Sexuality*.

300

with by interpersonal relationships or ethical codes. Thus it is no surprise that much of the conservative religious movement's backbone is made up of women or that it is driven largely by women's energy—women's donated office work, organizing abilities, church attendance, fund-raising activities. Many women like the church because it supports them in their struggle to continue the home–family value system—i.e., it supports them as long as they stay in the home (or at most combine home with career only after children are in school; women with young children who want to work are sometimes made to feel ashamed of "shirking their responsibility"). But there is something appealing about the desire, at least on the part of some men, to continue a tradition of "family" values—i.e., humane values. If only these men could learn not to make those values conditional on women's secondary status, on women's subservience—and their own dominance.

The Two Cultures: Women Live Bi-Culturally

Women here paint a picture of widespread gender stereotyping and condescension to women—even in their most intimate moments with men they love, which can make the impact even more devastating. The dynamics of this situation in personal life have been only cloudily seen up to now, perhaps for lack of the kind of massive documentation provided here—documentation that is an indictment of the traditional gender system with its unfair emotional "contract." That contract (the still-not-eradicated psychological counterpart of the centuries-long legal domination of women by men) exploits women emotionally while not even acknowledging that this is going on, insisting that women who "complain" have "complexes," not real problems created by a real social ideology which is negative to women. There is not "something wrong" with women—women don't have a "problem," a "bad attitude"—but there *is* a problem in the society: that is, the attitudes of the dominant "male"-oriented viewpoint (especially as sanctified by much "psychological theory") toward women as a class.

Women are engaged in profound questioning about how they can go on living with this situation, what to do about it. Their choices seem to be: leave the relationship/marriage, keep struggling to "get him to see," or tune out, become less emotionally involved, i.e., take on "male" values in love relationships. Or restructure their lives fundamentally.

If women have different beliefs about what a relationship should be, are operating on different premises and define their priorities differently from most men, then it is obvious that a struggle is likely to ensue eventually in most relationships. We have heard women state that most men don't believe in such behaviors as empathic listening: trying to understand without judging and being emotionally supportive are basic to what having a relationship means; at least they do not offer these things. Instead, most women say men seem rather to think of a relationship in terms of "being there," with the man "of course"

302

psychologically dominant (although most men would be quick to say that they do not *intend* to dominate women they love). Listening emphatically, drawing the woman out, supporting her projects are not first priorities in most men's definition of relationships. Though both women and men at least do agree that physical affection is a number-one priority, in most other ways their value systems differ. (There is also another manifestation of these differences: most women say that men do not connect sex with love relationships the way women want to, and also that men do not see why having a fight should get "in the way" of having sex.)

Most women are surprised when men don't respond with fairness in a relationship, following the general rules of give and take, and most are even more surprised when a man begins to use a relationship for his own emotional support, not seeing (even when it is pointed out to him) that he is getting this but not giving it back. The problem is that many men have a double standard for their behavior with women and their behavior with the rest of society: since women are "less" or the "other," the same rules, many men unconsciously believe, do not apply. And as the pattern of men's unwitting gestures of inequality, followed by women's "bringing up the issues," which in turn is often greeted with gender-stereotyped remarks, continues, women become more and more dissatisfied, and begin to disrespect men, since it is difficult to respect someone who is unfair.

Why is this so? Why do men and women have such different ideas about relationships? Why does men's value system see love as something a "real man" wouldn't take as seriously as his job, his "honor as a man," and so on?

"Women's" Culture and "Men's" Culture: Two Worlds

Women and men really live in two different worlds, with two inter-locking sets of values. In the personal sphere, these values work out to mean that women nourish men, while men believe they have no duty to nourish but only to *be*, to achieve. Men generally expect the world to want and value them for *themselves* and for their work.

These semi-articulated beliefs (seen not as "beliefs" but as "how things are") have been built into theories of behavior, psychology, "human nature," religion, etc., over several thousand years, until they seem "obvious"—and trying to find the language for unraveling the assumptions is like Alice trying to walk through the Looking Glass.

Historically, the situation is now volatile: with most women working outside the home as well as in, the two value systems are in conflict, as men apply the values of competing and winning to relationships (in and out of marriage)* and women wonder whether (as with the idea of wearing male-type business suits) they should adopt "male" values in love too, give love a lesser place in their world than they often want to do (for example, not "insist" on connecting sex with love). The weight of society is on the side of women adopting "male" values, since these form the dominant culture: men are the "standard of reality," the reality-testing point.

In other words, the problems between women and men in personal relationships have not been overcome because there is a cultural conflict going on.

The two cultures:† an historical tradition or a biological given?

If women have a separate "sub"-culture, is it based on biological difference, or historical tradition?

There is no need to posit a biological difference between "male" and "female" "human nature" to explain the two different value-systems defined by women here and by men in *The Hite Report on Men*, nor does the existence of these double cultures in any way prove that they are inevitable/or a product of "nature." In fact, they are not biological; they are historical: two separate historical traditions that have grown up over centuries. We have very little information regarding ideologies which preceded our own in history, but we do have enough to know that there *were* different ideologies: Adam and Eve were the first ideological lesson for the West in the version of gender differentiation which grew out of the Indo-European frame of reference as it came to the Mediterranean basin.‡

---

* Karl Marx predicted that in a capitalist society the values of the marketplace would eventually penetrate everything, even personal life.
† For other discussions of whether or not there are "two cultures," or depictions of "woman's voice," see the works of Jesse Bernard, Joan Scott, Mary Daly, Carroll Smith-Rosenberg, Carol Gilligan, Elizabeth Petroff, and others included in the bibliography. Certainly a well-developed "female" culture and value system is implicit in what the majority of women are saying in this study, and in women's and men's statements in the two previous Hite Reports.
‡ See Elaine Pagels, *Adam, Eve and the Serpent* (New York: Random House, 1988); also Marija Gimbutas, *Goddesses and Gods of Old Europe* (Los Angeles: University of California Press, 1982).

That these two cultures are in conflict now, and how this conflict will be resolved, how the transformation will be made to a new world-view is one of the momentous questions of our time.

"Men are the reality, women are the role"*

As the song from *My Fair Lady* says, "Why can't a woman be more like a man?" So *we* might ask—"Why can't a man be more like a woman??"

Men, it seems, don't want to be "like women." The general presumption is that women, to "gain equality," should try to learn from men, drop their "old values" and become more "like men."†

The emotional contract reflects this general presumption of men's psychological superiority: men have the edge in psychological power and status in relationships just as they have higher status in the outside "work" world. Men are seen by society as somehow more "legitimate" and psychologically "right." Men's opinions and actions are given much more credibility than women's, which are more likely to be criticized or scrutinized. In other words, the culture considers whatever men do the "norm," a somehow unquestionable "reality," while seeing what women do as a "role," and one with inferior characteristics at that.

Women's value system, always "second-best," is currently under very strong attack. There is great pressure on women to "realize" that "men are better," more "normal," for women to throw off their "old-fashioned" values about love, "grow up," become more like men in their view of the world. (At the same time, men still expect women to be supportive, loving, and nurturing of them.)

The reality is, in fact, that both systems have important values—there is not one "reality" and another group of people who need to stop thinking the way they do and get in touch with "reality." And "women's" systems of values (belief in nurturing, putting relationships first in life) has been providing most of the love and emotional support the "male system" has been running on.

Part of many men's disdain for "women's" value system comes

---

* This is true even in language, where "man" stands for "men and women" in many "humanistic" book titles and television "educational" programs; and "he" is the "correct" pronoun to use when discussing behavior in the abstract. All this has been shown to have a profound effect on kindergarten girls and boys. It also has a profound effect on personal relationships between women and men.
† Doesn't this sound something like the nineteenth-century presumption that the West would "civilize" the natives in various colonies, expecting the "natives" to drop their own "superstitions" and become "rational," like us?

out of the belief that "men are the reality, women are the role"—i.e., a woman without role training (or, for some, hormones) would just "naturally" be like a man. But this contains the assumption that men are not just as heavily laced with role training, and that their beliefs and behavior patterns are not just as much culturally or historically fabricated. And even for many of those who agree that men's behaviors might be culturally produced or emphasized, the assumption is still that men's characteristics are superior. But men's "psychology" or value system is just as much arbitrarily fashioned as "women's"—whether through history or a long ideological legacy and "role-indoctrination." Men's way of life is not "natural" or somehow "right," the bottom line of "reality" for measuring the behavior of the whole world. In fact, now, in the late twentieth century, if we want to invigorate our "system" and have it continue, we may well have to reassess what it is that our culture and political tradition are all about, what they stand for—and whether we are being true to the best parts of them.

If most women are put on the defensive in their private lives about their values and behavior (and this has been increasing during the last twenty years), what should women do? Argue back all the time? How can a woman feel good about herself in a relationship if she is fighting an endless inner war between who she is and her loved one's perception of who she is? Love relationships with men can be emotionally dangerous for women, since our philosophy makes it hard to stop giving, even when it has become more than we can afford.

"Masculinity": a heroic tradition?

Glorious, heroic images of masculinity abound in history—mythic figures who sail out to find their destiny, rescue their countries, create great science and art. These heroic efforts seem to imply no negative attitudes toward women—except, of course, women were not allowed on any of these expeditions. The heroic quest has been a male preserve.★

To be "male" seems to have two traditions: masculinity as being courageous, brave, and noble—and masculinity as being macho with women, aggressive and competitive with others, "conquering nature,"

★ There are also, it must be said, a few noble images of women contained in standard history books, those of women ruling their countries—Catherine of Russia, Empress Maria Theresa of the Holy Roman Empire, and Queen Elizabeth I of England, to name those best known. But generally, when not born to it, the role of hero has been reserved for men. When Jeanne d'Arc lived a heroic life on her own initiative, and in male terms, she was eventually inquisitioned and killed.

justified as "natural behavior," "human nature." Which is the "real" masculinity?

How can such a tradition as the noble male—going into space, building mathematical systems, discovering the laws of the universe—exist side by side with the lowly tradition of oppressing women—keeping women out of educational institutions, excluding women from power in governments, and generally treating women as second-class, often less than fully human?* How is one to reconcile in one's mind that a great tradition could also contain the least noble of traditions?

Historically, the classical Greek state, which is so admired for its balanced ideas of government and philosophy, was, we must remember, *not* balanced: it was a male democracy—excluding women and slaves from free speech and government, already containing the stereotypes of the "talkative" woman (Socrates' wife was said to "nag" him), the only philosophical women or women of letters being categorized as "mistresses." (Does this mean they had lovers? That they were not married? That famous men were attracted to them, and they allowed these men to make love with them? Men who have lovers are not categorized by history as "lovers," and yet women are frequently presented by the history books as no more than "mistresses," "harlots," or "courtesans.")

Has there always been this split in the culture's choice of possibilities offered to men? Or is the "macho" side of being male more with us today? Gore Vidal once quipped, on being asked what he thought about "masculinity": "Oh, masculinity—I hear they had a bad outbreak of it down near Tampa, but I think now they're getting it under control."

What Is the "Male" Ideology† and Why Does It Make It So Hard for Men to Love?

What is behind the "male" system that makes men emotionally distant—at the same time that it makes them need love desperately, precisely *because* of this emotional isolation, *because* they are so cut off

---

* Early Christian "scholars" debated whether women had souls, just as in the Freudian tradition "analysts" now wonder whether women are "masochists." In fact, the American Psychiatric Association, in 1986, designated a new category of disease (there being only fourteen categories altogether), "masochism." While women in the field have protested this, it has been basically adopted by the all-male board of review.

† It is important to point out here that this ideology is not something a man is automatically part of just because he is anatomically male. The "male" we refer to in the phrase "male" ideology is cultural: men who adopt the cultural style of masculinity as domination.

from their feelings? Many men are racked and torn over how to relate to women they love, in deep anguish over their personal lives and love relationships.

Obviously, men want love; they look to women for love, are angry if women are not "loving," and 90 percent get married by the age of twenty-seven. Rarely are men the ones to bring up divorce. Men want a home, and warmth, just as women do. But they also have deeply ambiguous feelings: real closeness is a threatening state of emotionality that most can't afford. Men learn that a "real man" never completely lets his guard down, or loses control of a situation; a man must continually assert his "independence" or "dominance." Real closeness is forbidden for men because it makes them vulnerable.

It is often said, "It's the mothers' fault if men are macho—they bring up boys that way." But this is an aggressive remark, simplistic, and not really to the point at all; after all, the fathers, by the example of not being home, or by their emotional distance when home, also "bring up the boys." The real problem is the ideology with which we live, the entire system which teaches men that to be "real men" they must follow "male" codes, other male examples—not create their own way.

The basic tenets of the "male" ideology are only beginning to be understood—since for many centuries male behavior and personality and male-designed religious and state systems, were thought to grow out of "human nature," rather than being part of a belief structure which one could stand back from and analyze.

Hierarchy: the essence of the "male" ideology

One of the earliest and still repeated stories, by which the hierarchical system of unquestioning obedience to authority is explained to Jews and Christians—by which it is ordained that one must not put personal feelings of love before duty and obedience to the rules of this hierarchy—is the biblical tale of Abraham taking his son up on the mountain, where God has commanded that he kill/"sacrifice" his son—with no explanation given. The message is: obey and don't ask questions. As a reward for their obedience to this hierarchy, men in other parts of the scriptures are promised rulership over women, children, and "nature"; women are told, "Wives, be obedient to your husbands."

Even today, men are told in one "nature" special after another on television, and in many biological textbooks, that they have a "natural" tendency (right?) to be "dominant," to rule—as part of a "natural instinct." The assumption that men are more important

308

than women, that they have more right to be "in charge," that their thoughts are more "rational," "clear," and "objective," underlies much of the culture. In other words, the "male" ideology is still all around us, and still tells men that if they follow the expected patterns of behavior of the "male" hierarchical system (show "loyalty"), they will have all the "natural" rights of men to be dominant over women, children, and the planet. Thus the concept of "male pride."

The conceptualization of democratic government, as its ideas were developed during the Enlightenment and the French and American Revolutions, was in part a reaction against this hierarchical view of unthinking obedience to a ruler who was king because of his lineage and "the right of God." Men should no longer be *told* what they should do: now *all* men were thought "educable," able to think for themselves. Still, this new system of equal rights and dignity for "all" was only for men.*

The psychology of being "male": "someone has to be on top"

According to the "male" ideology, hierarchy and fighting for "dominance" are part of "nature"; therefore there can be no such thing as equality—"someone has to be on top." For this reason, the very idea of equality with women is interpreted unconsciously by many men to mean a challenge to their "dominance." A man should "keep a woman in line," keep her from her propensity to try to "run things." It is a mental construct that sees women as "the other,"† and makes men apply different "rules" in their relationships with other men than in their relationships with women.

---

* As Mary Midgley describes it, "Essentially, much of today's trouble (women's rebellion) is a nemesis for the vast ambitions of the Enlightenment. Many of those who proclaimed . . . high ideals of human freedom and equality instinctively protected themselves from disturbance by tacitly applying these ideals only to a limited group—namely, white males. This protective habit went so deep that remarks on its inconsistency tended simply not to register; they sounded frivolous and unreal . . . And the issue does indeed centre in the United States, whose founders, by giving it a constitution devoted to Enlightenment ideals, loaded it far more openly than other nations with a painful choice between profound change and rampant hypocrisy" (*Times Literary Supplement*, August, 1983).

"Freedom" in the "male" code means that a "real" man should be "independent," should not be "told what to do"—especially by a female. Surely, Thomas Paine in the eighteenth century could not have had in mind the propping up of the modern "macho" personality when he exalted the "Rights of Man." And yet, this "democratic" language is what is being used today to make some men's insistence on being dominant sound righteous.

† The famous phrase and theory of Simone de Beauvoir.

But if women want equality, of course, they *have* to "challenge" "male" dominance—and do so daily. But if most men do not believe that there is such a thing as equality (since in a hierarchy someone has to be "on top"), it seems to them that what women are "demanding" is "dominance" or "power." And if men cannot understand equality, perhaps women in frustration will have to wind up doing this.

The "male" ideology, based on dominance, and the "female" belief in love and nurturing thus create a tragic pattern in many individual lives—a man being "full of his right," condescending (even unconsciously), while a woman is trying to "talk," understand, explain, draw the man out, and somehow "make it all work." Often the two remain locked in this struggle throughout the relationship, at an unclear, basically undefined, and therefore inescapable impasse.

Why are many men so confused when they fall in love?

In *The Hite Report on Men and Male Sexuality*, many men describe being brought up to avoid discussing their emotional lives, and their surprise and emotional confusion when (usually in their teens or twenties) they do fall in love. Many picture a really "masculine" man as being in control of his emotions, rational and "objective" above all else—to the extent that they actually feel uncomfortable being "in love." There is an inherent contradiction for them between staying in control of their feelings and loving another person—which they fear may make them "weak," "soft," and vulnerable. Although men often enjoy being "in love" temporarily, basically many are uncomfortable and say that the sooner their less rational feelings are "gotten rid of," the better.

Thus men's ambivalence about love involves not only a desire for "freedom," but also grows out of a fear of their own feelings flooding over them—a fear that is often reinforced by parental injunction. Thus boys are often advised by their fathers (or even mothers): "Don't marry the first girl who comes along just because of your feelings. Others will come along later." Or: "Make the right decision, son. Don't let your feelings (sexual) carry you away," implying that it's "just sex," that a boy may let his first sexual feelings make him think he is in love. (Isn't he?) Or another frequent piece of advice reported by men: "Success is much more important. (There will always be women.)"

In other words, the ideology of masculinity deeply affects men's ability to love and be close. If a "real" man should be a tough, rugged, independent loner (like the Marlboro man), how can a man accept a relationship or marriage without feeling split: if a man "should" be independent, but is not (in fact, is married, in love, or in a relationship), how can he not feel constantly torn between his feelings of love for his wife/lover and his concern that he should be asserting his dignity as a "man," his independence? He may see the relationship as a constant test or threat to his "dominance" (only by having "dominance" in a love relationship can a "man" retain his masculinity . . .); a man should not become a "wimp" or be "dominated by a woman" if he falls in love. As one woman puts it, "Most single men appear to have deep fears about loving women. They fear that loving is not 'macho.' They can let a woman love *them*, but try to keep their own feelings in check, hold back. It's a wonder they don't all get sick more than they already do."

For all these reasons, perhaps the deepest love a man feels for a woman can also bring out his deepest hate or fear, because his love is threatening to his ideal of autonomy—perhaps he doesn't want to feel that connectedness, even if it feels *good*. A man may feel very conflicted if he interprets his feelings as dependency, neediness—even "weakness." In fact, according to *The Hite Report on Men*, most men say they did not marry the women they most deeply loved.

Thus, many men are trapped, tragically, in a kind of permanent isolation and aloneness by a system which offers them "dominance" (and says their only alternative is not equality, but "submission"!) in exchange for holding back their feelings, keeping their emotional lives in check, suffering loneliness as they attempt to judge every situation "rationally"—and wind up with no one to whom they can talk, really talk, about their feelings. Eventually, they often lose the women in their lives, too, who come to resent them and withdraw emotionally and sexually.

What Are the Values of "Women's" Culture?

"When I'm in love, I feel like I'm part of them—and they're part of me. If they're upset about something or if I do something they're upset about, it bothers me terribly until we can talk about it and resolve it.

Women's philosophy and "sub"-culture have been forged over the centuries by women's personal thoughts, their discussions with other women about their relationships, families, and inner feelings of love—and in their practical experience of what it takes to make a family function emotionally. Its values include working with others (rather than emphasizing competition), valuing friendship, listening with empathy,

311

not being judgmental, trying to bring out the best in others, nurture, not dominate.

One woman describes the qualities in "women's" "Weltan-schauung," way of looking at life, that she admires:

"I admire the quiet work of women, their defense of interpersonal peace—doing decent things when they don't get much credit for doing anything. I want to see women move into the world and rebuild the bridge between private spheres and public works, which was destroyed by industrialization. How about the hundreds of women going to graduate school in chemistry? Right on! I'd like to see private morality extended to the earth; I hope that women retain some of the knowledge they gained raising children and shoring up civilized human relationships when they are out in the dogfight."

Another describes the qualities in her sister that make her feel close, qualities she would also like to find in a man in a love relationship:

"The closest I feel to anyone is my sister—she's who I turn to in time of trouble. She doesn't try to solve my problems, just helps me sort them out and solve them myself. There is nothing I can't share with her, nor she with me. I feel good when we're together. I like best her total lack of making judgments about anyone or anything and the fact that she'll listen to anything I want to talk about."

And one woman says what almost all women say: how much easier it is to talk to other women:

"I am nineteen, white, a college student in Des Moines, Iowa. I am creative, angry, sensual, intelligent, and a great cook. I value love, respect, gentleness. Right now there are two people that I am closest to, one a woman, and one a man. The man is my lover, and although I am living with him and try to talk to him about everything, he doesn't understand some things very well. The woman is my best friend, and we talk about everything."

When asked what women contribute to the world, most women say that women are givers—women take care of humanity:

"Women in general care about others and work to make life better. They give of themselves."

"What things about women do I admire? Their marvelous human-ity, their genuine caring about people, their nurturing, sharing, gener-osity, willingness to give of themselves."

Women's descriptions of themselves frequently reflect characteris-tics of being a giving person, supportive:

"I derive much happiness from doing nice things for other people. It gives me a sense of purpose and makes me feel needed and wanted."

"I am a mother and a wife. I like to cook, garden, and enjoy nature. I have a deep concern for the welfare of others. I am creative and active. I love animals. I am a family person—all that I do is for my family and with my family. I want to go through life helping as many people as I can in a quiet way. What makes me happiest is watching my daughter grow and develop, and seeing and feeling the love within our little family unit. I feel the greatest love for my husband when he's holding our child."

Are women "better"?

By stressing the positive, nurturing qualities that women believe in, and that they are asking men to consider taking on, are we falling into the trap of saying that women's moral sense is superior to men's? No, we are not saying that women are, or have been, perfect, "saints" who love everyone, without a vicious bone in their bodies. However, the nurturing qualities that women have developed in the home may be more appropriate, in fact the needed antidote for the emphasis on aggression that has come to characterize the dominant "male" system.

Although we are not saying that women are inherently "better" than men, women do have a right to be proud of their values and their philosophy—which they have worked very hard to refine. In this study, women are seen subscribing to a belief in the importance of caring about the feelings of others, a philosophical system based on the primacy of human relationships and cooperation. This is not dissimilar to what women seem to have said in psychologist Carol Gilligan's study, *In a Different Voice*, in which attachment and bonding emerge as the basis of women's moral sense. Women should be respected for this system, not put on the defensive.

Women have worked out their philosophy in the area of love and family relationships because this has been the traditional area of women's primary concern: if men have been urged to go out and succeed in the world, women have been urged to succeed in personal relationships and having a family. Women's speculations are no less dense or profound because they are focused on love or relationships, instead of "abstract" discussions of "politics." The moral and strategy issues are essentially the same.

Women's thinking about relationships is leading women to ask deeper questions about the nature of society

Women at this time in history are thus staging a very complex debate over whether or not they will continue to define love as their primary focus or their primary role in their lives in the future, how they should deal with "male" attitudes and the compromises they are often expected to make, whether men should learn to change their focus to be more involved with love, or whether women should find other parts of life more interesting, stop being "overly concerned" with men and love, and see the rest of life as more important.

Women Are Faced with an Historic Choice

Women are under great pressure now to give up their traditional values, as redefined over recent years, and to take on "male" values, not be "overly focused on love." But most women, after the attempts of the last ten to twenty years to "have sex like men" (not connect sex to emotions or a "relationship") and to "feel less," "love less," have not found these ways of life satisfying. Most women feel uncomfortable taking on these values; they feel they cannot live this way and maintain their own integrity, be true to themselves.

Moreover, even when women, despite their preference for their own value system, accede to the pressure to take on "male" values, and *do* act in a "male" style (stop nurturing), men often berate them for it. Some women are caught in a no–win situation: no matter what they do, they are put down. This has made many women do a lot of thinking about what can be done to change things.

As women run up against the male gender system time and time again in their relationships, trying to break through, make real contact, they begin to ask themselves deeper questions about the "male" system and why men behave as they do. In other words, the pain in their personal lives with men they love leads many women to think about *why* love is so difficult—and then to ask themselves a whole spectrum of questions.★

★ Women's re-thinking now is going on at the same time as women are also drastically changing their economic situation. Within the last ten years, the number of women taking jobs and starting businesses has escalated so rapidly that in fact women as a group are no longer dependent on men: although most women still have relatively low salaries (and day care is expensive), more women than ever have enough resources to make it on their own, even if only minimally. The consequences of this large-scale change will obviously be enormous and are as yet only in the beginning stages.

As women try to figure out relationships, they often start by questioning themselves, asking themselves if *they* are doing anything wrong; then they may try to figure out the psychological make-up of the men in their lives—a man's individual psychological background. This often then leads a woman to look at the structure of her lover's family, his parents' relationship—and finally, to look at the overall social structure, the whole system and how *it* got that way. Asking themselves so many questions about themselves and the men in their lives thus leads women to think deeply about the whole culture—and, frustrated with their relationship with men, often also to become angry and frustrated with the society itself.

It is not simply by chance that we look at the basic values of our society here through the lens of personal relationships.* Rather, it is in fact essential to look at the fundamental beliefs of our society as they exist within individuals, and in relationships between two people, because it is individuals and these very relationships that form the building blocks of our social system: the way we form relationships with others IS the social structure. It is the way we build governments, corporations, the structure of work and home—everything. Without examining these basic beliefs and conflicts about how relationships are made, what they are at the deepest level, we cannot possibly unravel what is going on with our society on a "macro" level, e.g., in domestic politics or international relations.

As women struggle with men to change the whole aura and understanding of relationships, they are pitting themselves against the entire "male" system. The result of this struggle will determine the values and direction of the culture for the foreseeable future.

Could the "female" or "love" value system (the family value system) disappear?

If women give up love as a basic value (since women have carried this "home" or "love" value system more than men), will love/family disappear as a way of life? And are millions of women now waging an inner struggle over whether they should do just that—urged on by the constant attack on and ridicule of "women's values," plus the fact that continuing these loving (defined as "giving") patterns, being "givers," doesn't "get them anywhere"? Almost all the "liberal" media are urging women to stop being so "feminine," to get "smart," be more aggressive, be more like men. If they were to do so, this could mean the complete

---

* Men's views of these relationships can be found in *The Hite Report on Men and Male Sexuality*.

victory of the "male" ideology. But will men like this victory? Will it be good for society—or will life become harsher, more unfriendly, and the world a less hospitable place in which to live?

This is the point of the revolution we are at now, a turning point, in effect. Will women go along with the "male" emotional value system, making competition and coldness (staying "in control") their watchwords, since they are so ridiculed for being too "emotional"? Or will women, somehow, manage to keep their tradition of nurturing and warmth alive, even "underground," as a secondary culture, living bi-culturally: acting one way when they go to work, and another at home? Or will the set of values women have carried for so long be lost altogether? Do we care?

Seeing the World through New Eyes: the "Other" Transformed

Some women are beginning to express a new choice—to say that the choice is not simply between taking on "male" values and keeping "female" values, but that a third choice is for women to keep their own value system of believing in caring and nurturing as a way of life, but to change its focus. While most women still believe in loving and giving as a primary value system, something they admire in others too, many now question whether the best, the most important, expression of this loving and giving is or should be "being there" for a man.

Some women, while keeping their belief in love, are diversifying it, shifting its focus away from individual men who still don't see them as equals, and applying its emotional strength to a whole spectrum of relationships, even to work and politics. There is a difference between giving up on love relationships with men for the moment, while still keeping our belief in love, trust, and kindness as a basic way of life—and giving up on love by adopting cooler, more distant "male" values and behaviors.

As women, will we take with us our belief in love, giving, and understanding as we are more and more involved in the running of the "outside" world?

This is a turning point for the culture, a historical moment. Most of the pressure is (as always) on women to change. Will men see that a new direction is possible for them? Will women push for their own beliefs, their own value system, or will we decide that changing society

316

or even our own relationship is too difficult, and settle back into the "male" superstructure?

In effect, to reassess one's idea of love and how one expresses it, how one defines it, and whom one should choose to love, is to call for a complete re-evaluation of the culture and its world view. All of these issues are interconnected: by working on/improving/solving some of our problems in "love"—its meaning, and especially seeing how it is often destroyed by the emphasis for men on competition and "winning"—by taking these issues seriously, we can solve some of our political and economic problems as well, and create a more positive framework for society.

Friendships between Women: A Different Value System

Women describe their friendships with other women as some of the happiest, most fulfilling parts of their lives. Eighty-seven percent of married women have their deepest emotional relationship with a woman friend, as do 95 percent of single women. These relationships are extremely important—a frequently "unseen" backdrop to women's lives that is nevertheless as solidly "there" for them as the air. Women rely on each other, knowing they can, in moments of crisis, or just for daily emotional nourishment and fun—being alternately children, mothers, sisters, and pals to each other, sometimes all on the same day. There are moments of letdown, even betrayal, but these are the exception, not the rule. And yet it is expected that women will consider their friendships to be much less important than love relationships with men, or, especially, marriage.

Women Love Their Friendships with Other Women

Ninety-four percent of women speak of very close and important friendships with other women:

"I have lots of wonderful women friends. After I broke up with Dave, I threw a 'Girls' Club Party' for girls only, with champagne, pastries, and all kinds of beauty aids—facials, henna, manicures, everything. It was to thank all the great girls in the world."

"Women are the most important people in my life. My close relationships with women have kept me going where all else failed."

"She was my first true love, and my most important. Knowing her helped me find myself."

"I think close friendships turn you into a higher being. You want to excel, live up to others' expectations, develop higher expectations of yourself. The worst thing that somebody can do to me is not to give me credit for what I can do (be non-supportive) or bore me. That is something that my close friends never do."

318

Women's descriptions of their friends brim over with warmth, admiration, and affection; the overwhelming majority of women when they describe their friends express feelings of great enthusiasm and happiness:

"We do a lot of talking and laughing. I like her honesty, and sense of the humor and irony of life. She's non-judgmental. She has helped me through difficult times, just by being there for me to talk to, by listening and caring. With her, I feel like myself. I have an identity that feels right."

"My best friend listens but does not condemn, accepts me as I am. Usually what we do together is meet for lunch or dinner, drinks, talk for hours at her house or mine. I feel her presence, comfort without words, total understanding even if I don't understand, miss her when we don't get together."

"She is my age, we are in an all-women's college. She is very supportive and a very good listener—not at all selfish, very funny and attractive. We go out for coffee, just sit and talk—or we choose some really different place to go and just do it. She is very spontaneous, and we share a lot of laughs. I always feel thrilled to see her—of all of my friends, I love and respect her the most and no matter what different paths we take—we always have things to say to each other."

"My best woman friend is someone who I know would operate in my best interests, and support my point of view in my absence. Together we enjoy everyday life, talking, mostly, or rehashing our views as to the nature of this existence. We have made a pact that regardless of whether we are in a relationship with a man, we will always have time for each other."

"We have been friends for thirteen years. She's smart, but not academically educated. She knows me like a book, I can never fool her. She makes me aware of things about myself I don't even realize, she makes me think but won't solve my problems for me. When we are together we talk for hours. When we are together for the first time after a long while, I feel like there is a strong bond between us, yet there are also many things that have changed."

"My best woman friend is vivacious, talented, humorous, full of energy, insightful, aggressive, and interested in my well-being. We see each other less now that she has a baby, but we still make a point of talking several times a week."

"She's helped me through many crises and is the first person I turn to for support and/or advice. She is the woman I've loved the most. When we spend time together, I usually hang out at her home so we can enjoy all our kids together (she has four daughters). We also make a point to spend time alone, without kids—we'll take a day and just take off—go out for lunch, shop a little, walk around town checking out art shops and talking—mostly talking. That's what's best about it. We're able to talk about anything and everything."

"We have been friends for twenty-nine years. She is the mother of two daughters and stepmother to two more, plus she has a career (finance). She progressed from being just another paper pusher to being head of her department. What I like most about her is her willingness to listen when others talk. Although she has her own opinions, she hears the other person out first, before offering her viewpoint."

Why Are Women So Happy with Their Women Friends?

Emotional empathy and subtle communication between women

"We always know what the other one is feeling."

Ninety-two percent of women say it is easier to talk to other women than to most men:

"Women feel a common bond for each other and relate better to each other's problems. My husband takes everything like a personal threat to his security. I couldn't tell him anything I tell my best friend."

"It is easier to talk to women than to men. (Some women, and some men.) On the whole, women understand more, can relate more, and aren't squeamish about details. We offer help to each other because we can talk more easily, and the encouragement often makes us stronger individuals. We care more and love more, and aren't afraid to show it to our women friends. Men can be good friends too, but they just don't seem to understand the *human* side of feelings by putting themselves in the other person's shoes like women do. I think the statement is both sad and true. It's healthy to have a close female friend that one can talk to about anything, but your husband should be your best friend too, someone you can share anything with. It seems those couples whose marriages last and are happy are the ones who are each other's best friends."

"I find it easier to talk to women because men hide behind logic when an emotional response is what is needed. We all need someone to laugh with us, feel happy with us, and cry with us. If I could talk to my husband and he to me as my best friend does, we would have a super-hot thing."

"It is easier to get through to women. It is easier to reveal your emotions to women. Men are not close to their own feelings, so they have difficulty when it comes to interacting with women who have their guards down."

"The thing I like best about Jane is that I can talk to her about absolutely anything under the sun. Nothing shocks or surprises her. Jane's listened to me talk through tons of difficult times, fights with my folks, my separation from Keith—his stay in the hospital. I've helped her think through a long-drawn-out divorce, her relationship (now two years old) with her subsequent lover, and the recent death of her father. We always have a good time when we're together. We're free to be ourselves no matter how good or bad we may feel, and then all of our problems don't seem so bad."

Women have developed among themselves a way of relating that makes it possible to have intensely close relationships, to share intricate inner thoughts, and to have a large repertoire of feelings expressed and understood. How women talk together is different from how women and men talk together, in most cases. Women have a special communication with each other which is more detailed, more involved in searching out, listening for and hearing the other's inner thoughts—working together to explore the feelings one is trying to express.

Women's friendships: often emotionally closer than love relationships with men

Over and over, women say that their friendships with other women are more open and spontaneous, that it is easier to talk, that women are rarely judgmental, are good at listening and giving feedback, and that this is helpful in thinking through problems and ideas. When women describe these friendships, their tone of voice changes, lightens up and sounds freer.

Women are each other's basic support systems, whether single or married. Throughout their work, their achievements, their major decisions, difficult times, and changing relationships, women are being cheered on, encouraged and believed in by their friends.

Here the dynamics of women's caring and giving work to women's advantage: women do not wind up feeling drained, since the support is mutual. The giving is not taken advantage of, considered "soft" or "weak." The idea of any given conversation is to understand and help draw out the other person, not (as in some "male" interpersonal patterns) to "judge," decide if the other person is "right," or win the point. Most women are more receptive and give more "acknowledging" feedback: "I heard you and understand what you are saying."

Is it harder to "talk to" a male lover because there is more vulnerability in a love relationship than a friendship? Or is it easier to talk to women because women are less competitive, prefer to be supportive? While it is true that love relationships are more intense and demanding—"I think the quality of love I give this man I am in love with is much more selfish and demanding than that I give to women," as one woman says—the fact that women believe that the basic role of a friend or lover is to listen and understand, not dominate or judge, goes much further in explaining why more men also say women are their best friends, rarely other men. In fact, most married men say that their wives are their best friends—but most married women, as just seen, say they only wish their husbands could be their best friends.

Most men, as they explain in *The Hite Report on Men and Male Sexuality*, when they need someone to talk to, turn to women as friends, not to men. Ninety-three percent of men in *The Hite Report* say that after school they do not have a close male friend; 89 percent of those over age twenty-five say that their best friend is a woman, or, in fact, their wife. Men rarely turn to other men for friendship—to have close friends they can talk to. This clearly indicates that women's way of relating is preferred by both women and men when they want a close companion to trust, talk to, and be open with.

Why, then, is so much fun made of women's being enthusiastic, non-combative, talking with their friends? Why are women put on the defensive, their conversations referred to as "gabbing away" and "girl talk"? This is merely the dominant ideology proclaiming itself superior—when in fact the dominant ideology relies on this very talk and enthusiasm *from* women, counting on women to be non-aggressive, "loving," and caring—to give men emotional support.

Women believe listening and supporting the other person is one of the basic ways in which love is shown; they feel it is inappropriate to be competitive, distant, or not tuned in emotionally (mentally absent?) in a personal relationship. Many women have developed skills in observing and tuning in to the inner thoughts, wavelengths of others, whether male or female. This skill is one of the great cultural resources of our society. However, this skill can be very dangerous for women individually when used in a non-equal relationship—one in which they are not getting

322

their emotional or intellectual needs met in return, i.e., the man is "starring" in the relationship, with the woman as the non-listened-to supporting cast.

Women say their friendships with each other do not leave them feeling drained, as do many of women's relationships with men, even when quite emotionally involved. Women's ideology works well when it is in contact with other women, because, while women's "giving" is met in many men with a "men have the right to take" attitude, in a relationship with another woman the two "givings" work to mutual advantage. In other words, "giving" to other women works, because women are "giving" back.

Even class or "marital status" differences among women are not as difficult to overcome as gender divisions: women say they can still talk to other women with more ease and feeling of acceptance, being "heard," than they can to most men, including the men they love/who love them the most.

This style of listening without judgment, "being there" emotionally, registering having "heard" and understood another person, can serve as a new model for men's relationships with women, and with each other. Just as women have made major shifts in their lives in the last ten years, men too can with great benefit make shifts in their personal lives by learning these new attitudes.

Talking about men: are women "using" their friends, or trying to understand another culture?

While most women enjoy telling and hearing from their friends about what is going on in their love relationships, 22 percent complain that their friends talk "too much" about their love lives or "boyfriend":

"What I've always disliked about women friends is their constantly talking about their involvement with men. It bothered me that we didn't talk enough about our *own* plans and problems."

Of course, there are many more ambivalences and interesting dynamics, difficulties and jealousies, between women friends than there is space to discuss here; see the special issue of Women's Studies International Forum, "Rethinking Sisterhood: Unity in Diversity," edited by Renate Duelli Klein, vol. 8, no. 1 (Oxford: Pergamon Press, 1985), and Janice Raymond, *A Passion for Friends: Toward a Philosophy of Female Affection* (Boston: Beacon Press, 1986).

Women and Power: We May Love Our Women Friends, But Do We Take Them Seriously?

"I've never spent much time hating any woman for long (except my mother for periods). I am easier with women. Does that mean that along with the rest of the world, I don't take them seriously enough?"

Do we think women are as important as men? As powerful?

Sometimes women say they feel hurt if their friends take the men in their lives more seriously—or put men first, just because they are "men":

"I'd never do what my friends do to me: plan something with me weeks in advance, but if their boyfriend asks them somewhere, break our plans. For instance, my one friend who is married, she planned to go to a show with me two weeks in advance. Two nights before the show I called her and asked her what night for sure she wanted to go, Friday or Saturday. She nonchalantly says, 'Oh, me and my husband are going to that show Friday.' No mention of me at all. I was left out in the cold. I know he's her husband and that's great, but the least she could have done was ask me to join them. She didn't. Before she was married she wanted to go to a show with me, and he wouldn't *let* her! That's too possessive."

"She always waits for me to call, and makes no plans for us to spend time together anymore. I think she thinks that once you have a guy or are married, everything is different."

"She has a boyfriend, so we don't do anything together. All my friends are married or have boyfriends, so I don't do much of anything with any of them anymore except talk on the phone once in a while."

"I really hate to say this (or I should say, I feel guilty about saying this) but I can't stand a woman who wants nothing out of life except to find a man who'll sweep her off her feet to servility and baby making. What's strange about this is that one of my closest friends is this way. We've been friends since sixth grade, before feminism was part of my vocabulary."

Eighty-three percent of women complain that their mothers and fathers brought them up to think less of themselves than of the men around them, to mentally serve and wait on men:

"My mother certainly did show me how to be 'feminine': don't be tough, don't be strong, be 'nice,' polite, passive, assume you are wrong and everyone else is right. Always put others' needs before your own. Oh, and it's an absolute duty to be as pretty as possible."

"I felt from as long as I can remember that my brother was treated more generously, lovingly, and unequivocally than I. While I remained the class honor student, he was not penalized for getting C's (although his IQ was tested as the same as mine). The rules he had to keep were more relaxed. He was given money for 'owning' pigs and cows, which was a kind of pay for his hours spent in the fields with my father (and he *did* truly work). But I worked also, just as many hours! During those years my mother worked outside the home, I did the majority of the housework and often cooked midday dinners for as many as a dozen farm helpers at harvesting times (I was twelve and thirteen). My work was not rewarded with the ownership of animals: I had no money. I deeply resented my brother and always felt my mother did not understand that. My mother did not think that my daydreams could come true. Her lack of faith in me and amused (not exactly cruel) attitude toward my ambitions made me very angry. I often had fits of shouting about it and consoled myself in my bedroom listening to the radio."

"My mother is much more loving and kind to my brother than she ever was to me. She prefers him. Many times she won't send me a birthday or Christmas present because she says she wants to get him something really special. She's got a blind spot where he's concerned. I just always knew that boys were more special."

Most women hate it when they see women giving men more respect than other women:

"I admire women who can love other women and not be ingratiating with men. I hate women who have split personalities—one for their women friends and one for their men friends. I admire a woman who loves who she is and doesn't try to live up to someone else's expectations."

Fear of the power of the "male" system

"I really think something has to be said about this. This has to be stopped—I mean, women's trashing of each other when they feel they have to choose between hanging on to a man's shirttails and ditching their women friends and women they work with. We are afraid of men. We are afraid that they will hurt us, fire us, say bad things about us—or if it's personal, not love us, call us names, and so on. But why should we apply a double standard to men?—we let them trash us and then we treat them nice, but with women, we would never do that. We are sucking up

325

to men's power when we do this, not standing up for ourselves. It's only natural to be afraid of power that can hurt—but it's something we've got to fight. We've got to be brave. We can beat this system if we just stand up to it—and love each other, be loyal, don't ever let each other down if we are right."

Most women's only real complaint about their women friends, whom they frequently admire in every other way, is that they can be "wimps" in the face of possible male disapproval:

"My friend is great—except sometimes in the face of male authority."

"What my friend does that I like the least is not to be frank about her feelings if she thinks they'll be offensive or negative to men."

"My best friend—I love her sense of wit, her truth to her own values, and her loyalty. She's just, unfortunately, wimpy in the face of men when we're together in groups."

"Women love, they suffer without blame, they are patient to a fault. But I dislike their lack of self-esteem and their belief that they are not at least equal if not superior to men. Through this belief they are taught early to play games, and use sex to get what they need. However, they deserve it without having to do this."

Fifty-eight percent of women say that they sometimes find their friends afraid to "challenge" or openly disagree with men's ideas or anti-woman remarks in public—or find that their friends are afraid to take the lead in conversation, state forcefully their opinions, etc., in groups. In other words, many women are still hesitant to act in a non-subservient manner in public situations—i.e., "challenge" male "dominance" (being in charge) publicly. (And women have testified amply to their often well-justified reasons, i.e., men's reactions.)

Noble thoughts and extreme transcendence—men only?

Do we take women's and our own intellectuality seriously? As one woman says, meaning to praise her friend, "I find her wise and strong. She likes to talk about deep things." What does this mean? In a man, would "deep thinking" be considered a philosophical-intellectual personality? But in a woman, does it somehow have the flavor of an "earth mother" connection—i.e., related to a biological "nature" or "inner wisdom"—rather than the "pure intellectuality" of men?

Can We Trust Women's Power Yet? Are We Strong Enough?

Are we strong enough economically and socially now to stand in for male "power figures" with each other? Can we trust our power yet?

As one woman puts it, "I'm twenty-three. Women my age have taken to assimilating male behaviors because we basically think they are better. We've been raised to look up to men and naturally try to 'mirror' them. Like, I repeat, how I want to be single and on my own, I act like I am emotionally 'in control' most of the time—but do I really feel that way? Or am I just watching football because it makes me look uncool not to like it?"

If women try to join "male" culture—since it has the prestige and is the dominant one ("if you can't lick 'em, join 'em")—will this solve our problem, get us status? No, because we will still not be men, we will only be ratifying the "male" system by our behavior. (Therefore, do we have to "win," "dominate" with *our* culture, just to get "equality"?)

Since men have more economic and political power than we do, don't we still have to keep our ties with this system, no matter how we are treated? As Connie Ashton-Myers puts it, "Can any woman seriously question an assertion that her status ultimately depends on her pleasing, in one way or another, a male or set of males in control of some social institutions, from the multinational corporation to the smallest nuclear family? And this arrangement has been perpetually nurtured and reinforced within the patriarchal family."*

There is such a thing as a legitimate fear of male power. Can we separate understanding men from copping out, fearing them—and save our integrity, our dignity, our value system? The challenge is to continue our valid feelings of love and still devise a way of facing down the system.

Are we afraid to challenge male power?

"Every little girl is told to be a good girl!! Be nice! *Don't make waves!!!* That is what it means basically."†

* She continues: "How has [patriarchy] persisted? It functions with the cooperation of women themselves who today strike bargains similar to those struck in prehistoric times . . ." Connie Ashton-Myers reviewing Gerda Lerner's *The Origins of Patriarchy* (New York: Oxford University Press, 1986), in Coordinating Committee for Women in the Historical Profession newsletter, vol. 17, no. 1 (February 1986).
† In Russia, girls are given a similar message; girls who show overly "independent" or rowdy behavior may find themselves sent for a stay in a labor camp for girls with "wayward" behavior (Desmond Smith, *Smith's Moscow* (New York: Knopf, 1976).

We may not be afraid anymore to live our own way, by our own rules. But do we still fear challenging "male" dominance in society? This would not be surprising, we may fear confronting men or male power directly—with good reason. However, in the past hundred years, when we did work together, we *did* win such things as the right to vote, equal employment legislation, and we were almost able to pass the Equal Rights Amendment to the Constitution, which may now be won in the 1990s.

Can women be power centers in society now? Can we trust each other enough? Will we stand up for each other?

Do we take our relationships with other women seriously enough now to use them as a power base, a form of solidarity?* This is a question which affects all of our futures, and the status of women for generations to come—because if we can't take each other as seriously as we take men, then we will not have the solidarity to change things. Respecting each other, we will be much more powerful.

But if we can't count on our friends in public, if we see them bow to "male" power in public, how can we respect them? And we may feel we too must hide our thinking, continue existing on two levels, knowing the dominant "reality" and also knowing our interior thoughts about it, but rarely voicing those thoughts or doing anything to change the system. Because, beneath it all, we feel we have to continue to respect/fear men who run the system too much.

As one woman describes this feeling in herself, and coming out of it, "I used to feel like I had to be 'nice' all the time (I hate to admit it, but especially to men) until one day I caught a glimpse of myself in a mirror, being kind of obsequious and fawning. From that moment on, I decided to be me, even knowing full well that I would not be as attractive—or 'non-threatening'—to men. But I just didn't have a choice, and still be able to live with myself."

The "male" ideology has tried to breed in us a form of passivity, especially in public situations. For example, if we voice an opinion, we may be seen as trying to "dominate" the situation, or the men present. (However, if we are silent, we may be seen as "wimpy"!) It may be hard for us to speak out and make our thoughts part of the

---

* As a woman in the documentary film *Bread and Roses* put it, after organizing women garment workers in the 1920s, "We weren't just nice girls anymore; we were vigorous people who wanted to change society."

world when we are taught that men's thoughts are more "profound." We are frequently discouraged by men from stating our views, told not to "challenge" the status quo in even the smallest way, by being reminded how men hate "ballsy," "aggressive" women. We become, unconsciously, "man pleasers," and change our behavior around men so as not to be "outspoken," or seem to challenge them—i.e., so the man can be (or seem to be) the leader, dominant.

Most of the time we tell ourselves, what does it matter anyway? I can get my way, or get my point across, another way. (And so, women are "rewarded" by being called "manipulative.") In other situations, we go along with the system because it can be fun—i.e., in a "dating" situation, going out to dinner, letting the man invite us, take us, etc.

Another reason for our reticence, in addition to male pressure not to be "aggressive," "strident," or "nagging" (!), is that many women have a fundamental desire for more grace in life, less hostility and competition. If the only way to have that, part of us says, is not to speak up around men, not to "challenge" men's touchy "dominance," so be it. But this brings us back to the philosophical dilemma of how to handle aggression without being overrun.

We have seen that women are fighting for their values in personal relationships; however, the less aggressive patterns of the "female" philosophy may not be automatically suited to "win" against an aggressive ideology such as the "male" system. This has been a persistent problem for women, or indeed for any society which is more peace-loving, or does not at times have the capacity to defend itself. For example, Poland, which refused to maintain a great standing army although the other countries of Europe were building theirs, was, as a result, partitioned three ways in the late eighteenth century.

How much "aggression" is good as a personal quality? Do we want to change this part of our value system? Women, especially women "at home," or "mothers," have been called "wimpy," but this is in part a "male" ideological view of the "peacemaker" role women have had—in fact, the role women often see as part of their idealism, their honor. Most women in this study believe women's interpersonal values of nurturing, listening, sharing, enthusiasm, non-aggression, and caring should be preserved. And that this is quite different from being "wimpy," even in the face of "male" power. If Gandhi and Martin Luther King could practice non-violent resistance, so women feel that they can too—in fact, feel that they have been doing so for far longer. What forms of resistance are appropriate for us in our situation?

Being Proud of Each Other and Supporting Each Other: The Key to Changing Our Status

When asked the most important advice they could give other women now, women frequently say to love and respect each other and ourselves:

"My advice to women? Love yourself and each other, the rest will come."

"Open your eyes. Value your women friends, love yourself and each other first. Don't be afraid to be strong and define *yourself*. We are great!"

"Love yourself, be active to help this world become a place in which you want to live. But enjoy the means of doing so, don't just live anticipating the future."

"Make sure you always have a support group of women. Women are bright and strong and emotionally expressive, loving and motivated. They have a fullness men lack."

Do we take our friends seriously enough to write them into our wills? One woman, at least, takes a female relative this seriously:

"The most important relationship with a woman in my life is with my youngest sister. She is the beneficiary of my will and I feel she will give my possessions the most thoughtful consideration in disposal."

Others say that women must help other women professionally:

"I had a mentor relationship with a woman who chose me as her successor as a Symphony Guild president. She spent great amounts of time grooming me for the position, and at the same time she had in me someone with whom to share her frustrations. I continue to feel great warmth toward her and feel that she truly cares about me as an individual. Because she is very busy with her job and with a difficult family situation, we have lunch only a couple of times a year now. Still, I have enormous gratitude toward her for believing I had the potential for leadership at a time I did not know it, and she partly did it by expressing her own self-doubts to me and seeking my advice—treating me as an equal before I actually felt equal. Eventually, she and I and a couple of other women who were equally willing to accept major responsibilities in the volunteer sector (leading to major business positions) became a kind of elite group in our small city. We are not intimate friends but have great respect for one another and feel a closeness and concern about one another's continued self-realization (including in emotional ways)."

But other women complain that, while women are good as friends, they generally don't have enough knowledge of the world to give practical advice, or offer "connections"—therefore women can't be taken as seriously:

"What's missing in my women friends is that I have no mentor. I don't need a role model. I make my own role, but there is no one that has similar experience, there is no one who has done what I've done and can clue me in or encourage me, or give me ideas. All my friends are younger—much different, or at earlier stages of their lives. They have sympathy, empathy, but no concrete help."

One woman puts down women who have these negative attitudes to women, who do not support other women, and calls them "male-identified":

"Some women don't bond with each other, or worry about women's issues—they want to be 'smart,' and compete in 'serious,' traditional 'men's' areas, the 'real world' . . . they are brainwashed. They are male-identified. They don't see that the point is to make/reveal the larger world—that women's thoughts are just as valid."

Women now *do* support each other, more and more, as we have seen here: over 80 percent of all women have their closest emotional relationship with another woman.

This is not to say, of course, that all the women we know are perfect, that *we* are perfect, that all the women we know are our friends, or that all the women we meet have all the wonderful, nurturant qualities described here. And yet, even with women who can snap and be condescending, we have much more in common than we might wish; the shared experience of being a woman in a gender-oriented society creates a strong underlying bond—if not always respect. Many women are still male-identified in their thinking about other women, and may take out their general frustrations on women as the weakest, most convenient target, the safest, the least threatening group to be aggressive against.

One woman describes this commonality she shares with her mother through all the ambiguity, "I identify more with my father because he has always had a job and I do too; I want to be more like him than I want to be like my mother. But my mother I can talk to in a way I never could my father. She is always there for me—not on every level, but for bottom line survival, I *know* she is there. She is the one I turn to when I've got to be *sure*."

We offer each other a great reservoir of strength for all kinds of purposes in our lives. We must not be ashamed of the love we bear for one another. By respecting each other, putting each other first, recognizing who we are, we will change our status.

Toward a New Vision of Sexuality

Female Eroticism: What Was Women's Sexuality Originally Like?

What would women's sexuality be like without a society to shape it? Do we know? Women in the first Hite Report asserted that women have a right to "undefine" sexuality, to redesign it individually; that we have a complete right to say "no" to sex; and that we may not really know yet what "female sexuality" is.

Is sex basically "intercourse"—or an individual vocabulary of activities? *The Hite Report on Female Sexuality* in 1976 argued for undefining sexuality*—both the physical "acts" that we define as "sex" and the cultural atmosphere surrounding "sex." Sex could become an individual vocabulary of activities, chosen to show how we want to express ourselves at a given time, with a specific feeling and meaning—an individual choice of activities, not always necessarily "foreplay" followed by "vaginal penetration" (why not call it "penile covering"?) and intercourse, ending with male orgasm.

The Judeo-Christian tradition has had a very narrow idea of what "sexuality" should be, mostly relating to reproductive activity. It spelled out, both in the Bible and in rabbinical and papal encyclicals, how often one should have coitus, with whom, when, and so on—thus certainly giving the impression that coitus is the central act of "sex," and that it is, furthermore, the central connecting point, the nexus, between the two genders—their most important relationship. Interestingly, the Bible does not speak of female orgasm, only male orgasm. Is this because it is only male orgasm which is necessary for pregnancy and reproduction?

---

* In other words, *The Hite Report* stated that what we think of as "sex" is not a biological given, but an historically and culturally created phenomenon. Much ridicule was heaped on this idea by parts of the popular press at the time—and again when it was reiterated in *The Hite Report on Male Sexuality* in 1981.

Undefining Sex: An Individual Vocabulary

While women, as documented over and over in *The Hite Report on Female Sexuality*, may love having intercourse with men they want to have intercourse with, orgasm or no orgasm—the idea that one *must* have intercourse, that this *must* be one of the activities when you caress a person, does not make for spontaneous expression or freedom of desire, an open way of translating feelings into actions. And as long as the "male" ideology persists, and sees women as "scores" or mothers, the atmosphere around physical pleasure will not change. We will not be free to discover and feel, design new types of sexuality that celebrate the richness of the whole spectrum of what "female sexuality" and "male sexuality" can be all about.

We still haven't undefined sex enough to permit an individual redefinition of sexuality—or is it that we haven't changed social conditions enough yet to allow ourselves to feel free enough to do this?

As this was summed up in *The Hite Report on Female Sexuality*: "Although we tend to think of 'sex' as one set pattern, one group of activities (in essence, reproductive activity), there is no need to limit ourselves in this way. . . . Our definition of sex belongs to a world view that is past—or passing. Sexuality, and sexual relations, no longer define the important property right they once did, children are no longer central to the power either of the state or the individual. Although all of our social institutions are still totally based on hierarchical and patriarchal forms, patriarchy as a form is really dead, as is the sexuality that defined it. We are currently in a period of transition, although it is unclear as yet to what . . ."★

Can women, even now, define sex on their own terms?

If understanding our own bodies well enough to know how we have orgasms and not be inhibited from telling this to men is a "sexual revolution"—and in fact, it is a profound change from the days in which, after sex, a woman would go into the bathroom and close the door and masturbate—still, the fact is that almost every man with whom a woman has sex continues to expect that sex will center on intercourse/penetration—almost as his automatic "right." Although many men now understand most women's need for clitoral stimulation, still, generally most men continue to see "penetration" and

---

★ *The Hite Report on Female Sexuality* (New York: Dell, 1977), p. 527.

intercourse/coitus as the only "real" definitions of sex. This is not to say that women don't enjoy these activities, but that the focus on these activities, their glorification over all others by society, is as much a matter of ideology as of physical desire.

And—Do Men Really Enjoy Their Definition of Sexuality So Fully?

Although it seems so obvious, do we know what "male sexuality" really is? After all, it is impossible for us to know exactly how much of what we see men do is "natural" "male sexuality" and how much is learned or reinforced behavior.

The current definition of "male sexuality" (as a driving desire for "penetration") is quite clearly culturally exaggerated. "Male sexuality" comprises a much larger, more varied group of physical feelings than what we call "male sexuality," which has been so narrowly channeled by the culture.

Surprisingly, when looked at more closely, the definition of "sexuality" put forth by the "male" ideology is actually quite negative. This is surprising because it is often thought that men are very "pro-sex," while women are "anti-sex." In fact, women are more pro-sensuality, most women think in terms of a much broader concept of sexuality than the reproductive model we have come to believe is "natural"—while the basic "male" ideology refers to sexuality as a "body function," an instinct, an "animal feeling" of pleasure—the "opposite" of spiritual feeling. In this value system, "animal feeling" is somehow not respectable, something "without soul" (animals in early Christian tradition did not have "souls")—brute "bestial behavior." While the point here is certainly not to say that sex must always be "sweet," not passionate, the idea of sexuality as completely cut off from feeling—sex as something "subhuman" that animals (who have no feelings?) do and therefore not part of our humanity, part of a whole person—is a rather strange definition of sexuality, and probably not the most erotic one we could espouse.

"For men—to be penetrated not only physically but emotionally . . ."

A part of the double standard not frequently cited is what may be an alienating pressure on *men* to have frequent sex, and to think and see the world in mostly compartmentalized sexual terms. In fact, the "male" ideology (and the life cycle it creates) robs men of the chance to enjoy love, by warning them against "confusing" a passionate attraction with "love," warning them against real closeness, saying "you can't trust women," "don't let your sex drive confuse you," and so on—stating that a "real man" should be "independent," remain "free" and unmarried for as long as possible, watch out for being "tied down." "Real men" should go after/want to have sex with as many women as possible, as often as possible. "Real men" don't fall head over heels in love. The result of all this training of men to control their feelings is that many men become alienated from their deeper feelings.

The re-invention of "male sexuality" was discussed in *The Hite Report on Male Sexuality*, with many men seeming to feel on a gut level that somehow they were missing out—that no matter how much sex they had, they were left feeling unsatisfied on some level. And yet our culture's lessons to men have been so strong that few men have been able to go past them, to create their own personal sexuality or to transcend the double standard. But a new sexuality and identity is certainly possible for men.

This is by no means to downgrade men's traditional "lust," but to redefine it: "Passion is one of the most beautiful parts of all sensuality—the desire to "possess, to take, to ravish and be ravished, to penetrate and be penetrated. But is physical love real love? While love is caring, love is also passion and desire, the desire to belong to, to mingle with, be inside of another. Part of love is a sheer physical feeling—a desire not only to have orgasm and 'sex,' but to lie close while sleeping together, to inhale the breath of the other, to press chests (and souls) together, so tightly, as tightly as possible; to lie feeling the other breathe as they sleep, their breath grazing your cheek and mingling with your own breath; to smell their body, caress their mouth with your tongue as if it were your own mouth, know the smell and taste of their genitals—to feel with your finger inside them, to caress the opening of their buttocks. What is love? Love is talking and understanding and counting on and being counted on, but love is also the deepest intermingling of bodies. In a way, body memory of a loved one is stronger and lasts longer than all the other memories."★

★ *The Hite Report on Male Sexuality* (New York: Ballantine, 1982), pp. 610–11.

Continuing Controversies Over the Nature of Female Orgasm: The Politics of Coitus

But haven't women made profound changes in their sexuality over the past years? In terms of the stimulation for orgasm, yes, to some extent. The idea that most women need some form of clitoral or exterior (non-vaginal) stimulation in order to orgasm, as documented in *The Hite Report* (1976), has now been accepted by women (and by gynecologists and counselors) on a large scale—both in the United States and in many other countries.

As early as the 1950s questions were raised about whether vaginal intercourse alone leads to orgasm for most women, in particular by Albert Ellis in his essay, "Is the Vaginal Orgasm a Myth?"[*] Another pioneer was Anne Koedt, who, in 1970, wrote "The Myth of the Vaginal Orgasm," an essay which was later published in the anthology *Radical Feminism.*[†] In Germany, in 1975, Alice Schwarzer published *Der Kleine Unterschied*, also attacking the idea that women should be expected to orgasm from simple vaginal penetration.

In 1973, Dr. Leah Schaefer published, as part of an earlier Ph.D. thesis done at Columbia with Margaret Mead and others, in-depth interviews with thirty women about their sexual feelings which demonstrated that it was more "normal" for women not to orgasm from simple coitus than "abnormal."[‡] In a psychological study published in 1972, Seymour Fisher,[§] although not describing this as "normal," stated that two-thirds of the women in his study said they could not orgasm during coitus per se (although they could in other ways), while one-third of them could. Dr. Fisher tried to connect this "ability" to orgasm with whether or not the women had been encouraged to achieve in general by their fathers—since, among all the variables, this was the only correlation he found. Finally, in *The New Sex Therapy*,[**] in 1974, Helen Singer Kaplan also questioned whether it is correct to label the large number of women who do not orgasm from coitus alone (but do orgasm in other ways) "abnormal."

The Hite Report on Female Sexuality, in research extending from 1971 to 1976 and including 3,500 women, found that two-thirds of women

[*] Albert Ellis and A. P. Pillay, eds., "Sex, Society and the Individual," *International Journal of Sexology* (1953), pp. 337–49.
[†] See Anne Koedt in Ellen Levine and Anita Rapone, eds., *Radical Feminism* (New York: Quadrangle, 1973).
[‡] Leah Cahan/Schaefer, *Women and Sex: Sexual Experiences and Reactions of a Group of Thirty Women as Told to a Female Psychotherapist* (New York: Pantheon, 1973).
[§] Seymour Fisher, *The Female Orgasm* (New York: Basic Books, 1972).
[**] Helen Singer Kaplan, *The New Sex Therapy* (Boston: Little, Brown, 1974).

do not orgasm from intercourse but orgasm easily in other ways—and went on to call into question, on the basis of women's statements, the definition of "sex" our culture has considered a biological given. *The Hite Report on Female Sexuality* also documented the many ways women have of reaching orgasm easily during self-stimulation (masturbation), saying that these stimulations should be included as part of what we call "sex," and considered as important and exciting as the activities which lead to male orgasms.

It is astonishing to see that even today Masters and Johnson classify women who can orgasm easily in other ways, but do not orgasm during simple "vaginal penetration," as having a "sexual dysfunction." Although they state that they believe clitoral stimulation is important for women's orgasms, they believe a "normal" woman should get enough "indirect" clitoral stimulation from simple intercourse (coitus) to lead to orgasm. They do not believe manual stimulation should be necessary."* They say this in the face of the evidence in *The Hite Report on Female Sexuality*† and other studies, evidence that intercourse alone is not enough stimulation for most women to orgasm. In fact, there is no point in labeling women "normal" or "abnormal," depending on whether they orgasm from "vaginal stimulation" or "clitoral stimulation."

It is interesting to speculate as to why Kinsey did not go into this subject, since it has been "common knowledge" for so long that "women have a problem" having orgasms during "sex"—i.e., intercourse/coitus—and that women could orgasm much more easily from clitoral stimulation or masturbation. However, aside from two or three oblique sentences, Kinsey does not address the topic. In private correspondence, however, it is said that he did discuss this matter, and that he believed clitoral stimulation by hand or mouth to be by far the easiest way for women to orgasm.‡ In other words, "Although the 'problem' had been known for some time, it was not until research was done for *The Hite Report on Female Sexuality*, and given a culturally related analysis, that the ideological misunderstanding of female sexuality was made clear, on the basis of scientific evidence," as Dr. William Granzig, past president of the American Association of Sex Educators, Counselors and Therapists, has put it.

The most advanced information presented recently has been the

* In 1986, Masters and Johnson published *The Art of Human Loving*, reiterating their earlier position, although they have done no survey work to back up their claims.
† This study has been replicated in Norway, Sweden, and Brazil, with the findings regarding orgasm being basically the same. A similar study was undertaken in England, also based on *The Hite Report* questionnaire, with the same basic findings.
‡ See also James Jones' forthcoming biography of Kinsey, done through use (among other sources) of the archives of the Kinsey Institute in Bloomington, Indiana.

anatomical drawings by illustrator Suzann Gage which show the interior clitoral system in detail.* One can begin to understand the anatomy of female sexuality much more fully through these drawings, which Freud would surely have appreciated; as he said, perhaps all his theories on female sexuality would turn out to be inaccurate, since the interior anatomy of women's sexual organs was not known at the time he was writing. We are still learning about this interior anatomy, especially the structures beneath the skin. The Gage drawings are available in *A New View of a Woman's Body*, the best source for information at present.

Reintegrating Sexuality and Spirituality: Toward a New Sexuality

In traditional Western ("male") philosophy and religion, the body has been seen as separate from the mind, soul, and, in consequence, "sex" has likewise been presented as without context (except that of conquest or reproduction?), its meaning removed from mutual expression of feelings, cut off from the rest of life.

For most women, however, this body/mind split hardly exists; for them the body and spirit are united and sex is inseparable from emotion. As one woman describes love, "Love is a longed-for feeling of unity, bliss, fulfillment. A strong feeling you feel for someone right from the beginning—a feeling of well-being all over. Sexual passion and the desire for a relationship are indistinguishable." And another: "I usually feel the closest after we make love, because it is an expression of all the wonderful and closest feelings I have towards her. When we make love, I feel as though we are a total entity—I can't tell where she leaves off and where I begin. It seems to be a 'complete' feeling, capturing my emotions, my intellect, and my physical awareness."

Thus most women feel that passion includes not only the body but also the mind and the emotions; when they speak here about a "passionate connection," they are not referring to just a feeling of lust. As one woman puts it, "There are more passionate and less passionate relationships. The passion is involved in every part of knowing the person, not just the sex. And many women, referring to a deeply passionate attraction when speaking of "falling in love," also include transcendent or spiritual feelings.

* See the anatomical drawings by Suzann Gage in essay on "Men and the Clitoris: A Moment in History," pp 190–1.

To try to downgrade this to "mere" lust is again a problem of language, reflecting the philosophical biases of Western history. The phrases we have to work with in English are "lust," "loving," "caring," and being "in love." But love as sexual desire, love as caring—are these really the categories women feel? Or are many women here describing passion as an intensity of the mind and body felt all at the same time in a kind of ecstatic mingling?

Some feminist philosophers* have questioned whether the mind/body split has ever existed for women. Certainly, the evidence of this study is that the majority of women—although, of course, they know the difference—do not feel such a split. Women often see and feel things "holistically"—i.e., as wholes, rather than dualistically, as the "male" ideology does. And this in spite of the fact that images reinforcing the "male" ideology's separation of sexual and motherly love are all around us, reflected particularly in the Eve/Mary split—the "good" woman and "bad" woman of the Judeo-Christian tradition;† "good women" are mothers, asexual (like Mary, who bore a child without having sex), and "bad women" are sexual and pleasure-seeking (those who "eat the apple of carnal knowledge" and "lead men astray"). Such stereotypes pervade popular slogans and motifs, and indeed women and even girls in high school, as seen in this study, are still continuously having to fight their effects, as boys treat them with disrespect during and after sex. And though girls and women themselves may interiorize these images and face a split identity, wondering which "type" they are before they are even old enough to know that they need not choose between pre-existing stereotypes, women continue to resist abandoning their own definition of passion.

As seen before, the "male" ideology implicitly holds that the way men do things is somehow "reality," "the real world," whereas how women do things is a "role." So, in this way of thinking, if women connect sex and feelings, this is a "role" they have been taught, one they should drop, not a "reality" or part of "nature." "Natural sex" is what men do—i.e., see no need to connect sex with emotional life. In fact, however, most people (men as well as women) probably experience a passionate attraction to someone, falling "in love," as both physical and emotional—although men in particular (but women, too, since the "sexual revolution") are encouraged to label these feelings "only physical," "just sex." But almost all women continue to hold that these

* See Alison Jaggar, *Feminist Politics and Human Nature* (Totowa, N. J.: Held, 1983), and unpublished papers presented before the Society of Women in Philosophy.
† During the Middle Ages, perhaps as many "bad women" as Jews during World War II were exterminated, in a concrete attempt to "cleanse" the world of "wicked women."

early feelings of attraction include both physical and emotional elements, that there is no way to separate them. This leads to the situation in which a woman, after a short time with a man, may say she is ready for an emotional relationship—whereas the man usually takes much longer to reach this conclusion.

Is women's connection of sex and feeling a "moralistic" holdover that keeps us from our "true hedonism," if not "repressed" by culture and religion? Or is it that the mind/body split in the area of love and sex has never fit human feelings or human experience? After all, men also say that sex is much better when you love someone (see *The Hite Report on Male Sexuality*)—although they would still feel comfortable having sex without feelings more often than women.

Actually, in the earliest civilizations, before the "Garden of Eden," sexuality may have been not only an individual behavior but also part of spirituality, religion, sometimes even part of religious rites; then reproduction and the feelings leading up to reproduction were seen, rightly, as part of the mystery of rebirth of life. Even in Greek times, the remnants or descendants of this early religion, the "Mysteries," included sexual/religious rites. In other words, some of the meanings of sexuality were probably once religious, related to the worship of reproduction, the sacredness of the re-creation of life.* Thus seen, women's resistance to separating sex and feelings may have an entirely different cast to it, as something with roots in the distant past—in a different philosophy. And it may presage a very different future.

* See Marija Gimbutas, *Goddesses and Gods of Old Europe* (Los Angeles: University of California Press, 1982). See also Colin Renfrew, ed., *The Monolithic Monuments of Western Europe* (London: Thames and Hudson, 1981).

Women Loving Women

Love Relationships between Women: Another Way of Life

Is there a difference in the way women in gay relationships define love, compared with the types of love we have seen so far?

This *is* a separate culture, and yet it is also, inevitably, influenced by the culture at large. Speaking of this, one woman in her twenties asks, "*Are* women better? There are women I meet who are like 'soul sisters'—and then there are those who are just like most men—cold, distant, unable to communicate, using people, not taking other people's feelings into consideration. Have a lot of us been co-opted by male views of power—power as necessary to make a relationship attractive? We don't have many alternate models. Still, intense and maybe over-analyzed as they have been, I think my relationships with women have been closer and more rewarding than any relationship I have ever had with a man. Maybe we're not perfect, but we're definitely onto something."

Another woman, in her fifties: "People in the women's movement said the problem with relationships is that men are so macho—i.e., they never apologize and they don't ask about feelings. So gay relationships should be a lot better, because both women have the same basic equality. Is it easier to get along? I would say yes. The best types of relationships are same-sex relationships, especially between women. They have the best chance in the world: they are more equal, and time together is much better quality. But even with all this going for them, there is no way that disputes won't come up. What you learn is to negotiate those disputes, and try to remain a team anyway. Women understand this better, the team concept. I could never have a relationship with anyone except a woman. I think that's the best way in the world to go."

341

Listening on another frequency

"The conversations with Anne-Marie would be so complete and involved—like 'Oh, this dinner we're going to, I have really mixed feelings about it. How do you feel about it?' And then we would speculate on our thoughts, talk about it. Or if we were having a fight, one of us would say, 'You're really taking advantage of me,' and then the other would say, 'Tell me why—explain to me how you feel about that—tell me what you mean, in depth,' and then she would listen to me for five or ten minutes—she might complain about what I said, but still she would listen. That's the relationship I had with her.

"I think that your identity develops through these discussions. Even though when you have two women together who are extremely introspective and always examining what's going on, it can be really too much, the constant questioning—still, it's great."

Is love between women different? More equal? Do women get along better together than female/male lovers? Or is this the wrong way to put it: is what we are looking at here a different culture, of which we should ask different questions?

One woman remarks, "I think this is a window on a world that most women have no conception of whatsoever—an all-woman culture."

A note on statistics
Eleven percent of the women in this study have love relationships only with other women. An additional 7 percent sometimes have relationships with women. One of the most surprising findings is the number of women over forty, most of whom were in heterosexual marriages earlier in their lives, now in love relationships with women for the first time. Sixteen percent of women over forty have love relationships only with other women, and 61 percent of women over forty now living with another woman, as lovers, were previously married. Of the total "gay" population, 31 percent are in relationships, 52 percent are living together, and 17 percent are single.

What is love?

"How do I love her now, after ten years? I love her mind, her body, her abilities. She's very brave and strong, exceptionally brilliant, and a beautiful woman."

"Our love feels like a stream that flows on and on, growing ever stronger and deeper, giving me a sense of peace and center. Her sense of humor always makes me laugh; her constancy and the knowledge that she is eminently dependable give me strength; the wonderful sparkle of my passion for her—the sense of joy in her just being there—is a daily joy for me. We live near each other, we sleep together, bathe together, wash each other's hair, and rub suntan lotion on each other. I love the warmth and intimacy of that. We sort of roughly share money, whoever has some shares—we're both poor. We generally tell each other everything—intimate things, memories, dreams. We are monogamous."

"When we make love, she makes me feel as though I'm the most beautiful woman in the world. She plays with my long hair and tells me how sexy she thinks it is. She tells me she loves the shape of my breasts. I especially love it when she whispers, 'You are so soft.'"

"My lover is the one I live with twenty-four hours a day, and go on holiday with. She is a spark strange to me. Close, but from far, far off, like no light I've ever seen. A sound that constantly catches my ear, and sets my mind reeling. I am in love with her comfortably, vigorously, and for a long term. I love her too. She is my lover, my soul mate; the one I think about when I see a certain smile, when my heart sings—a sister I have known from centuries ago. We were together once, and it was easier or more difficult than it is now—but someday, some life, it will not be hard; it will be as natural as it feels. I'm in love with her *depth*, her sparkle. It makes me secure to know I'm deeply loved."

"My lover is beautiful, courteous, intelligent, well read, and attentive. Her political and spiritual views are important to her and similar to mine. I feel happy when we are together, we have a lot of exciting adventures. For example, she had an idea of how we could start a business and get rich, and we are working on that now and have a good chance of succeeding. We live together and have a pleasant lifestyle. We don't fight but we do argue sometimes. As time passes things are working out. Our biggest difference is opposite tastes in silverware design—that and a few more serious issues! I have a greater fear of intimacy, which is slowly diminishing. I work too many hours. I neglect her sometimes and she suffers in silence. She is developing her assertiveness, and I am becoming more attentive. We share very well."

Thirty-nine percent of gay women in relationships are currently "in love" with their lovers—as is the following woman:

"I am twenty-five years old, black—in love with a thirty-two-year-old woman. She's all I think about, I can't sleep, can't think straight, she's just constantly on my mind. I would like to settle down with her and be comfortable, also financially. My lover feels the same for me. When she first kissed me and told me she wanted me too, I was so happy. Being in love with her is a challenge—it's joy, pain, frustration, hurt, learning, happiness all rolled into one. My favorite love story is my own.

"I've been in this relationship for two years. I have one nineteen-month-old daughter from a previous relationship. She has one child from her ex-husband. The most important part of our relationship is communication, passion, love, and sexual intimacy, in that order. Worst is we lack time together. She lives with her relatives. If I could change things, I'd move into my own place and invite her to come with me. I love and adore her.

"I broke up with a man I used to date before I became gay. He's the father of my child. One day he just took off. I went through a lot of changes, but after a while I came to the conclusion it's his loss, not mine. I came out of it O.K. I was good to him and there was no appreciation for it. To me women are more sensitive, lovable, affectionate, better to get along with, and more faithful. I feel more emotional commitment when I have sex with a woman. This feels better to me.

"My lover is the woman I have loved the most and hated the most. She's sweet, loving, generous, kind, stubborn, selfish, good lover, confused. Not really sure what she wants out of life. We see each other often, we go shopping, to movies, out to lunch, events, etc. We talk on the phone about everything. We have a good time most of the time—except when she likes to make me jealous. I guess she likes to see how I react and if I care.

"I feel a lot of passion usually when we are out to dinner or a movie and we start teasing each other. My passions go wild. I like to explore all parts of her body, especially breasts and vagina and clitoris. The taste and smell really turn me on. Usually I orgasm the best with oral sex. Sex with someone I love is much more fulfilling.

"My woman feels it's not necessary to have a man or a lover or a baby to be a whole, complete woman. I agree. You can be a woman without any of these. A lot of women feel you must have a baby and a man in your life to be whole. I don't. You can just be yourself."

Coming Out Is Hard to Do—But Most Women Sound Very Happy about It

Women coming out can be very shy:

"I am eighteen years old, blonde hair, blue eyes, medium build, and am very creative with the way I think and act. I'm in love right now with a very beautiful woman, but I don't have the guts to ask her how she feels about me, which leaves me pretty much confused. If I get up the courage to talk to her about the way I feel for her (even though I think she knows already), I hope we can come to some agreement for a relationship (we've been to bed together already once)."

"Just recently, I have begun to include women in my choice of sexual partners. My relationship with my friend has grown much more important. We have made love. When we made love, she stared into my eyes and whispered my name. We masturbated each other. With her I loved sex. This is especially significant because, in the past few years, I have not enjoyed sex very much. I love to touch her body. It is so thrilling."

Most women under twenty-five who have recently come out feel good about their lives, but often are told by others they are "doing something wrong," "making a big mistake":

"I am twenty-two years old. I recently informed my mother that I am lesbian. She took the news horribly!! She believes the only way I can be happy is to marry and have children. This really shocks me, as she is very miserable with her life. Although she is usually quite understanding about most things, she could not deal with the fact that I was a lesbian at all; to her that represents total failure!"

Or women *themselves* feel they have "wrong thoughts" and desires:

"On the one hand I feel that I have certain bisexual tendencies, but on the other hand I don't. I love making love with a man but I just have this curiosity about women. There, that's it. It doesn't sound like that much of a problem, but it bugs me. I have alluded to this 'problem' with my fiancé but we really haven't talked about it. I feel I am accepted and understood by him, I guess, but I still can't reveal a few thoughts and feelings to him because of my own insecurities.

"I began to tell him something a while ago . . . but I couldn't. I hinted. The reason it's weird is because it has to do with sexuality and we both are open about that. But this specific aspect of myself cannot be shared unless I am comfortable with it myself. I guess I'm not. It's not that he wouldn't accept that aspect of me—or understand it—*I* don't accept it or really understand it myself. (How's that for being vague!)"

345

The period before coming out is often filled with agony, inner doubts, and a feeling of loneliness, caused by trying to make oneself "fit in" to heterosexual "norms":

"I wasn't gay in high school and knew no one who was. I should say, I didn't *know* in high school that I was gay. I didn't like high school. I was lonely, never felt like I fit in, didn't date. I felt like being intelligent was boring and lonely. I started dating boys in senior year in high school, had a few sexual experiences, and then came out to myself at nineteen—so my heterosexual career was short-lived. (I have, however, had a few heterosexual 'interludes' since.) I wanted to be with boys so I would feel normal, but still didn't feel normal—the sex I had was to be tolerated and rarely 'fun.' It was much better with girls (at twenty and later). But even then, even with girls, it took me a while to become really sexual—the excitement was still unusual for me and transitory for a long time.

"In high school I became aware of my attraction to other women, but I quickly forced it out of my mind, telling myself, 'Everybody has these feelings, it's O.K. if you don't do anything about it!' I never considered that I might actually be a lesbian, since lesbians were obviously sick and deviant and I was neither."

"High school was rough for me. With boys, I was nervous, I liked them, even liked kissing some, but found them very aggressive and not very attractive physically. Being with a girl was ecstatic. Although I was gay, I didn't really know what to do with it, so I was pretty much in the closet. I didn't like feeling abnormal. I was loneliest my whole life before I came out. My parents never knew I had sex at fifteen, but I came out to them as soon as I came out to myself. My mother was more upset than my father, who accepted me regardless."

"When I was in high school (five years ago), I felt ugly, fat, left out, and weird. I think it was related to my emerging lesbian sexuality and my realization I was not about to fit in. I then transferred to an alternative, open-concept school where most of the kids were outsiders—super smart, gay, or from unusual parents, etc. I felt happier—like I fit in most of the time—but still I had problems. My mother was stricter and I had an earlier curfew than my friends. They all laughed at me. I was always between things—my mother's wrath if I arrived home late or my peers' laughter.

"I dated boys from fourteen to sixteen. I felt it was a social necessity, but it always made me feel sad and alienated because I knew I was gay. (I fell in love with another girl at age twelve and we shared some physical affection. I was unable to admit to myself at sixteen that I loved her far more than any boy.) My first straight sex was at eighteen, and my first lesbian sex too. But my parents were proud when I dated boys. They never noticed my women lovers. I felt awful about that because I knew I was a fake.

"Leaving home was splendid. I wanted nothing more than to live freely and openly as a lesbian and explore all the other wonders of life. And that's what I'm doing!"

But when the decision to "come out" is made, the picture changes almost immediately; the amount of enthusiasm and pride expressed by almost all lesbian women is remarkable: 94 percent feel only positive about their decision to "come out."

Eighty-six percent of women describe their first love as important, serious, beautiful—whether they have been "out" for one year or twenty:

"I 'fell in love' in my last year of college with a classmate. I was floored when I realized what was happening to me emotionally. I said to myself, 'You're in love with another woman, you are!' I was shocked, surprised, and very pleased to *at last* have 'fallen in love.' I was shocked because I knew that falling in love with another woman was not considered normal, surprised that I was doing something considered abnormal by society, since I'd always been a very popular girl, dated the star basketball player in high school, a summa cum laude in college. But with those boys I had not fallen in love, and very in love I was with Jane. She was my first *love*. I always liked sex, but after Jane I preferred women and sought them out, while men sought me out. I wonder if my aloofness from them, untouched emotionally, increased their pursuit; if it did, that didn't impress me."

"I came to be a lesbian when I was about twenty. I kind of knew all along as an adolescent that I had homosexual feelings, but chose to date boys to cover up my feelings. When I was sixteen, I had a terrible crush on a cheerleader that I worked with in a restaurant. After a time, we became friends, and about four years later, lovers. The entire relationship lasted nine years and was very intense and passionate.

"Sex with women is much more of an emotional feeling and a closeness that I just haven't found with men. It's much more than a different physical touch, it's an inner intensity that can't be equaled. There are no rules or expected sexual behaviors involved. It's the freest kind of love I know.

"By the way, my mother thinks my lesbian lifestyle is great! I like my mother very much, I admire and respect her and think she is one in a million. I can't think of too many seventy-year-old mothers who think their daughter's lesbianism is great and support her lifestyle. I think I am very much like her—enthusiastic about life and always running in high gear. I like my mother's enthusiasm for life and her open-mindedness."

Women Over Forty: Becoming Gay for the First Time

One of the most surprising findings in this study is the number of divorced women in their forties and fifties who are having love relationships with women and finding this a comfortable, in fact, excellent, way of life.

Amazingly, 24 percent of the gay women in this study were having a lesbian relationship for the first time after age forty; this represents a definite departure from past statistics. The following woman, previously married and with children, describes this change in her life:

"Throughout my life, my women friends have been strong, courageous, beautiful people whose friendship has meant more than nearly anything else. But never in all of my forty years had it occurred to me that I might love a woman in a sexual way. I have hugged and kissed woman friends, we have wept and laughed together, struggled through our respective marriages and divorces together, worked together. But never did I realize that I would feel physically attracted to a woman. It did not occur to me that I might have the ability to love a woman. I have engaged in conversations in which I espoused the theory that human beings would be bisexual if social barriers had not restricted their thinking, etc. But those conversations were intellectualizing on my part.

"Now suddenly, a new world has opened up to me. I've asked a thousand questions, with dozens yet unasked. I have learned and experienced so much joy and dazzling pleasure that I find it difficult to understand why I didn't discover it before.

"Two years ago, I moved to this state to take on a new job. Since I was here, I had been celibate the entire time. My job was so time-consuming and full of pressure, I had little time for myself. My daughters are older and require attention from me in the evenings. After weeks also of evening meetings and late nights at the office, I preferred to be at home with them, rather than looking about for men.

"About this time, through some gay friends of mine. I happened to meet a very special woman. In the beginning, I had no intentions of looking for anything other than female companionship with her—we had mutual interests and would share records. This turned out to be the most wonderful relationship of my life so far. It has literally revived me, and brought me back into the world of feelings, happiness, relaxation—intimacy and love. My daughters think we are just friends—that is all I am prepared to cope with with them right now.

"I still think of myself as single, and probably always will. I treasure my singlehood almost as much as I treasure my self-identity. I love being single. The happiest times in my adult life have been when I was single. My lover wants for us to live together and make a long-term commitment, but I am not interested in giving up my freedom. I doubt I'll ever give it up.

"All of her touching excites me. My breasts and nipples are the most sensitive, and she can bring me the closest to orgasm this way. But it is the clitoris which holds the magic. I'm tempted to say that orgasm is the best part of our sex. However, I did orgasm with my husband and it was not as exquisite as it is with my lover. It is the quantity and quality of holding and affectionate touch which I share with my lover that makes it all so different, so wonderful."

Another woman, age forty-two, describes the "magical quality" of her life now—in contrast to life with her ex-husband:

"I'm a relatively well-adjusted, happy, healthy, loving middle-aged woman, deeply in love, probably for the first time, and closest to my lover—another forty-two-year-old woman.

"There's a glow—a magical quality—to being 'in love' which gives all of life's experiences more joy and delight. It may not be necessary for everyone, but I wouldn't have missed it. We have compatibility on every level—physical, mental, emotional, and spiritual—which has been the key. In the past when I loved someone, my husband and two other men, we only ever connected at one or two levels.

"My love and I have lived together for two years, and we had known each other at work for four years before. Companionship, total intimacy (including exquisite sex), and economics, all are considerations in our partnership. We've been able to save money, make major purchases jointly, and share our house while renting the second. We have taken all our vacations together, including a study tour of Europe and trips to visit relatives and friends. Our physical intimacy and passion is more tender and gentle, slower but deeper and more powerful. We fall asleep every night with arms and legs intertwined.

"For the first time, the loving seems equal—I have always felt that I gave far more than I received. Now I feel totally loved and secure—and so does she. We enjoy everything about our life together—cooking, dishes, garbage—are all easy and effortless—not the power struggle of my married years. Going to bed at night or for an afternoon nap is our favorite activity—just for the snuggling, holding, and sweet talking.

"Talking is relatively easy and equal. She's learning to ask for what she needs—knowing that it's finally O.K. to ask—that happiness is not related to total self-sufficiency as she had thought. We are both sharing all parts of ourselves—without withholding, judging, or criticizing. Years of therapy and growth experiences before we met had prepared us for a close and deep relationship—but we hadn't found a partner with the same background and expectations until now.

"When I got married in 1961 at eighteen it was because I hated dating and living at the dorm or at home. I found a sweet, sensitive, sophisticated man and decided I'd do better if I were married. Although we eventually divorced, I believe that my choice was good—I have yet to meet a man with his strengths and qualities.

"Yet later, when my son was an infant and my marriage was very unsatisfying, I cried myself to sleep frequently. I didn't see divorce as a possibility because I took the vows 'deadly' seriously. I was the loneliest when my son was young and we lived in the mountains with no neighbors and I commuted forty miles to a job with no kindred souls.

"For most of our marriage I was the primary wage earner and it was a problem for his ego. The decision making was 'equal' but the earning wasn't and I was always reluctant to veto his wishes—not wanting to 'emasculate' him with money. We always lived on the edge of financial disaster—we overspent and had no savings.

"Most men forty and over are very threatened by the women's movement—feeling that if women gain something, men will have to give up something. My husband had very mixed feelings. Intellectually he supported women's issues in church, school, and work settings—but at home he was hostile about helping with housework, cooking, and other 'women's work.' His head and his heart were not together.

"At two points during my twenty-year marriage I experimented with affairs. One was with a friend's husband (they had just separated). But the sex was no better and he was no more capable of intimacy than my husband.

"My current partner is the most important relationship I've had. This is the happiest and closest I have ever been. It's almost too good to be true—beyond any dream or fantasy I ever had of marriage or life with a man. It's the first relationship that does not require 'working at'—it's been effortless for two years. In addition, I've had several deep and lasting (ten-plus years) friendships with women.

"I admire women's ability to endure—to survive and make a good life for themselves and their children despite the political and/or personal climate that men have created. Eleanor Roosevelt and Margaret Mead were early role models. More recently, I admire Shirley MacLaine and Gloria Steinem—would like to be like them in ten years. All four have made real contributions.

"I am very grateful to the women's movement for giving a political and historical perspective to the feelings of powerlessness and desperation that we all experience privately—thinking something was wrong with me—I didn't fit into the mold.

"To women today I say: love yourself first and don't eliminate women as possible partners in life!"

Loving Women: Does This "Make" You Gay?

Where is the dividing line between gay and straight affection for a friend?

"I was closest to my college roommate. It was pre-women's movement. She was humanistic, loyal, tender. Funny. She was one of the most 'together' people (hackneyed, but it describes her) I've ever met. She and I were inseparable. I sketched her in the nude and even had some sexual thoughts, but didn't take them very seriously. Men were the object of the day. She and I have lost touch. She got involved in community work in a large city and I moved to the country. We met a few times but she was way ahead of me. She was a role model to me—very human and didn't look down on me in the least. We were partners in all kinds of 'crime.' Nice craziness!"

"At one time I thought I was 'in love' with my roommate and I talked to her about this. She said it was normal to have those feelings, especially after coming from the bad situation I did at home. We tried lesbian love at one time but it wasn't for us."

Gay women describe their love for their best friends

Some gay women have close women friends who do not know that they are gay—but many more have close women friends who of course know, but continue long platonic friendships together:

"I am in love again at present—but I am not closest to my lover. My new relationship only started about two months ago. I am closest to my best friend. I am not afraid to show her *any* side of me."

351

"We are fellow professionals and interested in the same things—everything! We travel, sail, talk, work. Get together at least several hours a week."

"I don't have a best woman friend, I have four! I love their sense of humor, openness. We go to the movies or dinner, once or twice a week. They listen to me and they like me."

"My best friend is intuitive, intelligent, and very sensitive. She is not a very strong woman emotionally, but is supportive and nurturing. I like the fact that I feel comfortable enough with her to show her any side of me."

When is love for another woman "gay," and when is it friendship?

Where is the "borderline" between being "in love with" one's friends and loving them—and does it matter?

"My best friend and I have hiked together, traveled, read philosophy, Zen, and holistic health together, worked, talked, played together for six years, and developed a deep (but non-sexual) love for each other which we were sure would last forever. I had never loved anyone so intensely. We spent most of our time together though I was married (she was alone). She is very intelligent, funny, beautiful, and we went through so much pain and pleasure together. My relationship with my current lover ultimately destroyed our friendship, which had begun to become sexual only in the last two months before it broke down. It would have broken down even if it hadn't become sexual: we were always 'lovers' in a sense, and the intrusion of another woman was too much. The loss of that friendship was/is like a death to me."

"My best friend is the reason I answered this questionnaire. I love her so much and I don't understand it. She's helped me through some of the lowest points of my life. She's encouraged me to be the whole person I am today. We probably had an affair without sex. I can't ever say how much of the happy, healthy me of today I owe to her. She helped me to find out what I want and who I am. When I'm with her things are great. We enjoy each other. I love her the most of any woman in my life."

"As I've grown up I've had many crushes on women—some of which have turned into good friendships (nothing sexual). I believe women can be attracted to women sexually as they are to men. This doesn't mean you're gay—it's merely a physical attraction. Usually I find this physical attraction dies as soon as I get to know the person well and become friends."

352

"My best woman friend and I are so compatible and feel very comfortable around each other. She is very honest and open, very accepting, and doesn't try to change me. She lets me be. We communicate so well. Our love for each other has been very strengthening. We have both helped each other with difficult situations to make major moves in our lives.

"We also have been sexually attracted to each other, but decided not to act upon it. We have used it to become closer emotionally. I love her and hope that we remain close throughout the years. We have even talked about being the 'life mates' of each other. Why do people have to be married or lovers to spend their lives together? I feel that two friends can make that commitment."

Fear of loving and desiring another woman: Do some heterosexual women love their women friends more than they love men?

Women often feel emotionally closer to other women than they do to men, as seen earlier. Eighty-nine percent say they wish they could talk to the men they love in the same intimate and easy way they can talk to their best friends. Descriptions women give of their best friends contain a remarkably happy and loving tone of voice.

On the other hand, most women feel that they are basically "heterosexual"—i.e., they do not feel "attracted" to women physically, sexually, but see them as basically psychologically accessible, or possibly soul mates. If one took away women's remaining economic dependence on men, and men's dominance in the larger society, would women still feel that they "should" be "heterosexual"? Or are women getting another kind of closeness, a non-verbal closeness, in their sexual relationships with men? On the other hand, are some simply psychologically attracted to the power men have, feeling themselves powerless without a man to "help" them in society?

This is not to imply that "all women are gay underneath it all" but to point out that women can re-examine their preconceptions about what a long-term gay lifestyle means, and whether or not one can find security and happiness there.

Being Woman-Identified: A Valid Alternative

"There are a lot of qualities women assume they can get only from men that they can get from a woman too, if they just tried it."

Perhaps women don't feel they can find permanent security with another woman, as with a man; if so, this may be a false idea. Of course, being gay doesn't have the status of being heterosexual, or being part of a nuclear family—whatever the shape of that nuclear family psychologically. But women, as we see here, *are* giving each other a great deal of emotional and even financial security (economic cooperation). It is quite possible for a woman to live her entire life in this woman-to-woman culture. Indeed, 92 percent of women over thirty-five who are doing so say that this is providing them with an excellent base for their lives.

Women sum up the pleasures and importance of loving other women:

"Falling in love is not as important as not falling out of love. These relationships I share with women with whom I am forever in love—with or, probably, without sex—are the relationships I value above all others. The lovers who are closer than friends; friends deeper and more multifaceted than lovers. The ones I will always meet up with again, and know they are somewhere out there in the world; not forgetting our love; using it to strengthen them."

"My experience has been that women are more caring and more honest in relationships than men are. They are much more satisfying. As the Alix Dobkin song goes, 'You can't find home cooking in a can, or clean air in a traffic jam, You can't find a woman's love in a man. Never in a million years.' Love between women is much different for me than with men. There is no comparison! Sex is also much different—much softer, sweeter, and real."

"I believe a love relationship between two women is far more serious than one between a man and a woman. Women run on a higher emotional level than men will let themselves, and they get to deeper levels with each other."

Another World, Another Culture

Women's lives together have a rich texture at once all their own, and at the same time, filled with many of the same human problems heterosexual women face. And yet, there is a feeling here of looking in on a special culture, another way of life, breathing a different air. The existence of this world is a great cultural resource: it provides a place of strength and beauty to draw on, opening up for all the pleasure of diversity and new ways of seeing things, being together.

Why should anyone have to defend lesbianism as a way of life? In fact, as historian Carroll Smith-Rosenberg has written in her study of women in nineteenth-century America, one can see things just the other way: in fact, "to see heterosexuality as an artificial construct imposed upon humanity [would be] a revolutionary concept."* Who is to say which is more "natural": to love the opposite or one's own sex? Greek men of ancient times would certainly have been hard-pressed to give an answer. Perhaps it is even more important here to ask why it has become so taboo for women to hold hands even in friendship, or to demonstrate physical affection as they did in Victorian times. Once again it seems imperative for us to review our entire concept of sensuality—as well as our priorities in terms of friendships/feelings for other women.

Many, many women here have expressed the deepest feelings of love, joy, passion, and sorrow for the women they love. A passage by the poet Judy Grahn says something about the deepest longings of all our hearts, describing intense feelings of closeness for her lover, feelings which transcend death.

> a funeral: for my first lover and longtime friend
> Yvonne Mary Robinson, b. Oct. 20, 1939; d. Nov. 1974
> for ritual use only†
>
> wherever I go to, you will arrive
> whatever you have been, I will come back to
> wherever I leave off, you will inherit . . .
> whatever we resurrect, we shall have it
>
> we shall have it, we have right
>
> you have left, what is left.
>
> I will take your part now, to do your daring . . .

* Carroll Smith-Rosenberg, *Disorderly Conduct* (New York: Alfred A. Knopf, 1985).
† Judy Grahn, *The Work of a Common Woman* (Trumansburg, Pa: The Crossing Press, 1978), pp. 102–103.

lots belong to those who do the sharing.
I will be your fight now, to do your winning
as the bond between women is beginning
In the middle at the end
my first beloved, present friend
if I would die like the next rain
I'd call you by your mountain name
And rain on you

want of my want, I am your lust
wave of my wave, I am your crest
earth of my earth, I am your crust
may of my may, I am your must
kind of my kind, I am your best

tallest mountain, least mouse
least mountain, tallest mouse

you have put your very breath upon mine
i shall wrap my entire fist around you
i can touch any woman's lips to remember

we are together in my motion
you have wished us a bonded life

Marriage and the Nature of Love In the "Age of the Family"

A classic question or decision women and men have had to contemplate is whether they want to—or can—marry someone with whom they are "in love," or whether they think it is better to choose someone who seems to provide safe, stable companionship with less volatility, less of the vulnerability they may feel with someone with whom they are "in love." Surprisingly, there have been no large-scale studies which attempted to statistically correlate the results of type of love with how many marriages and relationships actually work out.*

Women often debate with themselves the meanings of these feelings: What is "falling in love"? Is it just sexual? Is caring, learning to understand someone over time, more "real," more "mature"? In fact, 82 percent of the women in this study are asking themselves why they are in the relationships they are in, what kind of love it is they feel—whether it is the "right" kind.

When women think about getting married, or when a marriage or relationship isn't going well, they wonder if it is their fault—whether they have made a mistake: on the one hand, if they are in an "in love" relationship, they can think perhaps they are "messed up," not being "rational" and "mature"; on the other hand, if they are in a "reasonable," low-key relationship, but "still not satisfied," they may blame themselves for wanting "security" too much, being "too dependent."

Are the stereotypes and assumptions about what kind of love works in relationships accurate? One theory holds that falling "in love" is "unreal," one is "projecting" on to the other person; that the only "real love" is getting to know a person over time. Others believe that a more low-key or steady love is not love at all but merely "taking care of" someone, a security-oriented definition of love, formulated to prove one can "make a relationship work."

* Schwartz and Blumstein correlate other factors. See Pepper Schwartz and Philip Blumstein, *American Couples: Money, Work, Sex* (New York: Morrow, 1983).

According to the first theory, falling in love does not work for long-term relationships because it is "juvenile" (the two people don't really "know" one another, and therefore mature love is not possible). And yet just the opposite case could be made—that it does not work because the two people care *too* much, and so their feelings are too easily wounded, and this is what creates the tension, leading to flare-ups and explosions. On the other hand, countering *this* argument, it could be said that while it is true that passionate "infatuation" makes people susceptible to easily hurt feelings, it also makes them care about overcoming lapses in communication, and makes them want to try to scale any barriers to reach each other.

If the intense feelings of first love *are* transitory, why is this so? One theory is that falling in love really shuts out the world for a time; when the world forces itself back in, this is when the "in love" feeling dies a little. Do some couples find a way of keeping the outside world out, building islands of time and space apart for only each other and their innermost thoughts? Times to re-create closeness? Or, as many people believe, does the so-called love-yearning expressed so well by Mahler end or change when fulfillment or togetherness is achieved?

Most of the women in this study do not marry the men they have most deeply loved. This was also true of men in *The Hite Report on Male Sexuality*: most men did not marry the women they had most passionately loved. But this did not make their relationships "happy," as we have seen. Women, as seen here, hope that by avoiding the highs and lows of being "in love," they can make a relationship more secure, if not inspired, and a better setting for living and raising children.*

The constantly heard assumption that "in love" marriages don't last and that more low-key love relationships are more stable and do last has no basis in statistical fact, as demonstrated here. Further, in marriages that *do* last, there still remains the question of level of happiness within the marriage. As we have seen, even a quiet love, a supposed "safe haven," can turn out to be filled with arguments (or silences). While the turbulence associated with being "in love" can be difficult, the

---

* But, most women (as opposed to men, who often don't even *like* feeling "in love," because they feel "out of control") do like being in love. However, as one woman puts her final thoughts on the matter, "Being in love to me is thrilling, exciting, it's magic—but it can also turn your life upside down, and put you in a confused state of mind. It can be extremely painful and heartbreaking. I don't regret ever having been in love—but who would want to *live* with it???" Women, as opposed to men, however, do not generally pride themselves on their "rationality" and "objectivity" in making their choice of marriage partner. For men, it is often a matter of pride not to have picked someone with whom they were "in love" for marriage, since, according to men, the decision for marriage should be based on more "rational," "objective" considerations.

daily problems demonstrate that most typical "loving" marriages also contain the unequal emotional contract, which is condescending to women, harasses women while also putting great emotional demands on them, expecting them to provide love and support. Of course, such relationships can easily lead to eventual alienation and frequently finally to a kind of emotional death.

In other words, the supposition that if contentment replaces passion, the marriage will be more stable is not borne out by the research of this study. Here most women say their marriages are not based on being passionately in love, and yet their satisfaction levels remain low. Therefore it is logically impossible to say that passion is the cause of instability in relationships.

What this study shows is that the dynamics that kill love basically involve inequalities in the emotional contract. The emotional contract itself must be changed before relationships can be stable *and* happy—whether based on "loving" or being "in love."

Statistically, in this study, marriages and relationships are most likely to break up when the man refuses to discuss issues and problems which the woman finds to be important, and this goes on over a period of time, so that alienation grows. As the emotional distance widens, most women restructure the emotional relationship inside the marriage and the nature of their feelings. We do not know, for the most part, how relationships (whether "in love" or "loving") would fare without the interference of the unequal emotional contract.

Democratizing the Family: New Emotional Arrangements Within Marriage

There are myriad types of emotional arrangements within marriages, but there are three basic new models of what the psychological arrangements should be: (1) the emotional intimacy model (most women would prefer this type, if they could achieve more equality and closeness with their husbands); (2) the "home-base" model, usually emotionally distanced, but working on the level of "being there"; and (3) the teamwork model, in which the partners actually work together and their work/business is the focus of their life together; this third type of marriage is still quite rare.

In other words, first, there is the marriage in which intimacy, emotional and psychological, is the primary goal. This is the emotional arrangement most women are trying to get their husbands to adopt—and the way of life most women would prefer. (And they do it with their women friends.)

Then there is the marriage that provides a "home base" for the rest of one's life: "being there" is all that is really required. The traditional marriage, still so prevalent, as seen, is not the same as the new "home-base" marriage because in the traditional arrangement, the woman is providing a stable base for the husband and children to go out from and live their lives, but the woman herself has little room or time for her own life; the marriage is not a stable base for her; she *is* the home base for others. It is not a backdrop for her life, it *is* her life. In the "home-base" marriage, the emotional contract remains intact, with male distancing and harassment of women continuing—but usually the woman doesn't care so much anymore, as she has placed her primary emotional interest elsewhere.

Finally, one woman describes the team concept of marriage: "Last winter we had saved up enough money so that we had the freedom to concentrate on our own work without having to worry about money. We worked in the studio until very early hours. Working together, with our dreams, free to use our true abilities, was wonderful." Other women are starting small businesses with their husbands as partners, and find these team marriages very exciting.

Why do so many women have "home-base" marriages?

"My relationship with my husband is the center of my life because it allows me the freedom to move outside of it but to return for sustenance. It gives the children a space to grow up in. It provides a solid economic base, companionship. It allows me to pursue my career without abandoning my children (my husband is there)."

Although this woman sounds as though she has ultimately made a practical choice about how to organize her life, most women in home-base marriages have developed them after giving up on creating a more emotionally intimate marriage.

The promised emotional intimacy of marriage is a phantom for most women at a time in history when men are taught more than ever to deny their emotional lives, to be "rational," "scientific," and "objective" above all else. Men are constantly downgrading the importance and validity of emotions, so that for women to be constantly trying to bring men back to a level of more emotional openness becomes an endless occupation, overwhelmingly involving—i.e., a great deal of emotional work. Therefore, many women who remain married are now making a sort of new arrangement by developing the home-base or distanced marriage: in a way, they are making marriage *their* home base now, as so many men have always done—taking their freedom to go outside of it as much as they want, for work, friends, and lovers, while still using it. This is a workable way of life for a woman, as long as she does not care "too much" and is not longing for a deeper emotional contact with her husband.

The feeling is inescapable, as we see throughout all of these comments on marriage, that love relationships as a whole could be so much better:

"In my marriage, I can be a homemaker, have kids. I can still live my own life. He ignores me, so I make the best of it. My husband is happier than I am, only because I leave him alone and don't nag him. I still feel frustrated."

"We've been married twenty-three years. The best part of being married is the physical warmth and comfort. The worst is the frequent anger I feel. Marriage is more drudgery than I thought—I mean the housework involved. We married because we hated being apart and wanted to be together. I'd do it again and plan on staying married because I love having my children."

Here is a very typical answer from a woman as to why she likes her marriage and plans to stay there; it is very general and really doesn't explain anything, but it is exactly the kind of answer most women give:

"I like just spending time with my husband. Whether it's vacationing or working in the yard, going out to dinner, cooking together, lying in bed, reading, even talking (if the subject is not too sensitive or controversial). My husband tells me he loves me often. He does not tell me I'm beautiful, desirable, or wonderful—I wish he would. I would like more intimate talk. I have not shared most of myself with my husband nor has he shared himself with me. He has said that feelings and emotions are private and need not be shared with anyone."

In a nutshell, women's most usual reasons for "liking" and "disliking" marriage come down to such things as the following:*

"The best part of being married is the companionship and being together. The worst part is having a job *plus* the job of running

* Statistics show that married men are healthier and live longer than single men, but these statistics do not hold up for women.

the house—my husband refuses to help. We have been married two years."

"The best part of being married is having a companion to go places with you. Perhaps the financial security is even better. I'm just out of school and it's tough."

"I like the companionship but loathe the bossiness, always having to consider the other person in social plans, and I dislike losing my credit at banks or businesses because I'm the wife. It is unfair to assume the woman automatically takes a back seat to her husband."

If these are the bottom-line reasons for being married, the reasons half of women are staying in their marriages (the other half are divorcing, although they often try another marriage), it is easy to understand why many women sound somewhat resigned, and give themselves only a "five" or so when asked to rate their happiness on a scale of one to ten.

Double Lives: Leaving a Marriage Emotionally

Women are deserting marriage in droves, either through divorce,* or emotionally, leaving with a large part of their hearts.

As we hear married women talk about their lives here, we see that almost 90 percent are putting their primary emotional focus elsewhere. Most women have begun to give up on creating the amount of emotional closeness and intimacy, the equal partnership, that they had wanted in their marriages. Most, after an initial period of trying, have gone on to find other places to invest their emotional lives. Woman after woman, after the initial years of "trying to get through," gives up and begins to disengage quietly, gradually, perhaps even unnoticeably.

Is this what women really want? No, not at first, at least—but many women come to feel they have no choice: "How I have come to handle it is, I just don't focus so much on it anymore. Then if I am disappointed, it doesn't matter so much. I roll with the punches. Maybe the love will build back up over a period of time. If not, it's better to have other parts of my life I am involved in. Then everything goes smoother."

Most women separate themselves emotionally in these cases without really even trying; it just happens. They find themselves drifting away, no longer able to relate to the "other" person in the relationship, who

---

* Ninety percent of divorces are brought by women, not men.

does not seem to see them or what is happening, and who remains withdrawn, "unknowable," distant.

One woman describes the stages like this: "At first, I pretended I didn't care about my husband as a bitter response to his own uncaring attitude. Eventually, for my own sanity, I stopped pretending and I didn't really care. I was worrying myself *sick* over him, and I decided I had to worry about me!" But she, like many others, did not actually leave; she chose to stay but to move her emotional focus, her inner life, elsewhere. Most of the 50 percent of women who stay married eventually use their marriages as a sort of "home base"; they are not staying because they have the emotional relationship they want.

This 50/50 division is striking—almost as if women are poised at a turning point, at the moment of deciding their future. Women ask themselves: Should we adapt marriage to our lives, using a "male" model, that is, using it as a relatively non-emotional home base, as many men seem to do—or will some better way be created out of our thoughts, a more perfect vision of what relationships can be?

The situation is complex: women often think of leaving marriage . . . but to leave marriage is to go—where? While women may be frustrated with trying to create love, openness, and intimacy with men who don't return them, or do so only sporadically—after which a woman has to start the "opening up" process all over again—when women do "give up on love," and turn away, as nearly half do, many still come back to try again, remarry, always torn, always asking: Why is it like this anyway? Why is it so difficult?

The injustice of the larger society is reflected in the basic assumptions of the traditional emotional contract in marriage, and yet there often seems to be no other place to turn for warmth and love. As seen elsewhere, the "singles world" of dating and relationships is certainly no better. Women have marvelous relationships of emotional closeness with their women friends, but most women do not want to look to women for physical intimacy. Classically, women have often turned much of their emotional focus toward their children, to share emotional warmth with them, and many still do so, but this is not complete.

The seeming lack of anyplace else to turn, and sometimes the lack of hope of finding a better relationship with someone else, are what make many women stay in their marriages and try for a compromise, even if they are emotionally alienated. Even if a woman does not find emotional closeness, she can use the relationship for physical affection, general companionship (someone to have dinner with, if not talk . . .), and someone to have children with. ("This can be distracting for several years, anyway," as one woman puts it, "because they make a lot of noise!")

Facing this impasse, women—whether they decide to stay or to leave—frequently ask themselves if their expectations are too high; "What is the best one can expect out of life/love relationships?":

"It's like life just offers you quicksand all around you. I feel sorry for the ones that just sink. I was in a very destructive relationship for two years. When I left the last time, I still cried every day, I missed him so much. But I knew I was doing the right thing, and eventually I felt better. Now I am really glad I left."

"Do all relationships end up this way? There you are, after ten years, just putting up with the other's faults? And sex is boring, the hurts of the past make you sarcastic and mean, etc.? There's a lot of mediocre love in the world. Or are most of us just scared of living?"

So, women often go through stages in their relationships: first, there may be bickering, "bringing up the issues," a woman trying to stand up for her rights to keep the emotional channels open; next, if a woman decides to give up on trying for emotional intimacy but doesn't want to leave home (after all, it is a place to belong, perhaps the place where she and her children form a unit with their father), she may, like many women at that point, design another life for herself, a separate life, a life outside the home.

In fact, the majority of married women are leading double lives: 90 percent of women married more than four years say that their relationship with their husband is not the main source of their emotional gratification—or expectations. Double lives are important for women, and necessary; one might say that for many women, they are the only way to live with a man and love both him and themselves at the same time.

The British film, *The Red Shoes* (1949), in which the main character is forced to give up her career as a ballerina by the men who "love" her, is a moving portrayal of the many pressures on a woman to choose between self-expression and marriage. To force a woman to choose is really to put her in an impossible situation—indeed, a life-threatening situation.★ But the truth (not depicted in the movie, but true nevertheless) is that even if a woman does *not* choose a double life, does choose to put her marriage before her "life"; by the very fact of her feeling pressured to choose, making ongoing choices (against herself, in favor of loyalty), she becomes alienated from the one she wants to love, the one she has

★ Even if this is "only" her emotional life—or her identity, her self-expression.

made the choice in favor of. Why should such a choice be necessary? Why are women supposed to "prove" love in this way? And paradoxically, having chosen to remain "loyal," she may find herself lonelier than ever, because she cannot reach him and she has no other outlets: the harder she may try to reach the one she loves, the further away he may seem to be.

What kinds of "second" double lives are there? First, jobs, careers, and going back to school are many women's preferred new "second" identity. As one woman puts it, and she represents many, many more, "My greatest achievement, even though I'm married, is my work and my ability to support myself. I gain recognition for what I do in life. My salary (!) shows that I am considered somebody, worth something to the world. I love my children and my husband too, but my work is what makes me feel like getting up and getting going in the morning."

Despite the popularity in the media of stories of women who "give it all up" and return to twenty-four-hour-a-day homemaking, the trend statistically is the reverse: the number of women working outside the home is steadily increasing—and most women like it, according to this study. While some younger, never-married or just-married women do find the idea of staying home with babies for two or three years appealing, most discover that after that, they want to "go back out to work into the world." They often worry that they will have trouble reinstating themselves.

Although the pressure of being torn between work and home for women is often portrayed as simply a problem of too little time (and there *is* too little time, if women continue to do most of the "housework" as well as "outside" work), the pressure comes also in great part for women from the emotional strain of feeling depleted by being asked to give too much, with not enough emotional support for one's own "starring" role.

Another vitally important type of "second" life for the great majority of women is women's close friendship with other women. In fact, the primary emotional support of most married women is their best woman friend. Women describe these friendships, as in the following: "I love talking to my best friend. She is so much easier to talk to than my husband. He gets silent or seems to feel threatened if I really open up and start talking about things. She just listens and I can tell by the way she reacts she is interested and understands. She always seems to know the right thing to say."

Traditionally, as noted, many married women have also turned much of their emotional focus toward their children. Women have been alternately ridiculed for doing this (called "smothering"), or put down for *not* doing it—not being "loving enough," not devoting themselves to their families sufficiently, working outside the home, and so on. Even after children are grown, the closeness often remains, as here: "My relationships with my adult children are more satisfying than what I have with my husband—even though we still live together, and I spend all my time with him."

Still another way many women have found to have second lives is through therapy or psychological counseling. Since their relationship with their counselor is private, secret even, women can express another part of themselves, create a different life in this setting, apart from the world. They can, with a good persona, explore any thoughts, no matter how "forbidden." In this way, perhaps the fact that so many women are in therapy (a disproportionately large number compared to men) can be seen as positive: that is, while the medical establishment may see "therapy" as "treatment" of a woman with "problems," women may often see it as creating a new life, a new philosophy—a way of making clear and visible their own inner reality, the way they see things which seems to find no validation or recognition in the outside "real"/unreal world.

Finally, a classic way women have separate lives is through extramarital affairs. As this study showed, 70 percent of women married five years or more have affairs—and the average length of these affairs is four years. This is a clear indication that these women have two separate and different lives going on side by side, and are not just involved in "sexual flings" (even though they usually are not "in love" either). Many women seem to feel that in an affair they somehow have more equality—maybe because they are not "owned" or maybe because the man does not think so much in terms of gender stereotypes—for example, does not assume (as in the singles world) that the woman is looking for marriage.

Are "home-base" marriages the answer?

"Home-base" marriages are an improvement which women have created for themselves over the traditional marriage in which the woman provided the "home base" for the man and children, but herself *had* no individual life: she *was* the home base. Still, can women be happy over the long term living with such an emotionally alienated situation at "home"? Even if they are finding emotional fulfillment elsewhere?

One woman describes this type of marriage in her own life, but with an undertone of frustration: "I got a job and have really started enjoying it, especially the time out on my own and having my own money. But my life with my husband is no different than it has been. It is still a matter of two unlike people on two opposing paths attempting to live a semblance of parallelism. He lives his life, and I live mine."

Most women, ideally, would desire a different emotional structure in their marriages (even though they would like to continue working and making money independently). However, they find that their partners resist the emotional restructuring required. So women go along struggling, often bisecting themselves emotionally (if they stay in the relationship)—trying to become accustomed to the arrangement. While they believe that the purpose of a marriage should be emotional intimacy, they decide, finally, that if one cannot have such intimacy, marriage can at least produce a base from which to live one's life. For the moment, for some women, this may be a workable solution. At the same time, however, this new "home-base" marriage also represents women *leaving* marriage—emotionally and psychologically, with their hopes and dreams.

More and more women resent having to bisect themselves like this. Where will this lead?

Redefining marriage: progress or cop-out? Does "liberation" mean rejecting marriage?

Various theorists have made the case that, since marriage generally exploits women, requiring more domestic services (cooking and cleaning) than single life, as well as loss of various legal and financial rights, if women were truly "liberated," they would give up marriage. Since most women have continued to marry, it is implied (often by the media) that they are "uninterested in liberation," backsliders, "traditionally oriented"—just proving what women's fundamental "nature" is, after all. But this argument leaves out the important factor that no matter how "liberated," "independent," or "self-defining" women become, women/people will still want to make a "home," belong somewhere —and the institution said to be equivalent to home in this sense in our society so far is "marriage."

Men too, with their vociferous denial of interest in "commitment," have been rebelling against marriage as a way of life (at least, verbally rebelling) for at least half a century, complaining that they feel restricted in it. As one man writes, "Marriage seems so impractical. It cuts off one's interaction with a lot of the world. Even getting into a 'relationship' is so demanding—and how long can one be expected to pour so much energy into just one person?" One of the first manifestations of men's alienation from marriage in the twentieth century was James Thurber's cartoon putting down a giant, possessive wife (whose body took over the whole house); then later the "playboy philosophy" and then the "sexual revolution" with its single male movie heroes and rock star idols. However, it often seems that the media approve of men's tendency to denigrate the idea of marriage, since men are "questing" after Meaning, Themselves—but look down on women who are against marriage as "unnatural," "man-haters."

It has been said for twenty years that "marriage is dead." Now people often say they marry "because of children." But the real reason for the continuing popularity of marriage, for both women and men, is that almost uniquely in our society, "marriage" holds out the promise of not being left alone in a very cold and competitive world, where it often seems that individuals don't matter very much. What we need is a new "home," a new concept of what "home" is and where to find it—those feelings of happiness and peace we long for.

Was There Marriage before Patriarchy?

Is marriage a "natural" institution? Or was it invented? Would people "naturally" want to marry—even without the current social structure? Was there marriage before patriarchy?*

The problem with general discussions in the media of "family" issues—i.e., the cry "the family is dying"—is the assumption that only with the nuclear family can we have a "civilized" world, because it has "always been this way," "even in the Paleolithic caves."

But is this true? *Was* there "marriage" before patriarchy, that social order in which women were declared to be the possessions of first, fathers, and later, husbands—the aim of which was to produce children who would "belong to" the father and take his name? or were the earliest families, in fact, mothers and children? And did inheritance and name go through the mothers, as some paleoanthropologists and archaeologists now believe?†

"Marriage" as we have known it for centuries has been legally

---

* Some gay couples express the desire to "marry"; is this because of the cultural atmosphere around them—or an impulse to make a public ceremony of those feelings?
† There is no evidence to suggest that the patriarchal family has always existed; in fact, much evidence exists to the contrary, that indeed the earliest families were women with children/clans. See the work of Richard Potts of the Smithsonian or David Pilbeam of Harvard University.

defined in terms of property and inheritance.★ Were there ceremonies celebrating personal romantic love in pre-patriarchal times? No one knows—and yet, surely people have always wanted to mark the passages of life in some public way; one can only speculate on what the nature and meaning of those celebrations—if any—may have been.

Just so, we cannot yet imagine, perhaps, what our future (post-patriarchal?) institutions and celebrations may be. But we can say that "marriage," even a reinvented marriage, should not be pushed on people as the only real way to "real happiness" or involvement with the world. Many women in this study are quite happy in other ways. We can have great self-expression and love through our work, our friendships, our children, our love for many things: the earth, plants, flowers, the animals who share the planet with us—and our "pets." Depths of feeling, investing oneself passionately in *something*, seems to be what matters to be happy.

Marriage as a longing for home

Marriage, despite the high divorce rate (and the unhappiness rate), remains an important institution in our society.

Why do women return to marriage? Even after the pain and turmoil of various relationships, the emotional ups and downs, many women still come back to look for something—what?

What *is* marriage in our society? The repository of all the hopes each one of us has to be not alone, to have affection and warmth and stability and meaning in life. To be seen as someone special, real, important beyond being "productive" in society, someone understood and valued as a human being, not just a production unit. There are no similar alternative institutions, none even close (although there should be)—and so no matter how bad things are, we keep regravitating to marriage as we know it, trying to reinvent it. But there is a lot to be said for living "alone," with a network of friends—even though the mythology, the magical aura surrounding "marriage" is not there yet for other ways of life.

★ Various Marxist theorists have of late tried to define marriage in terms of labor, as a way of giving women's work a measurable value in the system. Even sex has been considered a form of production, labor, in order to be placed within the theoretical analytical system. But rather than making women's activities at home fit into a labor-analysis, this wage-production framework for conceptualizing political reality should be transcended and a new analysis developed. See Joan Kelly, "The Doubled Vision of Feminist Theory," in *Women, History and Theory: The Essays of Joan Kelly* (Chicago: University of Chicago Press, 1984), part of the Women in Culture and Society Series edited by Catharine R. Stimpson.

We have asked, "Are women happy in marriage, or not going after their dreams?" Women may be answering softly that perhaps now their dreams lie elsewhere. The promise, the hope, the desire is still there—for the perfect, great, intimate love that will last and be happy and lead to a family—all of it. But it is doubtful that women will ever again see love in the same way.

Is the "Age of the Family" Over?

If women are alienated from men, and beginning not to see marriage as their primary emotional support or definition, what will this mean for the society? If women leave marriage, emotionally or physically, does this mean that the age of the "home" and "family" is over? Would the end of this "home" be good or bad? What *is* home, after all?

"The family is the basis of our society; without it, the society will crumble"

Would the dissolution of home as we know it be a disaster? Or would it be a good moment, a time of reorganizatiion, rethinking, a chance for re-creation of a basic social institution along better lines—a good basic social reorganization, shifting the values of the overall society? If men no longer find there can be a hierarchical family, could this influence for the better their view of how the rest of the world is shaped?

The current assumption—correct in many ways—is that the nuclear family is the linchpin of our whole system, and that without it, the society as we know it will be in jeopardy. It would indeed be in for a big change. But would this be a bad thing? Are we, in fact, in the midst of a transition back to the mother–child family? Statistics on female single heads-of-households certainly make a strong case for this.

Thus, it is mostly a male fear that without the nuclear family, the system would collapse; all that would be left of the society would be a market economy, with millions of isolated individuals jockeying for position. Many men wonder,★ would there be no place one could go for relief? for an atmosphere of trust?

This brings out an interesting point: has society been counting on marriage (i.e., on women) to counteract the harshness of the "outside

★ In newspapers and the popular media, and in the previous *Hite Report on Male Sexuality*.

world" with its competitive "male" system/values to make that world bearable for men? In that case, the system—that hard, "rational" system—has been running on women's spiritual energy (or, as others might say, "off women's backs"), and this in turn would explain the fear *men* have that if women are no longer there to fulfill the "home" role . . . what will we have? An atavistic mass, with no one feeling very valued in life. Of course, if the dominant value system changed by taking on some of "women's" values, one might not have only one's "nest" to rely on for comfort, because the "outside" world would not be so violent.

But if, under the "male" ideological system (perhaps especially in its present, winner-take-all market manifestation), individuals have no one to "come home to" who values them and shows appreciation, understanding, "sees them," can this lead, in a hierarchical society like our own, in which only the ones "on top" really count, to an escalation of the social violence already present? This at least is the nightmare.

In fact, a case could be made that "home" values are preindustrial values that survived because they were tucked away from the world in the "home" and that these values became an "anachronism" when most work began to be done in factories (and not the home) during the Industrial Revolution. They were values in a "time capsule," waiting to be rediscovered.

In any case, now that the main action is not in the "home," women too live increasingly outside it, and the market system has caused the prestige accorded things made and done at home to decline—home life and work life are being penetrated by the same values. Women are under pressure to take on the values of the dominant workplace, the dominant society, the "male" ideology.

Now, therefore, is a good time to scrutinize those values, as well as the values of "women's" culture or *Weltanschauung*, to see which parts of them, i.e., the stress on cooperation and teamwork, might be helpful in solving some of our current problems. Somehow, what we need is a new vision, a more valid framework, for redefining our relationship with work, with each other, and with the planet that supports us.

B. F. Skinner has asked in a recent issue of the *American Psychologist*, "What is wrong with daily life in the Western world today?" His answers are less than profound, but the question goes to the heart of things, for it is not only our manufacturing units that are in trouble, and our fiscal policy, and our international relations, and our natural environment, but our very daily lives, our relations with each other. Similar worries have been focused on the "home" in the popular media, i.e., why are there so many divorces? Why don't couples get along? Why is there incest, and violence between spouses—and so on? In fact, the entire value system must go under review to discover what it is that is making people—especially men—behave in such violent and aggressive ways, whether the reference is to sullen "workers" or angry husbands or aggressive drivers. And this is a large part of what the dialogue among women here in this study is about, what women are asking themselves and each other and the world.

"The family would lose its central personality—the mother . . ."*

Women have been the centerpiece—some would say "altarpiece"—of the home for a very long time. Although women have not always been very happy, nevertheless, the continuance of this institution did seem—for a while at least—to represent a world of permanence, an eternal order of things. Strangely, it was women, the less powerful of the genders, who were the basis of this aura of stability—the place men always "came home to"†—like Ulysses to Penelope: the end of the journey was to be admired and appreciated by a woman.

Even if women have been coerced into presiding over the home (by such means as economic and legal subjugation and the pressures of public opinion), still, it is amazing to think that by leaving the home, as women are doing (whether physically, through divorce, or emotionally, by simply ceasing to care), the linchpin of society is slipping—or at least some people feel it to be slipping. "Women" (or the idea of "woman") were, in Western "male" ideology, the most permanent of realities, fixed in the role of retiring, devoted, selfless motherhood—a symbol. That symbol was ideologically powerful, even though women themselves as individuals have had very little power.

Some right-wing theorists warned in the 1970s that if women left the home, left their "place," they would lose what power they had, and still not gain a position of equality in the "outside" world. Others, feminist theorists, have worried that if reproductive technology becomes more and more advanced, men will make babies in tubes and therefore not need women anymore, leaving women even more powerless, redundant. Both analyses are based on seeing women's reproductive/creative powers as our basic means of status in the society. Would we be foolish not to rely on our traditional "stronghold" in the future? Or is it eroding anyway? Have we decided we cannot live this way anymore, with our choices

---

* William H. Chafe, *The American Woman: Her Changing Social, Economic, and Political Roles, 1920–1970* (Oxford: Oxford University Press, 1972).
† Is this also the function of Mary in the Catholic religion?

so circumscribed? Do we also see the perilous position the larger society is in at the moment, the precariousness of all our futures in these times, because of the ideology the society is operating on, and does this add to our feeling that we want to be, must be, involved in solving the problems?

Here is another choice women are facing, then: should we continue to base our "power" on our capacity to re-create life? (If men have re-created life in the test tube—admittedly with our eggs—have they finally become the "equals" of women, that is, they can now create life too?) Or should we turn to the larger society and insist on our claim to equal "ownership" of the system, an equal right to design and name the means of production, the philosophy, the art and culture, all of it?

Longing for love

What is home? Where is it? How many people have at one time or another found themselves standing in the middle of their own living rooms, but being unhappy, shouting, "I want to go home!"? And how many people living in apartments, instead of houses, feel "This is not really a home, this is an apartment"? Shouldn't a "home" be physically permanent? Now at the end of the twentieth century, it is so rarely permanent: we move frequently, and we divorce frequently.

Much as we try, and much as statistics tell us that the stable-for-a-lifetime nuclear family is not the "norm" anymore, something in us still feels that we want "it"—and that we have failed, we are "wrong" if we do not "make it work," have that particular home. And yet, as seen, many women inside that kind of "home" do not feel nourished or cared for—or even connected. Many feel tremendously lonely and angry. And men, as seen in *The Hite Report on Male Sexuality*, are often angry with it too.*

Home is a state of mind; home in an emotional sense tends to creep up on one. It takes a while for affection to grow, increments of trust and counting on someone or a place or a certain situation—until one day, "it" really *is* home. And this is what women are trying to get to, in a way, when they "complain" that men won't get close to them: because, then, there is no "home."

Can we reorganize the home and family so that it is more than, as some have called it recently, just "the feeding and sexual gratification of

---

* Even while the world was changing all around them, becoming industrial or now post-industrial, and men were frequently having to learn new jobs, men could always return "home to a woman."

two production units"? Yes, heterosexual love relationships can become much better, but there is no reason why they alone should be taken seriously, counted on as "home." Each person knows in fact where her or his heart lies, where she or he would go this minute if they could—where home is. It should be seen as positive that now we have the choice of creating "home" where we find it—not having to make ourselves fit into the "right grouping of people," in the proper "box" for living.

If "home is where the heart is"—where one feels loved, "seen," and we remember this, it will help us to stop thinking that a "home" must consist of one man, one woman, and 2.3 children. Re-creating home will take more than men "helping" women with the dishes; men will have to re-create themselves—respiritualize themselves, be able to believe in women, stop worrying about dominating. Women, having been in the home for so long, may not want to put so much effort into it again so soon. It may take women a while to begin to trust men again.

We need a new concept for the basic structure we call "home," as part of the re-evaluation of the purposes of the society in general. What *is* our social philosophy today, the overall purpose of the society? Economic production? Stable "families"? To provide a place guaranteeing the individual's right to a search after meaning, or the "pursuit of happiness"? To rescue the planet and change our relationship to nature, while the planet will still support us?

It is clear that women's great inner questioning is part of large cultural change—one that women are playing a central role in, as those with another perspective to offer, alternative possible solutions to current problems. The society needs a new infusion of idealism and dreams—a redefinition of goals. As women think through their personal lives, try to understand them and the men they love, they are critiquing this world, and envisioning a new one. Women are going through a revolution, and they are taking the culture with them.

A Cultural Revolution in Progress

Women's Thinking about Relationships Is Causing Them to Question the Whole System

What is going on right now in the minds of women is a large-scale cultural revolution. Women everywhere are asking themselves serious questions about their personal lives. These questions are growing initially out of their desire to have closer, more satisfying relationships with the men they are with. As their frustration with these relationships increases, many begin to ask deeper and deeper questions—finally, not only about love, but about the entire system.

As woman after woman lies in bed at night wondering, "Why did so and so not call?" or "Why doesn't my husband turn over and talk to me about this thing that he knows is on my mind, or at least that I told him is on my mind?" she begins thinking, analyzing all the possible answers. First, she may wonder, "Is it *me*? Is there something wrong with me?" Next, she may try to figure out the psychological makeup of the man she is with, his individual psychological background. Then, to understand this, she often begins to look at *his* parents' family structure—and then next at the overall social patterns that made *them* that way—until finally, in her searching, she comes face to face with the whole system, and asks herself how *it* got the way it is.

In other words, the pain in many women's personal lives, or the built-up frustration as women try to figure out a relationship (or deal with the loneliness inside it), leads women to a series of deeper questions about *why* love is so difficult—why men behave as they do, why a man can be sometimes loving, sometimes cold and distant—*why*? And the question, "Does it have to be this way?" Pondering these questions, women are developing a rather clear-cut and detailed idea of what it is they really want out of relationships—what they think are the right bases for human relationships and for the society as a whole.

Women's dissatisfaction: driving social change

As women think through these questions, they are causing everything to change. Recognizing the problems, thinking through the issues, women are becoming different from what they are analyzing. Having to analyze a thing so deeply removes one from it, and so women begin to feel removed from the current system, things as they are. It is impossible to ask these questions and not change, to stop the process inside oneself: seeing the situation, a new level of understanding and awareness takes place which cannot be undone, and so one is—whether one wants to be or not—transformed—changed forever.

The feelings of alienation women are describing here in their personal lives are leading to the formulation of a new set of political goals and philosophical beliefs, a new philosophy, based on women's traditional point of view, modified by the changes women have made during the last twenty years.

Women are in a struggle with the dominant ideological structure of the culture. As women see their relationships and their lives different-ly—*become* different—many are no longer content to live biculturally. And wrestling with themselves on many issues, they also discuss these matters with their women friends—comparing relationships, asking what is the best one can expect out of life, and how to interpret men's actions. These discussions between women are part of a very important process of creating and maintaining a specific value system.

Finally, these changes in thinking are all happening in conjunction with women's new economic situation which has been called "the quiet revolution."* Within the last ten years, the number of women with jobs and businesses has increased so markedly that in fact women as a group are no longer essentially economically dependent on men. This is a startling development—and one whose implications have only barely begun to take hold. Although many women receive extremely low salaries (and day care is expensive), more women than ever have enough resources to make it on their own, if they have to—even with children, and even if only minimally. The 50 percent divorce rate, mostly initiated by women, and the "feminization of poverty" mean that women today would rather leave a relationship than stay and put up with a negative situation.†

---

* So referred to by Elizabeth Dole, and later by *The Economist.*
† The "feminization of poverty" is a phenomenon that has been misinterpreted: it is caused not so much by men leaving women as by women choosing (now that they have an alternative) to leave men, even if they have to be poor. A large number of women are refusing to stay in bad situations any longer.

The Other Transformed

Forty years ago, Simone de Beauvoir aptly described women as the "Other"—as defined by men and men's view of the world. Now, women have taken that position as Other and transformed it, turned it around, making of it a new vantage point from which to analyze and define society. No longer are women an "other" knocking at the door to be let into society. Women now have gone beyond this point, reaching a stage where they no longer want to integrate themselves into "men's" world so much as to reshape the world, make it something better. From "outside," we are in an advantaged position to do just this: we can understand and interpret the system we are distanced from more clearly than those at its center.

Women's re-evaluation of themselves and of the culture is part of a process that has been going on for some time, for over a century.* During the last twenty years, this change, which could be called a revolution in women's definition of themselves and of society, has been occurring in stages.† Stage one began with women "demanding equal rights." Stage two was women trying to take a place in, join, the "male" world. And stage three, now, is women consolidating their own value system, examining and discussing the society as we know it, accepting some values of the dominant culture, discarding others—leading to the cultural struggle currently in progress.‡ The fourth stage of revolution would be to change the culture.

The stage of women "demanding equal rights" was superseded by the current stage when women discovered that "equal rights" would mean integrating themselves into the "male" value system. Women, as we have seen, are under great pressure to give up their traditional (even if newly redefined) values and take on "male" values (such as giving up relating sex to feelings so much, etc.). But many women

---

* The feminist tradition in France has been traced back five centuries to Christine de Pisan, a French writer who defended women in the 1500s. See Joan Kelly's *Women, History and Theory* (Chicago: University of Chicago Press, 1984).

† These do not refer to Lenin's or Trotsky's or Betty Friedan's stages.

‡ Women's re-examination of our situation began with "equal rights" but has evolved into much more than this. As Evelyn Fox Keller has commented, "We began by asking a few simple questions about equality, and it was like unraveling a ball of knitting; the more we looked for the beginning, the more we unraveled, until finally we are undoing the whole thing." Thus, questions women have raised about "equality" have led to discussions, examinations, and reconceptions of the nature of methodology in the sciences/social sciences, the philosophical understanding of "truth," the various definitions of "science," and so on.

feel they cannot do this and be true to their own beliefs; for example, most women do not want to be competitive and continually relate to others in terms of one-upmanship.

As one woman put it, "Women can only have 'equal rights' if they adopt the whole male value system. But most women cannot do this and maintain their own integrity; women would have to compromise themselves." "We are not trying to say anymore that we want to be just like men," another woman states. "We are women, not a cloned version of 'men' or the society's version of who we are! We refuse to accept these terms."

The result is that women are faced with having to redesign the whole system. Many, as seen, solve the problem (temporarily?) by living double lives—bisecting themselves to keep things going. But, while many women are in fact trying to make decisions about combining their culture with the "male" culture, trying to see which values are workable in both systems, most men are not trying to fit in with women's "ideology." Nor do they see why they should. They feel women are supposed to adapt to *their* ideology.

Women as a Force in History★

Women's thinking is revolutionary: redesigning their personal lives and the nature of relationships, women are deciding what they do and do not want life to be, clarifying their own philosophy. Where we are going is still unclear—but that is one of the exciting things about what we are seeing here—that there are so many individuals participating in this reformulating of what is going on, so many points of view.

Of course, in any value system there will always be debate, as, for example, in the "male" system there are "democratic," "conservative," and "liberal" points of view, and so on; it is not that we have to pin down exactly what every woman would think or do were she to run the government, or what she thinks and believes now. However, one thing *is* clear, and that is that the spectrum of women's thought represents a different cultural outlook from that represented by men in *The Hite Report on Male Sexuality* and in other works.

Cultural change, then, is something we are all in together now, as at night when we go home and try to accommodate our needs to his *but* still insist that he meet us halfway; or when we talk to our friends; or when we work at a standard job but try to do it our own way. In

★ As Mary Beard put it so aptly in her 1927 work.

this manner we are all changing society, developing a new consensus of what is valid philosophically as a way to live.

The "male" ideology and the psychology of a culture

What is the "male" system, and how does it affect men? Why do men think and behave as they do?

The "male" ideology is the dominant frame of reference for Western civilization. In fact, it is the basic building block of almost all current societies, no matter of which religion or state system—Eastern, Western, or non-aligned; Islamic, Christian, or "atheist." And so, the "male" ideology is, in a way, everyone's ideology, although women live biculturally, also knowing the rules of their own belief system. Racism, gender prejudice, and class divisions may all be different varieties of this basic "male" ideology, which is essentially an ideology of hierarchy.★

Now, the question is: is this ideology biological, "natural" (because "women have children" and because "when men compete, some are stronger and smarter"), or is it part of an historical cultural system spread by a warlike group (the Indo-Europeans) which expanded out of the East in succeeding waves, between approximately 15,000 and 5,000 years ago? *Have* women always and everywhere been "dominated"? Were women, through the centuries, the "weaker" class? If we begin to consider prehistory (history before written language), which is at least ten times as long as what we call "history," we may find a quite different picture of social attitudes and family structure.

Hierarchy: "Human Nature" or an Ideological Construction?

Is a hierarchical social structure necessary, or is it antiquated and out of place in an age of democracy? Do hierarchy and inequality keep popping up in all kinds of societies because they are "human"—or is this behavior exaggerated by a "male"-hierarchical ideology?

As noted earlier, one of the most important ways through which the hierarchical system of unquestioning obedience to authority (or "what is") is transmitted to Jews and Christians alike is through the biblical tale of Abraham taking his son Isaac up on a mountain where God had

★ Does the noble part of this tradition—the positive, outward, socially interested side of the masculine—have to include the anti-woman ideology? Can a group only define itself by making itself "special" and excluding others?

commanded that he kill or "sacrifice" the boy. Abraham is given no reason other than that the Lord commanded it, and that therefore it was "right." From this, Abraham learns that he must obey the system and not ask why the rules are the rules. He must show his loyalty by not questioning authority. This system rewards men, especially "upper class" men, with elevated status.

Today, this elevated status continues to be reinforced in men by the daily use in the English language of the pronoun "he," the adjective "his," and the generic term "man" to refer to all humans. Further, as noted, men are reminded in "nature" specials on television (and popular biology textbooks) that they have a "natural" tendency (therefore "right"?) to be "dominant," to "rule"—that "competition for dominance" is "part of their natural behavior." But even if this were true in some species of animals, it is certainly not true in all, and who is to say which is the "model" for *our* species? And even if it were "natural," would this make it "right"?

Applying democracy to the family

Most men, while they would probably say they believe in democratic government, have not stopped to think that they have not applied the same principles to the family. Many seem to assume that women are not capable of being equal, and that men/husbands know what is best for women.

But, in fact, with the promulgation of the idea of equality and democratic government during the Enlightenment of the eighteenth century, the idea of man as Automatically-Head-of-Society-and-the-Family became an irrational part of the system, i.e., if power was not derived from the authority of God and the scriptures, but now rested on the innate ability of each individual in a democratic system—on what did male authority in the family rest?

Since belief in gender superiority went so deep in the ancient "male" ideology, this glaring inconsistency was not widely questioned until relatively recently,* beginning in the nineteenth century—and then, for the most part, by women. Indeed, rather than men recognizing the error of their ways, in the nineteenth century many men "found" support for the idea of male superiority in "science" (or popularized science).†

---

* Although as early as 1776, Abigail Adams asked her husband, working on the new American Constitution, "not to forget the ladies" (in a letter); he declined to comply. And, even earlier, such women as Christine de Pisan had written of women's rights in the fifteenth century.

† And in a new psychological theory. See Shulamith Firestone, *The Dialectic of Sex.*

The Darwinian,* nineteenth-century version of "male domination" succeeded the old idea of the God-given inherited right of kings (and men) to rule, in the following way: humans, it was said, had come to dominate other animals as we evolved, because we were superior; similarly, within our species, it was claimed, males "naturally" competed with females and each other for "dominance"; therefore, if we have a social structure in which men are dominant, this is clearly proof that males were and are "naturally" superior, i.e., stronger, "smarter,"† and so on. (Similarly, adherents of slavery in the eighteenth and nineteenth centuries argued that blacks were slaves because their "natures" were to be lazy and dependent, and that they were happy that way, etc.) Darwinian competition was also used to "justify" sharp divisions between social classes in the nineteenth century, and continues today as the framework for theories of "free competition in the marketplace."

All this is not to say that competition such as in games, normal trading, etc., is not part of life, but that cooperation has been left quite underemphasized. Many biologists and primatologists and even economists are now trying to make up for this by showing how important the cooperative forces of nature and society are.

In any case, the competition theme is a central point in the "male" ideology: "real" men "naturally" compete for a spot in the hierarchy, *must* compete (or they are "cowards" and "wimps"!). This is one of the most important credos of "masculinity." In fact, without a belief in competition as a ruling force of "nature," men would not be able to continue their hierarchies, including looking down on women, and still feel morally righteous about them.

And there is an underside to all of this for men too: by having to close off one side of themselves to women's equal humanity, blind parts of themselves to their inhumanity to women through the general social system, not "see," in order to be loyal to the men's hierarchy, men coarsen themselves—deaden their sense of justice.

Men live with the interior knowledge, conscious or not, that by ruling, they are dominating someone, i.e., women. Since they live with/have to look at those with less privilege every day, they must develop a way of not really "seeing" them. Men know on some level that they are not superior, and they know that this gender division is

* Or, Darwinism in its popularized form.
† For part of the nineteenth century, it was commonly assumed by the scientific community that the brains of males were larger than the brains of females. However, when the opposite turned out to be the case, this "fact" could no longer be used to justify male authority, and so the issue was quietly dropped.

unjust—so the question becomes, how to live with it? The answer is, learn not to really "see" it.

Research from *The Hite Report on Men and Male Sexuality* shows that most boys, between the ages of eight and fourteen, go through a stage of learning which involves forcing themselves to disassociate from, stop identifying with, their mothers. They are forced by the culture to "choose," to identify henceforth only with things "male," not to retain any "female" ways about them, for this would "ruin their chances" in life. This is a period of great stress for boys, who often feel guilty and disloyal for thus "leaving" the mother; many never recover fully.* And so, boys go through a stage of first identifying with their mother, then next, having to break with that identification and learn to keep a distance, disassociate themselves, ridicule women/their mother, dominate them/her, and finally, reach the stage where they can rule, dominate with no qualms. *This* is the psychology of men which should be studied. But it is not; instead, the questioning is focused on women: "explanations" are sought for the so-called "problems of women."

Finally, this learning process, living with this knowledge of injustice built into the system, means that gradually men lose their ability to *see* injustice, and also to be just, to recognize justice and expect it of themselves—because they have been so carefully educated by the "male" culture to turn a blind eye to injustice on a massive scale. Living with this forced blindness leads to cynicism: idealism about life is impossible in such a situation. Thus, the "male" ideology breeds negativity toward life, finally becoming a blight on the culture.

How big a part of the "male" ideology is seeing women as second-class?

If part of the "male" ideological system is the assertion that men are "better" than women—smarter, more "rational," that they are more important, more capable of running corporations, launching campaigns, building things, being philosophers (because they are more "rational" and "scientific"), and so on—how big an investment do men have in seeing women as "less," "second best? Obviously, quite a substantial

---

* A large part of teenage boys' "mean and nasty" crazes are attempts by them to deal with their culturally imposed guilt; i.e., if one is "bad" already, one might as well glorify being an outlaw, being really tough and cruel, etc. Thus, the glorification of being mean and nasty as being "really male" (for example, as frequently seen on MTV and in children's monster or war toy commercials) comes because men (by definition) can never be "good."

one. But is it logically necessary to the overall ideology? Is being "anti-woman" making men continue to try to keep women subservient, and thus the deeper definition of the "male" ideology—or is seeing aggression as "natural"?

Which came first: the "aggressive belief in competition for dominance" side of the "male" ideology—or owning women? Some say that the idea of some "owning" others came about when men first wanted to control female sexuality and thus "own" their offspring, be sure the children were "theirs." Perhaps this is true: the "male" ideology is obsessed with keeping the genders separate. This may be in part because men would lose control of inheritance and reproduction if women had choices of other family systems and were not forced to be so focused on men, or so loyal to "male" institutions.

What is "male pride"?

To play devil's advocate for a moment, why shouldn't men look down on women? Men have built the bridges, the mathematical systems, the rockets and so on. Do men feel that, since they have built all this—the universities, great music, etc.—they have every right to be proud of what "they" have done?*

But does a twenty-year-old male have a right to "male pride"—as he personally had nothing to do with all these achievements? Isn't his "male pride" just a matter of taking advantage of "class" privilege? Is most "male pride" a cover for the ideology of men as dominant? Men as having the right to "possess" all they see?† Man is the sun, with the world and women as his province, which revolves around him at his bidding? "Male pride" essentially means: do not challenge a man, do not challenge what he says or does, or you are challenging the male world, and all the power behind it.

Women also have the right to take and build on the good parts of "male" culture, because, after all, young men don't start with

---

* Perhaps some men look at women's position the way the victors looked at the Germans after World War I: women cannot be admired, have no right to be proud and independent, because they are/have been owned, captured, defeated. As one woman answers this "men have done it all" point of view: "Sure, they have been nurtured and made comfortable by women—it helped them be all they could."

† Did communism, as an idealistic system in theory of "give to all according to need," try to do away with the "taking" aspect of the "male" ideology? Even earlier, Christianity emphasized a turn-the-other-cheek, love-thy-neighbor point of view, especially in Jesus' teachings, downplaying the earlier idea of a wrathful God to whom "men" owed blind obedience. Thus humanism, the "Rights of Man," and even communism as an ideal can all be seen as outgrowths of Judeo-Christian *ideals*.

"nothing" either; they build on the cultures before them. And women have contributed substantially to what has been built; also, in a profound sense, women may have built much of the pre-patriarchal tradition which merged with later patriarchal cultures. For example, the idea of "justice" of the classical Greeks (portrayed by the figure of a woman) was not pulled out of thin air, but undoubtedly harked back to a long and rich tradition of debates over what "justice" is and how society should operate.

When looked at more closely, in practice "male pride," more often than being related to courage and bravery, means that men should not be "challenged"—i.e., assertions of "male pride" are really usually a demand for dominance. "Male pride" is considered a supreme value, which must not be tampered with. What we are looking at here is not "human nature," as it is so conveniently called by those who would like to justify the status quo, that is, men dominating society because they are superior, but an endlessly repeating ideology, created by a certain group/groups at a certain time in history. Beliefs teach rules which dictate their own logic. But this does not mean they *are* logical or right.

Shakespeare's *The Taming of the Shrew* illustrates the "it's all biological" school of "masculinity." It and similar stories should, if used in high school English classes at all, be noted as examples of psychological problems growing out of a particular culture, a specific ideological point of view. Classes should not be led to believe that these characters represent "human nature." If so, the story in fact eggs boys on to make just such things as "taming the woman" the "test of their dominance" or "masculinity"—which they are told is a "biological urge," an urge they have a "right" to feel and act on, that they "can't help" but display.

Men's fear of being "in love"

What does the ideology of "masculinity" tell men about how to deal with love in an ongoing, *mutual* relationship? Nothing. It only tells men to be dominant, to dominate relationships, and to make sure the woman doesn't "dominate" them. This explains many men's fear of being "in love" and displeasure when "overcome" with feelings for a woman. A "real man" must separate himself; assert his "pride" and "dominance" before all else.

Thus, the opposite side of the coin of a "masculinity" defined as being "tough," "able to take it," is that most men also are afraid to express emotions or be too close to women, lest they seem "weak." To put it another way, the split between love and reason in classical Western thought (with "love" decreed to be "feminine," and "reason" masculine") makes it difficult for many men to love without inner conflict.*

Most men in *The Hite Report on Male Sexuality* were seen to have enormous inner conflicts over their love relationships—but few doubts that they were doing the "right thing" when they chose in favor of "reason" and against "irrational" feelings of love and attraction, whether physical and/or emotional and spiritual. Most men were proud of their ability to resist their feelings. At the same time, there is a logical contradiction in this denial of emotion: men may hold demeaning attitudes to women's "emotionality," but most still rely on women's emotional support to get them through.†

Change is a Catch-22 for men

While many men are extremely sensitive to ethical and moral issues, the closest many have come to developing an "ethical" position for themselves vis-à-vis woman has been to believe men should take care of women. While it is praiseworthy for men, or anyone, to take care of others, this does not resolve the basic issue. If men are to be fair-minded, they must look at the overall system and completely overhaul its idea of what an ethical relationship between men and women would be.

But change is a problem for men, because to give up "dominance" may mean being seen as "unmasculine"—but to question the value of domination is the only way to improve "masculinity," or society. How can men, given this no-win situation, change their ideology? (And besides, as has often been said, who wants to give up "power" if they don't have to/aren't forced to?) The first step is for men to look inside themselves and understand their lives and their philosophy better.

---

* Where did this particular dichotomy come from historically? To assume it sprang out of "nature" would be to stay within the parameters of the current ideologically defined "reality." It would be interesting to explore, historically, the various strands of this mind/body division in other Indo-European societies, compared with *pre*-Indo-European thought and culture—although what we know of these societies is as yet fragmentary. Quite a few languages of these earlier societies (what languages or signs are known) have yet to be deciphered (such as Linear A on Crete).
† Men's emotionality is encouraged in such events as the Superbowl, which is all-male, a glorification of the male, and one of the rare times men are really allowed and encouraged to be emotional; many women feel they become "overly emotional" about it.

The Current State of World Affairs: The Connection between "Male Pride," a Hierarchical Social Structure, and International Terrorism

One could make the statement—seemingly exaggerated at first glance—that political terrorism for "independence" and some men's terroristic attitudes toward women are all part of proving "masculinity"—as unfortunately defined by patriarchal cultures around the world.*

The "male" ideology in its current phase, with its acceptance of the increasing amount of violence in the world and toward the natural environment, and its seeming lack of emotional concern for individuals, its focus on power and "dominance," is allowing aggression and terrorism to run riot. If the "male" ideology prescribes that competition is "natural," why *shouldn't* anyone use any means at hand to "win" in the competition for "dominance"—since power and winning are all that are respected in the final analysis anyway? In the current political situation, terrorism is a built-in consequence, a logical outcome of the "male" ideology with its focus on hierarchy.

As the feeling intensifies through increased media communications that the world is small, that we are a global village, the belief increases that one individual doesn't really matter very much, that we are expendable. Every day, as television shows us so many parts of the world, we cannot help but realize how "small" we are as individuals—that some nations and some individuals are very rich and powerful, while others are very poor. The poor and powerless can *see* the others, the rich and powerful, day after day on television, and in newspapers. This reminds them/us forcefully of their/our position, reminds us that the dominant ideology only respects power—and this knowledge increases aggression, as aggression seems to be the only way to be heard. And in a very terrible way, this is true. Disruptive acts are almost the only way for a small state or individual to get its/his(?) voice heard, or for a small state to make a point, in a hierarchical world system.

Within the system now (whether the world/state system or the "male" system as individual women encounter it with men) other alternatives are limited or closed off. A new system should be devised in which small countries and/or women are not driven to such desperate states of mind, to a feeling there is no other alternative than to fight or remain powerless, because those in power (or the man in the relationship) won't listen.

---

* This could be seen as a male version of the feminist precept, "The personal is political."

It is significant that terrorists are mostly male: is this a sign of the poverty of the "male" psyche (as created by the "male" ideology) in which men can't talk out their troubles (which would be "weak"), or can't facilitate cooperation with those around them (because they are taught to judge and compete)—or is this a sign of the "powerless" ("power is wrong") mentality of women, who would be afraid to show anger, be "unloving" or "aggressive"? Here we have our dilemma again: which system is "right"? Without stopping to analyze all the possible answers here, it can definitely be said, at least, that it is a weakness and a failure of the "male" system not to deal with all the possibilities and complexities of a very diverse world—instead insisting on dominating and trying to control the diversity which could be so productive and so harmonious. Valuing people and their feelings is perhaps the basis of democracy in government; why can't men now begin to apply this idea, valuing each individual equally, to their own personal lives and political opinions?

Origins of "Male" Domination

Did the "male" ideology have an historical beginning, was there a time and place when this social system with its hierarchical ideology and religious structure (as differentiated from the more egalitarian pantheon of the Greeks, the Egyptians, probably the pre-Greeks, and others) became established? Or is "male" domination a "normal" function of male hormones—i.e., testosterone levels make men restless, "aching for a fight," loving a good battle? Haven't these hormonal influences been exaggerated by those who would wish to rationalize aggressive masculinity as "natural"; to say that "male" "human nature" as we know it is "natural," and therefore "male" dominance in the social structure is also "natural"? Almost all the academic and scientific disciplines are currently involved in exploring these arguments, finding pieces of evidence.

Others argue that "male" domination originates not from "male hormones" but from the "biological" nature of the family; that is, as we have heard (ad nauseam), women "have" to stay home to take care of their children, leaving men to go out and defend them, get food. However, it has been shown that in gathering–hunting societies women do most of the gathering, and also that the majority of the food is gathered; therefore, women in some societies in prehistory probably provided most of the food. Also, there is a current debate in anthropology regarding whether the rest of the food was hunted or scavenged.*

On the other hand, perhaps male domination is not biological at all but the result of an historical accident—certain tribes with this ideology winning key battles, battles won in fact *because* of their having this ideology: an extremely competitive, combative, and warlike group could easily be the victor over less militaristic, more peaceful societies.

We do not know enough about prehistory (the time before writing, or writing that has not been deciphered or was perishable) to trace the various strands of philosophical thought back much further than 3000 B.C.† But we know that high forms of art and culture existed at least as long ago as 35,000 years, as the Ice Age art exhibit appearing at the Museum of Natural History in New York, and featured as the cover story of *Newsweek* in the fall of 1986, demonstrates.

The Old Testament of the Bible makes an important point of repeating, in stanza after stanza, the lineage of certain people, *because it wants to establish the tradition of descent through fathers*, not through mothers. What does this imply? That *maternal* descent may have been traditional for preceding millennia, as suggested by lists of female names found on clay tablets in Crete and elsewhere. The Old Testament also inveighs against the worship of female gods (who were popular in Canaan‡ and elsewhere)—thus also implying the existence of a possible important status for women, at least in religion, in competing ideological systems of the time.

Primatologists and fossil paleoanthropologists (those who study bone fragments of primates and humans one to two million years old) now believe that the "first families" were almost certainly mothers and children living in a clan grouping—the father being a later addition.§ What contribution did pre-state societies in which women may have had a more important, or even the leading role in "governance," the making of rules, weighing justice, have in forming the tradition of states seen later in history? How did "chiefdoms" become a male-dominant system?

---

* Richard Potts, paper delivered before the American Anthropological Association annual meeting, 1985.
† The original Hebrew God was pictured as being wrathful and aggressive in the earliest parts of the Old Testament. However, one historian has questioned the male role offered to men by Adam; in *The New York Times Book Review*, John Boswell of Yale University has written that Adam is really a kind of non-person, a passive being who doesn't really do much except succumb to Eve's temptations, she being the major actor. This is an interesting viewpoint, and might corroborate the belief of some that in earlier history (or prehistory) women were held supreme and were those in charge of society.
‡ Ba'al, referred to only by name in the Bible, was in fact a female deity.
§ Roundtable discussion, Institute for Human Origins, University of California, Berkeley, November 1986.

Archaeologists studying pre-Indo-European culture have added many more questions to the puzzle: Crete probably was not a patriarchy, and indeed, many of the civilizations around the Mediterranean basin in prehistory had long traditions of holding sacred female creation figures, or "goddesses." Archaeological sites such as Çatal Hüyük in Anatolia (Turkey, near the Mediterranean) had no walls around the city for defense; therefore, was the point of view of these societies less warlike?* If so, this could disprove the "male" ideology's position today that "aggression" is a large and "natural part" of (biologically ordained) "human nature." In fact, contemporary society is urging men on a daily basis to be aggressive and competitive, not "soft"—deemed to be the two basic "natural" opposites of human behavior. Another spectrum is not seen as possible, nor another composition of "human nature"—either in the past, as having once existed, or for the future.†

Loving Men at This Time in History

"I want to love him and be close to him, but I just can't, the way I used to be. He can't understand what I'm talking about half the time, it seems, and when I try to insist or explain it more to him, he gets irritated. So I have to just let it go—let go of him, my dreams, love him for who he is, even if he can't understand a lot of who I am. I feel I see him clearly, who he is and how his life became what it is—but he doesn't know me the same way."

Can one be as close as one dreams one can be? Is what's "out there" in contemporary society an atmosphere conducive to letting love relationships develop? If society separates the two genders so decisively that it impedes love—a kind of supracultural version of Romeo and

---

* Is classical Greece one of the crossover points, culturally, between earlier goddess-centered, less martial "states," such as Crete, and the warlike trend of the tradition? No one is sure; some scholars speak of invading Indo-European tribes with a warlike ideology who had invaded northern India two centuries earlier, coming then into Greece and later Italy, pushing the indigenous populations to the south, where they continued their traditions of goddess worship (usually with many deities) up until the historical period of the Roman Empire and even later. Of course, a supremely hierarchical system must not be a multi-deity system, but a "one god above all" system—the point which the Hebrews made so much of. For a discussion of the changeover in Greek mythology, see Jane Harrison, *Prolegomena to the Study of Greek Religion* (United Kingdom: Merlin Press, 1981).
† See S. Hite and Robert Carneiro, abstracts, 1985 annual meeting of the American Anthropological Association.

Juliet, the two genders made to promise to believe in different ways of life and to distrust one another—what is an individual to do about it?

It is not that women think men are the enemy—but many women do think that men who live by the "male" ideology are the enemy. In a way, this book, besides being a redefinition by women of who they are, what reality is, is a massive plea from women for men to stop living by their current rules and rethink what they are doing to themselves, to women, and to the planet.

If men could only see how their belief system is hurting them too, how it is possible to lead a different life, they might—they probably would. In a way, most of them do understand on some level: the majority of men in *The Hite Report on Male Sexuality* say that after high school their best friends are their wives, or the women they know—because they find it impossible to really talk to other men. This is a clear indication that men *do* understand that no one can live with the "male" system alone—an indictment by men of their own system.

How alienated *are* women from a system based on the "male" ideology (in which women in the United States are not even considered for the office of President, and receive so much less money and status for their work)? How far has this process gone in women's minds? Are women so dissatisfied that this is the reason for the high divorce rate—are more women than ever now leaving marriages because they refuse to live any longer with a man or a system that classifies them as less, less important, less intellectual, less rational?

As individual women go through this process of struggling to understand what is making love so difficult, they often find themselves gradually and painfully saying goodbye—with deep regret and sadness—to a belief in the possibility of the kind of love they had wanted with men. Also, many find they have gradually lost faith in the entire "male" cultural system itself.

This process of leave-taking usually happens in stages. First women bargain with themselves: "O.K., so I won't ask him to do the laundry or pick up the kids anymore—it's not worth it. I love him, he's a man and you just can't expect all this overnight, but I love him and I can enjoy him—and where else could I find a better lover, or a man who loves me as well?" When even this bargain doesn't really work, next to go is a woman's belief that she is loved "well." Still, she stays, because "I still love how well we know each other, what we have built up over time, and I hope he believes in this too . . ." and so on. With each bargaining chip in this interior dialogue, a woman gives up one more emotional tie

390

to the man until she realizes, finally, that she *is* in fact *alone*, living by herself, emotionally.

As women struggle with this inner dilemma, questioning themselves daily about the same issue, the feeling often is: "I am giving more than he is emotionally, trying harder to make it work. Why doesn't he try harder, seem to want to meet me halfway? Does he even understand that he is not? Will the relationship ever be better? Am I a fool to continue it? Should I keep on struggling? Give less energy to it? Should I *leave?*"

This state of inner questioning, alienation, and frustration many women are experiencing—whether they stay in their relationship or leave—represents a long goodbye not only to the man in question but also to "male" culture and to our allegiance to that culture's hold on us. In the process of leaving a man, whether emotionally or physically, so many women, as we have seen, go through layers of self-questioning about the meaning of love, relationships, life, the nature of family, work, what life is all about—all the basic philosophical questions one has to confront to make major decisions. And as women's thoughts about these inner questions seem to raise more and more questions, women are piece by piece analyzing and seeing "male" culture for the first time. Through this independent thought, women are shifting their allegiance from the frame of reference that has for so long dominated everything.

It seems, based on this research into private life, that women today are already moving into a different frame of reference. While most are doggedly trying to get men they love to change, they are relying more and more on their women friends as major supports and primary relationships.

One woman comments on the transformation she sees in her own mind, having gone through all these emotions in relationships:

"I think the solution is that we have to mentally transcend the whole thing. It's not a question of to be with men or without them. The real solution is when you reach a stage where somehow or another it's just not the biggest worry in your life—it's a different way that you see the world. You live in another sphere, which is to become whatever your interests are, and maybe men are part of it and maybe not, but it is not *the* feature. Female friendships are definitely a part of it—I don't mean that now women should give up men and live only with women and follow some feminist party line, that's not it . . . I mean you live somewhere else emotionally—love can be there and become more or less important in your life—but you don't get your identity through a man."

Should Women Take a Mass Vacation from Trying to Understand Men?

"I sit here in this argument, discussion, thinking to myself, surely you will say what I need to hear next, or give an opinion on this, your feelings about this . . . and yet you don't. And no matter for how many hours or days or years you don't, I can never stop listening, never stop hoping, waiting for, hearing your reply in my mind. And sometimes I think the frustration of waiting to hear your opinion, what you think, really think, will drive me mad."

One woman, at a very trying time in her life, wrote the following:

"Single women should boycott men—have a national strike! All these games are so demeaning to women! Barbaric on the part of the men and pathetic on the part of the women. They plot, 'Should I do this or that, how can I get him,' etc., etc., etc. Men's attitude, even with AIDS, is: 'New York is a candy store.' I think women should live together and raise children together—period. Men have a way of approach and avoidance (distancing)—you know, first, romantic seduction and candlelight, the chase—but then, to *live* with a woman? How? Why? Who cares? New York is a candy store—and women are the candies, treats for men—not people.

"Even very nice men are full of stereotypes and dangerous preconceptions that can injure a woman's basic sense of self. Think of the nastiest names you can to call a man and they all relate to women—i.e., 'pussy-whipped,' 'dominated by a woman,' 'he's a momma's boy,' 'son of a bitch,' 'fuck off,' and so on.* Men's attitudes are so bad, so impaired, and they don't even realize how negative to women they are. They think they *love* women! It will take some massive action to make them start realizing, start thinking about all of this—like a national strike, or a boycott, a new version of *Lysistrata*. But women (any woman who is) should stop humiliating themselves—and married women too—just to 'have a man'! It's holding us all back!"

---

* See Dr. Janet L. Wolfe, "Women," in A. Ellis and M. Bernard, eds., *Clinical Applications of Rational-Emotive Therapy* (New York: Plenum, 1985).

The gradual wearing down of an identity: a betrayal of yourself?

"Women haven't yet begun to fight for their rights in personal relationships"
"If you're giving all and getting nothing . . . get out."

In fact, some would say that women should stay away from love affairs with men until we can change this emotionally draining system. The reason: if women are brought up with "love as their destiny" (i.e., to think that love is the most important goal in life), and men are not—*and* if women believe in love as giving, and men do not—then the system itself, with its two ideologies of "male" and "female" behavior, supports men in "starring" in relationships and in the outside world, with women supporting them emotionally and domestically.

Does this system make women angry? Yes—but often this anger is stymied because "women have no right to anger": a "good" woman is loving and giving, not "nagging" and "demanding." How can a woman be "loving" and change her situation at the same time? Will she have to give up her image of herself as a caring, understanding person, and worry that she is "bitchy" or unpleasant if she "insists" or "complains" to a man that she wants to change the relationship, or tells him that he has to change?

Women as Revolutionary Agents of Change: To Transform the Culture with Our Values

Do Almost All Women Feel Generalized Repressed Anger at Men and "Male" Society for Dominating Them?

How do women feel coming up against this "male" code of behavior, with its wall of hierarchy?

Do most women feel some form of generalized anger at men, for being in control of the society, the home, their lives, everything—having more power, more status, more influence? And is this independent of how they are or are not treated as individuals by the individual men in their lives? This would be only logical, after all; women would have to be cone-heads as a group not to have some of these feelings. Undoubtedly, this makes even the slightest remark which seems condescending maddening to a woman who has to fight this in every aspect of her life—and worst of all, at home too.

Why shouldn't women be mad at all of history for keeping them out? Can we really celebrate the Declaration of Independence with the same glee that men do? Is it really ours? And how happy can we be, enjoying Richard Strauss's music, when we know he had such misogynistic views? Is history really *ours*? Or is our history only really beginning—even though there were great women during all periods, known and unknown, remembered and forgotten?

Would women ever spontaneously just become so angry that there would be an unstoppable expression of centuries of pent-up feeling, a dam bursting?*

---

* Do women really feel this much dissatisfaction? As a reporter for National Public Radio commented with regard to a 1986 *Women's Day* study of married women: "If we saw this much dissatisfaction in any other sector of the population, we'd be talking about revolution."

394

Such things do happen suddenly, to the puzzlement of historians, who ask, why *then*, when the conditions had been there all the time? Why the French Revolution *then*? Or why the revolt *now* in South Africa, when the situation has been discriminatory to blacks for a long time? Why the solidarity and show of strength now?

Would women ever reach such a point of frustration that they would become even more politically active, even violent? Could the situation be anything like the situation in South Africa, with women ready to fight for their rights and for their belief in how the society should be run, their right to a complete part in the government? Or is our policy of non-violent resistance better?

In a way, the position women are in is the same as that of some terrorists: some have been explaining their situation for years, trying to talk, etc. Finally, they become so frustrated that they begin to say, "Well, I'll make some trouble and then they'll *have* to listen." It's a phenomenon similar to somebody in a family who's not getting through, a child maybe, who starts throwing his or her plate on the floor during dinner. When you can't get through, after a long enough period of time, out of frustration, either you take it out on yourself and become suicidal, self-destructive, or you challenge the society—and one way is to become "terroristic."

Many women's anger is seen coming to the surface here. Do women have the right to "revolution"? Or, if "women can't be angry," "it's not ladylike," would this be impossible? Many women today feel like they don't fit in anymore, either "at home" or at work. At home, they feel guilty and "unprogressive" for being "at home"; while at work, a woman has to prove she is "just as good as a man," but still does not receive equal pay or equal opportunity. This makes women somewhat like a group without a home, without a place to be—a large displaced population, a people without a country.

If women don't fit in anymore, and are a majority of the population—as in fact they are—wouldn't this make women a potential revolutionary segment of the population?

"Kept Waiting For Too Long?"

An editorial in the London newspaper *The Guardian* (reported in the *International Herald Tribune* on August 31, 1986), while speaking of the mental state of blacks in South Africa who are waiting and striving for equality in their country, applies in some rather startling ways to women's quest for equal rights:

"South Africa [is] in an unstable equilibrium. The massively discontented Africans lack the unity and strength to overthrow apartheid, with its overwhelming apparatus of repression. But the power of the security machine is not so great that it can go where it likes without meeting resistance stiff enough to exact a steady toll on the human (mostly black) instruments of white domination. Such a stalemate could last for years or decades.

"The answer to the overriding question as to what kind of South Africa will emerge in the end becomes clearer the more the blacks are made to wait before they come into their inheritance. The bitterness in the townships is piling up even as more and more whites tell the opinion pollsters that they recognize majority rule as inevitable.

"The nature of the African government that emerges on that day will be directly related to what it has to endure and overcome to achieve power. If the outcome displeases the whites and their supporters in the West, they have only themselves, and President Botha and his ilk, to blame. Black resistance to apartheid is no longer just a law-and-order problem, if it ever was."

The injustices making for instability are clear. As the United Nations Decade for Women Conference in Nairobi in 1985 declared: "Women do almost all of the world's domestic work, which combined with additional work outside the home means that many women work a double day. Women grow about half of the world's food, but own hardly any land. They are concentrated in the lower-paid occupations and are more vulnerable to unemployment than men. In the area of health, women provide more health care than all the health services put together. Women perform two-thirds of the world's work, receive one-tenth of its income and own less than one-hundredth of its property."

The conference called for recognition of the value of women's unpaid labor, by asking governments to invest in services to women in the ratio to which they make a contribution to the national economy. This is estimated at 30 to 85 percent of the GNP, depending on the country.

There are interesting echoes here of women's assertions about men. Many men seem to have a tendency to let things get to a crisis stage by walking away (from a "complaining woman" or a "complaining people") until the group is so alienated that the government/man is faced with a catastrophic, black-and-white situation; people/women are forced to choose either to use force to gain equality, or to leave the person or the country altogether.

One woman correctly reminds us that we are still in the midst of a revolutionary process that is not over:

"Women are magnificent, resourceful, strong, brave, creative. Sensitive, warm, intelligent, and they communicate on altogether a different, more fluent and intuitive level than men. They are more self-sacrificing and nurturing, and if anyone will ensure the survival of this planet and this species, they are the ones. They are the backbone of this world economy. The ones whose unrecompensed, unceasing labor has made a decent standard of living available to so many.

"I'm a radical feminist at the cutting edge of the women's movement which is just beginning and which will create the most fabulous global revolution you've ever seen, 53 percent of the population, rising against patriarchal-hierarchical thought. My advice to women? Rise up! Take power! Don't be afraid! Listen to women."

Or, as Christabel Pankhurst, the English suffragist (1880–1956) tells us, "Remember the dignity of your womanhood. Do not appeal. Do not beg. Do not grovel. Take courage. Join hands, stand beside us, fight with us . . ."

"To Make a World in Which More Love Can Flourish"

Could the values of "female" culture serve as a framework for a revolutionary philosophical movement?

"How much, if ever, have institutions corresponded to the imaginative ideals that women created, love as women have imagined it? How much have women really imagined what all the possibilities are?"

—ELIZABETH PETROFF*

* S. Hite and E. Petroff, "Controversies over the Nature of Love," American Philosophical Association, annual meeting, 1986.

This study states many women's philosophical case for a new organization of human relationships—and therefore of the society.* Women here are questioning the human condition, saying it can be better than it is.

Equality and interaction as a social framework are not just idealistic dreams. Cooperation and teamwork are viable ways of organizing society. Nevertheless, it is often heard that women are "too emotional" to run governments, that "women's" "soft-hearted," cooperative ideals would not work on a global level in government or international relations. And yet, how can a system which has brought us to the brink of nuclear war and ecological disaster call another system unworkable or impractical?

If the "male" value system has brought us to the edge of annihilation, whether by nuclear war or destruction of the equilibrium of nature, it is time to look at other possible social organizations. In large part it is the interpersonal patterns of the "male" ideology, with its constant encouragement for men to use competition for dominance as the means of "resolving" disputes, that has led the world to the situation in which it now finds itself, with total destruction possible.

"Women's" philosophy truly does contain other ways of resolving disputes, or preventing them before they arise, i.e., the subtle negotiating process described earlier. In the midst of the very real problems with which society is now faced—problems the current system does not seem to be able to address adequately—it is time to take a serious look at "women's" alternative philosophy.†

---

* Indeed, how people make relationships is the basis of the social structure; or, "the personal is political," the social structure in microcosm.
† Of course, not all women are "just" and "kind," while many men are; it is not one's biology that creates these characteristics. However, women's shared experiences do tend to create certain understandings and ways of relating to the culture, just as do men's.

How Would This Transformation in Culture Occur?
How Does Change Happen?

Are revolutions about changing thinking, or taking power?

What if we *did* take seriously what we feel we know? What if we did try to establish generally what seems to us to be a better way of doing things? Remembering that women *are* a majority of the country, and that there are many men too who believe in the values of caring, fine-tuning relationships both at home and in business or global politics, keeping situations working for all parties involved before crisis situations develop, surely, with the majority of women and many men believing in these principles, we could make quite a try at it.

Why don't we? Why do we let the situation continue as it is? Because it is the way things have "always" been, with the "male" ideology dominant, a star fixed permanently in its heaven? How hard *would* it be to change? If women would support each other, as individuals and in economic and political alliances with each other, it could be fairly easy. If women would decide to cooperate on common goals, we could do anything.

On the other hand, do we have to "do" anything? If a large percentage of the population knows something is wrong with the ruling system, that it is unfair, and understands the antiquated ideology (the "male" ideology) behind it, this is already an enormous psychological change that cannot but have a tremendous impact—especially in combination with women's rapidly accelerating economic independence. Simply by thinking this way—not seeing men as more powerful, not feeling pressure to "get a man," not giving in to "male" power in the system, whether it is in a personal emotional relationship or at a bank with a male executive—each such woman is making change happen now: if a large part of our population is inwardly critiquing the overall system, separating themselves mentally from it, then that new mental life *is* a new culture. Or is this too simple?

Another theory of change is that revolution happens when the beliefs of some infiltrate or convert the beliefs of the many: "We have to convert them—show them our system is superior." By trying to change men in our personal relationships, will women change the larger society?

Sometimes the reverse happens. To make an analogy with politics: in what was known during World War II as the "Stockholm syndrome," referring to Sweden's attitude to Germany, a group often gradually comes to love and identify with its captor. On the other hand, sometimes a culture that is dominated by another politically and militarily *does* still manage to have its culture become dominant eventually. For example, the Romans were "civilized" by the Greeks (but the Greeks had more prestige than women do). Christianity was adopted by the Romans through an imperial decree—but did the imperial decree come about because of Christianity's underground popularity? Would it have eventually died out, even with its popularity, without the imperial decree? Traditions in Germany were changed by Christianity, but many of the old traditions survived simply because of their popularity and the strength of people's belief in them. Perhaps there has never been an example quite like our own.

There is tremendous pressure, as we go into new areas, to take on "male" colors, "male" beliefs, downgrade ourselves and our own way of life. Perhaps we ourselves fear trying out our own "sub"culture on the larger system, especially on a political level. But the "female" system, with its storehouse of humanistic values emphasizing mutuality and cooperation, is a cultural treasure. And we have not thrown out "male" values in a wholesale way: over the last twenty years of large-scale and historically important questioning of our values and identity, we have taken from the "male" system whatever was of value to mesh with the "female" system.

Some say we can best fight for our rights by electing political candidates: if "power only respects power," the more women become members of political groups, the more likely it is that we will see women candidates selected by the parties for major political office. And if we vote for them, we will see them elected. Others suggest that we form an alternative party. After all, the Green Party was started in Germany quite recently by a woman, Petra Kelly, and has had a great effect on German politics. The Green Party deals especially with issues of ecology and nuclear war. In Iceland, where women have been much more active than in the U.S., a feminist party won 10 percent of the vote and six seats in Parliament. In Norway, half the parliament has recently become female, due to women's organizing. And, as Corazon Aquino, in a speech at Harvard University on September 21, 1986, stated, "Women led the change of power in the Philippines by using non-violent protests."

On the other hand, something in the political system in the U.S.

and elsewhere seems to create a tendency to select women who are as "tough as the guys"—which is what "women's" philosophy is trying to examine and change. So the political system, as it is, can contain a built-in contradiction for many women who do not like fighting for power. Still, many people do believe that women in general would be more idealistic in the running of government than men tend to be—better suited to office, in fact. As one man wrote in *The New York Times* on Sunday, March 8, 1987, "Would women be as corrupt, aggressive and exclusive as men [in recent politics] if given the opportunity? I think not . . . men are unwilling or unable to give up a role, a way of behaving that was once necessary . . . [which] creates conflict with other men . . . [Women's] preference for negotiation over fighting, their abhorrence of violence, their inclination to compassion . . . are the qualities needed for leadership in the twenty-first century."

The principles of mutuality in relationships, such as women use with each other, are the essence of good diplomatic skills, which could be well used in government. The United States and now other countries seem constantly to find themselves in situations with "third world" countries in which they must choose either supporting non-humanitarian "right-wing" dictators or seeing the government "fall" to a "left-wing," supposedly egalitarian philosophy (communism) which, however, often leads also to a violent, non-humanitarian "left-wing" dictatorship. But why do these situations reach such an extreme point?

These confrontational situations in the world are remarkably similar to those seen in women's private lives with men. "Sticking his head in the sand," as one woman describes her boyfriend's reaction to her discussions about their relationship; so some governments refuse to listen to the "demands" of disenfranchised women or small countries, thinking the problems will all just "go away" (that the really smart people are the ruling elite of men around the world). These attitudes lead to more and more seething resentment, until it is too late to resolve things productively, whether in the world political situation or in the home.

But old-style politics, running for office, may not be enough. What about creating a new, non-aligned coalition—a *philosophically* non-aligned coalition? Should we start a different kind of organization—combining politics, economic boycotts, and ecology issues? In a way, "women's" revolution is not so much aimed at politics or the political system (although we would like to have half of

the Congress women) as it is at economics, ideology, and philosophy.★

Women have a great deal of economic power—collectively, an enormous amount. Women now would be financially able to form a network
to support other women and women's projects/corporations, etc. Could
we form collective corporations, go into business with each other?

Other theorists, going in an entirely different direction, say women
can force change by paying most attention to the politics of private life.
Some women (sometimes called "feminist separatists") call on women
to boycott men, that is, stop having relationships with men, remove
their emotional support from men who have not changed—in other
words, remove their energies from men entirely, stop supporting the
"male" system in all areas, including emotionally—in work, in love,
and any other way possible.† This is a tactic that could clearly have a
profound effect if large numbers of women did it.

In fact, while most women would not think of themselves as "separatists," the high divorce rate, with most of those divorces being initiated
by women, and women's emotional "leaving" of many marriages, even
if staying physically in them, does resemble this actual position.

Will non-violent resistance work?

All of these strategies we have been looking at are forms of non-violent
peaceful resistance. Will they really work, or are we fooling ourselves?

Is it so simple as to say that since we are 51 percent of the population,
if we begin to see ourselves as forming the core of society, the center
of history and philosophy—as men have done for centuries—then this
will automatically change things? Or must we face male power, enter
into a real confrontation, force men to stop dominating us and to share
power?

After all, for centuries, women have been half the population and
have lived with a "sub"culture of separate values, expressed more or
less overtly in different times and places—but this alone did not change
women's second-class status. History shows us that simply being a
majority—even with the heightened sensibility we have today—is no

---

★ One of the goals of this new coalition could be the "de-violentizing" of America's media
culture that is sent around the world.
† Within feminist circles, the separatist call at times had the unfortunate consequence of
causing women who did fall in love or were married to feel somehow ashamed; and so, as
if it were not enough to have the "male" culture calling women "masochists" for loving
"too much," now some feminists seemed to be calling others "masochists" or implying
that they needed their consciousness raised if they were with a man.

guarantee: for example, even though women got the vote earlier in the century, our status did not change—certainly not sufficiently.

Can we change women's status by "convincing" men to "give" us our rights? Or are we just kidding ourselves, taking the easy way out? With the French Revolution and others, it was finally necessary for people to show strength, to actually take power to change things, because those in power wouldn't listen, wouldn't *hear*—exactly as women have described.

At times in history, peaceful or less militaristic movements have triumphed over larger forces. For example, Gandhi was able to found a movement which eventually, along with other factors, ended British rule in India. The Bible speaks of David and Goliath—although David used the same means as Goliath—namely, force (he was smaller and with less power, but did win). The non-violent protests of the civil rights movement are of more relevance; however, while they have "raised consciousnesses" of both blacks and whites, the concrete factors in the lives of most blacks have not changed sufficiently; most blacks still have lower income, higher unemployment, less education, higher infant mortality rates, and no blacks are chosen as candidates for President by major parties.

According to historian Michael Howard and others for centuries before him (Clausewitz, for example), arming oneself, being ready for a fight, is the only way to "enforce peace," to keep from being taken over. Of course, if we could live with a basic ideology different from the currently dominant "male" ideology, this might not be true of "human nature"—we might not all need to have the arm-or-be-eaten psychology. However, living as we do in the current situation where hierarchy is a way of life and competition and aggression are rewarded, how does this affect the strategy women must use to change the situation?

Are we pacifists by choice—or are we *afraid* to fight?

If women have been dominated by men for centuries, the question goes, "Why have women stood for it?" "Why haven't women revolted?" Women have accepted their own oppression, men say, and this is used to "prove" women's basic "passive" character, women's supposed lack of leadership ability, women's innate recognition that men should lead! Therefore, this is a question we should consider seriously. Should we fight? Do we make it easy for men to continue, not change, because we don't frighten them, i.e., they believe they can count on our "peaceful" beliefs to keep us from making a revolution or taking power?

Another way of changing the culture, then, is to have the kind of revolution that men usually make to take power, to force men/the culture to change. Bruno Bettelheim showed in his concentration camp studies how quickly a person's orientation and view of life can change when the circumstances and power dynamics around her/him change radically; women in power, boycotting men, would have this effect on men immediately. And it would change forever our perception of ourselves and our power. We would never ever again think of ourselves as powerless.

As Janet Sayers has put the issue in "Feminism and Science,"* "Feminism can no more secure equal power and status for women with men in . . . society solely through drawing attention to the unreasonableness and injustice of present power imbalances between the sexes than was the eighteenth century French bourgeoisie able to secure its rights simply through demonstrating the irrationality of aristocratic rule and privilege. . . . The bourgeoisie only secured the rights of the men of its class through revolutionary overthrow of the physical and ideological forces whereby the aristocracy held power. It remains to be seen whether feminism can only secure equal status for women with men in society through revolution."

A militaristic strategy?

If women did assume militaristic tactics toward attaining their rights, would this change women's basic ideology of non-aggression—and therefore defeat the whole purpose? Or is this only the argument used by those who would encourage women to stay in their place, trying to scare us off by saying "power corrupts"?

These kinds of decisions are always hard, whether faced by nations or by individuals. How does one deal with aggression, keep a place of respect and dignity in the world? There do seem to be times when one has to fight, even if one doesn't want to.

In his analysis of the position of women in the twentieth century, written in 1972, historian William Chafe† describes in detail the patterns of "women's liberation" from the 1920s to the 1950s—and at the end of his argument, seems to be saying that the *ideology* of "women's place is in the home" (woman as second, not supposed to lead) has so far been too strong to be overcome. While Chafe is far from a radical, he (without intending to make this implication, perhaps) states over

---

* *Women's Studies International Forum* 10 (2).
† William Chafe, *Women and Equality: Changing Patterns in American Culture* (Oxford: Oxford University Press, 1972).

and over that only the "substantial upheaval" of World War II, and not any "propagandizing" by "feminists," changed women's basic situation—i.e., World War II brought significant numbers of women out of the home and into the work force, giving them an independent income—and this included women of all ages, not just, as before, mainly women who worked when they were single before they married. This financial independence, Chafe implies, brought them a certain amount of general independence and thus "liberation." But according to his analysis,* it was only "compulsion" or "substantial upheaval" that forced change for women on the society.

In this assertion, then, he is (without meaning to, probably) calling for revolution on the part of women—i.e., his study would imply that women are fooling themselves by believing that any amount of talk or "consciousness changing" will create lasting, fundamental change in women's status. He has argued that our patterns are repeating themselves, that evolutionary change in such a fundamentally embedded ideology is impossible, especially with a vested interest—i.e., the "male" ideology (not Chafe's terminology)—consistently working against it.

Women's Honor—Our Own Code

Women are now of a revolutionary spirit, but we are non-violent by "training" and/or belief and disposition. Most women don't want to fight militarily—and are not convinced it would work anyway. Women in power, it is quite possible, would be "just like men"—although this is not necessarily true, as the nature of our consciousness could change this. But the worry is that a "political revolution" might only repeat the patterns we have, replacing one hierarchical structure with another.

Political change, without ideological change, seems only to create the same hierarchical power structures it means to eradicate. For example, capitalism and communism both turn out in practice to create hierarchical states, because the underlying assumptions are those of the "male" ideology with its basis in hierarchy, defense of turf or dominance, focus on status.†

---

* And that of others, such as Alice Kessler-Harris and Ruth Milkman.
† Freud reached the conclusion (which he did not want to reach) that this system is inevitable, because (he believed) there is a human aggression instinct. Marx held that aggression is just a function of economic modes of production in history and thus not inevitable. The position of this work is that aggression and competition are not inevitable, not because they are merely a function of economics, but rather because they are part of an entrenched and very ancient ideological system.

A non-violent philosophical framework

How can we change the dominant ideology, and our status now, if our system dislikes aggression? Perhaps we should take a cue from a black civil-rights song that proclaims: "I know one thing we did right, was the day we started to fight." The question for us is, what kind of fighting will really work?"

First, the fight has already begun, as women everywhere are now fighting being owned, fighting for a different way of life in thousands of ways—in legal suits for jobs, asking why not about jobs and positions that are dominated by men, and in the millions of personal struggles with men, asserting their dignity. To know all of this is crucial for women now, for everything one of us does has an impact on women we never saw and who never saw us.

There is no one way of fighting that is right; finally, *all* ways are right—being reflective, introspective, thinking, fighting, voting, running for office, boycotting products—as long as somehow one's voice is heard, one's opinion is registered. We must act with courage. Those who do nothing are inviting repression; those who act boldly will see the results of their work. Even just among one's friends, to make what you think, really think and believe, known and clear means a lot.

We have something valuable to give the world now—our belief system, our philosophy. Our knowledge of how to give, how to love, is a richness we can diffuse throughout the whole culture.

Ideological Revolution

"Women of the world, unite! You all *know* what's wrong—but it's wrong not only with *your* personal life, it's wrong in the entire system."

So, if it is not (not only?) "power" we want, but major philosophical change, then the rethinking we are doing, and the devising of a clearly articulated alternative, is the kind of fighting that will make a lasting difference—along with all the rest.

Struggles for hierarchy and dominance won't stop being perceived as the most basic form of behavior, or be replaced by cooperation, without a revolution in consciousness, a revolution in what is known as "personality structure" (which is essentially the spectrum of possible personalities created by any given social structure). We badly need a revolution in thought and behavior patterns on every level, an important change in consciousness.

Some feminist philosophers have been working on questioning the values of the "male" system, analyzing possible alternative world views, trying to think beyond Western philosophy or patriarchal philosophy as we know it, with its parameters so narrowly limited by classical Greek thought and the Judeo-Christian tradition's tightly patriarchal values. Other female scholars are working in anthropology and archaeology in order to increase our knowledge of possible alternative social systems*—counterarguments to the idea that "all societies are male-dominant" and that all we see in front of us is the result of "human nature" rather than certain ingrained philosophical and cultural positions, behavior created by society. Women are researching new information, rather than saying, "Well, women have always and everywhere been dominated—so maybe they like it that way," which has been the position of more than one major academic school of thought.

In fact, now, after twenty years of work and rethinking in various fields, women have formulated new ways of viewing almost all fields of thought, including psychology, biology, philosophy, history, primatology, and anthropology—and this process is ongoing. There has been a cultural revolution, a revolution in thinking, which has caused a renaissance in almost all the disciplines, and which is still going on—perhaps has hardly begun.

Still, while women in most academic disciplines and many feminist writers have done great work in critiquing "male" culture, women's building of a new way of looking at things, reformulating their philosophy, can be said to be most importantly taking place now in the thought and actions of women everywhere—as seen in this study.

The interesting and important thing about this revolution is that it is not just being made by an isolated group of people; it is women and some men everywhere who are thinking these thoughts. For women these issues are pressing, since many women meet the "system" every day in the faces of men they love: the exquisite pain and contradiction women experience receiving men's double messages lifts many beyond the daily to the highest plateaus of thought and reflection. Thus, as we have seen, it is in large part the behaviors of men they love which has led to the crystallization of the level of awareness women are now expressing—an awareness which cannot be removed from the history of consciousness.

* See, for example, Alison Jaggar, *Feminist Politics and Human Nature* (Totowa, N.J.: Held, 1983); Sandra Harding and Merill B. Hentikka, eds., *Discovering Reality: Feminist Perspectives on Epistemology, Metaphysics, Methodology and Philosophy of Science* (Boston: D. Reidel, 1983).

The current statistics on marriage and divorce confirm these findings—and are strangely symbolic of the moment we are in: 50 percent of women leave their marriages, 50 percent stay, even if not emotionally satisfied. We are clearly at a turning point, half in and half out of a new time. The picture is striking—almost as if women were pausing, stopping a moment for reflection, half way out of a door, still turning to look back, bidding goodbye to the past, before setting out on a journey.

This journey in consciousness is further impelled by women's new economic situation—which in turn was/is being created by women's new view of things: the great majority of women are now financially independent for the first time in history. Seventy-five percent of women now have jobs, earning just enough money to be independent (although not well off, by any means; women still make only 66 percent of what men make, according to U.S. Bureau of Labor statistics). This independence, in addition to our belief in our own worth and importance, means that we are at a new time and place in history. And we have created this situation for ourselves: women have pioneered the jobs and the ideas.

A New Philosophy

"I think women are really re-designing the world. The next century is ours—mentally and in every other way."

This philosophical revolution, which Jessie Bernard has named the Feminist Enlightenment,* is the biggest realignment of thought in two centuries or more. It is extending democratic ideas and a different sensibility into love relationships, science, and politics.

This is not only a "female revolution" but a general revolution: to fight for women's rights and dignity is to fight for an entirely different ordering of the social structure, based on a different understanding of personal relationships.

Just as the Enlightenment built upon older structures, transcended them, adding new dimensions to the philosophical framework of the society and the understanding of "human nature" (out of which grew the idea of democratic government), so in the same way what women are doing now is enabling society to take another philosophical step forward.

* Jessie Bernard, *The Feminist Enlightenment*, work in progress.

This new philosophical questioning applies not only to Western society: it is a critique of hierarchical social systems that exclude women (and others) and the thought patterns created out of these systems all over the world. Women are creating, on an international scale, a global critique of "male" ideology. Women are questioning how social organizations and governments are formed, how "leadership" is decided on, and want to change the belief systems behind those choices.★

In fact, gender may be the basic, original split that needs to be healed to alter society, to lessen aggression as a way of life. Women are re-integrating "female" identity, leaving behind the double-standard split that began at the beginning of patriarchy, with Eve, followed by Mary as her opposite—and beyond this, trying to end/overcome the opposition between "male" and "female" emphasized by our culture. And this questioning of gender hierarchy leads to a questioning of all kinds of hierarchies, such as those based on race and class, not just gender.

Not "the human condition"—not forever . . .

Would it be too simplistic to blame all our problems on the "male" ideology, with its hierarchical and aggressive motifs?

What *is* the cause of human brutality and injustice? Communism says it is the system of "capitalism," the West says it is the system of "communism," Islam says it is Western materialism, feminism says it is the ideology of "patriarchy"—and others say it is just "human nature," that evil tendencies are always there, that there is an ongoing fight between good and evil.

Of course, there *are* people in every system who are "not like that," everyone agrees—people who are multi-sided, generous, open, thoughtful, idealistic, and honest.

It is tempting to say—or at least it should be pointed out—that patriarchy, the "male" ideology especially as it has been developed over the last 2,500 years, may be a very large part of the problem, because it may be *the* system underlying all the other systems. If the system we now have is "human nature," and not an ideology, if the system as we now know it is something growing out of our very biological natures, and not an historical system which, once entrenched, becomes hard to dislodge—"reality" seems to mean living with an increasing amount

★ See the bibliography for feminist magazines founded by women in "non-Western" countries.

of violence, massive inequity in global food distribution, in health and educational opportunities—and a grating friction in people's personal lives, plus destruction of the natural environment, not to mention destruction of each other in hurtful psychological games.

If all this is true, then there is nothing to be done except for each person to retreat to her or his own mountaintop and hope for the best. But we do not have to believe this.

Many people (both women *and* men) do hope for, have a longing for, a different way of life—for more politeness, more civility, more warmth—less hostility and aggressiveness. It is a challenge for us to somehow rise above the "natural" hostility and triviality of daily life at the moment, given the current psychologies created by the dominant culture as we know it.

Another world (or perhaps several) is possible, another landscape, full of fauna and flora, both in nature and in the human imagination—positive mental constructs not yet discernible to our "human nature as competitive" belief system. If hierarchy is the basis of all our institutions now—from religion to the state,* to the family and to love relationships—this need not last forever. It is just that our view of what is possible is temporarily obstructed.

A new spirit: the "other" now as seer

"Feminism didn't work? My god, it hasn't even started! We are Luther posting the statements on the cathedral door, we are Jeanne d'Arc with our army to defend ourselves. We no longer believe in the male gods; their power over us has ended."

This is the resistance, the beginning of the change—when the Other describes the dominant society, its ideology, for the first time, names truly what was before taken to be "human nature" and inevitable. Now, it is named as a belief-system, and so it is possible for new beliefs and reflections of reality to spring forth.

What is it, finally, that we hope for? A way of seeing things that would value each individual, recognize each individual's unique contributions, empower each individual—ending the psychological circle of hierarchy and competition. A new social contract not only with each other but also with the planet and the other creatures who share the earth.

This alternative system, with its new spirit and aura, is still in the

---

* The U.S. Constitution was an attempt to balance a government, rather than structure it hierarchically—one of the few lasting examples in history.

process of formation. Like a star, twinkling with light and motion, it is radiating out waves of energy to all around it, particles of light and illumination. This is the third step of the process that has been building for so long, and one that will continue far into the future.

Scholarly Papers Pertaining
to the Hite Reports

Philosophical Reflections on the Hite Reports

Joseph P. Fell, 1984, Harris Professor of Philosophy, Bucknell University

As a philosopher I believe that the task of ethics or moral philosophy is to determine what the real and pressing needs of human beings are and then to determine how these needs can be fairly and justly met. The first requirement for moral philosophy is thus actual knowledge of human needs, knowledge which, historically, has not been easy to obtain. The Hite Reports are concrete empirical studies in which thousands of individual human beings, women and men, express some of their deepest needs and satisfactions and frustrations in their relationships with each other. This is powerful and profoundly moving material. It is powerful because the Hite Reports are a medium that has made it possible for a large number of human beings to speak openly and candidly about needs the expression of which society has tended to censor or limit, and the satisfaction of which society has often condemned and punished. It is profoundly moving in the way that all human revelations of deep and persistent but frustrated needs are moving. It's not too strong to say that I find in the Hite Reports a massive cry of the human heart, a cry for the open recognition of the fundamental needs so eloquently revealed.

This open recognition is a historical and moral necessity. We find ourselves in the midst of a vital struggle to revise a long history of repression of the distinctively human need to be able to express our needs, together with unjust condemnation of our attempts to fulfill them. The historical and moral importance of the Hite Reports lies precisely in their challenge to this history of repression and suppression, which has kept us ignorant of each other's deepest feelings. Nothing is more tragic than human beings misusing the brief time they are allowed on this earth by suppressing their own needs, by failing to recognize each other's needs and so failing to fulfill each other.

Responsible and moral treatment of each other and of ourselves requires knowledge of others and self-knowledge. We must know what each other's deep, often unexpressed needs are if we are to treat each other humanly, responsibly, justly, lovingly. And I must know that others have deep-seated

415

needs like mine if I'm not to mis-know myself and so condemn myself as a freak or a misfit or a depraved animal. The Hite Reports are essays in knowledge of others and also in knowledge of ourselves. In them we have a classic example of how science and morality can go hand in hand: they offer a knowledge of human beings directed at a future in which we may better fulfill each other because we better understand each other.

The Ideological Evolution of Sexuality as Related to Gender

Shere Hite, 1984, American Historical Association Annual Meeting

There have been many "histories of sexuality"; the reason this symposium refers to "sexuality as related to gender" is because it is not the various customs and mannerisms relating to orgasm, intercourse, oral sex and so on that we are trying to document and follow over time; rather, we are trying to follow (as clearly as possible, because it is a very thinly discerned thread so far) how the *idea* that there was/is one "correct" form of sexual behavior—that is, heterosexual reproductive behavior—came to be the focus of so much attention and pressure. Accordingly, our two questions here are:

(1)   When did intercourse/coitus become the basic definition of what we know as "sex"? Were there other, more diffuse forms of "sexuality" earlier? What was sexuality like in some of the earlier, non-father-oriented social systems of pre-history?

(2)   The other basic question, inextricably intertwined with the above, is, when did women's sexuality come to be seen as "evil"? Was it with the story of Eve as the temptress in the Garden of Eden?

Was the definition of sexuality ever different?

One constantly hears references to the "male sex drive." It is, it seems, supposed to be a "natural" biological constant of male anatomy, existent since the distant ancestry of "man." Secondarily, the "male sex drive" is presumed to be oriented toward the male search for and penetration of the female vagina, with the aim of ejaculation. Rarely if ever in modern times has it been questioned that sex as we know it—that is, something called "foreplay" followed by "vaginal penetration" (why not call it "penile covering"?) and ending with male ejaculation into the vagina—is "the" basic definition of "sex." The nature of female sexuality is and has been much more a matter of debate, but in general, it has been presumed that it would fit in with a need for, and fulfillment by, the "male sex drive."

However, the fact is that what we call "sex" has a history too, and was certainly not always defined as we define it.[1] How we define it is part, a subhead, of our general social structure. Of course, many classical historians have pointed out the differences between, say, Greek expressions of sexuality and our own. But I am referring to even deeper and older differences. In 1976, both the first Hite Report and Foucault's *History of Sexuality,* volume 1,[2] made a case—his more "elaborate," mine more pointed—for a realization that sex has not always been defined in the way we define it, that it is tied to culture, and that there is a need to re-examine what it is we call "sex" and why.

Both Foucault's work and *The Hite Report on Female Sexuality* were saying, in different ways, that not only was sex defined differently in the past, but probably there was no concept of "sex" equivalent to our own in early societies; sex is a social construct. As the *London Review of Books* puts it, Foucault was saying that, "To think and act as if having certain organs determined gender and behavior, or as if sexuality and personality were totally conditioned by an orientation toward particular ways of using these organs, is a recent way of conceiving [or conceptualizing] human beings. [Foucault's] history is intended to show us that what we mean by the term 'sex' is not obvious, and that we take too much for granted in assuming that our experience must be the way it has been always and everywhere for others. He plays with the thought that there has been 'sex' only since the nineteenth century, and that we would be better-off in the future not wanting to 'have sex.'* His view is that 'sex' is a socially and historically conditioned concept, one formed by abstracting from the diverse and multiple phenomenal manifestations of 'bodies and pleasures.' "[3]

These are, of course, points made both in *The Hite Report* of 1976 and the second part of the trilogy in 1981. It is quite plausible that both Foucault and I were influenced by the intense philosophical debate going on during the early 1970s in both U.S. and French feminist circles on gender issues. However, Foucault does not seem to undermine the feminist critique of sexual definitions, nor the historical context which feminist analysis sees as the crux of the matter.

Feminists have long pointed out that the restrictions and elaborate rules placed especially on female sexuality by the Judeo-Christian ethic grew out of a need for men in "patriarchal" societies (that is, societies in which fathers were the legal owners of children) to establish with certainty their own paternity of a child; this made it necessary for the man to "own" the woman, control her sexuality, limiting it and her overall status in many ways.

The Hite Report of 1976 was in the feminist tradition, and contrasted women's ability to orgasm easily during oral or manual clitoral stimula-

---

*As *The Hite Report on Female Sexuality* put it, we would be better off "un-defining sex."

tion with the pressure on women to orgasm "the right way," i.e., during intercourse "with no hands." However, *The Hite Report* also went further, theoretically, to question whether intercourse/coitus had always been seen as "the main event," the most basic, "natural" definition of "sex"—and asked whether, instead, this definition had only come in after the connection between coitus and reproduction became known, or even centuries later, when there was a desire on the part of a society (such as the small, struggling tribes of Israel just after the Babylonian exile) to increase reproduction.

In summary, the philosophical thrust of the Hite Reports is to put sexuality into an historical perspective—and also to designate its current definition as "foreplay" to coitus as part of a particular philosophical system.[4] Was intercourse the focus of sexuality before children were "owned" by fathers and it became necessary to be able to prove paternity for inheritance purposes? Or were "sexuality" and reproduction two distinct forms of activity, such as they often were even in classical Greece? The Judeo-Christian focus has always been on the nuclear family-couple (Adam and Eve, or Mary and Joseph, although the latter didn't "have sex") as the basic models for emulation, the desired pattern of behavior, the social core. The Old Testament spent a good part of its verbiage inveighing against other forms of sexuality, even if only indirectly and/or mixed in with prohibitions against "worshipping false gods" or goddesses; the impression is quite clear that the Old Testament does not wish the Hebrew people to practice the more diffuse forms of sexuality of the surrounding societies, such as the Babylonian and others.*

It seems clear from the fact that so many laws, social mores, and religious teachings were placed around sexuality—particularly reproductive sexuality—that it was not "natural" for sex to be defined only in that way. In other words, if "sex" as we know it—i.e., "foreplay," followed by intercourse to male orgasm—is "natural," why would we need laws telling us that "fornication," other forms of sex, are bad? Although the Old Testament may not have specifically used prohibitions against masturbation, homosexuality, anal intercourse and so on (this is a matter of scholarly debate) the fact is that quite early on the rabbinical interpretations, and certainly the later interpretations of the church fathers, were that these things are taboo. The Bible does indeed urge people to have intercourse and reproduce, just as Plutarch urged the citizens of Athens to have sex with their wives at least three times a month.† The fact that any urging was/is needed implies that the supposed

---

*Although it is not clear to most reading the Old Testament, such as to myself as a child, many of the names of the "bad gods" that one should not worship are female goddess names, popular in the surrounding societies.
†Even as late as classical Greece, husbands had to be encouraged to have sex with their wives three times a month; much more of their time was spent in the company of men, and sex be-

physiological "drive" could not be counted on, at least during early historical times, to lead in just the right direction, that is, to focus itself basically on coitus. Perhaps too many people found oral sex more enjoyable, or perhaps dancing under the moonlight into a final frenzy was more to the liking of others. Probably there was no one institution known as "sex" for many millennia; "sex" (our current institution) being something that grew up as defined by the need of men to know their children if they wanted to ascertain certain paternity.[5]

Another way of approaching the question is this: the statistical side of the first Hite Report showed that the easiest and most common way for the majority of women to orgasm is via stimulation of the pubic or clitoral area, or sometimes the vulva—usually not combined with intercourse or penetration of the vagina. Women almost always orgasm once or many times during masturbation, which most women can easily do. Only one-third of women can orgasm easily during coitus "with no hands."[*] But if most women can orgasm so easily during clitoral/vulval stimulation, why has there been a stereotype in society that women have a "problem" having orgasm? It is not women who have a "problem," but society that has had a problem accepting the type of stimulation most women need for orgasm, during the institution we call "sex."

Why hasn't the activity by which most women orgasm most regularly and most intensely—that is, clitoral stimulation by hand or mouth—been given as much attention and glorification as coitus? Why hasn't it been considered as important and valuable as coitus and male ejaculation? (Of course, coitus is connected to reproduction, and female orgasm is not necessary for reproduction, so coitus contains these religious overtones.) However, in terms of spirituality, many people, men and women, feel that oral sex is much more intimate than intercourse.

The fact that there is no word for "manual clitoral stimulation," which is the activity necessary for a large number of women to orgasm, shows the ideological bent of our long historical definition of sex. College students always laugh when I mention that if a woman wants a man to stimulate her clitorally, what should she do? Look at him and say, "Please stimulate my clitoris manually?" Heaven help her if she has to repeat it.

---

tween men, and with boys, was considered "natural" and a sign of manhood. As Sarah Pomeroy, the classicist, points out, ". . . sex between husband and wife [was more] an obligatory duty fulfilled by procreation—rather than an intimate emotional encounter."[6]

*Masters and Johnson, although they pointed out the central role of the clitoris in female orgasm, still believed that women should receive enough "indirect" clitoral stimulation from "male thrusting" during coitus to lead to orgasm—although they state that they have not "cured" the majority of cases of women who complain they can orgasm outside of coitus but not during.[7]

Another sign of the lowly status of women's sexuality in Western "traditional" society relates to menstruation. The woman was undoubtedly right who stated that if men had menstruation, it would be celebrated as a national holiday, and considered a mark of strength and virility: "My blood! See how it flows, how it gushes, how strong I am, how much I can bleed!" But with women, it has been considered something to hide (like the stimulation necessary for orgasm), a "shameful" secret. As the advertisements of this century have told women, "He'll never know your secret!", alluding to the supposed "embarrassment" of menstruation. But menstruation in pre-history must have been seen as part of the general mystery of reproduction and the creation of life, the female cycle—something to celebrate, the blood "holy," certainly not something to be ashamed of, but something vital for life and rebirth.

How old, in fact, is the word for "clitoris"? What is its origin and derivation? Although it is usually taken to be a term from the classical Greek, the *Dictionnaire Etymologique de le Langue Grecque* does not contain the word "kleitoris" (the modern Greek term); in effect, it is not a word of classical Greek. A French philologist, Marcel Cohen, on fragile evidence, suggests that a search in India might be fruitful, since one of the Isot books of Aristotle, in a passage dealing with the Indus River, describes a dark precious stone called klitoris. Another possible pathway is from the ancient Egyptian k^3t, meaning "vulva." In Somalia, "kintir" means "clitoris," and there are at least six Sanskrit and Hindi terms for clitoris: "kurah," for example, means swell, sprout, bud, while "bhagkosha" is literally "vulva treasure." The Dravidian languages of southern India contain "kut" (in Kota), which is related to words for banner, crest of a bird, nipple, and so on. Cohen believes that "kleitoris" originated outside of Greece and bears the strongest resemblance to synonyms in living Ethiopic languages. But unfortunately, in fact we do not know where the word "clitoris" originated, or how long ago.[8]

On the other hand, the word "vulva" was an ancient Egyptian hieroglyph of an inverted triangle, and was widely used. This sign seems to hark back to the original "V" or inverted triangle seen on most of the Venus or creation-figurines, and thus may be the most ancient term we know of referring to female sexuality.

It is remarkable that neither the Bible nor the oldest Indian works such as the Rig Veda mention either masturbation (male or female) or the clitoris directly in any way. But almost all animals masturbate from time to time (as those with pets will know), and children explore and discover themselves from an early age. Certainly people during ancient times must have done the same things. Why are they not mentioned, in either a positive or negative context?

Gender in ancient societies

The question just posed of whether sex has ever been different leads us to the further question, has society ever been radically different with regard to gender relations, i.e., has society ever been non-nuclear-family based, and/ or non-paternity-oriented?*

Despite some excellent scholarship, many anthropologists and socio-biologists have asserted recently (and been widely accepted as accurate) that gender roles have always been defined basically as our society defines them: that is, that woman has always been woman-as-mother-in-the-home, and man has always been basically man-as-hunter, going "outside" into the broader world "against" which he would display "conquesting" characteristics.

Recently, however, the *New York Times* summarized the growing questions in anthropology and archaeology as to the accuracy of the notion that hunter-gatherers were predominant for most of pre-history and formed the early background of the modern nuclear family. (In other words, the implication of these now-questioned theories is that since the family has "always" been mother-father-child, current roles are more or less part of biology, or at least of strategical "human nature," and therefore unquestionable to human life.) The fact is, however, that—although the nuclear family has many good attributes—still it is an historical and not "integral-to-human-nature" configuration, carved out of eternity; other forms of family and social organizations can provide warmth and beauty too. Just as the "family" is seen as being a biological phenomenon, so gender roles have rarely been seen as being truly historical.

As the *New York Times* put it, "New examinations . . . of fossils from Ilduvai Gorge in Tanzania, one of the world's best-known archaeological sites nearly two million years old, suggest that the hunter-gatherer life style might have developed later in human history than previously thought, and that the social patterns associated with that way of life might be less central to 'humanness' than is often asserted. . . . Many anthropologists have theorized that the home bases of early hominids were the crucible in which the development of nuclear families, extended childhoods, language and other unique attributes of human culture was spurred. But . . . new analysis calls into question the oft-repeated theory that humans lived the hunter-gatherer way of life—with its attendant family structure, division of labor between the sexes, and interfamily sharing of food and other tasks—for 99% of man-

*These descriptive terms are preferred to the more heavily emotionally laden terms such as "patriarchal" etc., also because these traditional terms seem to have accrued many varied and imprecise definitions over the years.

kind's history, from when hominids first began chipping stones into tools until the invention of agriculture some 12,000 years ago.

"Rather than being integral to the emergence of humans as distinct animals, and hence representing the 'natural' condition of the species, the base-camp/hunter-gatherer pattern might have developed only gradually and reached its familiar form in later stages of cultural development . . . 'We simply do not know as much as we envisioned when it seemed appropriate to extrapolate a human hunter-gatherer model back two million years,' said Richard Potts of Yale University."[9]

And so we can ask, what happened during pre-history—that is, the period starting two million years ago until about 7000 B.C., when we have the first fragments of formal writing? What happened? Just because there was no writing, perhaps only signs and symbols as Alexander Marschauck and others have pointed out, does not mean there was not a very complex level of "civilization," or many such complex philosophical structures that came and went over the millennia.[10]

Regarding sexuality, it is interesting to note that tens of thousands of Paleolithic (35,000–10,000 B.C.) European cave paintings do not contain a single image of copulation, either human or animal.* Was this because the women or men who made them did not yet know that copulation led to reproduction? Did they connect childbirth more with "female mysteries," and with the mysterious changing of seasons of nature, than with coitus? Were they more concerned with developing a calendar to tell them when to expect frost or new plant life by painting ferns and plants as seen at different times of the year, and animals with and without horns, also at certain fixed times of the year, as suggested by Alexander Marschauck?

Creation (or "Venus") sculptures found all over Europe since about 25,000 B.C. seem to imply a female deity. Did these early, "pre-literate" societies worship the female creation ability? These figures are found plentifully all over Europe even as far as Russia, and certainly seem to imply this: after all, wouldn't it have been natural for people to worship or revere women's birth-giving processes and stages, especially if there was as yet no understanding that intercourse led to pregnancy? It must have seemed magical, divine, that women had the power to reproduce themselves—and not only in a female version, but also in the male version as well! This fact alone, it seems, would have served to make women be seen as the givers/creators of life, and therefore magical, honored, and deified.

This type of philosophical system seems to have continued until just

---

*Joseph Campbell disagrees, and cites one example. However, there were hundreds and thousands of depictions of vulvas and breasts compared to these few possible examples of copulation or the penis.

before the classical period in Greece (and perhaps later in northern Europe). John Chadwick, one of the two men who deciphered Minoan Linea B (A remains undeciphered), writes, "There can be no doubt that from Early Helladic times onwards the cult* of the Earth Mother dominated religious life all over the Aegean world; and this continued into the classical period under a variety of names. The conclusion that *Potnia* [later Athena] was the Mycenaean name for this figure is inescapable . . ."[11]

But if a female deity was worshipped, did this mean women had a higher status in society, and how was social/sexual organization different? Dr. Sarah Pomeroy, a classicist, writes, "Mother goddesses were prominent in the Bronze Age cults of Minoan Crete . . . Minoan statuettes of females wearing flounced skirts and blouses revealing the breasts, as well as fresco painting of the period, allude to the primacy of the female in the religious sphere . . . [However], the existence of the mother goddess in prehistory has been seriously challenged in recent years. . . . Some scholars claim that to attempt to connect a hypothetical earth mother of prehistory to mother goddesses of classical mythology is fallacious . . ." remarking especially that ". . . it is impossible to draw any conclusions about social systems in pre-history in the absence of written documents from the time or with the archaeological evidence now available."

But, she continues, "For the classical scholar, the mother goddess theory provides a convenient . . . explanation of the following puzzles: Why are there more than four times as many neolithic female figurines as male ones? Why do females predominate in Minoan frescoes? Why does Hesiod describe earlier generations of divinities as female-dominated, while the last generation, the Olympian, is male-dominated?" On the other hand, Pomeroy says, ". . . to use the mother goddess theory to draw any conclusions regarding the high status of human females of the time would be foolhardy . . . Christianity (has) demonstrated that the mother may be worshipped in societies where male dominance and even misogyny are rampant." Still, although it is impossible to draw any conclusions so far about social systems in pre-history, Pomeroy comments, ". . . then we must recognize that it is foolish to postulate masculine dominance in prehistory as to postulate female dominance . . . the question is open and may never be answered."[12]

How and when did "patriarchy" and the focus on coitus and controlling women's sexuality begin? No one knows, but in a sense, the earliest source of modern gender roles is the story of the Garden of Eden. What did/does the myth say? Adam and Eve are certainly a model for the nuclear couple. The relationship between the genders is seen here as primary; artifacts of

---

*It is unclear whether he is using the term "cult" as opposed to "religion," or uses the terms interchangeably.

earlier religions show the primary relationship as being between mother and children. (In fact, why create a myth with such strong gender-sexual messages and taboos if it is not a myth to instruct people regarding the basic unit of society?) The Garden of Eden is the quintessential gender story of Western history: already seen is the "battle between the sexes" (did one exist before?) including disrespect, enmity, blaming, etc. "Love" is not mentioned in this story.

Why was the female depicted as "bad" and "second" by the time this myth was formulated?[13] What had happened historically by then? Was the myth created at the same time that patriarchy or male ownership of children became prevalent—or later? Or was the story that declared women "evil," "too sexual" and "second" only theoretical and not yet the general practice and understanding of society: after all, the Old Testament was still fighting alternative images of women in the surrounding societies, calling them bad and not-to-be-followed. And, as Wendy O'Flaherty has pointed out, at just about the same time as the formulation of the Adam and Eve story, there was a similar myth in Mesopotamia, but in it there was "[a] good woman, a good tree and a good serpent."

Serpents and gardens had mythical meanings in many cultures of the times. The Egyptian god/dess Isis and Osiris, brother and sister, husband and wife, connected with the serpent and fertility; serpent gods in India were and are endowed with great wisdom. In fact, the serpent was everywhere a symbol of immortality because it could slough off its skin, and so is a symbol also of divine wisdom. Robert Briffault states that, "The belief that menstruation is caused by intercourse with a serpent is a common one; it attaches to the Garden of Eden myth and its Persian cousin." Possibly this is because the serpent is a symbol of divine wisdom, and to early people in pre-history, knowledge of how reproduction works or the cycles of female sexuality was indeed divine wisdom.

Regarding the garden, Wolfgang Lederer writes that the trees ". . . are about as universal as the serpent . . . The Persians, the Chaldeans, the Indians, the Chinese, the Toltec had trees of wisdom and life. Not by chance did Buddha receive his illumination under a tree . . ." Merlin Stone and many feminist writers have stated that the grove was a female goddess symbol, and typical worship site. Lederer goes on to say, "A word about the garden of Eden itself. Gardens, or groves, were of great religious importance among the Assyrians; they were sanctuaries of Ashtarte, the great Mother and divine harlot, who was honored by the faithful through sexual intercourse with her temple prostitutes. The cult was so popular in Israel that it lasted until the good king Hezekiah, in about 704 B.C., cut the groves down . . ."*

*Oedipus and the Serpent, Lederer, pp. 92–93, 632–33.

425

Or perhaps the story of Adam and Eve basically represents goddess-religion, now conquered by Indo-European invaders who believe in a male god, with the moral not that woman is bad, but that woman-oriented creation religion and its social order, lineage through women, is bad. Adam and Eve may have also represented the hoped-for triumph of individual sexuality over group/religious/anonymous/ceremonial sexuality. The earlier goddess religion may have had coitus or sexual display as one of its main rites, and so by integrating coitus into a new world model in the Adam and Eve myth, making it "bad," the worship of female cycles and reproduction (with its possible attendant social order) was now proclaimed to be "bad" and having caused the downfall, etc.

Enormous differences in the status of women existed in the ancient world. Egyptian or Babylonian women had a legal status far higher than that of their Jewish contemporaries. When classical Greece was having its heyday, women were kept strictly in the home, unable to participate in public life in any way (in that great "democracy"!). However, during the same historical period, in Southern Italy (the civilization of Magna Graecia, inherited from Crete slightly earlier), women were definitely the equals of men. While all the major gods in Athens were male, all the major "gods" in Southern Italy were female, just as they had been on Crete. In fact, the idea of equality of the sexes was declining from the ancient world, not increasing. The place of women in Greek myth also changed for the worse during the course of classical Greek history.*

Sexuality also has varied widely during these periods; on the basis of historical times alone, without discussing pre-history, we could make a case for a non-coitus-focused "norm" for sexuality. John Boswell noted that "sex" was not defined or categorized as we see it by the ancient world: "The literature of antiquity raises one very perplexing problem for the scholar . . . whether the dichotomy suggested by the terms 'homosexual' and 'heterosexual' corresponds to any reality at all. Terms for these categories appear extremely rarely in ancient literature, which nonetheless contains abundant descriptions and accounts of homosexual and heterosexual activity. It is apparent that the majority of residents of the ancient world were unconscious of any such categories." [14] (Are we to assume that women were waiting at home, totally focused on a desire for coitus? Or would this imply that women too had more than one idea of sexuality?)

Boswell questions, as I do, the idea that gender relations as we know them, and sexual "drives" toward the couple and the family—beautiful in-

---

*Many scholars believe that the change in Greece (originally Athena was born from the sea, later she was born from Zeus's head) with regard to the status of women took place because of the Dorian and/or Achaean invasions—Indo-European peoples from the East, who had a more "male dominant" ideology. A similar invasion took place in India.

stitutions as they can be—are the only forms of "reality" that have ever plentifully existed, or that somehow these "drives" are planted in the nature of the universe, biological givens.

In fact, it is my contention that not only was "homosexual/heterosexual" not an important distinction in the classical world, but that in the earlier, non-father-oriented world, even "heterosexual sexuality" (a phrase that certainly would not have existed) was not at all defined or focused basically on coitus, or "penetration" of the vagina by a penis; "rape" certainly did not exist until patriarchy. What later came to be known as the "mysteries" might have been a normal part of the physical/religious life of human beings earlier; or perhaps the "mysteries" were originally the initiation for girls into the fact that intercourse could lead to pregnancy, including an understanding and celebration of menstruation and female cycles, and other points of information about female sexuality (such as orgasm?).

Even as close to our own time as the sixteenth–seventeenth centuries in France, although coitus was definitely considered to be the basic definition of sexuality, the privatization of sex and the body was not yet completed. As Norbert Elias wrote in *The History of Manners,* in "On Behavior in the Bedroom": "In absolutist society of France (and earlier), bride and bridegroom were taken to bed by the guests, undressed, and given their nightdress."[15] This was part of an earlier custom in which the bridal bed had to be mounted in the presence of witnesses if the marriage was to be valid; in the later Middle Ages this custom gradually changed so that the couple was allowed to lie on the bed in their clothes—earlier they had been naked.

But by the eighteenth century, according to Elias, "The bedroom had become one of the most 'private' and 'intimate' areas of human life. Like most other bodily functions, sleeping has been increasingly shifted behind the scenes of social life. The nuclear family remains as the only legitimate, socially sanctioned enclave for this and many other human functions. Its visible and invisible walls withdraw the most 'private,' 'intimate,' irrepressibly 'animal' aspects of human existence out of the sight of others. In medieval society this function had not been thus privatized and separated from the rest of social life. It was quite normal to receive visitors in rooms with beds, and the beds themselves had a prestige value related to their opulence. It was very common for many people to spend the night in one room . . ." (pp. 163–64).*

---

*Elias adds further, "In other words . . . the lives of human beings are increasingly split between an intimate and a public sphere, between secret and public behavior. And this split is taken so much for granted, becomes so compulsive a habit, that it is hardly perceived in consciousness. In conjunction with this growing division of behavior into what is and what is not publicly permitted, the personality structure is also transformed . . ." (p. 190).

What is/was "natural" sex?

Early female-oriented religion probably contained sexual rituals because they celebrated reproduction and rebirth as the basic mystery of life. The religion of "the goddess" was focused on female reproductive, life-giving activity and saw this as the central mystery of all life, related to making the plants grow and life continue. (This is still the mystery of all mysteries, in fact.) The beauty of this early religion has often been misunderstood, and its connection with sexual acts painted as vulgar or pornographic, "pagan"—possibly because later, diluted versions which appeared in classical Greece or Rome were mixed with later attitudes. The body/mind split—mind being spiritual, and body "dirty"—had obviously not yet occurred in the female religions of pre-history; sexuality was not considered "lower" or "vulgar."

But would the earliest creation religion, just before it was known that coitus led to pregnancy, have celebrated sexual acts or just the stages of the female body/vulva as it was going through pregnancy? Was the earliest form of goddess-worship, during the creation* ("Venus") figures period, 25,000–10,000, not oriented toward celebrating coitus, but in fact, only celebrating the female body, and the mysteries of the vulva and interior? In fact, specially painted caves, as Marschauck points out, require the participant to enter through an uncomfortably small neck, even crawling (as in the Egyptian tombs) to reach a larger room. Could this have been symbolic of the vulva, the "vaginal canal," finally leading to the large cavern, the uterus/womb? Were female religious rites practiced by women in some of these caves, and were some of the caves painted by women? Or were men the basic bearers of this religion?

Another part of early sexuality, for which there may have been an entirely different name, was probably "festivals," or group dancing to ecstasy and/or sometimes orgasm, or other intense physical states—to express the spirit and emotions. This free-form dancing or physical display could bring on a feeling of exaltation and release. A very satisfying part of this was also, most likely, to be "seen" by the group in this way, to show oneself.

Personal sexuality—not connected with religious ceremony—has surely always been with us too. Originally, personal sexuality probably was an individual vocabulary of behaviors, chosen on any given occasion to express the feelings toward a specific person, or the mood of a specific day, etc.—not the rigid pointing finger we have, that once having had "foreplay" or a kiss, one must automatically move on to "vaginal penetration" to coitus and male ejaculation. Sexuality is malleable, plastic. Both men and women have an

---

*Professor Gimbutas prefers the term "creation figures" to "Venus figures," since "creation" is more accurate, and the term "Venus" reflects a later point of view.

urge for orgasm from time to time, and an urge to nuzzle and make physical contact—but how they socialize those feelings is cultural.*

Can we generalize the sexual behavior of early humanity from the behavior of other primates? Along these lines, it is important to remind ourselves that human females are the only mammals who have coitus during all times of the month; other animals usually have coitus only during estrus. When an estrus-defined period of coital activity ended historically for us is not known, nor the effects—perhaps it happened when we stood upright. Of course other primates do participate in *other* physical/sexual activities at all times of the month. A further note: in primates, coitus is as regularly initiated by the female "presenting" as by the male "initiating."

What about love? Did individuals during pre-history "fall in love," or feel a special attraction for another person? Was there individual, "nuclear" love between individuals—or were sex and attraction, as is sometimes said about sex in Polynesia, "a natural and non-mystified part of daily life" with no residual feelings of connection left over after "the act"? Jane Goodall has pointed out that our primate relatives do have preferences, and sometimes develop emotional attachments related to sex with each other.

The bittersweet quality of love must have always been there. At least in Greek times, not that far removed in time or tradition from the world of Minoan Crete, people did "fall in love" or feel an intense erotic attraction for a specific other individual, an attraction that lasted for some time. Although the institutionalization and "meaning" attached to these feelings probably did not exist in pre-history (did they have some other social meaning?), still the feelings Sappho and Catullus expressed have most likely always been felt:

> ". . . how many kisses are,
> You ask of me enough and more:
> As all the sands upon the shore . . .
> As all the stars which mutely shine
> On furtive lovers in night's gloom.
> Enough and more, such kisses will
> Drive your Catullus raving mad . . ."
>
> *Catullus*

"Like the very gods in my sight is he who
sits where he can look in your eyes, who listens
close to you, to hear the soft voice, its sweetness
murmur in love and laughter, all for him. But it breaks my spirit;

*Attributed to Betty Dodson, 1974.

underneath my breast all the heart is shaken.
Let me only glance where you are, the voice dies,
   I can say nothing.
but my lips are stricken to silence, underneath my skin the tenuous flame suffuses;
nothing shows in front of my eyes, my ears are muted in thunder."

Sappho

Notes

1. See Vern L. Bullough, *Sexual Variance in Society and History,* University of Chicago Press, 1976.
2. Michel Foucault, *The History of Sexuality,* vol. 1, Random House, 1978; Gallimard, 1976.
3. *London Review of Books,* Nov. 14, 1984.
4. Does building a cosmos which starts by shifting the ownership of children from women, or the extended family, to men, also bring along with it, inevitably, a greater emphasis on gender as the core unit of society? Our current philosophical system, our cosmos, is based on gender distinctions as its core; was this true of societies in pre-history? Or, was gender even more noted, since one bore children and the other did not? However, this may not have provoked a constant "battle between the sexes" (the battle so many refer to as "natural"). Perhaps before the need to know paternity, the relationship between the genders may have been less hostile, less aggressive, because there was no constant territorial battle to fight.
5. But how did society come to this state? Why did men want to "own" the children, and therefore women? Because owning the children would mean power? But why did men—and was it all men, or just certain tribes, or classes?—want power? Is the desire for power elemental? Or was all this perhaps the outcome of the domination of the West by certain warlike invading tribes from the East, the well-known Indo-Europeans? And is much of what we describe as "human nature" today the outcome of actual historical "accident"—that is, the social form of the group that happened to win that ancient series of battles?
6. Sarah Pomeroy, *Goddesses, Whores, Wives and Slaves,* Schocken Books, 1975, p. 87.
7. William Masters and Virginia Johnson, *Human Sexual Response,* Little Brown, 1966, and *Human Sexual Inadequacy,* Little Brown, 1972.
8. Thomas P. Lowry and Thea Snyder Lowry, *The Clitoris,* Warren H.

Green, 1976, pp. 164–70. M. Cohen: "Clitoris. Extrait de l'Annuaire de Philologie et d'Histoire Orientales et Slaves," t. V, 1937 (Melanges Emile Boisacq).

9. *New York Times,* "Theory on Man's Origins Challenged," Erik Eckholm, science section, Sept. 4, 1984.

The article further states, "Until the late 1970s, scientists tended to read back from the present, searching for similarities between the life styles of ancient hominids and modern remnants of hunter-gatherers in Southern Africa and Australia. But . . . 'Most anthropologists are now starting with the assumption that the past will be unlike the present,' said David Pilbeam of Harvard . . . now some scientists are trying, solely on the basis of scanty archaeological evidence, to reconstruct life at the very dawn of human existence. The fossil record does prove that about two million years ago hominids already had the ability to stand erect . . . and were making crude stone tools and eating meat . . . But the answers to other crucial questions—whether family groups foraged and slept alone or together, whether food was shared . . . whether males maintained lasting ties with their mates and off-spring . . .—are far less clear today than they seemed a few years ago."

10. Of course there is a question as to how much archaeological data or oral myth can be used to imply what went on in any given society, but improved techniques for dating and analysis mean that we can begin to know much more than before, even without formal writing. In particular, the period from 25,000 B.C. to 10,000 B.C. is beginning to open up as a real area of "history"/pre-history. New techniques include improved means of carbon-dating and scrutiny with an electron microscope of markings on bone fragments, the latter recently developed by Dr. Potts and Pat Shipman of Johns Hopkins.

11. John Chadwick, *The Mycenaean World,* Cambridge University Press, 1976, p. 93.

12. Sarah Pomeroy, op. cit., pp. 13–17. As to Pomeroy's question regarding whether archaeological remains and frescoes are enough evidence from which to imply some social behaviors or relationships, of course there would always be problems associated with this; however, we should remember that historians working closer to the present have also relied on such material, such as Philip Aries, and many historians do feel that this material is quite acceptable documentation from which to read.

Also, as to her misgivings about female goddess statues representing an equivalent high status for women in society, of course the difference between our worship of Mary today and ancient worship of "the goddess" is that, should our society be excavated, depictions of a male god and his son would also be plentifully found, giving an overall picture of our religious pantheon. The fact is, as Pomeroy points out, that female goddess figures overwhelmingly predominate in the excavations of an entire 20,000-year period. What does this mean?

13. There are dissenting views regarding Eve's low status: John Boswell wrote in the *New York Times Book Review,* summer, 1984, covering the book by A. J. Phillips, *Eve,* "Eve might be the culmination of creation, (as) she is created last in what is manifestly an ascending series; . . . Far from being a passive or secondary player in the central pre-Christian drama of human history, Eve determines the fate of her race, and does so as a result not of the excess of emotion or passion later attributed to her, but of intellectual curiosity. Adam, in contrast, is passive, his only motivation seeming to be his uxoriousness . . ."

   Why were the early Hebrew fathers, especially after leaving Babylon, so intent on stamping out the worship of the many god/goddesses of the times and proclaiming only one male god? It has been asserted by some scholars that Yahweh was originally both male and female, but that Hebrew only contained male or female pronouns, and so, although the god was both, the authors had to choose and picked "he," although it really stands for "he" and "she." This has been refuted by many scholars; see R. Reuter, P. Tribble, and Robert Alter. Basically, had the authors of the Old Testament had this intent, they certainly would have gone to some greater lengths to make this clear.

14. John Boswell, *Christianity, Social Tolerance and Homosexuality,* University of Chicago Press, 1980, pp. 58–59.

15. Norbert Elias, *The History of Manners,* vol. 1, Pantheon Books (originally pub. 1939, Switzerland), pp. 176–77.

Controversies over the Nature of the Family in Human Pre-History

Shere Hite, 1986, American Association for the Advancement of Science Annual Meeting

Hello, and welcome to this symposium.

The objective of this symposium is to bring into focus the current controversies in the field about the origins of gender values, the place of women and men in families, the nature of the earliest family structures known (if this is possible) and how we evolved our modern system of the nuclear family. Recent carbon-dating of fossil finds, along with re-thinking by David Pilbeam, Glynn Isaacs, Ruby Rohrlich, Adrienne Zihlman, Sara Hardy and others of the evidence on hand, had led to a re-evaluation of the long-standing assumption that "family" is a self-evident word which "naturally" means father-mother-child.

Was the family always "the family" as we know it? There are two basic points of view: that the first families, and thus the "natural" families, are nuclear, father-mother-children families; and the second, that the first families were mother-children families, with the father a much later addition in history. Possibly the role of intercourse in pregnancy was unknown until a certain era; possibly kinship structures were more conveniently arranged, with the mother's uncles, cousins, sisters and so on forming the "family."

The essential argument is over whether the basic social order as we know it—"human nature," some call it, hierarchical "patriarchy," others call it—has its origins in historical events or psychological and biological givens, like the fact that women can become pregnant and breast-feed children and men cannot, so therefore they are more "vulnerable" and "weaker," and more "biologically" attuned to "nurturing" and taking care of people.

Highly sophisticated investigations are going on in various fields, often drawing opposing conclusions. The archaeological record, while much more difficult to ascertain than the anthropological evidence, does seem to be in contradiction to what we might have assumed, as Marija Gimbutas, an archaeologist at UCLA who has worked in the field for over twenty years, demonstrates. Robert Carneiro, along with others, however, argues that the traditional view, that the nuclear family has always been the primary building block of society, is still clearly correct, based on the fact that according to the numerous available files (human area files), all societies today, including the most primitive, are patriarchal. Discussion and controversy among those on the panel should move all a step closer to synthesis in current thinking.

Of course, this is a topic of great contemporary relevance: the media constantly reports the changes going on in basic family structures, and new trends, such as "single mothers," women as heads of households, higher divorce rates, lack of desire to marry, etc. In the past ten years, the number of books written to advance the cause of, or defeat, numerous of the all-important micro-arguments within this macro-question (what is the future of the family?) have been enormous.

In anthropology, the deepest part of the debate is going on right now. Most anthropologists who study currently existing so-called "primitive" tribes, or hunting-gathering societies, insist that since almost all contemporary hunting-gathering societies have father-headed families, therefore the earliest families must have also been patriarchal. Little open-mindedness is kept for the idea that there may have been great variability in the past, although many (especially female) anthropologists have made brilliant critiques of standard anthropological theory; first they point out that since the greatest amount of food is obtained by women, who are generally the gatherers, it would be more appropriate to dub these groups "gatherer-hunters" than vice versa. Recently, it has also been shown (by Potts, for one) that much of the supposed "hunting" was really "scavengering," and so the myth of the "great hunter" which is so popular is something which can only be noted with amusement as part of a particular mind-set growing out of a particular culture.

Although plausible alternative behaviors that also may have led to regular food sharing have been presented by feminist anthropologists (Tannen and Zihlman), the basic features of the Man the Hunter model persist in anthropology and the alternatives have been ignored or dismissed.

Also, in the works of many anthropologists there is an implicit suggestion of a cultural community in gender arrangements from the earliest hominids into the present. This stance forcefully implies that contemporary gender dynamics are built into the species through unspecified evolutionary processes. Although most anthropologists and archaeologists research human life after the establishment of modern Homo sapiens, they inherit a picture of human social life and gender structures that appear to have been established for several million years, and thus gain "a false notion of objectivity" and security, when using these assumptions in their work. As noted by Conkey and Spector referring to one article, in particular, "Archaeologists appear to be objective, and are quick to point out that 'we have no idea how prehistoric human groups were socially partitioned,' yet in the very same article we read about casually made stone tools that indicated presumed occupation by women engaged in plant processing."

Another example, found by Conkey and Spector, discussing an article by Winters, ". . . when grinding pestles are found with females in burial contexts, they are interpreted as reflecting the grinding and food-processing activities of women. When such items are found associated with males, however, they suggest to Winters that the men must have manufactured these artifacts (for their women?) or utilized them as hammerstones in pursuing other (less feminine?) tasks. The same kind of reasoning is applied in the interpretation of trade goods. When found with males, Winters infers that this indicates men controlled trading activities. But when found with women, the association suggests only that women possessed such items, not that they participated in trade."

Assumptions about the nature of sexuality and the family: What is/was "natural" sex?

These same biases—almost always unconscious and unnamed—are also true of sexuality. Most of the disciplines that work with the question, "What is the nature of humans?" are permeated with assumptions, assertions, and statements of "fact" about sexuality which are based on unfounded assumptions.

Just as people used to assume males were sexually "aggressive" and females in all species of primates were "passive"—just so, they assume that the primary sexual motivation in all species is for heterosexual intercourse and reproduction. This assumption—for which there is no real justification—puts those in many fields in rather undefensible theoretical predicaments.

Scholars in several disciplines, consciously or not, are propagating cultural assumptions about sexuality in their interpretations of data, constructions of studies and methodologies, and reconstructions of the past. This is a cause for concern, as it has serious political and educational implications. It is my hope that this critique will contribute to new ways of thinking about what we do and what we can know about social life in the past.

According to Hite Report research and historical evidence, there is no reason to believe that only one basic definition of sexuality is possible, or that sexuality has always been basically defined as coitus. Although this definition (coitus) has always been part of the Judeo-Christian tradition, if such definition were completely "natural," why would this tradition have had to place laws and restrictions on other forms of sexuality? Primate research and reports of current gatherer-hunter societies tend to study their subjects as if this were the primary form of sexuality, often neglecting to investigate or report forms of self-stimulation or sexual practices with those of the same gender. This is particularly true when the various disciplines are attempting to gather data on the incidence of female orgasm. Also, the assumption of coitus as the basic expression of sexuality for all times and places and in all primates tends to reinforce gender bias regarding the relationship of males and females, and to reinforce beliefs that male-female relations were always central to all societies.

I have been quite surprised to see that in so many fields, some of the most sophisticated theories contain assumptions about the nature of sexuality which seem to be unexamined on the part of the writer. For example, the overwhelming majority of anthropologists in all areas (with some notable exceptions) seem to take as givens (1) automatic heterosexual attraction or "sex drive," (2) that the basic form of heterosexual sexual expression is intercourse/coitus, and (3) that female primates/humans want intercourse because they want to orgasm. Anthropologists, primatologists and others easily forget masturbation, oral sex, and cuddling—even though the writings of classical Greece are so near at hand, and even though the Old Testament clearly indicates that ancient societies such as Babylon and Sumer supported such diverse ideas of sexuality.

There is a constant unstated assumption built into research design that sex is now as it always was, that it is a biological "given," hardly affected by culture (only to the extent of with whom and where). For example, how many primate studies are now in progress to observe female orgasm during coitus, and how many are now in progress to look at the whole spectrum of sexuality and orgasm in that primate? Almost all the studies relate to coitus— and their outcome is awaited almost as tensely as one's own orgasm! This has been true also in anthropological investigations of current tribal life, with notable exceptions.

The question of female orgasm in primates has been hotly debated. For many years, up until 1976, the few researchers in this area said that female primates did not orgasm, only male primates. (Donald Symons stated this as a probability as late as 1981.) Of course, male orgasm is easy to see— first the erection and then the ejaculation—whereas female orgasm is not so easy. (And do researchers always know the signs to look for? But they could use Masters and Johnson's method of physical testing.) Suzanne Chevalier-Skolnikoff demonstrated in the mid-1970s that, while the stumptail monkeys which she studies did not orgasm during intercourse, they did orgasm easily and frequently by mounting each other and rubbing their external areas; she, however, apologized for this fact, and went on to *defend* her monkeys for not having orgasm "the right way," explaining various reasons why they exhibited this "abnormal" behavior.

No one, biologically speaking, knows the reason for the existence of female orgasm in the cycle of reproduction. It is not necessary for a woman to have an orgasm for pregnancy to occur—nor for a woman to reach orgasm to become excited. In fact, as some have pointed out, pregnancy may be *more* likely to occur if the woman does not orgasm, since the stage of excitement before orgasm creates a small lake at the upper end of the vagina (if the woman is on her back) in which the semen may rest, rather than possibly running out. Perhaps orgasm is a mechanism for the release of overall body tension, not just a sexual release.

The work of Marija Gimbutas, the archaeologist from UCLA who will be heard this afternoon (on her excavations in pre-Indo-European Southern Austria), demonstrates a point of view about sexuality which is amazingly untouched by contemporary stereotypes. Gimbutas believes, based on over thirty years of work studying artifacts and art produced between 25,000 and 5000 B.C., that the early so-called "fertility goddesses" were rather "creation goddesses," that is, that they represent religious or magic celebrations of women's ability to give birth—to give birth not only to their own gender but to both sexes. This was probably considered the central religious mystery of the time—magical and important. Probably for much of pre-history, the male contribution to pregnancy was not known, that is, the connection between male orgasm/coitus and pregnancy.

Implications of Hite Report research for investigations of data relating to the "nature" of the family

The first Hite Report (which is part of a trilogy*), published in 1976 and covering a study of 3,400 women in the U.S., presented several major conclusions:

(1) Most women require some form of clitoral or exterior genital stimulation for orgasm; only one-third of women can orgasm regularly through simple "vaginal penetration" with no additional stimulation.†

---

*The second Hite Report was *The Hite Report on Male Sexuality,* covering men's feelings about sex and also about love, relationships and marriage, and published in 1981 by Alfred Knopf; the third part of the trilogy will be published by Knopf in 1987.
†Only Hite and Anne Koedt have stated that "vaginal orgasm" is not the norm in women. While Masters and Johnson were of crucial importance in putting the anatomical existence of the clitoris (and stressing its role in relation to orgasm) on the map—they have held and still hold that most women, or the "normal" woman, should receive enough indirect clitoral stimulation from coitus to reach orgasm; however, they have described this as the "Achilles heel" of their treatment program, in that women coming to them with this "secondary sexual dysfunction" (only being able to orgasm with manual or oral stimulation but not with penetration) often cannot change this. *The Hite Report* showed that there is nothing "wrong" with women who do

(2) The definition of sexuality as we have known it—i.e., "foreplay," followed by "vaginal penetration," followed by "intercourse" and male orgasm —is a reproductive definition of sex, with an historical rather than a biological derivation. This definition was constantly mandated by the Old Testament, possibly in an effort to get the small, struggling Hebrew tribes to reproduce more rapidly.

(3) The definition of sex, by not including stimulation necessary for most women to orgasm, reflects women's generally lower status in the culture at large, and their lack of power to help define cultural institutions.

(4) Sexuality should be "un-defined" to become an individual vocabulary of activities and behaviors, which any given person may use when she/ he thinks they are appropriate to express her or his feelings at the time. They need not always include coitus.

In other words, statistically, the first Hite Report showed that the easiest and most common way for the majority of women to orgasm is via stimulation of the pubic or clitoral area, or sometimes the vulva—usually not combined with intercourse or penetration of the vagina. Women almost always orgasm once or many times during masturbation, and most women can do this easily. Only one-third of women can orgasm easily during coitus "with no hands." Why hasn't the activity during which most women orgasm most regularly and most intensely—that is, clitoral stimulation by hand or mouth—been given as much attention and glorification as coitus? Why hasn't it been considered as important and valuable?

The definition of sexuality has been very different

When did intercourse/coitus become the basic definition of what we know as "sex"? Were there other, more diffuse forms of "sexuality" earlier? What was sexuality like in some of the earlier, non-father-oriented social systems of pre-history?

One constantly hears references to the "male sex drive." It is, it seems,

---

not orgasm during intercourse; they are "normal." *The Hite Report* findings have been validated by being given the 1985 award of AASECT, and replication in three countries. Masters and Johnson made an enormous contribution through their anatomical observations; however, they fell prey to the ideological assumptions of our culture—achieving orgasm during intercourse "should" be normal, they thought, and thus carefully selected their sample for only women with a previous history of orgasm from both intercourse and masturbation. They then generalized to other women from their unusual sample. This was a natural enough mistake: they thought they would start with "healthy" women; but in fact, this assumption was fallacious. To be "scientific" in any field, we must look at what is "out there," and then base our conclusions on this data. In addition, the "G-Spot" theory of female *orgasm* has generally been invalidated—although all researchers agree that most women *enjoy* intercourse for its own sake, with or without orgasm.

supposed to be a "natural" biological constant of male anatomy, existent since the distant ancestry of "man." Secondarily, the "male sex drive" is presumed to be oriented toward the male search for and penetration of the female vagina, with the aim of ejaculation. Rarely if ever in modern times has it been questioned that sex as we know it—that is, something called "fore-play" followed by "vaginal penetration" (why not call it "penile covering"?) and ending with male ejaculation into the vagina—is "the" basic definition of "sex." The nature of female sexuality is and has been much more a matter of debate, but in general, it has been presumed that it should "naturally" fit in with a need for, and fulfillment by, the "male sex drive."

However, the fact is that what we call "sex" has a history too, and was certainly not always defined as we define it. How we define it is part, a sub-head, of our general social structure. Of course, many classical historians have pointed out the differences between, say, Greek expressions of sexuality and our own. But even deeper and older differences have been discussed to some extent in both my own work and that of Michel Foucault. In fact, not only was sex defined differently in the past, but probably there was no concept of "sex" equivalent to our own in early societies; sex is a social construct.

As one reviewer puts it, "To think and act as if having certain organs determines gender and behavior, or as if sexuality and personality are totally conditioned by an orientation toward particular ways of using these organs, is a recent way of conceiving [or conceptualising] human beings . . . We take too much for granted in assuming that our sexual experience must be the way it has always been everywhere for others . . . 'sex' is a socially and his-torically conditioned behavior, one formed by abstracting from the diverse and multiple manifestations and pleasures."

Feminists have long pointed out that the restrictions and elaborate rules placed especially on female sexuality by the Judeo-Christian ethic grew out of a need for men in societies in which fathers were the legal owners of chil-dren to establish with certainty their own paternity of a child; this supposedly made it necessary for the man to "own" the woman, control her sexuality, limiting it and her overall status in many ways.

The Hite Report of 1976 made a special point of contrasting women's ability to orgasm easily during oral or manual clitoral stimulation, with the pressure on women to orgasm "the right way," i.e., during intercourse "with no hands." In other words, if we were studying some other species, to be "scientific," we would ask, when do females usually orgasm, with which stimulation, and that would be considered "normal" for that species. But since we are studying human females, we say, if most women don't orgasm from intercourse, there must be something wrong with *them*—there is noth-ing wrong with the expectation. We are biased.

Has intercourse/coitus, *The Hite Report* asks, always been seen as the "main event," the most basic, "natural" definition of "sex"? Or, instead, did this definition only come in after the connection between coitus and reproduction became known—or even centuries later when there was a desire on the part of a society (such as the small, struggling tribes of Israel just after the Babylonian exile) to increase reproduction?

Thus, the philosophical thrust of the Hite Reports was to put sexuality into an historical perspective—and also to designate its current definition as "foreplay" to coitus as part of a particular philosophical system. Was intercourse the focus of sexuality before children were "owned" by fathers and it became necessary to be able to prove paternity for inheritance purposes? Or were "sexuality" and reproduction two distinct forms of activity, such as they often were even in classical Greece? The Judeo-Christian focus has always been on the nuclear family-couple (Adam and Eve, or Mary and Joseph) as the basic models for emulation, the desired pattern of behavior, the social core. The Old Testament spends a good part of its verbiage inveighing against other forms of sexuality, even if only indirectly and/or mixed in with prohibitions against "worshipping false gods" or goddesses; the impression is quite clear that the Old Testament does not wish the Hebrew people to practice the more diffuse forms of sexuality of the surrounding cultures, such as the Babylonian and others.

It seems clear from the fact that so many laws, social mores, and religious teachings were placed around sexuality—particularly reproductive sexuality—that it was not simply "natural" for sex to be defined only in that way. In other words, if "sex" as we know it—i.e., "foreplay," followed by intercourse to male orgasm—is "natural," why would we need laws telling us that "fornication," other forms of sex, are bad? Although the Old Testament may not have specifically used prohibitions against masturbation, homosexuality, anal intercourse and so on, this being a matter of scholarly debate—the fact is that quite early on the rabbinical interpretations, and certainly the later interpretations of the church fathers, were that these things are taboo. The Bible does indeed urge people to have intercourse and reproduce, just as Plutarch urged the citizens of Athens to have sex with their wives at least three times a month. The fact that anything was/is needed implies that the supposed physiological "drive" could not be counted on, at least during early historical times, to lead in just the right direction, that is, to focus itself basically on coitus. Perhaps too many people found oral sex more enjoyable, or perhaps dancing under the moonlight into a final frenzy was more to the liking of others. Probably there was no one institution known as "sex" for many millennia (or it may have been partially combined with religious rites)—"sex," our current institution, being something that grew up as defined by the need of men to know their children if they wanted to ascertain certain paternity.

Gender in ancient societies

The question just posed of whether sex has ever been different leads us to the further question, has society ever been non–nuclear-family based, and/or non-paternity-oriented?*

Despite some excellent scholarship, many anthropologists and socio-biologists have asserted (and been widely accepted as accurate) that gender roles have always been defined basically as our society defines them: that is, that woman has always been woman-as-mother-in-the-home, and man has always been basically man-as-hunter, going "outside" into the broader world "against" which he would display "conquesting" characteristics.

Now, however, questions have arisen in anthropology and archaeology as to the accuracy of the notion that hunter-gatherers were predominant for most of pre-history and formed the early background of the modern nuclear family. As the *New York Times* puts it, "Many anthropologists have theorized that the home bases of early hominids were the crucible in which the development of nuclear families, extended childhoods, language and other unique attributes of human culture was spurred. But . . . new analysis calls into question the oft-repeated theory that humans lived the hunter-gatherer way of life—with its attendant family structure, division of labor between the sexes, and interfamily sharing of food and other tasks—for 99% of mankind's history, from when hominids first began chipping stone into tools until the invention of agriculture some 12,000 years ago . . ." We simply do not know as much as we envisioned when it seemed appropriate to extrapolate a human hunter-gatherer model back two million years, Richard Potts says.

The earliest source of modern gender roles is the story of the Garden of Eden; Adam and Eve are certainly a model for the nuclear couple. The relationship between the genders is seen here as primary; artifacts of earlier religions show the primary relationship as being between mother and children. (In fact, why create a myth with such strong gender-sexual messages and taboos if it is not a myth to instruct regarding the basic unit of society?) The Garden of Eden is the quintessential gender story of Western history: already seen is the "battle between the sexes" (did one exist before?) including disrespect, enmity, blaming, etc. "Love" is not mentioned in this story.

In light of historical evidence, how can we dream of assuming that family was always the nuclear family as we know it? Even today, a large percentage of families are not "nuclear": men often leave their families, and women bring up children alone or with their grandparents. (What does

---

*These descriptive terms are preferred to the more heavily emotional terms such as "patriarchal," etc., also because these traditional terms have accrued many varied and imprecise definitions over the years.

it imply about women that men are more likely to leave their children than women?)

Why is the idea of the earliest families being woman–child so threatening? Would it be "terrible" if we found that the current social structure is not biologically ordained? That change is possible. We must confront our prejudices and see clearly if our research is to flourish and bear fruit.

Women and Love: Towards a New Feminist Methodology

Nancy Tuana, 1987, Columbia University Presentation of *Women and Love: The Hite Report on Love, Passion and Emotional Violence*

In her first study, *The Hite Report on Female Sexuality,* Shere Hite was an important founder of a methodology now central to the feminist tradition—listening to women's own voices. She was one of the first researchers to develop a model and theory of female sexuality arising out of women's *own* experiences, rather than attempting to force a preconceived model upon our experiences. This methodology of listening to women's voices is the foundation of Carol Gilligan's landmark study of women's moral reasoning in her *In a Different Voice* (Cambridge: Harvard University Press, 1982) and recent studies of women and reason such as Mary Field Belenky's *Women's Ways of Knowing* (New York: Basic Books, 1986), and studies of women's self-image, for example, Emily Martin's *The Woman in the Body* (Boston: Beacon Press, 1987). Just as Hite discovered through her first report that the then accepted models of sexuality were lacking, so other theorists, employing the same methodology, have discovered that our philosophical and psychological accounts of reason and morality have been distorted by the omission of women's perspective. Hite's new study, *The Hite Report on Love, Passion and Emotional Violence,* demonstrates that our models of intimacy must be re-examined.

There is much to be learned from Hite's new study. As we listen to women describing what they desire from intimate relationships and what they see as going wrong with them, we hear much discontent. But one who listens closely will also hear the beginnings of change. Women are clearly unhappy with the present state of their intimate relationships with men. Women want more verbal sharing; they want their male partners to express their feelings more often and to take the responsibility for doing so, not always relying on their partners to draw them out; women want men to care about their feelings, truly listening to them when they talk and encouraging such sharing. We also find that when women feel that such intimacy is lacking in a relationship they feel lonely, are upset and angry, and question the re-

443

lationship. We listen to accounts of failures and successes, pain as well as joy, anxieties and hopes, dreams and fears.

Hite's study is a valuable resource. It provides an exciting confirmation of the results of other psychological studies of intimacy, such as Lillian Rubin's *Intimate Strangers* (New York: Harper and Row, 1983). In addition, Hite points out directions for future research into intimacy. Her study, for example, reveals patterns of argumentation that exist within many relationships—patterns warranting further examination. Her study also uncovers important relationships between emotional and physical intimacy patterns between women and men—another fruitful area for further research. Furthermore, Hite begins to identify the socio-political structures that ground and reinforce such patterns; a context we must be aware of in order to hear and understand women's voices, as well as to discover ways to transform these patterns.

Hite's study will also be an invaluable resource to scholars. The sustained voices of women provide a text for examining the values and images women associate with intimacy and for uncovering the metaphysic that grounds them.

By listening to the voices of the women in this study we learn that women are looking for a new notion of intimacy—a notion of intimacy that does not dichotomize physical and emotional intimacy; a notion of intimacy that does not set up an either/or choice between women's values and men's values, but rather unites and transforms them. This is a voice well worth listening to.

But, perhaps most importantly, by listening attentively to the voices of these women and the voice of Shere Hite who helps us to weave these voices together, we can learn how to enhance our own intimate relationships.

Shere Hite as Sociological Theorist

Cheris Kramarae

The sociology of sex in "Western" countries has been based on several models derived, for the most part, from what are generally recognized as landmark events and publications: Havelock Ellis's work in establishing sexology as a science; Freud's (ambiguous, conflicting) theories of sexuality; Kinsey's research on sexual behavior; Masters and Johnson's physiological research; and Foucault's theorizing the relationship between sexuality and social structure. (See Margaret Jackson [1984] for a review of some of the male-defined models of sexuality which, she argues, reflect and reproduce the interests of male supremacy.)

Shere Hite has completed several extensively researched books (1976, 1981, 1987) on female sexuality, on male sexuality, and on women's relationships with husbands and lovers. As background for her analyses, she has listened to, read, and cited many sociologists, historians, and philosophers. In her last researched book she has taken the mass of stories and other responses to a carefully constructed questionnaire about the definitions of love from almost 4,500 women of differing race, ethnicity, age, sexual preference, and economic status, and has organized her analysis by the central themes of the women's statements. She deals with marriage, the nature of love, finances, housework, emotional lives, fighting, pressures on single women to marry, women's feelings about divorce, communication among women and among women and men, the purposes of being married, love relationships among women—and many other issues raised by women talking about relationships and love.

Since these are topics of interest to most humans, including researchers, we could expect that Hite's work would be frequently cited in related scholarship on all these topics. Her research reports show up the heterosexual bias of the supposedly pro-woman, liberal Ellis; counter Freud's theorizing; point to critical absences in the Kinsey reports; correct Masters and Johnson's reports; and before Foucault got around to it, set forth the theme that sexuality is historically and culturally formulated. Yet Hite's report is *not* usually included in academic reviews of sexuality. In a forthcoming essay I chronicle some of the reasons that Hite's research has not been accorded a landmark position in work on sexuality, nor in work on family interaction, divorce, and communication satisfaction (*Women's Studies International Forum*, 1994, special issue on feminist analyses of self-help manuals, edited by Victoria DeFrancisco). Her books are about male dominance, and male dominance and anger are explanations for the punishing treatment she and her work have received in the press, and for the absence of her work in academic work. Study of men's resistance to Hite's discomforting evidence can help lead to theories that are not discomforted by it. Her work can be especially helpful in understanding the centrality of satisfactory *talk* in women's definitions of love.

Some of the topics Hite deals with have been discussed by others interested in heterosexual marital relationships; for example, Mirra Komarovsky (1964), Lillian Rubin (1983), and Annette Lawson (1988) have also suggested that married women are more concerned about communication problems than are their partners. (Men want sex, women want love; men want the act, women want communication.) However, Hite has asked women questions about their relationships to men that no other published researcher has asked, and she has asked them in ways not traditional to sociological practices. Further, she has presented the answers in a way which encourages redefining sexuality concepts and practices. In my longer essay, I give the specifics of the negative media attention given to the Hite Reports.

Hite as a news event

We need to remember that the mass media does not treat many feminist scholars kindly. Looking at the exceptions can be instructive. For example, Carol Gilligan's research on moral development, when noted by the media, has been generally approved. Her work has been simplified to suggest that boys and girls, and women and men, come to make different kinds of moral decisions, which can be made to explain some of the "misunderstandings" between women and men. No need then to dwell overly much on male dominance and institutional hierarchies of power (Nancy Henley and Cheris Kramarae, 1991). Gilligan's work can be simplified and made to fit without challenging the structure, without bringing up issues of male dominance and institutional hierarchies of power. The same is true of Deborah Tannen's (1990) book on cross-sex talk, a book which the editors of the popular media have given very positive attention to, although it uses a combination of anecdotes and taped conversations with an unspecified number of people—not a methodology they would approve of if one believed that their criticism of Hite was really based on their assessment of her (much more carefully researched) study.

Hite, like Tannen, talks about "two cultures"—about women's and men's different forms of communication. But Hite also posits *causes* of the different cultures, and the suffering caused by men's focus on hierarchy and maintaining rank within that hierarchy. They are *hierarchical*, different ways of perceiving and talking—and that difference and hierarchy are maintained by men, partly through what research they value and what research they criticize.

Hite uses her fifteen years of research to also argue that a cultural revolution is taking place as women reassess their relationships to each other and to men. Actually, if we had more information about women's continuing revolution *through the years,* we might not be so frightened about publicly recognizing the findings and value of her work. She is not the first U.S. woman to initiate an extensive study of the sexual experiences of single and married women. Katharine Bement Davis published her study, *Factors in the Sex History of Twenty-two Hundred Women,* in 1929. One of her findings was that homoerotic relationships were common among the middle-class women in her survey. But by this time in the U.S., Freudian theories of sexual relationships were the accepted words on women's sexuality, and many of the respondents, understandably, described these partnerships in conflicted ways (D'Emilio and Freedman, 1988, pp. 193–94). Davis found that a small number of women were enthusiastic about marital intercourse, a larger group experienced it as difficult, and a majority thought that sex had an important but limited place in their lives. Davis asked many women about many aspects of their sexual experience. But today, for the reasons explored here, we know about Freud's few women and not Davis's many.

At the same time that we learn from Shere Hite's work, we need to continue to listen to words about white skin bias, homophobia, and hostility, and the ways they define sex for everyone. Many lesbians point out that if sex is defined as coital imperative then we need another word to describe the rich and varied expressions of emotional and physical intimacy as many women know them. For lesbian, bisexual, and heterosexual women all interactions are structured by power relations, including race and class restrictions; we must not pretend that gender—or sex—exists separate from these other, also socially imposed, categories and boundaries.

There is, of course, no simple, single way of discussing, defining, or theorizing sex or sexuality. In the past, female sexuality described in men's terms has seemed pretty strange and destructive to many of us. Satisfactory sex, as discussed by the women who responded to Shere Hite's questionnaires, usually involves an environment of satisfactory talk. Women are talking about connections which the men are denying. What the Hite Reports make very clear is that many, many women—heterosexual, bisexual, and lesbian—are encouraging men to see *and hear* personal relationships differently, and to change their values—and many, many of these women are encountering a great deal of resistance. That resistance, including the form it takes of hostile reviews of Hite's publications, should become a part of our analyses.

I think her work is valuable theoretically. Of course, what academics called *theory,* or *knowledge,* is dependent upon academic hierarchies established and maintained by men. Shere Hite's analysis grows out of and contributes to feminist explications of sexual relationships. It is not an obtuse analysis— and thus many traditional critics find it too clear and too "popular." In her wide-ranging, integrative analysis, she explodes many myths surrounding women's sexuality, provides an extensive analysis of the problems women have in maintaining loving relationships with men, explains the "hidden inequalities" present in women's intimate relationships with women (calling male hierarchies central to male ideology and the basis of all our institutions today), and discusses men's emotional withholding and reluctance to talk about personal thoughts and feelings as central to women's problems with relationships to men. She exposes systematic flaws in society (as suggested by her many respondents) and she posits gender hierarchy as basic to all kinds of hierarchies—such as those based on race and class. It all sounds like theory to me—and it all obviously sounds heretical to many traditional men.

Bibliography

Brant, Beth. 1985. Coming out as Indian lesbian writers. Ann Dybikowski, Victoria Freeman, Daphne Marlatt, Barbara Pulling, Betsy Warland, eds. *In the Feminine: Women and Words/les Femmes et les Mots.* Vancouver, B.C.: Longspoon Press.

D'Emilio, John, and Estelle B. Freedman. 1988. *Intimate Matters: A History of Sexuality in America.* New York: Harper & Row.

Foucault, Michel. 1978. *The History of Sexuality.* New York: Pantheon.

Henley, Nancy. 1977. *Body Politics.* Englewood Cliffs, N.J.: Prentice-Hall.

Henley, Nancy, and Cheris Kramarae. 1991. Miscommunication, gender, and power. In Nikolas Coupland, John Wiemann, and Howard Giles, eds. *Problem Talk and Problem Contexts: A Handbook of Miscommunications.* Sage.

Hite, Shere. 1976. *The Hite Report: A Nationwide Study of Female Sexuality.* New York: Macmillan.

Hite, Shere. 1981. *The Hite Report on Male Sexuality.* New York: Alfred A. Knopf.

Hite, Shere. 1987. *Women and Love: A Cultural Revolution in Progress.* New York: Alfred A. Knopf. Published in the UK as *The Hite Report on Love, Passion and Emotional Violence,* Macdonald Optima, 1991.

Jackson, Margaret. 1984. Sex research and the construction of sexuality: A tool of male supremacy? *Women's Studies International Forum.* 7:1, 43–51.

Komarovsky, Mirra. 1964. *Blue-Collar Marriage.* New York: Random House (reissued 1987, Yale University Press).

Kramarae, Cheris, and Paula Treichler, with assistance from Ann Russo. 1985. *A Feminist Dictionary.* Boston and London: Pandora Press (Unwin Hyman).

Lawson, Annette. 1988. *Adultery: An Analysis of Love and Betrayal.* New York: Basic Books.

Rubin, Lillian. 1983. *Intimate Strangers.* New York: Harper & Row.

Tannen, Deborah. 1990. *You Just Don't Understand: Women and Men in Conversation.* New York: Morrow.

Warland, Betsy. 1985. Surrendering the English language. Ann Dybikowski, Victoria Freeman, Daphne Marlatt, Barbara Pulling, Betsy Warland, eds. *In the Feminine: Women and Words/les Femmes et les Mots.* Vancouver, B.C.: Longspoon Press.

Controversies Over the Nature of Love

Linda Singer, 1988, Society of Women in Philosophy Eastern Meeting

The panic felt at any threat to love is a good clue to its political significance . . . women and love are underpinnings. Examine them and you threaten the very structures of culture.

Shulamith Firestone, *The Dialectic of Sex*

In a current and widely circulated cultural script, love, especially the kind that bound women to love, was just fine until feminism came along. Up until that point, love was uncontroversial, universally valorized, celebrated, and sanctified, not only as the highest form of private personal gratification, but also as that which provided the possibility of civilization as we know it. Without love, we would be doomed to live by the law of the jungle, condemned to a nasty, brutish short life in the state of nature. In this version of the story, love was especially unproblematic for women, who were willing to devote their lives, energies, and bodies to it as expressions of their deepest yearnings and highest desires. Women were especially good at love by aptitude, talent or design. Then feminism, a discourse of the unloved and therefore chronically resentful woman, came along and threw a monkey wrench into what had been a smoothly running machine, by turning love into a battlefield and a political stomping ground.

My concern is not to try to contest this story. Fairy tales, like all fictional forms, are not subject to logical or factual refutation. Fantasies and dream discourses articulate themselves in other than a propositional logic. With respect to this phantasmatic profection, the language, as Shulamith Firestone has alerted us, is also a political language of power and privilege.

Like any other ideological construction, love, and the discourses which celebrate and proliferate it, operates by effacing itself, and the strategic utilities it is designed to serve. As a product of patriarchy, love, especially the heterosexist erotic variety, has functioned, at least for the last several hundred years, as a way of mobilizing women's energies in the service of men, under the guise of desire and self-fulfillment. In love, as Simone de Beauvoir

450

pointed out nearly forty years ago, women freely choose their enslavement, eliminating the effort and expense of developing a technology of coercion. By constructing women as the emblems and exemplars of love, men are free to go off and pursue other ends—autonomy, separation, competition, success, war—while women are placed in a sphere outside, holding the place of love for men when they are ready and have time for it.

Because of the utility of this discourse for the maintenance of masculinist hegemony, there is a heavy investment in representing these arrangements as uncontroversial, i.e., not subject to serious challenge or contest from either side. This position is maintained even in the face of long-standing behavior and discourse on the part of men (including misogyny, battering, rape, familial desertion, and other practices clearly expressive of male contempt for women) that would appear to contradict this. But as with any ideological construct, it is less important that those advantaged by the political arrangements it naturalizes and solidifies believe in these projections, than it is to enlist the beliefs of those positioned so as to be dominated by it. In other words, it is culturally far more important to both represent and induce women to regard the sexual division of time, energy, and labor prescribed by the discourse of love as unproblematic and as something which could not or ought not be challenged or contested. Given the levels of social resources devoted to the construction of the discourse of love and systems for its circulation, we should not be surprised that this discourse succeeds in creating the kinds of subjects it works to produce. But we also should expect that its effects are not seamless and that the discourse of love has also produced critiques and resistances—specially, but certainly not exclusively, from women.

Feminist theory, at least in its second wave, has consistently questioned, challenged and critiqued the celebratory sanctity in which heterosexual erotic love has historically been cloaked. This critique is addressed both to the underlying logic which assumes that ultimate intimacy can be forged out of the union of opposites, and to its consequences, namely the claim that women become willful or desiring contributors to their own subjugation and effacement, on the ground that that is what love, especially love of men, demands. Armed with an array of unhappy material consequences of women's love for men including unwanted pregnancy, death and maiming through abortion, death and crippling side effects from contraception, battering, abuse and abandonment, as well as psychological suffering and trauma, feminist theory has sought to make love controversial, since failure to do so would amount to uncritical complicity with its fallout. As Firestone argued in 1972, ". . . (a) book on radical feminism that did not deal with love would be a political failure."

The corollary of this position is that any book or thinker which seriously takes on the question of love, i.e., which challenges the cultural privilege and politics embedded in this institutionalized form of social relations, becomes a target for what is often a full-fledged hegemonic deployment aimed at trivializing or de-legitimating the very question raised. If the primacy of heterosexual love becomes questionable or, even worse, suspect, then so do all the forms of biological, social, and political distribution which are based on it including heterosexist privilege, male dominance, the nuclear family, phallocentrism, and a rigid separation between the private and the public, the personal and the political.

Historically, these latter oppositions have been used to justify forms of behavior and exercises of power in love relationships, like rape, assault, manipulation and exploitation that would not otherwise be considered acceptable, on the grounds that any form of direct social intervention into this sphere would violate the parties' right to privacy and free expression, even in cases where it is clear that such activity is designed precisely to limit the freedom of the female participant. Because the private sphere created by the logic of liberalism as the site for heterosexual erotic love is constructed as a space organized by the concepts of individuation and choice, social obligations are further reduced on the grounds that women have freely chosen the situations in which they continue to participate, and therefore, at least in a certain sense, consent to the consequences to which they are subjected.

In defense of this very vital thesis, numerous theories have been offered to explain women's willingness and, in fact, eagerness to freely engage in such relationships, including Freud's infamous theory of female masochism, the theory of woman's ego development in a context of relatedness rather than autonomy, and various formulations which emphasize the passivity of female eroticism.

The political utility of such theories in part accounts for their widespread proliferation and circulation, so much so that their truth is often taken for granted, even by writers like Carol Gilligan, who claim to be speaking on behalf of women. The use to which these theories are put reveals a lot about the political function of love in late patriarchy, since their effect is either to naturalize women's subjugation through love, or to blame the victim for the consequences she suffers, while protecting the prerogatives of the perpetrators on the grounds either that their behavior is also natural, and therefore not subject to moral censure, or on the grounds that they cannot be held accountable for women's complicity with their aggressive tendencies.

Examine love and you threaten the very structures of culture, the structures that depend on normalizing male dominance and aggression, in part on the grounds that this is what women really want, and then using the persistence of heterosexual coupling under the rubric of love as evidence in support of this truism. This in part explains why most of those who seriously questioned or challenged the discourse of love in the last century have been subjected to wrath, hostility, and trivialization. This would include not only the treatment given to feminist texts like Beauvoir's *The Second Sex,* Kate Millett's *Sexual Politics,* and the writings of radical lesbians like Ti-Grace Atkinson and Jill Johnston, but also works as distant from feminism as those of Sigmund Freud, Wilhelm Reich, Herbert Marcuse, and Norman O. Brown, each of whom raised questions about the organization of eroticism proffered by the rubric of love.

More recently we have the case of Andrea Dworkin's text, *Intercourse,* which was subjected to a range of socially conspicuous challenge and critique that might fairly be described as overkill, i.e., out of proportion to what would have been the likely readership for such a text. Dworkin's claim that penile vaginal intercourse is a mechanism of domination was challenged from a variety of directions by feminists, anti-feminists, women and men. The most common strategy employed was to invalidate Dworkin's thesis on the grounds that it was couched in an indefensible anatomical essentialism, which attached erroneous political significance to male and female body parts. What the media barrage failed to foreground, however, was the essentialist assumptions and motives underlying the combative discourse to which this text and author were subjected, namely that challenges to the hegemony of intercourse must be violently resisted, as conspicuously and publicly as possible, because the perpetuation of this practice is essential to the existing social order.

In popular media, any evidence of the waning cultural influence of love is subjected to a critical eye and ironic discourse, even when the phenomena in question are not cast in the context of an explicit challenge to existing social arrangement. As an example, there was *Time* magazine's recent cover story "Is love doomed?", which focused on the life styles of urban professionals, which often leave little room for and attach only subsidiary priority to love and erotic relationships. Even though the motives here are represented in the conventional language of personal ambition and economic aggrandizement, the consequences are presented with irony and alarm, as they are also represented, albeit comically, in the recent Yuppie romance, *Baby Boom,* and the figure of the grotesque in another recent and very popular film, *Fatal Attraction.*

At a time when fear of AIDS and other sexually transmitted diseases would seem to offer both grounds and motives for revivifying the prospect of organizing eroticism as a monogamous practice undertaken as an expression of love, contemporary sexual politics is further destabilized by the persistence of contradictory theory and practice, theory and practice which, intentionally or not, resist, oppose or contradict the resolutionary rhetoric of love. To a certain extent, at least, these forms of resistance can be read as useful to the proliferative logic of the dominant position, offering occasions for its explicit articulation and defense precisely because it is under attack.

Because the discourse of advocacy depends on points of resistance to jus-

453

tify and occasion its evocation, the logic of this position demands a continual stream of appropriate targets in order to mandate its redeployment targets which have thus far included homosexuality, promiscuity, and teenage sexuality. Just as the saturation point with respect to these phenomena is being reached, in strides Shere Hite with her new book, billed as the third volume in the trilogy of Hite Reports, *The Hite Report on Love, Passion and Emotional Violence,* a work that has been subjected to at least as much hostile treatment as any of those I have previously mentioned, as has its author. I think the degree of negative critical response to this text, a phenomenon which has received widespread attention from both the news and entertainment communities, provides some clue to its significance, as well as to the importance of its subject matter. Therefore I think it is worth examining the criticisms of Hite's work against the grain, which is to say resisting their implications that such critiques ought to result in a dismissal of Hite's conclusions because her methodology, or sample, or interpretations are flawed. I think that the heat this book has taken gives us reason for taking its claims more seriously, on the grounds that if there were not some significant fear, or temptation to believe that much of what is represented in Hite's text was true, there would be little or no need to devote so much time, energy, and space to refuting or contesting its findings, or the manner in which they were produced.

The subtitle of this book, "A Cultural Revolution in Progress," helps account for both the quantity and intensity of the critiques, both because it situates the text within an oppositional or critical context, and because it enlarges rather than minimizes the implicatory consequences of the findings and the interpretations Hite draws from them.

The findings from which these larger implications are drawn, and the ones that have been subjected to the most extensive and hostile challenges, are those that indicate not only that women are dissatisfied with their heterosexual love relationships, but also that they are no longer simply enduring it, as good women were supposed to, silently. Rather, women are doing something about it, including openly articulating their dissatisfaction and the grounds for it, as well as abandoning or decentering these relationships through divorce, extramarital affairs, and changing their erotic affiliations. The narratives Hite reproduces also make clear that many women no longer live for love, or consider it the most crucial factor for determining their happiness.

As troubling as this evidence is for those who wish to argue that heterosexual love still goes on uncontested, some of the conclusions Hite draws from this evidence of female resistance must be even more disturbing. Most striking, at least to me, if not the media, is Hite's claim that women's demonstrated willingness to leave relationships that disempower them can be read as part of a sustained, albeit unorganized, movement away from a society organized around male dominance and other masculinist values, toward a society which enfranchises feminine values like care and relatedness. Although much of what is represented as the grounds and consequences of women's dissatisfaction with love has already been articulated in earlier feminist theoretical writings, some of which Hite cites as support for her conclusions, Hite's book seems to pose an even greater threat, in part, because her book does not speak with a single authorial voice, but rather represents the voices of the several thousand women whose responses to Hite's questionnaire are reproduced in the text. While the conclusions of feminist theorists might be more easily dismissed on the grounds that they represented an elite, singular, idiosyncratic and therefore atypical point of view, Hite's work avails itself of empirical research technique, and thus claims to speak not only for its author, but for the collection of women whose views are offered and presented. This, unfortunately, also casts Hite in the position of the messenger who brings bad news, and she is being treated accordingly.

Rather than acknowledging their anxiety in the face of Hite's conclusions, most critics have attempted to challenge and undermine them indirectly, by caricaturing the manner in which those conclusions were reached. In an effort to displace the significance of what the women in Hite's book say, criticism has focused on representing these women as atypical, and the survey results as tainted, because the sample of women whose views they summarize was not sufficiently random: either because the surveys were distributed by women's groups (and the typical woman is assumed not to be a joiner) or because the voluntary conditions of response to what is, admittedly, a very extensive and therefore time-consuming questionnaire, already reflects a bias, namely that only women with an axe to grind would bother to respond to Hite's queries in the first place. The happy and contented women who do not supposedly appear in Hite's text are being constructed, by the reader critic—a silent majority with neither willingness nor ability to share their contentment with the rest of us. On the basis of this tainted sample, tainted by comparison to the constructed one, it is argued that Hite's conclusions ought to be dismissed, because the procedures for arriving at them were "unscientific."

Part of what is interesting to me about this critical strategy is the way it foregrounds contradictions within the operative politics of knowledge. Traditionally, love has been cited as one of the few phenomena that stands outside of the mechanisms of scientific discourse and objectification, a point of resistance to the hegemony of technological and informational objectification. For a long time culture has not only tolerated but valorized the assumption that love was not the sort of thing that could be subjected to or analyzed in terms of scientific method. As evidence one may simply point to the texts which have been most influential in constructing our social expectations for love, from Plato's *Symposium* and Ovid's *Art of Love,* to the Old and New Testaments, and more recent romantic literature from the nineteenth and twentieth centuries, as well as the work of popular psychologists like Erich Fromm and Leo Bascaglia, none of which are or claim to be scientific and yet continue to function as socially authoritative prescriptive and descriptive discourses. Unscientific approaches are unproblematic as long as the discourse produced confirms and validates dominant sentiments, and does not disrupt underlying social utilities.

When a text like Hite's comes along, and hers is clearly neither the first nor the last, which challenges hegemonic sentiments by claiming empirical evidence of their waning influence, methodological considerations are brought to bear in a way intended to discredit what has been said on the basis of who says it or on what basis, without ever having to challenge the truth or significance of the conclusions as such. The strategic utility of the methodological critique is double-edged: it casts doubt on the credibility and integrity of the inquirer, implying in this case that her methods were intentionally biased and designed to be misleading or unrepresentative, while concealing the ideological biases and allegiances of the critic and the criticism, by cloaking them in the language of scientific neutrality. Such a strategy allows the intended audience to believe that it is only the inquirer, and not the critic, who has an axe to grind, or preconceptions to protect. The numbers game being played with Hite's book has also resulted in some interesting tactical reverses through which individual critics, or members of talk-show audiences, can, with a single stroke, make a claim that supposedly invalidates what thousands of women have had to say. How many women do there have to be before what we say is worth paying attention to?

But the numbers game is only one element in a larger strategic campaign to dismiss this text and thereby discourage a potential readership from confronting the text for themselves on the grounds that what the women represented in Hite's book write, whether or not they are typical, is not worth reading. It is worth remembering, however, that male entitlement to cultural visibility and authority is often construed on just the opposite basis. That is, by reference to some special and distinguishing mark that differentiates, hence privileges him with respect to the average observer on the basis of knowledge, access, or the uniqueness of his point of view. The authority of the critic comes from the fact that he is not an average Joe, but an expert.

I also cannot help but feel that this strategy represents another reversal, masking the concern that these responses are all too typical, and that too many women will identify and recognize parts of themselves in at least some of what the many women cited say. The critical barrage mounted against Hite's work has sought to operate as a self-concealing censorship mechanism, discouraging potential readers, on the ground that the text they are being offered is biased and therefore misleading. But the success of this strategy is predicated on a thin hope, a.d one that I take to be rather questionable, namely that if women are not presented narratives of dissatisfaction, such ideas or sentiments would otherwise never occur to them.

In re-reading the strategies used to try to discredit Hite's work, I do not want to leave the impression that the text is not open to certain kinds of critical readings. I myself question some of the language and logic operative in Hite's interpretations of the phenomena she recounts and their social and political consequences. But in the context of more immediate political urgencies, those differences don't seem all that important, and are better saved for another occasion. More important to address at this point are the reasons why any discourse of women's dissatisfactions with loving men must, it appears, be silenced, marginalized, or discredited. In examining those reasons we also come to realize how much and for how long the discourse of love as uncontroversial has necessitated and depended on women's silence. This can be an empowering as well as a painful insight, empowering to the extent that we recognize that the effort to silence women is also an indication of the power carried by our voices when we do speak. Powers to disrupt, intervene, and change the rules of the games women and men play.

Love in our age has been offered to an increasingly beleaguered, discontented, and anxious citizenry as a pacificatory moment of pleasure and solace in a world that is organized in increasingly inhuman and alienating ways. Love is therefore a significant mechanism in the apparatus of modern power which, as a number of social theorists from Marcuse through to Foucault point out, operates not through threat of coercion or death, but rather by the social construction and manipulation of pleasure, a technology of control by incitement. When women, who have been positioned as the emblems and place holders for love, confess to its failure, i.e., that we are not pacified in love but are rather mobilized in other ways by it, some crucial part of our social fabric starts to come apart at the seams. That is why Shere Hite has to be wrong. But if she is wrong, so is most of the feminist and other theory produced in our century that has challenged or criticized existing sexual and social relationships. If Shere Hite is right, however, about what's happening with women, there is some very confirming evidence for all of us who have been struggling to undermine the patriarchal organization of sexual difference. Evidence that our efforts at cultural revolution have not been in vain, they are in progress and may, in fact, have more power than we or the dominant culture and ideology usually give us credit for. At a time in our cultural history in which traditional codes of femininity are being recirculated as cutting-edge fashion, and where feminists are once again being caricatured as male bashers, any text that offers women a potentially empowering position within a discourse of love, that has historically been used for our domination, is worth taking seriously, not only as a mirror of the present, but also as a potential blueprint for building our future. If we fail to keep love controversial, we are doomed to the limits of the current situations and to forms of suffering and frustration with which many of us, I suspect, are all too familiar, because these disappointments are all too typical.

APPENDICES

Methodological Essays

1976: Introduction to
The Hite Report on Female Sexuality

Women have never been asked how they felt about sex. Researchers, looking for statistical "norms," have asked all the wrong questions for all the
wrong reasons—and all too often wound up *telling* women how they should
feel rather than *asking* them how they do feel. Female sexuality has been
seen essentially as a response to male sexuality and intercourse. There has
rarely been any acknowledgment that female sexuality might have a complex
nature of its own which would be more than just the logical counterpart of
(what we think of as) male sexuality.

What these questionnaires have attempted to do is to ask *women* themselves how they feel, what they like, and what they think of sex. This is not
to imply that the only thing that stands between a woman and "satisfactory"
sex is her realization of her own physical needs. "Sex" as we define it is part
of the whole cultural picture; a woman's place in sex mirrors her place in the
rest of society.

This book presents what the women who answered said—in their own
words and in their own way. The intention is to get acquainted, to share how
we have experienced our sexuality, how we feel about it—and to see our personal lives more clearly, thus redefining our sexuality and strengthening our
identities as women. This book is also meant to stimulate a public discussion
and re-evaluation of sexuality. We must begin to devise more kind, generous, and personal ways of relating which will be positive and constructive
for the future.

In addition, this book presents a new theory of female sexuality, which
unfolds gradually, chapter by chapter, and can best be understood by reading the book in chapter order. The first half of the book is devoted basically
to a discussion of orgasm, and the second half to a critique of our culture's
definition of sex.

The experience of receiving these replies has been enriching, warm-
ing, and enlightening—for me, and, I hope, for all who read them. What
these women have shared (anonymously), with so much love and honesty,

comes from the wealth of female experience that is usually hidden, but which foreshadows women's great courage and potential for the future.

It has been my privilege to conduct this project for the last four years, and it is with great joy that I present the results.

Shere Hite
February 1976

1976: Background of *The Hite Report on Female Sexuality*

One woman who answered wrote, "This is the most fascinating sex survey I ever participated in, but I am baffled how you could compile an essay type of study in an accurate form." Had I not written my Master's thesis on the methodology of the social sciences, undoubtedly it would have been more difficult than it was. Actually, it was difficult and time-consuming, but the results made it more than worth it. There were probably over thirteen thousand woman hours involved in analyzing the answers, plus at least another ten thousand put in by the women who answered the questionnaires.

Specifically, the information was analyzed in this way: first, a large chart was made for each question asked. Each person's answer to the question being analyzed was then copied onto that chart (which was usually many pages long), next to its individual identification number. The many days required to copy the 1844 answers to each question were actually very valuable in that they provided extensive time for reflecting on the answers. Once the charts had been prepared, it was a relatively simple, though again time-consuming, process to categorize the answers. Usually patterns had begun to stand out during the copying process, so that the categories more or less formed themselves. Then figures were prepared by totaling the number of women in each category, following which representative quotes were selected. This procedure was followed for each of the fifty-odd questions.

In addition, one main chart was kept onto which much of the information from other charts was coded for each individual woman, including preferred type of stimulation, type of masturbation, number of orgasms desired, age, and many other facts. This chart, which acted as a kind of hand-made computer, was the basis for the majority of statements in the orgasm, intercourse, and clitoral stimulation chapters.

Project Financing

There was no foundation grant or other funding involved in this project. Originally, extensive funds were not needed, as printing was inexpensive. Luckily, there is a free press (Come! Unity Press) in New York that makes space available for non-commercial printing—for whatever donation you can afford, as long as the material printed is free to everyone.* Eventually I printed all the hundred thousand questionnaires at this press, with the help of other women—in many different colors, and on many different kinds of paper, including scrap from old bingo score cards. Thus, until the analysis of the information was begun, the main expense of the project, besides paper and moderate contributions to the press, was postage, since over 75,000 questionnaires were mailed.

The larger the project became, the more apparent it became that the results could best be made available in book form. *Sexual Honesty, by Women for Women* was an early attempt to share these replies in the form of an inexpensive paperback. However, since paperbacks do not generally receive as much attention as hardcovers (in terms of publicity or book reviews), it seems that in the long run, the information in hardcover books reaches more people. As for contributing to the financing of the project, the book advance for *Sexual Honesty* was of course small and only contributed to the continuing printing and mailing of the questionnaires. It was really the generous advance, through the sponsorship of Regina Ryan, which made possible the time necessary for the analysis of the answers. The debt I owe to Regina Ryan is enormous. Without her perceptive understanding of the project and belief in its importance from the very beginning, and her unerring good judgment at so many points in the work, the wheels of progress would undoubtedly have ground to a halt many times.

Eventually, it also became necessary to borrow money from friends, some of whom went into debt themselves to loan me money. For this very important support for the project I am especially grateful to Cecile Rice, Michael Wilson, and Virginio Del Toro. However, since loans must eventually be repaid, and since book advances are in themselves a sort of loan, in a very real sense it will be the people who buy this book who will, in the long run, have financed this project.

I would also like to thank the women who produced this book. Not only were the questionnaires printed by women, and the replies analyzed by women, but some very talented women were responsible for the produc-

*Of course the questionnaires were always free, and *Sexual Honesty* was available free to anyone who wrote me for it. Unfortunately, the present book could not be offered free but many N.O.W. chapters are receiving free copies so that anyone who is interested, member or not, can have access to the book.

tion of the book. Again, without Regina Ryan one wonders what the fate of this book might have been. I cannot thank her enough. At every step of the way, her criticism was invaluable, and her long-term vision and enthusiasm regarding the project provided me with an infinite source of energy and encouragement. Lindy Hess was also extremely important in producing this book, and deserves a large amount of credit and praise for her skillful work in many areas and her intelligent and carefully considered criticisms of the book's content, which influenced the shape of the book. She was enormously helpful, and enormously kind, and I am very grateful to her. Suzi Arensberg took on the gigantic job of copyediting the manuscript, and did so in a remarkably sensitive, skillful, and thoughtful manner. Christine Aulicino is responsible for the book's beautiful design. Finally, had it not been for the women who answered the questionnaires, there would have been no book, and to them I sent my warmest greetings and my deep personal appreciation—and congratulations.

1976: Samples of Replies to Questionnaire for *The Hite Report on Female Sexuality*

Why Did Women Answer This Questionnaire?

One of the criticisms leveled at *The Hite Report on Female Sexuality* on publication was, "Wasn't it only women who were dissatisfied?" (who answered the questionnaire). Anyone who had seen either the original questionnaire, or many of the answers given, could not have asked that question, because opportunities were provided to express happiness, pleasure, and satisfaction in many areas of life, not just sexually. Couldn't it be just as possible that women answered the questionnaire to share what was positive in their lives, as well as to express their dissatisfaction? That a forum was provided for previously unvoiced thoughts, fears, and feelings about the most intimate areas of women's lives was bound to express some dissatisfaction. Perhaps the greater query should be, why so little expression of dissatisfaction, given the other details provided on how difficult the circumstances were in which women were attempting to have relationships. After all, how would men feel if they were told that around 70 percent of them were sexually dysfunctional because they didn't orgasm in a way defined for them by women! On any level that would seem unfair. But that women should have survived receiving sexual information like that, with any positivism at all, is nothing short of miraculous. And positivism there is—not an "I hate all men" treatise—in *The Hite Report on Female Sexuality*.

The design of the research in the Hite Reports was to find out what individuals (men too, in *The Hite Report on Male Sexuality*) actually felt and thought about things, not to impose preconceived ideas upon them. And the context from which details of individual sexuality were gleaned was also freely expressed, again by the individuals themselves. Much of what was asked could be answered quite factually, and was so. Not before this research was there the tangible information to refute previous definitions of female sexuality, for example, because no one had asked these questions before and in such a way that they could be freely—and anonymously—answered.

The penultimate question asked in *The Hite Report on Female Sexuality* questionnaire provides an answer to anyone asking "Wasn't it only women who were dissatisfied?" (who answered). This question was, "Why did you answer this questionnaire, and how did you feel about it?" Although there *are* expressions of dissatisfaction that influenced the decision to answer, and 3,019 women did, it is not the whole story by any means.

Why did women answer this questionnaire? ("Wasn't it only women who were dissatisfied?")

"Why did you answer this questionnaire? How did you like it?"

"I answered this questionnaire because I think the time is long overdue for women to speak out about their own feelings about sex. As for whether I liked it, I can only say it was a great relief to say these things out loud at last. I for one am heartily sick of reading what men have to say about my sexuality."

"This was a great questionnaire. I really enjoyed thinking about how I felt about things. Women need to communicate with each other so much more, because we can really give so much to each other."

"I answered because I like the whole idea of it—that for once a group of women are going to be able to say what we like and don't like and what we want and don't want. I am tired of having some man tell me what I should want and feel and what my sexuality is or should be."

"Because I believe the findings will be significant. Since this is anonymous and written, instead of verbal, one can be completely honest without any discomfort. I would find it very hard to have to *say* all these things to another person, and I'm sure many women would feel the same. I believe it's terribly important for all women to know what most other women experience—not just what the more sexually free women experience, like those who don't mind relating publicly their experiences, or who could manage to perform in a laboratory situation."

"I answered this questionnaire because I hoped that in some way it would shed some light for other women, so that they might not go through what I went through to realize they are not 'frigid,' 'inadequate,' or 'have something wrong with them.'"

"I really enjoyed this questionnaire. I found out a lot about myself and quite a few things are really clearer to me after writing them down. I sure didn't think it would take so much time but it was worth it."

"I answered it because I'd like to help add to our collective knowledge of ourselves, and it seems a good approach to begin to define female sexuality without theorizing. I trust the answers you might get more than the answers male gynecologists and male analysts have gotten on women's sexuality. We need to know, but we don't get to know with all the studies being done by men. I liked the questions—they made me feel very deeply about things."

"I suppose I just wanted to tell someone how I really feel and get it out in the open. My partner knows most of my feelings but not all of them. I would like to know more about sex, but most of the books I have read are not very revealing. They don't answer the important questions. I really hope that when this book is published it will answer these types of questions. I have found no such book or information yet."

"It was *great!* Had to do with *my* sex life, not how to please a man!"

"Before this questionnaire, I was content to end the sex act with my husband's ejaculation, sometimes feeling unfulfilled. I now demand more attention, and my husband is very happy to oblige."

"My husband has read through the questionnaire—but not through my answers—and I am going to try to discuss the questions with him, though some of them may be painful. I wanted to answer them all first, however, without getting any comment from him. Perhaps we can find out more about what each of us wants and needs, though that wasn't what the questionnaire was set up for."

"It helped me to be clear about my sexual needs. I am happy that it demanded my being explicit. It also succeeded in putting me in touch with areas of my sexuality that I need to work on in order to get more gratification out of sex. I'm thinking in particular about my inhibition in asking for what gives me pleasure."

"Glad to be able to say what I feel for once. Relieved. Cried some. P.S. I hope the good doctors learn something (smile)."

"I have a great deal of anger about my sexual hangups and a great deal of confusion. I am at a point of seeing how much of what I have learned of sexuality has really been slanted and sexist. I am trying to dump that garbage, and trying very hard to *listen* to what is in me."

"I answered it for cheap therapy, and introspection. I'm glad I did it—I was able to tie together patterns that I hadn't thought about before, despite the fact that I do think about these things and introspect a lot."

"The questions sure got me thinking about myself! I was slightly embarrassed writing out the answers, thinking at certain points the questions were too personal—if it hadn't been anonymous I never could have answered. I learned more than you have about myself."

"What I like best about it is the thought that I'm talking to other women."

"I am only grateful I don't have to sign this, as all hell would break loose if this ever got into the wrong hands. I can't say I liked answering these questions. I would die of embarrassment to do so in person. This way I don't mind. My only reason for doing so is to be of some help and that is all."

"I cried when I first read through this. There is so much I've lied about for so long; I'd already come to understand that, but wanted to fill out the questionnaire to make myself write it all down. Undoubtedly, you will have helped many women in just this way, and publication of the results will reach many more who, as I did, will read the truth they couldn't tell themselves."

"I wanted to make sure you had at least one questionnaire with my viewpoint. It was difficult for me to answer this, but I did so in the hope that I could reach someone out there."

"I answered because I think your results are going to be based on a 'skewed distribution' of super-liberal and radical reformer types—and for balance you need some 'straight' *happily* married folks!!"

"I thought that some input from a person who was extremely slow and conventional in sexual development might be helpful to you. Not being a swinger—I had to force myself to be frank in my answers. It was worth it."

"Anything that helps women define their own sexuality on their own terms, and thus have more control over their own lives, is something I want to be part of."

"After I wrote reams, you ask me why I answered this—hah! I feel that all people regardless of age and experience have to be more open and honest and learn from each other."

"Because I felt there were not enough statistics about women septuagenarians nor enough understanding of the widows' situation. At my age and without responsibilities I do not want matrimony, but I have a continuing sex drive. Also I had heart surgery two years ago, which has completely rejuvenated me. I want to live to the fullest extent of my capabilities."

"I have a twenty-three-year-old daughter, to whom I still owe much in the way of truth-telling. So, what I have to say here is for her as well as for all young women."

"Saw an ad in the paper, thought you should have the opinion of a middle-aged woman concerning her sexual attitudes. Interesting questions, thought-provoking; some were hard for me to answer because I had never thought about them. I would not have answered honestly without anonymity, and I would not have answered as carefully had it been a multiple-choice questionnaire."

"I've read the results of a few sex questionnaires before, and all the women seemed happy, well-adjusted, and in control—that is, they all had orgasms. I felt lonely, left out, and odd. I answered this because I wanted you to hear from someone like me who is still struggling with it—but putting up a good fight, too!"

"This questionnaire was hard to answer. I felt blanked out, confused. I didn't want to face what's hard to look at for me."

"Being non-orgasmic, sex is often on my mind and takes a lot of energy. So it helped me feel a little better to have a chance to voice my frustrations."

"I answered because I feel the women's point of view should be publicized. I have read many of the sex books available, and they are all written of the male, for the male, and by the male. I would like to ask Dr. Freud how many orgasms Mrs. Freud had?"

"I think real information on women's sexuality should be made available to other women. It's time we began understanding each other instead of only trying to understand men."

"I feel that I owe the women's movement a lot for my own personal sexual satisfaction, which I might never have discovered otherwise. That's why I filled out the questionnaire. I hope it shakes male assumptions to the roots."

"I feel very strongly that sexual education for women will be one of the greatest single factors in our liberation. That's why I answered."

"I answered because I'm sick of all the lies that are printed about women's sexuality—especially that of lesbians."

"I answered it because I am hoping it will be compiled to give a true, realistic picture of female sexuality. I get annoyed at all these men who write about women and how we should or shouldn't feel. They can't possibly know how we feel."

"I answered this questionnaire because I was intrigued by the idea of sex information collected by women from women. This project seems to me to have real constructive possibilities and I hope there will be more of the same in the future, and that women will just throw out old assumptions about their sexuality and try to find out what's really happening."

"I got the questionnaire from my mother-in-law's copy of *Sexual Honesty,* and I was moved and fascinated by the diversity of replies. Women telling it like it is! I'd never really thought before about how arrogant men are telling us what we feel or should feel. I felt for those women who wonder if there is something wrong because they don't have orgasms, as I had this problem for many years. I'm sure many women read the book and realized that they were not abnormal after all!"

"I thought this was a very good questionnaire. The different questions seem to give an opportunity to think about various aspects of sex from more than one angle. This type of study is much needed."

Is *The Hite Report* "Scientific"? Toward a New Feminist Research Methodology*

Shere Hite, 1978

Is *The Hite Report on Female Sexuality* scientific? This is a question that is often asked.

The question itself reflects a misunderstanding of the word "scientific." Having done my master's thesis on the application of scientific method to the social sciences, I am familiar with the history of scientific method. "Science" is a term which originally came from the Latin root "to know" and means basically systematized knowledge in any field, sometimes as part of a system of general laws. Anything which is investigated carefully and in a scholarly manner can be termed "scientific," although the term has many specialized meanings. The term "social science" came into common usage in the late nineteenth century when the humanities, overshadowed by the increasing prestige of physics, mathematics, and the advances of the industrial revolution, started to think in terms of developing similar methods for their own work. Whether this is possible, and how it should be done, is a question which social scientists continue to debate in the field, which is still very young.†

Thus, *The Hite Report is* "scientific." However, what this question usually means is, "Does *The Hite Report on Female Sexuality* contain a statistically representative sample?" There has never been a perfect sample in sex research. In the field of sociology, the two basic methods which have been employed are the taking of surveys, and the building of predictive models, usually based on existing survey material or data banks. Traditionally, the survey— "a sampling or partial collection of facts, figures or opinions taken and used to approximate the whole"—was the basic method of the sociologist, with a "random sample" being considered the most accurately representative. However, in sex research in particular, this type of survey has never been possible

---

*Excerpted from *AASECT* magazine, January 1978–79 (Journal/American Association of Sex Educators, Counselors & Therapists).

†See P. Connerton, editor, *Critical Sociology,* Penguin Books, 1976; E. F. Schumacher, *A Guide for the Perplexed,* Harper & Row, 1977; Stephen Toulmin, "From Form to Function: Philosophy and the History of Science in the 1950's and Now," *Daedalus,* Summer 1977.

on a large scale because most of the people chosen would not answer—due to the personal nature of the questions, and the lack of anonymity in this sampling procedure.

Was Kinsey representative? A second survey method, which was Kinsey's, is to select people who statistically approximate those ranges found in the general population (as to age, marital status, etc.) and use them as control groups. What Kinsey did—and Kinsey is the *only* person who ever attempted a straight-out large-scale *survey* of sexuality in the sense of aiming primarily for representative accuracy—was to question people from as many walks of life, backgrounds, and economic levels, etc., as he could to try to approximate a representative selection. Arguments continued for years as to whether he succeeded, but today his findings are generally accepted as accurate. Of course, Masters and Johnson did not do a survey; they did biological research on the basis of a highly selected population of 694 people. Obviously, a "study" of this kind is just as "scientific" as a survey, as long as it is precise and systematic; not being statistically representative is not the same as being non-scientific. This is true of my own work as well.

The Hite Report on Female Sexuality was never meant to be a traditional "survey." It contains answers from a wide cross-section of women, although it was never intended fundamentally as a survey. In fact, *The Hite Report on Female Sexuality* was intended as a new kind of social science. Its methodology was conceived as providing a large forum in which women could speak out freely (thus the necessary anonymity of the replies)—giving everyone reading those replies the chance to decide for themselves how they felt about things. The methodology was seen as a process, both for the individual woman answering the questionnaire, and for the person reading what the 3,019 women had written—a process of rethinking, self-discovery, and of getting acquainted with many other women in a way that had never before been possible—an anonymous and powerful communication from the women who answered to all the women of the world.

At the same time, I was able to use my background in cultural history to put what the women said into an historical and cultural framework, analyzing it from a political point of view, and ending with a new and positive woman-oriented way of seeing women's sexuality. However, thanks to the methodology, it is not necessary for anyone to agree with my conclusions regarding the women's answers: the book is nine-tenths unedited quotes from the women—so the reader can draw her/his own conclusions and disregard mine altogether if s/he so desire. This is one of the first research reports, in fact, in which we don't have to take the word of the researcher; verbatim reports are not usually given.

This methodology has the additional benefit of avoiding "telling" people what to think: it does not create new "norms" or stereotypes for women to

472

"measure up" to. An important drawback of scientific method as it applies to sociology and psychology in particular is that it leads to the establishment of "norms"—that is, so-called normal ranges of behavior. In a traditional study, the researcher organizes the findings into ranges of behavior; the largest sub-category is the "norm." To generalize for a moment, we can say that the publication of these "norms" tends in itself to create behavior; norms themselves can suggest or even dictate behavior. Measuring "what is" thus reinforces the status quo. Trying to build rigid "scientific" models of personality development, or to predict inevitable patterns of social behavior—and such models usually lack any historical perspective—works toward a narrow and conformist view of humanity.

In fact, essay questions have long been recommended in the social sciences as a way of going beyond quantification. Multiple-choice questions are designed more with a view to measuring behavior, since the results can easily be computerized and the possible choices of answers are pre-standardized. Or, if you want to be more cynical, pre-biased. Multiple-choice questionnaires have been accused of *telling* people what to think, rather than *asking* them. The entire procedure is structured in an hierarchical and authoritarian manner, although there are certain times when this procedure can be useful.

The essay questionnaire, as it was used in *The Hite Report on Female Sexuality,* on the other hand, is geared toward a deeper dialogue, toward searching for new thoughts and a more meaningful understanding. It is a more equal, more cooperative model, and also more difficult and time-consuming for the researcher. But it is very important. As one respondent wrote me, "Our society has belittled the individual's opinion, and needs to start respecting each person's uniqueness instead of searching for new categories in which to 'clump' people." In the research for *The Hite Report on Female Sexuality,* the individual, while answering, has a chance to grow and reassess her life; while reading others' answers now, everyone can get the benefit of many people's experience, told in a very personal and whole way.

So, finally, *is The Hite Report* representative? No one can be sure of the exact percentage of women in the United States who masturbate, for example. No one can be sure if the 70 percent figure for women who do not orgasm from intercourse given in my book is exactly correct; however, it seems clear by now from the reaction to my work that it is not far off. But since we are not searching for "norms" or statistical measurement, this becomes to some extent irrelevant. I do believe that *The Hite Report on Female Sexuality* includes the entire spectrum of women's points of view. However, I would consider the validity of the study to have been challenged if, after publication of the book, many women had written that their point of view was not included, or many women had spoken out saying they did not think the book represented their feelings.

To date, *The Hite Report on Female Sexuality* has been published in seventeen countries, and in not one country has any woman disagreed with the basic findings of the book, i.e., that women do not for the most part orgasm simply as the result of thrusting during coitus; that most women can masturbate to orgasm via clitoral/vulval stimulation when they choose to; that we must reassess the traditional ideas the society has held about female sexuality. And many, many more basic conclusions. In fact, thousands of women everywhere have written publicly and privately in letters to me that they felt the book spoke for them, and that they were relieved to find that they were not "different" from other women, or "abnormal." Although *The Hite Report on Female Sexuality* may not be statistically perfect—as no studies in the field have been—it is obviously not far off either. But most important of all, women of all kinds everywhere have found that it had an active meaning for them, that it went beyond being "just a report" and became a living sharing among human beings, enriching all who participated. This is what social science should be.

Who Answered the Questionnaire: Population Statistics and Methodology

Shere Hite, *The Hite Report on Male Sexuality*

Starting in 1974, before publication of *The Hite Report on Female Sexuality*, questionnaires were distributed to men in various parts of the country. The purpose of this early distribution was to test for errors of fact which might be incorporated into the study of female sexuality, and to see if there was a difference between social stereotypes of "male sexuality" and the way men feel. Quite quickly it was realized that there is much that is not known about men's sexuality, and especially about how men feel about their sexual experiences and personal relationships. Men's replies to this early questionnaire pointed the way to a second version of the questions, which was distributed in 1975. Four complete versions of the questions were undertaken in all, with the final version being the most heavily distributed.

Great emphasis was placed on reaching men of all ages, in all areas of the country, in all walks of life, and with all outlooks and points of view. The success of this effort, in most cases, is reflected in the statistics and comparative statistics which are found on the following pages. Basically, the distribution proceeded in three stages. First, the early distribution was done to explore whether men would be willing to participate in such a study and to see which questions had the most relevance for them. Answers to this first questionnaire, and suggestions for further questions, helped make this a questionnaire designed with the help of many, many men. Then massive distribution began in the form of mailing large numbers of questionnaires to groups across the country, including university groups, church groups, and men's discussion groups. The paperback *Sexual Honesty, By Women, For Women** also asked male readers to write requesting the questionnaire. Finally, the questionnaire was printed in its entirety in 1975 in *Sexology* magazine with the respondent being requested to return his reply to "Mr. S. D. Hite." The purpose of this was to learn whether any bias was

---

*An anthology of forty-five complete replies received from women, published by Warner Paperback Library in 1974.

created by replies being addressed to a woman researcher in other samples. In fact, comparison of this sample with others shows that there is very little or no deviation.

After publication of *The Hite Report on Female Sexuality* in late 1976, distribution intensified. In many interviews given to newspapers, television, radio, and magazines, the address to which men might write was supplied. In addition, a footnote in *The Hite Report on Female Sexuality* asked men to write for the questions. Many requests for the questionnaire were received from these sources, although not all men who requested them returned the form. Answers from men who had read *The Hite Report on Female Sexuality* comprise 15 percent of the total sample. In 1977, *Penthouse* magazine and *Houston Breakthrough* (a feminist newspaper) ran the questionnaire in its entirety. The answers from readers of *Penthouse* are included as a part of the 11 percent of replies received from men who learned of the questionnaire through a men's magazine.

Although many answers had been received by 1978, it was felt that certain population groups should be explored more thoroughly. The large number of answers received so far had also indicated significant new areas of interest to question. Accordingly, a new questionnaire was prepared, and distribution carefully planned to emphasize population groups which had not yet been sufficiently examined. These included certain men in certain age, race and ethnic groups, special geographical locations, and educational levels. Once again, distribution through men's clubs, church organizations, professional associations, and sports groups was accomplished by sending bulk mailings of questionnaires for members to individual chapters of these groups across the country, but particularly in the geographical locations which were, at that time, less well represented. This distribution continued intensively for fifteen months, with constant checking of population statistics to follow the progress of the samples. Replies were also sought during this period especially from men over sixty-five, black men, and the "disabled" population, whose sexual lives are so rarely acknowledged. Forty-eight percent of the replies received were from this fourth version of the questionnaire; the large majority of those who answered had not read *The Hite Report on Female Sexuality.*

Each reply which was received was given a number, and then the answer to each question was placed on the appropriate chart, a very difficult and time-consuming process. However, any attempt at condensation or computerization would have defeated the purposes of the study: to find more subtle meanings underneath the easily quantifiable parts of the replies, and to keep intact each individual's voice so that men would retain direct access to communicating their feelings with the reader, thus reinforcing the integrity of the study. After all the replies had been charted, the process of identifying categories was begun, along with the selection of representative quotes. Statistical computation was then possible.

In addition, many of the findings were broken down into several different populations, for purposes of comparison, including the following:

General Sample

Anonymous	34%
Non-anonymous	16%

Special Samples

Forms with return address to a male researcher
Anonymous	4%
Non-anonymous	1%

Men who had read *The Hite Report on Female Sexuality*
Anonymous	10%
Non-anonymous	5%

Men who preferred sex with men   Sex with both men and women
Anonymous	8%	Anonymous	3%
Non-anonymous	1%		

Military (Answers from men who were in the military service)
Anonymous	6%
Non-anonymous	1%

Answers from men who learned of the questionnaire through a men's magazine
Anonymous	8%
Non-anonymous	3%

All in all, 119,000 questionnaires were distributed, and 7,239 received in return. The standard rate of return for this type of distribution is estimated at 2.5 to 3 percent. In that this study elicited a return rate of 6 percent,* this was an excellent result, especially since these questionnaires were very long and very personal, requiring an investment of time and thought from the respondent. Even though the forms were demanding, it was felt that this was the ideal type of questionnaire for developing the kind of dialogue which would allow men to speak out and expand on their thoughts in directions which were personal to them—as opposed to being limited by a multiple-

---

*The rate of return is fractionally lower if replies from readers of *Penthouse* magazine are not included, as their distribution was done in a different form.

choice form, even though that kind of form enormously simplifies the work of the researcher. Although many men did not return the form, this does not mean that the study is "unrepresentative," for two reasons: first, because the majority of the forms were not sent to individual men, but were sent in bulk to groups and organizations, so that many forms may never have reached an individual man and may have been discarded as excess copies by the club or group. Secondly, although some men may have found the questionnaire too personal to answer, or may not have been interested, and therefore not have returned their forms, special care was taken (as just mentioned) to compensate for this by doing especially concentrated distribution in areas where the sample, at the mid-point of the study, seemed lacking—i.e., religious groups, some geographical locations in the South and Midwest, and older age groups, among others. As pointed out earlier, sufficient effort was put into this that the final statistical breakdown of the men who answered (age, occupation, religion, etc.) in most cases quite closely mirrors that of the U.S. male population. (See tables beginning on page 1060 of *The Hite Report on Male Sexuality*.)

A note on "scientific method"

In fact, there seems to be a widespread misunderstanding about the types and validity of methodologies available in the social sciences. Reviews and articles about *The Hite Report on Female Sexuality* frequently cited the methodology as "unscientific," and yet this is inaccurate, and shows a lack of understanding of the meaning of the term.[*] It is with the hope of clearing up this misunderstanding that excerpts of the following article, which appeared in the *Journal of the American Society of Sex Educators, Counselors and Therapists,* are presented, in addition to some new material.

Toward a New Methodology in the Social Sciences: Is *The Hite Report on Female Sexuality* "Scientific"?

"Scientific" does not mean "representative"

Is *The Hite Report on Female Sexuality* scientific? This is a question that is often asked. And yet the question itself reflects a misunderstanding of the word "scientific." Having done my master's thesis on the application of scientific method to the social sciences, I am very familiar with the history of scientific method and its various meanings, especially as they have developed

---

[*]Issues of methodology are also discussed in the Preface of *The Hite Report on Male Sexuality*.

over time. Scientifically, what this question usually means is, "Does *The Hite Report* contain a statistically representative sample?" To be "scientific" and "representative" is not the same thing.

"Science" is a term which originally came from the Latin root "to know" and means basically systematized knowledge in any field, sometimes as part of a system of general laws. Anything which is investigated carefully and in a scholarly manner can be termed "scientific," although the term has many specialized meanings. Scientific method involves the gathering, recording, and analyzing of facts with care and accuracy, the finding of relationships among those facts, and drawing logical conclusions from them. The term "social science" came into common usage in the late nineteenth century when the humanities, overshadowed by the increasing prestige of physics, mathematics, and the advances of the industrial revolution, started to think in terms of applying the same methods to their own work.

Can people be studied "scientifically"?

But is it possible to transfer the methods of the physical sciences to the study of people? To be "scientific" in the study of society has evolved to mean, basically perhaps, to be objective—to see the facts clearly and report them without distortion, with precision. This is important; however, it is a problem in the social sciences, because the researcher is a human being and cannot escape having a point of view, a personal value system. As social scientists from Max Weber to Gunnar Myrdal have pointed out, there is an inevitable relation between the investigator's values and how s/he practices social science. There is no such thing as a value-free scientist, and there is no such thing as a totally "objective" researcher. Those who would imply that they are purely objective are likely to be the least so. It is the responsibility of the social scientist to make her/his point of view ("bias") known from the outset.

In addition to the problem of the subjectivity of the researcher, there is also the difficulty that the "things" being studied, i.e., human beings, are very hard to measure and categorize in the way that classical scientific method did with such success in the physical world. Fortunately or unfortunately, human beings are for the most part more complex than "things," and to try to reduce them to measurable categories is frequently to distort them beyond recognition—and lose sight of the whole person entirely. Even if the measurements are relatively accurate (which is always questionable), there remains the significant question of whether measurement is the best way to understand human nature. Why do we insist on applying scientific method to people in exactly the same way as we have applied it to the physical world? The act of quantifying human behavior into a series of discrete categories reduces a complex whole to a group of oversimplified variables. And, like Humpty Dumpty, can these pieces ever be put back together again?*

Is *The Hite Report* a statistically representative sample?

There has never been a perfect sample in sex research. In the field of sociology, the two basic methods which have been employed are the taking of surveys, and the building of predictive models, usually based on existing survey material or data banks. Traditionally, the survey—"a sampling, or partial collection of facts, figures or opinions taken and used to approximate the whole"—was the basic method of the sociologists, with a "random sample" being considered the most accurately representative. However, in sex research a perfectly random sample has never been possible on a large scale because most of the people chosen at random would not answer—due to the personal nature of the questions and the lack of anonymity in this sampling procedure.

Was Kinsey representative? . . . What Kinsey did was to question people from as many walks of life, backgrounds, and economic levels, etc., as he could to try to approximate a representative selection. Arguments continued for years as to whether he succeeded, but today his findings are generally accepted as accurate. Of course, Masters and Johnson did not do a survey; they did biological research on the basis of a highly selected population of 694 people. Obviously, a "study" of this kind is just as "scientific" as a survey, as long as it is precise and systematic; not being statistically representative is not the same as being non-scientific.

The Hite Report on Female Sexuality used the same basic approach as the Kinsey studies, working to include as wide a cross-section of the population as possible, then checking this against the U.S. population statistics, to ensure that the study would be as "scientific" (i.e., representative) as possible. Although there have been assertions made that the women who answered may not have been "typical," in fact, when the statistics are studied and compared with the U.S. population statistics for women over fourteen, it can be seen that in most cases they are quite similar.

The Hite Report on Female Sexuality contained two significant differences in methodology from the Kinsey reports, which were thought to improve the study. First, whereas Kinsey and his (male) associates interviewed women face to face and knew the complete names and addresses of those they interviewed,† *The Hite Report on Female Sexuality* used an anonymous essay-type

---

*This is a question that is being asked more and more frequently in the social sciences. See P. Connerton, editor, *Critical Sociology* (Penguin Books, 1976); E. F. Schumacher, *A Guide for the Perplexed* (Harper & Row, 1977); Stephen Toulmin, "From Form to Function: Philosophy and the History of Science in the 1950's and Now," *Daedalus*, Summer 1977.
†For reasons which were valid at that time.

questionnaire, believing that women would feel freer to talk about themselves in detail if they were offered the protection of complete privacy and anonymity. In fact, many women who responded said that they had been able to write about things that they would never have been able to tell someone face to face, especially a stranger. The second significant difference is that *The Hite Report on Female Sexuality* presented not only statistical findings, but also offered many direct quotations from the replies to illustrate the findings—and so gave participants and readers direct access to each other. This was an innovation in social-science methodology. Its purpose was to avoid, insofar as possible, setting up rigid new "norms" which might seem to be telling women what they should feel, and instead, to give women a chance to re-examine and re-evaluate their lives, deciding for themselves how they felt, and what they agreed and disagreed with. In other words, the *Hite Report* methodology was conceived as providing a large forum in which women could speak out freely—giving everyone reading those replies the chance to decide for themselves how they felt about the answers. The methodology was seen as a process, both for the individual woman answering the questionnaire, and for the person reading what the 3,019 women had written—a process of rethinking, self-discovery, and of getting acquainted with many other women in a way that had never before been possible—an anonymous and powerful communication from the women who answered to all the women of the world.

As to comments that *The Hite Report on Female Sexuality* had a political point of view, this is in fact true—as it is true that every research project ever undertaken has a point of view. When this point of view coincides with that which is popularly believed, the point of view often is unnoticed—since it is accepted as "truth." Assumptions made in such studies are often unrecognized, even by the researchers themselves. For example, map makers and explorers in the middle ages assumed that the earth was flat—but no one called this assumption "unscientific." It is only when the point of view is new, or an alternative to the standard point of view, that it is considered "biased." In the case of *The Hite Report on Female Sexuality,* the point of view was woman-oriented, in that it let women define sex as they saw it, rather than assuming that the male definition of sex which had been predominant for so long was the only possible "correct" definition. For this, the work was described by some as having a "feminist bias." In fact, much of the previous research into female sexuality had been less than "scientific" in that, rather than taking the information that most women could orgasm more easily during masturbation or direct clitoral/vulval stimulation than during coitus, and concluding that therefore this is "normal," instead, previous studies started with the assumption that women "should" orgasm during coitus, and concluded that if they did not, there must be something wrong with them—that they were somehow defective, "dysfunctional," or psychologically or physically abnormal. Research was often geared to finding out what the cause of this "defect" might be. This was a "non-scientific," in that it was not objective, way of looking at female sexuality. No study is free of bias, or a point of view; the important point is to recognize this fact, and to clarify, insofar as possible, just what that point of view is.

So, finally, is *The Hite Report on Female Sexuality* representative? I believe that it represents the entire spectrum of women's points of view, and contains a high degree of representativeness. Indeed, perhaps since we are trying to avoid setting up new "norms" against which women "should" measure themselves, establishing perfect representativeness may not be the point. However, as mentioned earlier, comparisons of the study population statistics with U.S. population statistics point to a high degree of representativeness. And, on a less formal level, this accuracy is underscored by the fact that, to date, *The Hite Report on Female Sexuality* has been published in seventeen countries, and in not one country have women disagreed with the basic finding of the book—i.e., that women do not for the most part orgasm simply as the result of thrusting during coitus; that most women can masturbate to orgasm via clitoral/vulval stimulation when they choose to; that we must reassess the traditional ideas we have had about female sexuality—and many, many more basic conclusions. In fact, thousands of women everywhere have written publicly and privately that they felt grateful for the book, and relieved to find that they were not "different" from other women, or "abnormal." *The Hite Report* quite clearly speaks for many, many women. But most important of all, women of all ages and points of view have found it an invaluable tool in re-examining and exploring not only their sexuality but also their lives as women, and as part of a universe of other women.

Society for the Scientific Study of Sex
Annual Meeting—November 13, 1982
The Hite Reports

Wardell Pomeroy, co-author with Alfred Kinsey, *Sexual Behavior in the Human Female* ("The Kinsey Report")

When I learned I was going to appear here I went back to a review I did of *The Hite Report on Female Sexuality* made in November 1976 and published in S.I.E.C.U.S. To my surprise I found that I could almost have changed the word "female" to "male" and present the same review. *The Hite Report on Male Sexuality* is a 1,129-page book, a 1,054-page paperback, about 95 percent of which consists of direct quotes from her sample of over 7,000 males who replied to her questionnaire.

Because I am used to and involved with a taxonomic, statistical approach in understanding human sexuality, I was originally disturbed by Hite's approach, which is quite different. I changed my mind after reading the female Report as well as the male Report and now believe that focusing on understanding behavior, feelings, and attitudes adds an important dimension to the overall understanding of human sexuality which cannot be obtained in other ways.

I have some caveats, minor quibbles, the most serious of which is Shere Hite's use of adverbs such as many, some, a few, a tiny minority, and so on. Whether something happens less than 1 percent of the time or whether it happens 10 percent or 30 percent of the time, one can only speculate.

I quibble with Shere Hite about the advantage of a questionnaire versus a face-to-face interview—obviously I would because my Kinsey technique has been one thing and hers has been another. I really believe that for what we set out to do we were both right. It seems to me that for some things a direct interview is helpful, and in other cases, and in *this* case, it could not have been done in this way and needed a questionnaire approach.

She points out that many people had told her that they would have filled out a questionnaire and would not have been interviewed. Of course my experience has been exactly the opposite. I have had many people say they would be happy to be interviewed but would not fill out a questionnaire.

I hope that by this time you are not turned-off to The Hite Reports, because I believe they are very valuable pieces of work. I have suggested before and I will suggest again that I think there are five groups of people who need to read these books. First I think that women who have sexual problems need to read the book, and secondly I think that women who don't have sexual problems need to read the book; and thirdly, I think that males with sexual problems need to read these books; and fourthly, males without sexual problems need to read these books; and fifthly, I think that therapists with or without sexual problems need to read these books.

The many quotes from respondents answering her questionnaires are an extremely valuable part of her book. The extensive use of direct quotes from the questionnaires on a particular topic provides knowledge that has been largely overlooked and has been badly needed. For example, to say that ex-percent of females masturbate by clitoral stimulation is only the beginning. The many specific descriptions of clitoral masturbation given in great detail allow one to know what female masturbation is really like for these women, and do it better than any source that I know. Similarly, the many descriptions about what orgasm feels like are again the best and most comprehensive source in the literature. Previous reports have stated that orgasm can range from nothing more than a sigh to an epileptoid seizure, but here one is exposed to unique descriptions of many types of orgasm along this continuum. Almost all women and men will be able to find themselves in this book and this can be very reassuring.

In the course of taking some 18,000 sex histories for the Kinsey Institute, the very last question was always "What questions do you have, what can I answer for you?" and overwhelmingly the questions that we got were concerned with normality. Am I normal, is masturbation normal, is homosexuality normal, is sado-masochism normal, and so on, and I feel that people who are concerned with this whole issue can find themselves in The Hite Reports, can see that they are not alone, that other people have their feelings, their behavior, and I think this can be a very important, helpful tool.

Another of the contributions of The Hite Reports lies in the questions she is asking. Many of them are original, and hence the answers give us a unique insight into human sexuality. Let me just read an example of that for you. This is in the male book. She is asking about pornography:

Do you look at pornography? What kind? Did your father read pornography when you were growing up? Where and when did you see your first men's magazine? What is your opinion of the pornography you have seen? Do you feel it represents certain elementary truths about how men and women really are, both psychologically and sexually?

What do you think of the sexual revolution? What do you think of women's liberation? How has it affected your relationship? What do you get from women that you don't get from men?

—and so on and on. I think that the very fact that many of these questions haven't been asked before, and have been asked in great number here, is another added dimension to this book.

In closing, I would like to highly recommend this book as a thought-provoking and insight-giving treatise on male and female sexuality.

Devising a New Methodological Framework for Analysis and Presentation of Data in Mixed Qualitative/Quantitative Research

Shere Hite, 1985,
The Hite Report Trilogy, 1972–86

There were unique challenges to be faced in devising the methodology for The Hite Reports, which comprise a three-volume study of over 14,000 women and men in the U.S., 1972–86. First, although quantification was necessary as part of the final result, a simple multiple-choice questionnaire could not be used, since the theoretical concept for the project stated that "most women have never been asked how they feel about sex" and "most research has been done by men": therefore, it was important not to assume predetermined categories, but to design an essay-type questionnaire which would be open-ended. Also, the data-gathering was designed to protect the anonymity of the respondent. Secondly, compilation of data from essay questions is very difficult, if the data is to be carefully and rigorously treated; the methods used in compilation, refined over the three Hite Reports, will be discussed. Finally, and almost as labor-intensive as compilation and categorization of data, presentation of findings was planned to serve more than an informative function; rather than simply giving readers statistics plus the author's theoretical analysis of data, the aim was to create an inner dialogue within the reader, as s/he mentally conversed with those quoted. Therefore, large parts of text comprise first-person statements from those participating. The format of presentation shows how these fit into intricate categories of social patterns.

New Trends in the Social Sciences

The Hite Reports are part of an international trend in the social sciences expressing dissatisfaction with the adequacy of simple quantitative methods as a way of defining people's attitudes. More and more the social sciences are turning to various qualitative methods, attempting to find out what people are thinking in a more complex way than projecting into their minds on the basis of preconceived categories. Hite elicits from the populations she studies not only reliable scientific data, but also a wide spectrum of attitudes and beliefs about sex, love and who people are.

JESSE LEMISCH
Professor, Department of History
SUNY, Buffalo

The research methods of The Hite Reports pioneered many current research trends, including the mixing of quantitative and qualitative data. Originally criticized, these techniques are now widely copied by many in the field not only in the U.S. but abroad.

TORE HAAKINSON
Wenner-Gren Center, Stockholm

There is a growing and highly sophisticated literature critiquing social science methodology and, in fact, Western philosophical concepts of "knowing." Part of this critique is growing out of sociology itself, as predictive models have failed to materialize; and part of it grows out of feminist rethinking of the philosophical assumptions behind various disciplines. Two ground-breaking anthologies of feminist scholarship in this area are: *Discovering Reality: Feminist Perspectives on Epistemology, Metaphysics, Methodology, and Philosophy of Science* (edited by Sandra Harding and Merrill B. Hintikka);* and *Theories of Women's Studies* (edited by Gloria Bowles and Renate Duelli Klein).†

*D. Reidel Publishing Company, London, 1983.
†Routledge & Kegan Paul, London, 1983.

The issues are brought out in the following extracts from a fascinating article by Gloria Bowles, University of California, at Berkeley:

"On the Uses of Hermeneutics for Feminist Scholarship"[*]

. . . the one discovery of the decade which enables us to understand and to move beyond the tension between discursive inheritance of Western thought and the feminist perspective [is that] what counts as knowledge must be grounded on experience.

SANDRA HARDING AND MERRILL B. HINTIKKA (1983)

Thinking begins only when we come to know that reason, glorified for centuries, is the most stiff-necked adversary of thought.

MARTIN HEIDEGGER (1977)

. . . The scientistic world view, which sits atop the university and defines the social sciences and reaches even into the humanities, has as its goal the so-called "objective knowledge" of mathematics and the physical sciences. Only now are literary criticism, and many other disciplines, wresting themselves from "objective" analysis, whose primary result is a divorce of objective knowledge from evaluation. It is not that the Humanities are merely rebelling against their place on the bottom rung under the Sciences in twentieth-century intellectual history. It is rather that the Humanities are realizing that their subject matter is so thick with personal and interpersonal experience, with moral and evaluative judgments, that the "impersonal" and "value-free" methodological strategies of the Sciences are at best irrelevant and at worst a distortion of the subject matter itself. This critique of scientism/logocentrism in the Humanities, while not inclined to throw all objective analysis out of the window, has been primarily a "negative" critique which has analyzed the limits of this borrowed methodology. Feminist scholarship has not only stood critical in a "negative" sense of traditional conceptual assumptions, but has made the positive move of putting forth alternative epistemologies which use experience, intuition and evaluation (both of women as individuals and of women as a "class") as modes of knowing. Further, women *qua* women seem to stand in a sort of privileged position in regard to the formulation of such new orientations of thinking. A critique of scientistic thought is not so difficult for women, since we have always used ways of knowing in addition to reason. Throughout male recorded history, men have been the "takers," while women have assumed (or have been forced to assume) the role

[*]*Women's Studies International Forum,* December 1984.

of "caretakers." Women live in a world where little is impersonal and much is personal, where little is fixed or certain and much is ambiguous and volatile, and where little is value-free and much requires an evaluative response. We have long lived our lives in the intimately personal and non-objective context of the daily needs and concerns of other human beings. We bring all this experience, these skills and perceptions, to our scholarly work and into the academic community. Here we are confronted by the modern form of traditionalism in the scientific mentality and its dictatorial regulations.

In the contemporary academic community, due in part to the recently emerged and broadly based critique of scientism and to the accomplishments of feminist scholarship, this scientistic mentality has become increasingly difficult for traditional scholars to justify. . . . [It is in] the hermeneutic or interpretive tradition where one finds the critique of logocentrism in a powerful form. I am using the most inclusive term, hermeneutics (*Hermeneutik* simply means "interpretation" in German), to designate a constellation of methodologies which stand critical of the objectivism and scientism of the white male tradition. These are the loosely defined movements which have emerged in the post-war years in Continental thinking under the nomenclature of "phenomenology," "post-structuralism," "hermeneutics" and, most recently, "deconstructionism."

One need not devote one's life to a reading of Heidegger and Foucault and Feyerabend and Derrida (nor do I think Women's Studies scholars should) to see that these writers are saying what we as feminists have been saying all along—that there is something profoundly wrong with the tradition. . . .

For there are common points of interest in the ideas of hermeneuticists and feminists. The "hermeneutical circle," although it has different connotations for different thinkers, means essentially that there is no such thing as a "detached," "neutral" or "objective" place to stand when we know something. We are always speaking from a "prejudiced" (in the sense of prejudgment) and "interested" and "evaluative" posture. This is the circle, that we are intimately (personally, socially, historically) involved with what we claim to know. This is Heidegger on the nature of hermeneutical thinking:

But if we sense this circle as a vicious one and look out for ways of avoiding it, even if we just "sense" it is an inevitable imperfection, then the act of understanding has been misunderstood from the ground up . . . What is decisive is not to get out of the circle but to come into it in the right way. . . . (Hoy, 1982)

Traditional thought claims to be able to leap out of the hermeneutical/ interpretive circle and to speak of so-called "value-free," "disinterested," "objective," and "ethically neutral" knowledge. Thus, the hermeneutical/interpretive tradition says all efforts to deny the "circular" and "interested" and "evaluative" nature of thinking are conceptually confused or dishonest. Feminist thought, precisely because it acknowledges and asserts its "prejudices," must, from the hermeneutical perspective, be judged as one of the only available theoretical postures which holds good claim to intellectual integrity and sophistication.

Heidegger contends that the Western tradition does not know how to think; he speaks of openness, receptivity and listening. Both he and Derrida say that truth is to be found in absence or in the spaces between words, a theme common to French literature. Many Women's Studies scholars had our original training in literature; for us, there is both irony and gratification in the "news" that the new model for understanding is the expressive language of the text. Many scholars—not only literary critics but anthropologists and philosophers as well—are talking about the literary text which should replace the machine model as the locus of analysis. For example, feminine biologists have been questioning this model and now some prestigious men in the field are making the same thought. *It is crucial to realize that the literary text, in its paradigmatic form, is an imaginative narrative of those personal interrelations which have long formed the life-world and the existential reality of women.* [Hite's emphasis] Those who have proposed the literary text as the interpretive model have not recognized any special affinity between the literary narrative and the feminist perspective and women's life experience.

However, many white male thinkers are uncomfortable with the hermeneutic circle—and engage in endless discussions of it—because for them it raises the specter of total relativity, the fear that we will never be able to know anything in an absolutely objective and certain way. Male thought, with its linear habits, would thrust itself out of the circle. It is difficult for men to make the critiques of logocentrism; the few who are trying, from within the tradition, find it hard to embrace intuition and experience as viable ways of knowing. The struggle to affirm what they have been taught to denigrate is enormous. . . . As women, we are not so attached to old ways of thinking since we have been discovering our own. Thus it is that the critique of logocentrism in *Theories of Women's Studies* and other feminist works is more directed and unmediated—feels less cumbersome—than many contemporary male critiques. These feminist essays contrast, for example, with the introduction to a very fine book, *Interpretive Social Science: A Reader,* edited by Paul Rabinow and William M. Sullivan. It painfully and painstakingly elaborates "The Interpretive Turn: Emergence of an Approach," the only way out of a failed social science: "As long as there has been a social science, the expectation has been that it would turn from its humanistic infancy to the maturity of hard science, thereby leaving behind its dependence on value, judgment, and individual insight" (Rabinow and Sullivan, 1979). The authors mock that polarity, the "hard" and "soft" sciences. Through science, one moves out of the softness and the world of the mother into hardness, which is mature; one leaves a world of dependence, the proper sphere of value and insight. For these writers, it is not easy to say, many pages later: "We propose a return to this human world in all its lack of clarity, its alienation, and its depth, as an alternative to the continuing search for a formal deductive paradigm in the social sciences." . . . Significantly, what they do not say, these male writers, is that they are leaving behind a world of male thought to enter the province of female thought. A growing number of them have been able to make the critique of logocentrism; but so far none of them has been able to analyze their own sexism—and I mean sexism in its many guises, from the denigration of women in prose and in public to a complete ignorance or an appropriation of the enormous advances of feminist scholarship. Moreover, the bulk of male scholarship of the hermeneutic/phenomenological persuasion has been unable to move beyond the preliminary effort of a negative critique of the limitations and irrelevancies of the traditional scientistic methodology. When asked by traditional critics for their alternative ways of knowing, they have little to offer beyond interesting generalities. Some of these thinkers have said explicitly that it is not up to them, it is beyond their capacities, to offer positive alternatives. The problem, and the promise, is that they have not realized that these alternatives will come from us—feminist women scholars who stand removed enough from the tradition to see things differently.

Explication of Scientific Method as Used in Research for The Hite Report Trilogy

The main concerns of this research were described in the abstract of a paper presented at the American Association for the Advancement of Science annual meeting in May 1985,* entitled "Devising a new methodological framework for analysis and presentation of data in mixed qualitative/quantitative research: The Hite Report Trilogy, 1972–1986":

There were unique challenges to be faced in devising the methodology for the Hite Reports, which comprise a 3-vol. study of over 15,000 women and men in the U.S., 1972–86. First, although quantification was necessary as part of the final result, a simple multiple-choice questionnaire could not be used, since the theoretical concept for the project stated that "most women

*See published proceedings, statistical abstracts, annual meeting, American Association for the Advancement of Science, May 1985, Washington, D.C.

have never been asked how they feel about sex" and "most research has been done by men": therefore, it was important not to assume predetermined categories, but to design an essay-type questionnaire which would be open-ended. Also, the data-gathering was designed to protect the anonymity of the respondent. Secondly, compilation of data from essay questions is very difficult, if the data are to be carefully and rigorously treated. . . . Finally, and almost as labor-intensive as compilation and categorization of data, presentation of findings was planned to serve more than an informative function; rather than simply giving readers statistics plus the author's theoretical analysis of data, the aim was to create an inner dialogue within the reader, as s/he mentally conversed with those quoted. Therefore, large parts of text comprise first-person statements from those participating. The format of presentation shows how these fit into intricate categories of social patterns.

The Four Stages of Research

I.
Questionnaire design

One of the most important elements in the design of *Women and Love* was that the participants be anonymous, because in this way a completely free and uninhibited discussion could be ensured. For this reason, a questionnaire format, rather than face-to-face interviews, was chosen, with respondents specifically asked not to sign their names, although other demographic data were taken. That this anonymity was in fact an aid to communication with participants was verified in statements by respondents in each study, such as the following:

I would find it very hard to say all these things to another person, and I'm sure many women would feel the same as I. I am sick of reading various "advice" columns about what I should be feeling, but I have not found another forum for saying what I think myself, taking my own time, rethinking, not feeling any pressure to be perfect or "in" or anything. I am saving my answers; they have been very important to me.

The second choice to be made regarding format related to how the questions would be asked. In the sensitive realm of personal attitudes, a multiple-choice questionnaire was out of the question, because it would have implied preconceived categories of response, and thus, in a sense, would also have "told" the respondent what the "allowable" or "normal" answers would be. Although a multiple-choice questionnaire is much easier for the researcher to work with, it would have given a subtle signal to the participant that the research categories were equated with "reality," or "allowable reality," whereas the intention here was to permit women's own voices to emerge, for women to say whatever they might feel on the deepest level to be the truth of their situation, with nothing to intervene or make them censor themselves.

Also, the development of the questions in this study has always been an interactive process with the participants. (In a way, this was true of the Kinsey questionnaires as well, since Kinsey developed several questionnaires over his period of research.) In this study, questionnaires were refined and modified at the suggestion of those responding, so that, for *Women and Love,* there were four basic versions of the questionnaire used over several years.

Coming from an academic background with a strong awareness of the ideological elements in the definition of culture, and with a background in the women's movement which gave further emphasis to this idea, it was a constant matter for concern that questions are not simple questions, but always have several layers of meaning. For this reason, the methodology used here was designed to pay special attention to this issue.*

Many people hold the mistaken belief that multiple-choice questionnaires represent the height of scientific objectivity, in that they can be quantified and need no "interpretation." Nothing could be further from the truth. All researchers, no matter how careful or aware/unaware of their own biases, *do* have a point of view, a way of seeing the world, reflecting the cultural milieu in which they were brought up, and so on—and these assumptions are subtly filtered into categories and questions chosen. (Philosophically speaking, we are all/all life is "biased" and subjective; it is only by combining a mass of subjectivities—all of our "seeing," if you will—that we find, through collective sharing of perception, a "fact"; in other words, for example, we only "know" the sun will come up tomorrow because we have seen it come up every day, and we all agree that the probability is that it will come up again tomorrow.)

Thus, to design the categories of response for a multiple-choice questionnaire is a political act, unavoidably filled with subjective bias, whether consciously or unconsciously so, and whether the researcher considers him/herself to be "neutral" or "apolitical" and so on.† If a study wishes to find out what's "out there," it cannot impose prior categories on that "out there"; it needs to develop its research instrument through an exchange with "them," the participants, before proceeding. This was done in the current study by

---

*Points presented at a speech to the National Women's Studies convention, University of Kansas, 1978.

†As both Elie Wiesel and John F. Kennedy have pointed out, to be "neutral" or "apolitical" is, in fact, to be highly political, because one is endorsing the status-quo.

listening to respondents' suggestions and, indeed, eliciting comments from them as to their feelings about the questionnaire. In other words, there was an ongoing interactive process of sequential refinement in designing the questionnaires for this project. Less meticulous care for research design may mean that a researcher only reifies his or her pre-existing expectations as to the content of the opinions/answers "discovered."*

The difficulty of studying the emotions

As Judith Long Laws has said, "Most social scientists still avoid the study of feelings and attitudes, because of the difficulty in quantifying such studies, and the belief that this is the 'best' kind of social science. This is not always true; quantification is not always the best way to arrive at understanding. . . . The Hite Report was the first large scale set of data where women talked about their own experiences in their own voices."

For this reason, essay questionnaires—which are not less "scientific" than multiple-choice, and in fact are recommended for use whenever possible by methodology textbooks—were the research tool of choice. The goal of this study was to hear women's deepest reflections on the nature of love, and to learn how they see love relationships now in relation to the whole spectrum of their lives. The method was important also in that it enabled participants to communicate directly with readers sharing myriad points of view—in essence debating with each other throughout the text.

II.
Distribution of questionnaires and composition of sample

The questionnaire following this essay and similar versions were distributed to women all over the country beginning in 1980. Their purpose was to dis-

---

*In the case of *The Hite Report on Female Sexuality,* for example, the point of view was woman-oriented, in that it let women define sex as they saw it, rather than assuming that the male definition of sex which had been predominant for so long was the only possible "correct" definition. For this, the work was described by some as having a "feminist bias." In fact, much of the previous research into female sexuality had been less than "scientific"; rather than taking the information that most women could orgasm more easily during masturbation or direct clitoral/vulval stimulation than during coitus, and concluding that therefore this is "normal," previous studies had started with the assumption that if women did not orgasm during coitus, there must be something wrong with them—that they were somehow defective, "dysfunctional," psychologically or physically abnormal. Research was often geared to finding out what the cause of this "defect" might be. This was a non-scientific approach, not an objective way of looking at female sexuality.

In short, no study is free of bias, or a point of view; the important thing is to recognize this fact, and to clarify, insofar as possible, just what that point of view is.

cover how women/we view ourselves and our relationships with men and the world now, how we define "reality."

Distribution of the questionnaires was extremely widespread and pains-takingly done, in order to reach as many kinds of women with as many varied points of view as possible. In order to ensure anonymity, it was thought best to send questionnaires to organizations rather than to individuals, so that any member who wanted might be able to answer with complete assurance that her name was not on any list or on file anywhere. Clubs and organizations through which questionnaires were distributed included church groups in thirty-four states, women's voting and political groups in nine states, women's rights organizations in thirty-nine states, professional women's groups in twenty-two states, counseling and walk-in centers for women or families in forty-three states, and a wide range of other organizations, such as senior citizens' homes and disabled people's organizations, in various states.

In addition, individual women did write for copies of the questionnaire, using both the address given in my previous works and an address given by interview programs on television and in the press. However, if an individual woman did write for a questionnaire, whether she returned it or not was her own decision, therefore assuring her complete anonymity, as her reply was unsigned and bore the postmark and demographic information requested, such as age, income and education, but not name or address. All in all, 100,000 questionnaires were distributed, and 4,500 were returned. This is almost as high as the standard rate of return for this kind of questionnaire distribution, which is estimated at 2.5 to 3 percent. A probability method of sampling might have yielded a higher rate of return, but then an essay questionnaire would not have been possible; the purpose here was to elicit in-depth statements of feelings and attitudes, and multiple-choice questions would have closed down dialogue with the participants.

Finally, sufficient effort was put into the various forms of distribution that the final statistical breakdown of those participating according to age, occupation, religion, and other variables known for the U.S. population at large in most cases quite closely mirrors that of the U.S. female population.

Could the study have been done using random sampling methods?

"There are many forms of scientific methodology besides the random sample; those of us in the field know that there is no such thing as a random sample in sex research, but this does not make the work unscientific if, as in the Hite Reports, the study population is carefully matched to the demographics of the population at large."

THEODORE M. MCILVENNA
Institute for Sex Research

Almost no major research using essay questions today is done with the use of random samples. Most survey research now tries to match its samples demographically to the general population in other ways; for example, by weighting responses to conform to the population profile, somewhat similarly to the methods used here. But an even more important reason for not using random sampling methods for this study is that a random sample cannot be anonymous; the individuals chosen clearly understand that their names and addresses are on file.

Does research that is not based on a probability or random sample give one the right to generalize from the results of the study to the population at large? If a study is large enough and the sample broad enough, and if one generalizes carefully, yes; in fact, the Nielsen television studies and national political polls generalize on the basis of small, select, non-random samples all the time. However, in a larger sense, no one can generalize from their findings, even if one were to somehow miraculously obtain a completely random sample—the reason being that variables such as psychological state, degree of religious or political fervor and so on are not measured; thus there is no guarantee that those picked in a random sample, although they might represent the population at large in terms of age and income, would also represent the population in terms of psychological make-up.

III.
Analysis of replies: measuring and understanding attitudes and emotions

To go from essay statements to mixed quantitative/qualitative data is a long and intricate process.* Of course, some portions of the replies received are already in quantifiable form, i.e., questions answered with a "yes" or "no." But the majority of questions were not so phrased, since the intention, as discussed, was to open dialogue rather than to close it.

There is an ongoing and abstruse discussion in the field of methodology as to how best to study emotions, belief systems, and attitudes—not to mention how to quantify them. For example, not only is the question "How do you love the person in your current relationship? What kind of love is it?" a difficult one to answer, but also the answer is every bit as difficult to analyze and compare with other answers received, and in some cases build into statistical findings. Nevertheless, it is possible to do this, if such statis-

---

*Thus, in this study, there were over 40,000 woman-hours involved in analyzing the answers, plus at least 20,000 put in by the women who answered the questionnaire. This of course does not include the time and effort needed to turn the resulting compilation of data into a book.

tics are attached for the reader to numerous examples of definition by the participants, such as is done in this study.

Specifically, the information was analyzed in this way: first, a large chart was made for each question asked. Each person's answer to the question being analyzed was then transferred onto that chart (usually many pages long), next to its individual identification number. The many months required for this procedure were actually very valuable in that they provided extensive time for reflecting on the answers.

Once the charts had been prepared, the next step was to discover the patterns and "categories" existing in the answers. Usually patterns had begun to stand out during the making of the charts, so that the categories more or less formed themselves. Then statistical figures were prepared by totaling the number of women in each category, following which representative quotes were selected. This procedure was followed for each of the 180 questions.

In addition, one main chart was kept onto which much of the information from other charts was coded for each individual woman, so that composite portraits could be drawn and compared. Any attempt at condensation or computerization at an early stage of the analysis would have defeated the purposes of the study: to find the more subtle meanings lying beneath the more easily quantifiable parts of the replies, and to keep intact each individual's voice so that participants would remain in direct communication with readers, thus reinforcing the integrity of the study. After all the replies had been charted, and the process of identifying categories completed, with representative quotes selected, statistical computation was possible.

Analyzing data from essay-type questionnaires, then, is a complex endeavor, but there is no way, if one cares about accuracy and detail or wants to search out and understand the deepest levels of the replies, that lengthy testimonies such as these can be understood quickly—and it is precisely the possibility of reaching these deeper levels that makes the essay questionnaire more valuable for this purpose than multiple-choice. Although multiple-choice questions make the researcher's job easier, only through listening to an individual's complete and free response, speaking in her own way and with her own design, without restriction, can more profound realities be reached.

IV.
Presentation of findings: a new interactive framework

In lectures, Hite's approach is a kind of Socratic dialogue wherein participants are able to question their own prejudices and ignorance, thus learning by thinking through a logical idea for themselves—instead of being simply presented with a "fact." Her method in the Hite Reports is similar. Essentially she carries on an intense dialogue with her readers, making them question assumptions and sharpen their own thinking and critical faculties through identifying with the dialogue she is having with the printed responses. Her readers are thus stimulated to a process of independent thinking and evaluation.

LAWRENCE A. HORNE
American Philosophical Institute, New York

As theorists have pointed out, simple presentation of people's statements is not a rigorous approach to documenting "reality"; people's statements do not "speak for themselves"; there are assumptions and things left unsaid. True analysis requires a complex presentation of subjective data—not just, "people say this, and so that's how it is." For example, in the study of male sexuality, if most men said they have extramarital sex and that it keeps their relationship/marriage working, while it does not bother them—must the researcher conclude simply that since the majority say this, this is "how men are"? It would be simplistic to draw this conclusion. There are many elements in every decision, and it is the researcher's job to search out all the variables.

As it was explained by Janice Green, "In standard social science projects, one researcher's unstated and often unexamined or unconscious point of view is projected onto a research design, and then later also onto the presentation and interpretation of findings in a rather undigested way. In oral history, at the other extreme (such as that by Studs Terkel), [each bit of] data is allowed to 'speak for itself'—but there is still no clarification of assumptions, biases or other hidden factors."

Dialogue between participant and researcher

Most basic to the methodology of the Hite Reports is the separation of "findings" from analysis and interpretation. This is done by choice of research design, questions, and method of analysis, and, in particular, the style of presentation of the final analysis—that is, separating the analysis and interpretation of what people say from the quotations in which they speak directly to the reader. At times, in the text, participants debate with each other, in their own words; at other times, analysis of what people are saying can bring out several possible sides of a point; researcher and participants can agree or debate at different places in the text. In this way, the metaphysical dilemma of how much of what participants express is ideology, can also be addressed. As Janet Wolfe, director of the Institute for Rational Therapy, has explained, "This complex approach has confused some general media reviewers, especially as Hite's work is accessible to a wide audience. But this many-layered structure is another part of Hite's overall methodology, in that she means to involve as many people as possible in the dialogue (not presenting closed 'norms')—since it is, after all, a dialogue about social change."

The issue of class as related to presentation of data

Much of the important work of the last few years in women's history and sociology has focused on class and economics as the major point for analysis; however, the purpose here is somewhat different.

Although it is important to write about women in terms of class and race, and not to see "all women" as "the same," the focus of this study is not class but gender and gender ideology, that is, the experiences women have in common because of their gender. Also, this book is not built around comparisons of the attitudes of women in the various traditional socioeconomic groups for the simple reason that differences in behavior and attitude are not the major dividing line between women on these issues that some have theorized they might be. But even more importantly, the intention here was not to focus on class differences between women and what should be done about them, but on men's attitudes toward women and what should be done to change them, strategies women have devised for developing their own lives while still dealing with the overall society's view of them—and to find the similarities and dissimilarities in women's current definitions and redefinitions of their relationship with men and society.

Nevertheless, women in this study include a vast cross-section of American women from different socioeconomic groups and "classes." Great care was taken to ensure that statements by women from all classes are well represented throughout every portion of this book. Women's backgrounds will probably emerge to some extent through their manner of speaking/ writing. However, perhaps unfortunately, some grammar and spelling was "corrected" so that answers could be more easily read. While some replies were very appealing when their original spelling reflected a personal style or regional accent, it seemed that in print these misspellings looked demeaning to the writer, or might be seen as trivializing that respondent. It is hoped, however, that enough of the original syntax in the replies is intact so that readers will get a feeling of the wide diversity among the respondents.

Finally, it does seem that based on this research, there are large areas of commonality among all women. While clearly the experience of a poor woman is different from that of a wealthy woman, and so on, in fact, the emotional expectations placed on "women" as a group by the society seem to be much the same. From the statistical charts and from women's statements here, it is clear that, with regard to gender relationships, variables such as "class," income, education, and race are not nearly as influential as the overall experience of being female.

Note on the use of "many," "most," and "some" in the text

For ease of reading, not every statement in the text is given with its related statistic; therefore, as a guideline for the reader, it will be useful to know that "most" refers to more than 55 percent, "many" to any number between 40 percent and 65 percent; "some" indicates any number between 11 percent and 33 percent; while "a few" will mean a number between 2 percent and 11 percent. In addition, tables giving a complete breakdown for all the major findings (of which there are 120) can be found in the statistical appendixes in *Women and Love*. This is the largest amount of precise data given in any study since Kinsey; certainly Freud never attempted any such large sample. The Schwartz/Blumstein data, while covering relationships, contained less intricate and less numerically coded data relating to the emotions, although this was an excellent study.

Even though, for ease of reading, these general terms are at times used, it is felt that the context makes their meaning clear; in addition the extensive statistical appendixes include the precise data.

The Media and The Hite Reports: Reactions by Scholars in the Field

In the general popular media, there seems to be a widespread misunderstanding of the types and validity of methodologies available in the social sciences—not to mention the subtle debates discussed earlier in these appendixes. For example, even an important medical writer for *The New York Times* in 1976 opened a story on the first Hite Report with, "In a new, non-scientific survey of female sexuality . . ." The press has often made the mistake of equating "scientific" with "representative," and although both criteria are met by these studies, the press has at times insisted on the "non-scientific" nature of the work.*

---

*In addition, "hard science" is still considered by many to be truly the province of the "male," as Evelyn Fox Keller points out in her article "Gender and Science": "The historically pervasive association between masculine and objective, more specifically between masculine and scientific, is a topic which academic critics resist taking seriously. Why? . . . How is it that formal criticism in the philosophy and sociology of science has failed to see here a topic requiring analysis? The virtual silence of at least the non-feminist academic community on this subject suggests

Many commentators in the scholarly community have tried to inform popular writers of their mistake:

Mary Steichen Calderone, M.D., MPH; Founder, Sex Education and Information Council of the U.S. (SEICUS):

The subject of human sexuality is one that closes many minds to any objective approach to it, so much so that panic and anxiety often cause people who have only marginal scientific information to repudiate such an approach to its examination. Hite's has been such an approach. Her studies have given ordinary women and men opportunity to verbalize their long-suffered panics and sexual anxieties, thus making it possible for other reseachers and educators in this new field of sexology to understand better what has been going on in human minds, through the centuries, about a part of life that is universal and central to every human being born. We have an enormous store of information about the human reproductive system and its functioning, most of it gained in the past fifty years. . . . Hite's research, as with all research dealing with thoughts and feelings, cannot be expected to be analyzed with the same techniques as those that tell us what doses of what drugs give what results in what kinds of patients. . . . We are a scientifically illiterate people, and honest scientists such as Hite are bound to suffer as a result.

Robert M. Emerson, Ph.D., Professor of Sociology, UCLA; Editor, *Urban Life: A Journal of Ethnographic Research:*

Statistical representativeness is only one criterion for assessing the adequacy of empirical data . . . other criteria are particularly pertinent when looking at qualitative data. This is primarily the situation with Hite's research, [in which the] . . . goal can be pursued independently of issues of representativeness, or rather, even demands a logic that is at variance with that of statistical representativeness. The logic is that of maximizing kinds of or variations in sexual experiences, so that the whole range of such experiences can be described; the frequency of any such experiences is another matter, one that is linked to the logic of representativeness.

Much of Hite's work seeks to organize qualitative comments in ways that do not involve an exhaustive set of categories, but again directly convey the more significant themes or patterns, in ways that also identify and explore variations in and from these patterns. Here again, range, breadth, and variation are more important than strict statistical representativeness. . . .

---

that the association of masculinity with scientific thought has the status of a myth which either cannot or should not be examined seriously." (From Sandra Harding and Merrill B. Hintikka [eds.], *Discovering Reality,* pp. 187–205. Copyright 1978 by Psychoanalysis and Contemporary Science, Inc.)

John L. Sullivan, Ph.D., Professor of Political Science, University of Minnesota; co-editor, *American Journal of Political Science,* and editor, *Quantitative Applications in the Social Sciences,* Sage University Papers series:

The great value of Hite's work is to show how people are thinking, to let people talk without rigid a priori categories—and to make all this accessible to the reader. Hite has many different purposes than simply stating population generalizations based on a probability sample. Therefore questions of sampling are not necessarily the central questions to discuss about her work. Rather, it is a matter of discovering the diversity of behaviors and points of view. Hite has certainly adequately achieved this kind of analysis. If she had done a perfectly representative random sample, she would not have discovered any less diversity in points of view and behaviors than she has discovered.

Her purpose was clear: to let her respondents speak for themselves, which is very valid. . . . What purpose would it have served to do a random sample, given the aim of Hite's work? None—except for generalizing from percentages. But Hite has not generalized in a non-scholarly way. Many of the natural sciences worry a lot less about random samples, because their work is to test hypotheses. And most of the work in the social sciences is not based on random samples either; in fact, many if not most of the articles in psychology journals are based on data from college students, and then generalized. Interestingly, they are not criticized in the same way Hite has been.

In short, Hite has used a kind of intensive analysis method, but not of individuals—of attitudes and feelings. One might say she is trying to put a whole society on the couch. Hers are works with many different purposes, and scholars and readers can use them in many different ways.

Gerald M. Phillips, Ph.D., Pennsylvania State University; editor, *Communications Quarterly Journal:*

The Hite studies are important. They represent "good" science, a model for future studies of natural human experience. . . . There have always been serious problems for social scientists involved with studying human emotions . . . they cannot be catalogued and specified . . . the most advanced specialists have difficulty finding and specifying vocabulary suitable for objective discussion of human emotions and their impacts on individuals and societies . . . Hite has acquitted herself of this task remarkably well.

The major share of published studies in the social sciences are done numerically under the assumption that similar methodology produced truth or reliable generalizations for the hard sciences . . . What social scientists obsessed with "objective scientificity" do not seem to understand is that the hardest of scientists, physicists, for example, must engage in argument at the onset of their experiments *and* at the presentation of their data. . . . The problem with numeric measurement in the social sciences is, in the first instance, it works well only when the things being measured behave like numbers. Human data rarely stands still for measurement. . . . A major issue with which social scientists must cope in the future is how to describe and compare ephemeral numbers. . . . It is also the practice of contemporary social scientists to [unnecessarily] obscure their methodologies in complex mathematical formulae . . . [it would be better to give] a statement of what was discovered, presented as simply and succinctly as possible . . . a clear discussion of the theoretical basis for the study . . . and a clear description of the people studied [as in] the Hite model. Hite is a serious, reliable scholar and a first-rate intelligence.

Robert L. Carneiro, Ph.D.; Curator of Anthropology, The American Museum of Natural History, New York:

Hite's work can definitely be seen as anthropological in nature. The hallmark of anthropological field method lies in working intensively with individual informants. And though Hite used questionnaires, they were questionnaires that invited long and detailed replies rather than brief, easily codable ones. . . . And from these responses, presented in rich, raw detail, deep truths emerge—truths which, in many cases, were probably never revealed to anyone else before . . . for every question she presents a broad spectrum of responses. . . . One comes away from Hite's books with a feeling that an important subject has been plumbed to great depths . . . of inestimable value.

The Professional Voice

Shere Hite discusses The Hite Reports, Hofstra University, New York

I faced unique challenges in devising the methodology for The Hite Reports, which comprise a three-volume study of over 15,000 women and men in the United States, 1972–1987. *Women and Love: The Hite Report on Love, Passion and Emotional Violence* is basically a study of emotions and inner belief systems. There is an ongoing and abstruse discussion in the field of methodology (a subsection of psychology and sociology, which is not a specialty of every sociologist or psychologist), as to how best to study emotions and attitudes.[1] Should they be quantified at all? The questions, "How do you love the person in your current relationship?" and "What kind of love is it?" are difficult to answer and analyze, not to mention build into statistical findings. Thus, the methodology for The Hite Reports was carefully designed to use a new combination of elements which would bring out complex data, yet retain first-person narratives, original voices, which are related to a state of consciousness now, twenty years after the women's movement and at the end of the twentieth century.

Questionnaire Design

Many believe that multiple-choice questionnaires represent the height of "scientific objectivity" in that they can be quantified easily and need no "interpretation." However, this is fallacious reasoning, since, as Max Weber pointed out one hundred years ago, all researchers have a point of view, a way of reflecting the cultural milieu in which they were brought up, and these assumptions are subtly filtered into the categories and questions chosen. A strong case can be made that multiple-choice questionnaires (especially those asking about attitudes and emotions) only project onto respondents the researcher's assumptions.

In other words, simple multiple-choice questionnaires could not be used for this study because they would have implied preconceived categories of responses, and, in a sense, "told" respondents what the "allowable" or

504

"normal" answers would be. Multiple-choice questions would have closed down dialogue with the participants when the aim was the opposite—to stimulate dialogue between those participating, and later, between readers and participants. Although much easier to work with, such a questionnaire would have subtly signaled the participant that the research categories were equated with "reality" or "allowable reality," whereas my intention was to permit women's own voices to emerge. Specifically, during an historic period of questioning our own inner assumptions about society and the nature of relationships/personal life, my intention was to elicit in women's own words their deepest reflections on the nature of love, and to listen to and record them.

In addition to the use of an essay questionnaire, anonymity was crucial to the integrity of the study so that women could say anything they wanted, in their own words, without fear of being judged or seen as "foolish," "picking the wrong man," and so on. Thus, I chose a written questionnaire format, rather than face-to-face interviews, with respondents specifically asked not to sign their names, although other demographic data were taken.

The necessity for anonymity also dictated the methods of questionnaire distribution: it was not possible to do a "probability" or "random" sample because then anonymity would not have been possible. Only by soliciting replies through church, university, and other groups, letting members decide on an individual basis whether or not to respond, could they be assured of their total privacy.

Distribution of Questionnaires and Composition of Sample

While this study includes a vast cross-section of American women from different socio-economic groups and "classes," are they representative of American women? All in all, 100,000 questionnaires were distributed; 4,500 were returned. This is almost twice as high as the standard rate of return for this kind of distribution.

The confusion in some public commentary about the adequacy of this percentage can be explained: there are two basic kinds of questionnaire distribution. In one, the respondents are not anonymous; their names and addresses are known to those taking the survey and typically they have been picked because they are "representative" of the larger society. In this type of sample, a "probability" or "random" sample, the return rate must be at least 70 percent or more in order to include enough of the spectrum chosen in advance to remain "representative."

However, in another type of distribution, such as used here, where it is important that respondents have complete anonymity, people cannot be picked. Rather, questionnaires must be offered through various types of groups and at locations across the country, and responses allowed to be returned until the demographic composition begins to approach the general demographics of the population at large. Then, as is usually done in a "random" sample, the small missing statistical groups can be patched in.

Almost no major research using essay questions today is done via "random" sampling methods, since the return rates tend to be low (and, as mentioned, in a "random" sample, almost all of those chosen must reply to validate the sample). Most survey research now tries to match its samples demographically to the general population in other ways; for example, by weighting responses to conform to the population profile. This is why so many sociologists who are not specialists in methodology speak of the necessity of at least a 70 percent return rate. They are not familiar with the type of study done here or the methodology necessitated by a need for anonymous distribution. (Indeed, few studies require the kind of anonymity which is essential to The Hite Reports.) Also, many people do not recognize that *The Hite Report on Love, Passion and Emotional Violence* is basically a psychological study done with an exceptionally large data base—a cross, in fact, between sociology and psychology.

Why didn't The Hite Reports use small samples, the way most psychological studies do? Certainly Freud never attempted a large sample, nor do most psychologists working in research today. (Freud used a handful of upper-class Viennese women on which to base his theories of female psychology; typically, articles in psychology journals are based on samples of graduate students or others, of less than fifty people.) Perhaps some in psychology still assume that their samples need not try to approximate the larger population, since they believe (like Freud) that the behavior they are studying is biologically based. However, if one believes that a large component is created by the social environment and social pressures, then the largest possible spectrum of opinion must be looked at and debated—and other historical philosophical positions considered as well—in order to critique a society's definitions of standard "male" and "female" psychology. In addition, "what is" must also be measured against "what might be," insofar as possible. In any case, sufficient effort was put into the various forms of distribution so that the final statistical breakdown of those participating according to age, occupation, religion, and other variables known for the U.S. population at large closely resembles that of the U.S. female population.

Analysis of Replies: Measuring and Understanding Attitudes and Emotions

Analyzing data from essay-type questionnaires is a complex endeavor; compilation and categorization of such answers is quite labor intensive. However, the resultant data is rich: it is precisely the possibility of reaching deeper levels of introspection that makes the use of an essay questionnaire so important here, as opposed to multiple-choice.

Analysis of data in The Hite Reports involved an intricate process of, first, placing the answers of each respondent (who received an identification number) onto charts. After this, I began the process of locating patterns and categories existing in the answers and then prepared statistical figures by totaling the numbers of women in each category, following which I selected representative quotes.

Any attempt at condensation or computerization at an early stage of the analysis would have defeated the purposes of the study: to find the more subtle meanings lying beneath the easily quantifiable parts of the replies, and to keep intact individual voices so that participants can communicate directly with readers. After all the replies were charted and the process of identifying categories completed, with representative quotes selected, statistical computation was possible.

To replicate this study, the same procedure must be followed. One cannot, as in the *ABC/Washington Post* poll, simply turn the final statistical results into questions, provide these questions with multiple-choice answers, and then ask them over the telephone to people who are not at all anonymous, and claim to have "replicated" a study.

Presentation of Findings: A New Interactive Framework: Dialogue Between Participants and Researchers

Most basic to the methodology of these Reports is separation of "findings" from analysis and interpretation. This is done by choice of research design, questions, and method of analysis and, in particular, by the style of presentation of findings. I planned the presentation of data to serve more than an informative function. Rather than simply giving readers statistics plus my analysis of data, my aim was to create an inner dialogue within the reader, as s/he mentally converses with those quoted. Therefore, large parts of text comprise first-person statements from those participating. My statements further debate how these may fit into categories of social ideology.

Unique to this study, my viewpoint as the researcher is separated from the data gathered. A reader can find participants with whom s/he agrees and disagrees and may also choose to accept or reject my theoretical conclusions—because the reader is given access to the original data, i.e., the voices of those responding. This is virtually unheard of in research; usually one must simply accept what the investigator says. Freud's women were never allowed to speak for themselves. In fact, as sociologist Jessie Bernard has pointed out, where else can you find a sample of 4,500 women represented by their own voices?

In addition to first-person statements and the researcher's theoretical perspective, 170 tables giving a breakdown of the major findings are presented. Rarely has so much information been given about the way in which a study was done, and almost never has the actual data received been shown.

Science or Philosophy?

While as many scholars have praised the research methods as have criticized them, are arguments over methodology really the point? This is an interdisciplinary study, one which tries to show not only "what is," but also to illuminate a debate that is raging inside of many women and many relationships over values and the family, the definition of the self.

As Professor John L. Sullivan, a specialist in methodology, explains, the debate over representativeness really misses the point: yes, The Hite Reports are "good research." Yes, they are "scholarly," but more importantly:

The great value of Hite's work is to show how people are thinking, to let people talk without rigid *a priori* categories, and to make all this accessible to the reader. Hite has many different purposes than simply stating population generalizations based on a probability sample. Therefore questions of sampling are not necessarily the central question to discuss about her work. Rather, it is a matter of discovering the diversity of behaviors and points of view. . . .

Her purpose is clear: to let her respondents speak for themselves. What purpose would it have served to do a random sample, given the aims of Hite's work? None, except for generalizing from percentages. But Hite has not generalized in a nonscholarly way. Many of the natural sciences worry a lot less about random samples, because their work is to test hypotheses. And most of the work in the social sciences is not based on random samples either; in fact, many if not most of the articles in psychology journals are based on data from college students, and then generalized. Interestingly, they are not criticized in the same way Hite has been.

And so, while debates over methodology have their merit and their place, in the case of The Hite Reports, to argue over numbers is to miss the forest for the trees: what this study is really about, what women are really doing here, is carrying on a massive debate about "female psychology" and the ideology of our times, choices for the future and the values of life we want to continue. Are we forever and always the mothers and nurturers of society? Should we give up our age-old interest in emotions and in a special kind of intimacy and supportive relationships? Become more like many men, "join" the "male" world? Or, can we "join" that world only at our own and society's peril? Yet another possibility: can we "join" that world and still, as Martin Luther King, Jr., remarked in a somewhat similar context, by retaining our values, thereby change that world? Can a less competitive value system ever fully share in power?

It is probably for these debates that the Reports are attacked, and not for the "methodology." Whatever the advantages and disadvantages of the methodology I have chosen (and the research design has been cited as "revolutionary," "groundbreaking," and "a great contribution to research" by many scholars),[2] I believe that only through these means could I have elicited from women such deep and private testimonies, enabling us all to debate and re-evaluate our definitions of love and the self in this important historic period of massive social and ideological change.

Notes

1. Dr. Gloria Bowles, University of California at Berkeley, has discussed the new trend in social science research in *On the Uses of Hermeneutics for Feminist Scholarship* (hermeneutics is the science of interpretation and explanation):

    "Feminist scholarship has not only stood critical in a 'negative' sense of traditional conceptual assumptions, but has made the positive move of putting forth alternative epistemologies which use experience, intuition and evaluation (both of women as individuals and of women as a 'class') as modes of knowing. . . .

    "Throughout male recorded history, men have been the 'takers,' while women have assumed (or have been forced to assume) the role of 'caretakers.' Women live in a world where little is impersonal and much is personal, where little is fixed or certain and much is ambiguous and volatile, and where little is value-free and much requires an evaluative response.

"Traditional thought claims to be able to leap out of the hermeneutical/interpretive circle and to speak of so-called 'value-free,' 'disinterested,' 'objective,' and 'ethically neutral' knowledge. . . . Feminist thought, precisely because it acknowledges and asserts its 'prejudices,' must, from the hermeneutical perspective, be judged as one of the only available theoretical postures which holds good claim to intellectual integrity and sophistication."

2. Among such scholars are: Mary Steichen Calderone, M.D., Founder, Sex Education and Information Council of the U.S.; Robert M. Emerson, Professor of Sociology, UCLA; John L. Sullivan, Professor of Political Science, University of Minnesota and editor of the authoritative textbook on methodology, *Quantitative Applications in the Social Sciences* (Sage University Papers series); Richard Halgin, Professor of Psychology, Amherst; Gladys Engel Lang, Professor of Communications and Political Science, University of Washington; Professors Nancy Tuana, University of Texas; Frank Sommers, University of Toronto; and Jesse Lemisch, SUNY, Buffalo.

**Shere Hite invites readers
to participate in her future
research. Please write to her at
the following address:**

**PO Box 5282
FDR Station
New York
NY 10022
USA**

Acknowledgments

I was a graduate student at Columbia University in New York when the anti-Vietnam War movement was at its height, and the women's movement a year or two just ahead. I was lucky enough at that moment in my life of questioning so many things to find others who were also asking questions. Where did I find them? In the early women's movement, where the debate was flourishing with an intensity I have rarely seen. So it is this movement I must thank most of all for helping me with the work I have done – hundreds of women, some of whom have been my closest friends now for twenty years, and who never cease to amaze and excite me.

I know when I try to thank people, I will never thank everyone. It is wonderful but painful to go back over all these years – I think of all the people I wanted to know better and didn't.

But first, I want to thank my aunt, Cecile Rice – who has acted as my mother from the time she told me about menstruation, and my grandmother, who cared for me for most of my life until I was fourteen. (When reporters asked her what she thought of my first book, she was quoted as saying, "Well, Jesus was a feminist too, so she is just fine.") To my grandfather, who walked me, cuddled me, loved me, picked me up after school and was always ready to help, and who later paid for my schooling even though he himself never set foot inside a college nor even thought about it, I send my love.

For intellectual and sisterly companionship and encouragement, I want to thank Barbara Seaman, Regina Ryan, Kate Millett, Ti-Grace Atkinson, Syd Beiner, Jesse Lemisch, Naomi Weisstein, Janet Wolfe, Andrea Dworkin and Erica Jong. Barbara Seaman first introduced me to her editor at Knopf, Regina Ryan, who helped me raise the money to do the five years' research which made the first Hite Report possible. Dorothy Crouch, president of New York NOW and an editor at Warner Books, encouraged me to distribute my early questionnaire, and then published a book full of questionnaires.

For editing and conceiving of this book, I owe a great debt to Liz Calder, Mic Cheetham, Harriet Griffey and Candida Lacey. Greater colleagues and friends I could never hope to have.

For their press conference presentations concerning my work, held at Columbia University in 1987, I want to thank Sue Rosenberg Zalk (CCNY), Harriet Pilpel, Richard Halgin (Amherst), and Nancy Tuana. I would like to thank Dr. Leah Schaefer, Dr. Mary Calderone, and the NOW sexuality committee of 1976, for their stirring presentations at my press conference on female sexuality in that year; I would like to thank Martin Sage for his help in preparing the press conference, as well as my publisher, Macmillan.

For the significant award for distinguished service I received in 1985 from the American Association of Sex Educators, Counselors and Therapists, I would like to thank Shirley Zussman, Bill Granzig, and the board for their speeches on my behalf.

I thank Katarina Czarnecki of Macmillan Publishing for establishing an excellent international publishing base for my books, and for being my friend. I thank Harriet Pilpel, Mike Sirkin, Howard Wilson, Joel Roth, and Steve Kaufman for their many kinds of counsel, advice and legal help, as well as being my friends. I would like to thank Tom Bolan for helping me sue a reporter who was the source of many unfounded and malicious stories about me and my work (as well as that of other feminist activists and writers), stories which are still unwittingly used in the backup files and 'standard wisdom' of newspaper stories.

Bob Gottlieb and Regina Ryan were the editors instrumental in making it possible for me to publish the results of my research. They both, as well as Corona Machemer at Knopf, believed in my work and championed it, waiting patiently over the years it took to research the books, and then involved themselves creatively and intellectually in helping me identify and clarify the essential themes. Lindy Hess's enthusiastic and invigorating editing on the first Hite Report will never be forgotten. Veronica di Napoli worked with me night after night, tirelessly, at the offices of the publisher, to send out fliers and book review copies to hundreds of publications, as well as offering many other acts of friendship.

ACKNOWLEDGMENTS

Corona Machemer was the editor for the final year of editing of *Women and Love: A Cultural Revolution in Progress* (the third Hite Report, and the one which "caused all the controversy", and for which a defense committee was formed). She and Nicholas Latimer, as well as Bill Loverd and I, had the 'pleasure' of holding onto our hats while the storm of controversy blew around us, including reporters calling the publisher and asking him to 'withdraw the book from the market'.

I have a special place in my heart for some of the friends who have helped my work in other non-categorizable ways, and I would like to thank Julian Prose (Eros Gyula), Irving Lazar, Hollie Wright, Lin Crouch, Kate Colleran, David Jones, Calla Fricke, Alan Nevins and Leah Fritz.

I want to thank the brilliant women who formed a committee to defend me during the attack on the third and most recent Hite Report (1987–88, Women and Love: A Cultural Revolution in Progress) and who held a press conference at an annual meeting of the American Studies Association, issuing a statement presenting their view of the media attack on me and the report. They include Barbara Ehrenreich, Naomi Weisstein, Barbara Seaman, Ruby Rohrlich, Gloria Steinem, Joan Ringleheim, Phyllis Chessler, Kate Millet, Ti-Grace Atkinson, and Florence Rush. This event was written up by *Chronicles of Higher Education*, and by Liz Smith in her national newspaper column. I thank both of them, as well as Laura Cottingham, who did creative investigative reporting about the reporters who were 'reporting' on me, for the *New York Observer*. Louise Armstrong pointed out the craziness of the media attack in her article in *The Women's Review of Books*, and early on showed that this attack clearly pointed to there being a new backlash against not only me but against feminism and women's rights in the United States. Susan Faludi in her spectacular 1992 *Backlash: The Hidden War Against American Women*, also pointed this out in her discussion of the attack on me. I also thank Cheris Kramarae, distinguished professor at the University of Illinois, for her writing and analysis of my work, as well as Linda Singer, Professor of Women's Studies.

To compile the research for all three Hite Reports, I have had to raise enormous sums of money. Eventually, the money I used for research and compilation of the data was more or less paid off by sales of the books – so that, in fact, the public has always funded my research. But without seed money in the beginning, these studies could never have been done. I supported the research originally with a book advance and with loans from friends. For these loans, I want to thank Regina Ryan, Virgilio del Toro, Michael Wilson, Syd Beiner, and Cecile Rice. For loans after the attack on my third book made my cash flow quite difficult, I want to thank with particular gratitude Dr. Janet Wolfe and Professors Jesse Lemisch and Naomi Weisstein. My deepest gratitude to Come! Unity Press, especially Lin and Debby.

Eventually, over 15,000 people, ages thirteen to ninety-seven, have participated to date in these projects, and I must thank them, above all. Women's and men's openness and sharing of their personal lives in such depth, over so many years, has enriched and sustained me both in my work and personally.

Groups who have distributed questionnaires over the years are too many to name, and have my gratitude. They include chapters of the National Organization for Women, chapters of NARAL, women's or student centers of the Universities of Florida, Indiana, Illinois, California, Kentucky, Oregon, Texas – and many, many others.

My express thanks to Gustav Mahler and Richard Strauss, Richard Wagner and Kirsten Flagstad, Puccini, Mirella Freni, Licia Albanese, Sergei Rachmaninoff and George Jellinek, among others, for their inspiration and companionship.

I want to thank my lovely dog who has kept me company for many wonderful hours in my life, listening to my ideas great and small, offering sympathetic understanding and enthusiasm.

I owe my husband Friedrich Horicke – a brilliant musician and scholar, with a profound knowledge of archaeology, politics, classical music and literature – a great debt of gratitude for his fearless response to the media attack on me in the United States in 1987–88 – and his intelligent analyses of the events, as well as physical presence in various threatening situations during that time. He has my thanks and my love.

Shere Hite, London, November 1992

Index

INDEX

Library of Congress Cataloging-in-Publication Data
Hite, Shere.
Women as revolutionary agents of change: The Hite reports and beyond / Shere Hite.
536 p.   cm.
Rev. ed. of: Women as revolutionary agents of change:
selected essays in psychology and gender, 1972–1993.
Includes bibliographical references and index.
ISBN 0-299-14294-9 (pbk.)
1. Women—United States—Sexual behavior. 2. Men—United States—
Sexual behavior. 3. Sexual behavior surveys—United States.
4. Sex (Psychology) I. Title. II. Title: Hite reports, 1972–1993.
HQ29.H58   1994
306.7'0723—dc20   93-39168